CAREGIVING SYSTEMS
Informal and Formal Helpers

Social Strucure and Aging

A series of volumes edited by
K. Warner Schaie

CAREGIVING SYSTEMS
Informal and Formal Helpers

Edited by

Steven H. Zarit
The Pennsylvania State University

Leonard I. Pearlin
University of California

K. Warner Schaie
The Pennsylvania State University

LEA

LAWRENCE ERLBAUM ASSOCIATES, PUBLISHERS

1993   Hillsdale, New Jersey   Hove and London

Lawrence Erlbaum Associates, Inc., Publishers
365 Broadway
Hillsdale, New Jersey 07642

Library of Congress Cataloging-in-Publication Data

Caregiving systems: informal and formal helpers / edited by Steven
    H. Zarit, Leonard I. Pearlin, K. Warner Schaie.
        p.   cm. — (Social structure and aging)
    Includes bibliographical references and indexes.
    ISBN 0-8058-1094-3 (c)
    1. Aged — Care — Congresses. I. Zarit, Steven H. II. Pearlin,
Leonard I. (Leonard Irving), 1924-   . III. Schaie, K. Warner
(Klaus Warner), 1928-   . IV. Series.
    DNLM: 1. Caregivers — Congresses. 2. Aged — Services for-
-Congresses. 3. Aged — Medical care — Congresses. 4. Aged — Home
care — Congresses. 8. Home Nursing.   WT 30 C2718]
HV1451.C329   1992
DNLM/DLC
for Library of Congress   92-2192
                                                                CIP

Books published by Lawrence Erlbaum Associates are printed on acid-free
paper, and their bindings are chosen for strength and durability.

Printed in the United States of America
10 9 8 7 6 5 4 3 2 1

Contents

Preface

This is the fifth volume in a series on the broad topic of "Social Structure and Aging." It is the edited proceedings of a conference held at the Pennsylvania State University, October 13–14, 1989. The conference series grew out of several planning meetings conducted at the Social Science Research Council by a committee chaired by Matilda White Riley, which called for the systematic exploration of life-course development as a process that is interdependent with social structure and social change. When I assumed the leadership of the Penn State Gerontology Center in 1985, I was pleased to be able to identify as one of our goals the implementation of the social structure and aging conference program.

The four previous volumes[1] in this series have dealt with the impact of social structure on aging in psychological processes (Schaie & Schooler, 1989), social structure and aging in cross-cultural perspective (Kertzer & Schaie, 1989), the impact of social structures on the development of self-efficacy over the life span (Rodin, Schooler, & Schaie, 1990), and the effect of social structures on health behaviors and health outcomes (Schaie, Blazer, & House, 1991). This volume was designed to highlight the social structures that facilitate and support caregiving for the frail and disabled elderly.

---

[1]The four previous volumes are as follows:

Kertzer, D., & Schaie, K. E. (Eds.). (1989). *Age structuring in comparative perspective*. Hillsdale, NJ: Lawrence Erlbaum Associates.

Rodin, J., Schooler, C., & Schaie, K. W. (Eds.). (1990). *Self-directedness: Cause and effects throughout the life course*. Hillsdale, NJ: Lawrence Erlbaum Associates.

Schaie, K. W., Blazer, D., & House, J. S. (Eds.). (1992). *Aging, health behaviors, and health outcomes*. Hillsdale, NJ: Lawrence Erlbaum Associates.

Schaie, K. W., & Schooler, C. (Eds.). (1989). *Social structure and aging: Psychological processes*. Hillsdale, NJ: Lawrence Erlbaum Associates.

One of the major concomitants of human aging is the increasing risk of physiological and psychological dysfunctions. A consequence of such dysfunctions is the loss of fully independent functioning and the resultant need for the provisions of formal and informal systems of caregiving. Whether or not such systems can provide effective support for the frail and disabled older person is affected greatly by a variety of social structural variables as well as individual behaviors that mediate favorable or adverse outcomes.

To address these issues, the editors commissioned chapters that review central aspects of both formal and informal systems of caregiving. The volume examines informal systems of care by considering cultural perspectives (such as generational relationships in Black families), comparisons across disabilities as they affect parental caregivers, as well as longitudinal perspectives in following caregivers of Alzheimer's patients over time. With respect to formal systems of caregiving, the focus is on innovative systems of care (such as social health maintenance organizations and home-care services). Finally, patterns of formal service utilizations and the barriers to the use of formal services are examined. Each of the primary chapters is followed by comments from experts drawn broadly from the behavioral and social science disciplines. As with previous volumes in this series, I think that we have been successful in bridging disciplinary boundaries and we hope that this effort continues our endeavors to permit better communication across disciplines and encourage more effective research on major societal problems related to human aging.

The other editors and I are grateful for the encouragement and financial support of the conference that led to this volume provided by Anne C. Petersen, Dean of the College of Health and Human Development, and Charles C. Hossler, Vice-President for Research and Graduate Studies of the Pennsylvania State University. We are also grateful to Barbara Impellitteri and Barbara Labinski for handling the conference logistics and to Alane Stiner for her work on the indexes.

K. Warner Schaie

I

INFORMAL SYSTEMS
OF CARE

Introduction to Part I

Caregiving families emerged in the 1980s as a frequent topic in the media, in discussions of public policy and long-term care, and especially in social and behavioral research. This attention reflects the central role played by informal caregivers. With the dramatic growth of the older population and the increasing number of people who require care, families remain the first, most reliable, and most acceptable source of assistance. Furthermore, informal caregivers often facilitate the linkages with formal providers, such as physicians, hospitals, community long-term care services, and nursing homes.

The attention to family caregivers has usually highlighted the stressfulness or burdensome nature of some types of care. Both the popular and the research literature have frequently emphasized one type of caregiving situation (e.g., a daughter caught between the demands of two generations, or providing care to someone with Alzheimer's disease). But families, care arrangements, and the context of caregiving vary greatly. Even the degree to which families find similar events or problems stressful can differ considerably, both in baseline comparisons and over time.

Our examination of informal care systems focuses on three issues that address variability in family caregiving: (a) culture and its influence on intergenerational relationships and caregiving, (b) comparisons of caregiving across disabilities, and (c) changes in caregivers' experiences over time. Although they are not exhaustive of the variety of caregiving situations or experiences, these topics explore major dimensions of the caregiving situation that are often neglected.

Elena Yu and her colleagues describe caregiving patterns and beliefs in Shanghai. They propose major differences in the impact that care has on

3

families as a result of cultural and structural differences in the Chinese family. Expanding on this issue, Lucy Yu explores traditional Confucian beliefs about family responsibilities and compares attitudes and practices of three groups of Chinese: a group living in the People's Republic, recent immigrants to the United States, and an American-born sample. Burton and Sorensen use conceptualizations of time to explore how inner-city African-American families address pressures for care of elders, young children, and sometimes also their young adults who have multiple problems. Morycz provides a commentary on cultural perspectives and caregiving, suggesting the central role that culture plays in informal care.

Although caregiving research has focused primarily on the elderly, normative and nonnormative caregiving occurs at other times in the life cycle. Examination of these situations can identify common themes as well as critical differences with care of older people. Toward this goal, Avison and his associates examine family caregiving in four contexts: (a) assisting a developmentally disabled child, (b) caring for a child with cancer, (c) Care demands for a normal child in a female-headed single-parent household, and (d) assisting a mentally ill adult. Matthews explores some of the issues and problems involved in comparing different caregiving groups, and the implications for research and intervention.

Although caregiving is typically studied at one point in time, it involves an ongoing process in which relationships, responsibilities, stressors, and stress may change over time. The advantage of longitudinal studies is demonstrated by Schulz and his colleagues, who examine patterns of change in depression among caregivers assisting someone with Alzheimer's disease. Smyer considers issues in the measurement of change, including inter- and intra-individual patterns of change and stability.

Pearlin and Zarit close this section by examining conceptual and methodological issues in caregiving research, assessing the current state of the literature and proposing some promising approaches for new lines of inquiry.

1

Caregivers of the Cognitively Impaired and the Disabled in Shanghai, China

Elena Yu
San Diego State University
William T. Liu
University of Illinois at Chicago
Pacific/Asian American Mental Health Research Center
Zheng-Yu Wang
Paul S. Levy
University of Illinois at Chicago
Robert Katzman
University of California, San Diego
Ming-Yuan Zhang
Guang-Ya Qu
Shanghai Mental Health Center, Shanghai, China
Fen-Fui Chen
Pacific/Asian American Mental Health Research Center
University of Illinois at Chicago

To date, caregiving in China is not yet widely recognized as an important research issue. Demographically, the proportion of persons 65 years and older is not expected to increase by large amounts before the year 2000 (Martin, 1988). And, in a society steeped in the historical tradition of Confucianism for thousands of years where the legal system, including the present constitution itself, has made the family primarily responsible for the care of the elderly, informal caregiving of the impaired is not yet perceived as a social problem. It is assumed to be available. Nursing homes—as we understand the terminology in the United States—are, for the most part, practically inaccessible to, if not nonexistent for, the average person in China. What are widely called "homes for respecting the elderly" (*Jinglao yuan*) or "sanitorium" or "nursing homes" (*Liaoyang yuan*), albeit designed with group activities and a modicum of medical services, actually resemble congregate housing or retirement homes in the United States. However, access to these homes is limited to a select group of disabled, childless, and kinless elderly. That it is a privilege and not an entitlement to be housed in these institutions is evidenced by the extremely small proportion of ordinary citizens found in such homes. Hence, for a large majority of the Chinese, the family remains a critical, if not the only, source of social support in old age. But, given the need for both husband and wife to work in the modernizing economy plagued with hyperinflation, and the push for the young to succeed in the socialist society, who actually *is* caring for the impaired elderly? What descriptive profile do we have of the caregivers? How do they feel about the persons for whom they are caring? Last, but not least, who are the care recipients? These are the questions that form the basis for this chapter.

Two types of caregivers are examined here: those who care for the cognitively impaired and those who care for the physically disabled. Of interest are the sociodemographic profiles of the caregivers and those of the care recipients, the frequency with which certain behavioral characteristics of cognitive and physical impairment occur, the levels of tolerance that caregivers have towards the care recipients exhibiting such behaviors, and how these tolerance levels are associated with the caregivers' characteristics.

BACKGROUND

Several theoretical paradigms in the social sciences have shaped research on family care of the frail and chronically ill elderly in the U.S. Themes of family abandonment and social isolation of older adults — dominant from the 1930s through the 1950s — have been counterbalanced by nearly four decades of research demonstrating the strength of family networks and the availability of social support to the elderly, as well as the presence of intergenerational reciprocity, even though increasingly large numbers of older Americans are living alone (Kovar, 1986; Lee & Ellithorpe, 1982; Litwak, 1985; Shanas, 1979a; Shanas et al., 1968); thus was coined the phrase "intimacy at a distance," attributed to Rosenmayr (1977). The idea that institutionalized care is "better" able to meet the needs of the frail and chronically ill was soon replaced by the realization that the informal support system actually provides more assistance than do formal organizations (Branch & Jette, 1983; Brody, 1981; Brody, Poulshock, & Masciocchi, 1978; Cantor, 1975, 1980, 1983; Shanas, 1979a, 1979b). Meanwhile, the idea of "substituting" informal for formal care is now being supplanted by the prevailing notion that both types of care are necessary to meet the needs of the noninstitutionalized elderly (Dobrof & Litwak, 1977; Litwak & Figueira, 1970).

At present, the bulk of the literature on caregiving has shown that women are more likely than men to be engaged in the care of the frail and the chronically ill and to attend to the personal hygiene needs and household chores of the elderly (Horowitz, 1985a, 1985b; Stone, Cafferata, & Sangl, 1987). While caregivers' stress and strain have been reported in numerous studies, efforts made to quantify the burden of care and level of stress have not produced the expected magnitude of empirical evidence for emotional strain, even though several studies have shown that role overload and role conflicts are endemic in most caregiving activities.

In this chapter, we explore the question as to whether, in a socialist country like present-day China, significant differences exist in the caregivers of the cognitively impaired versus those of the disabled. Which, if any, of the care recipient characteristics are associated with the caregiver's intolerance toward the behavioral manifestations of cognitive impairment and physical disability? Are some caregivers' characteristics significantly associated with their tolerance toward the care recipient's behavior? What are some of the common denominators and unique cultural features of caregivers in China, compared with the U.S.? What are the implications of these findings for long-term care of the elderly in China and the U.S.?

METHODS

The opportunity to do a preliminary study of Chinese caregivers emerged as a result of a large-scale longitudinal psychiatric epidemiologic research program of Alzheimer's disease and dementia in Shanghai, China. The program was a collaborative project of three institutions: the Shanghai Mental Health Center — a World Health Organization (WHO) Research and Training Center for Mental Health in China; the Pacific/Asian American Mental Health Research Center, formerly funded by NIMH and housed at the University of Illinois at Chicago; and the Alzheimer's Disease Research Center at the University of California, San Diego. Conceived in 1984 as a result of a U.S.-China Symposium on Aging and Mental Illness organized under the leadership of William T. Liu and Ethel Shanas, the study took more than 2 years to prepare.

Data Collection

Data collection began in 1987 and consisted of three phases. Phase I is a community-wide epidemiologic survey of cognitive impairment using a probability sample of 5,055 noninstitutionalized elderly adults, aged 55 and older, who are representative of the population in the same age group then living in Jing-An District of Shanghai—the largest city in China. The survey instrument included not only questions to determine the presence and degree of cognitive impairment, but also questions aimed at ascertaining the physical and mental health status of the respondents. Phase I is also called the "Dementia Screening Survey" or the "Shanghai Elderly Study."

Phase II is a reinterview of all of the positive cases of cognitive impairment obtained from Phase I, in order to arrive at a clinical diagnosis of dementia in general, and dementia of the Alzheimer's type in particular. In addition, a random sample representing 5% of the total number of negative cases of cognitive impairment was combined with the positive cases and reinterviewed, in order to assess the clinicians' accuracy in diagnosing dementia and to calculate the sensitivity and specificity of the screening instrument, using the clinician's diagnosis as the Gold Standard. Data obtained from this phase were then weighted to produce estimates of the prevalence of dementia in Jing-An District of Shanghai.

Phase III is a reinterview, after 1 year, of the age group most at risk for developing dementia—namely, persons 75 years and older. The reinterview consists of two phases, the first to perform a repeat assessment using the same Chinese Mini-Mental Status Exam (CMMSE) screening instrument, and the second to obtain a repeat clinical diagnosis of dementia and subtypes of dementia. This phase is also called the "Incidence" study ($n = 1621$). To avoid contamination of findings from one phase of the study to the next, the interviewers were deliberately kept uninformed about the results of each previous phase of data collection.

The Caregiver Interview

As part of the Phase I epidemiologic survey of dementia, all respondents who fell within a predetermined cutoff score (20 or less) on the CMMSE used for screening cognitive impairment were *not* interviewed directly. Instead, the most knowledgeable caregiver of the targeted but presumably "cognitively impaired" elderly was identified in order to conduct a proxy interview about the elderly's health status and a caretaker interview about the burden of care. This interview is called the "Caregiver's Interview." Likewise, a subgroup of persons ($n = 212$) who could not be tested with the CMMSE screening instrument because of physical disabilities or identifiable illnesses (other than dementia) was also administered the caregiver's interview. For lack of a better word, we call them the *disabled*. The singlemost important factors that

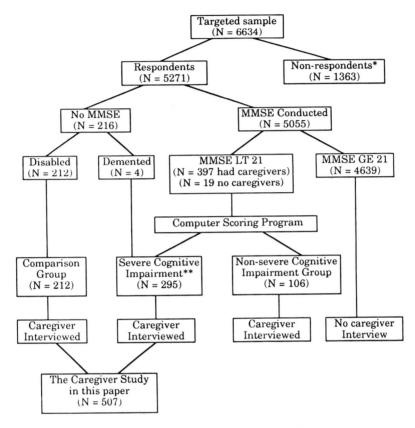

FIG. 1.1. Caregivers' study in China: Shanghai epidemiologic survey of dementia. (*These consisted of 1202 persons who were travelling or on vacation, 85 who moved, 34 who died, 18 who were seriously ill, 21 who refused to be interviewed, and 3 who actually did not live at the address indicated [called "empty household registers"]. **Includes 4 persons who were so severely demented that the MMSE could not be conducted.)

led to their inability to take the CMMSE were deafness (75% of the disabled cases); blindness (8%); paralysis or speech impediment (8%); and health, mental health, and other problems (9%). Figure 1.1 illustrates the various stages involved during Phase I that enabled us to obtain our sample of caregivers in Shanghai, China.

The interviewers were psychiatrists and nurses at the Shanghai Mental Health Center, the Shanghai Psychiatric Hospital, and their satellite health stations. The interviewer training sessions lasted 10 days, with Chinese-speaking U.S. researchers (E. Yu and W. T. Liu) serving as training faculty.

The CMMSE

Because data on the clinical diagnoses made by neurologists, psychiatrists, and neuropsychologists were not yet available for analysis at this writing, we based this chapter entirely on a subset of the Phase I dataset. The Chinese Mini-Mental Status Exam[1] (CMMSE) was culturally adapted by the present investigative team specifically for this study based on the original Mini Mental Status Exam (MMSE) developed by Folstein, Folstein, and McHugh (1975). The total possible correct scores range from 0 to 30.

Translation and back translation of the MMSE were made by bilingual and bicultural members of the investigative team, following the procedures described in Yu et al. (1989). Parallel translations and back translations were also conducted in China by a team of bilingual clinicians. The two versions were pretested on site using 159 community residents in Chicago's Chinatown and 150 noninstitutionalized elderly in Hong-Kou, Shanghai. The final Chinese version of the MMSE used in Shanghai was constructed on the basis of findings obtained from both pretests. On the whole, most items in the original English version could be translated and used meaningfully without modifications. However, some minor changes were required on certain items in order to adapt the instrument to the Chinese culture and language. An example of a cultural adaptation is the question on time orientation. Whereas in the United States, the items were scored with reference to the Gregorian calendar, in Shanghai so long as the response was correct according to either the Gregorian or the lunar calendar system, the answer was scored correct.

Scoring Procedure for Determining Caseness

The sequence of items and the scoring procedures between the CMMSE and the MMSE are identical, except for minor modifications, as mentioned previously. A SAS-Mainframe computer program identical to that used in the Epidemiologic Catchment Area studies was applied to the Shanghai CMMSE data in order to calculate comparable rates of cognitive impairment as those published by the Yale-New Haven ECA team of investigators (Weissman et al., 1985). The program uses two parallel scoring systems to classify the level of impairment on the basis of the total number of errors. One scoring system treats unanswered questions as errors, the other as missing values. Each of these two systems classifies the respondent as having a severe cognitive impairment if the number of errors is 13 or higher, and

---

[1]A copy of the CMMSE is available from the first author; send requests to: Elena Yu, Division of Epidemiology and Biostatistics, Graduate School of Public Health, San Diego State University, San Diego, CA 92182.

mild disorder if there are 7–12 errors (see Appendix A). When the two scoring systems agree with each other, the presence of cognitive impairment is considered to be "definite." When they disagree, cognitive impairment is labeled "possible."

MEASURES

For purposes of this chapter, two types of impaired elderly Chinese are identified and compared—the cognitively impaired and the physically disabled. The former are persons 55 years and older who were classified as having *severe* impairment ($n = 295$) on the basis of the aforementioned SAS-mainframe computer program; the latter are those in the same age group who had serious hearing or vision impairment, full or partial paralysis, speech impediment, or serious illness ($n = 212$). Their conditions were independently evaluated by collaborating psychiatrists and health practitioners.

The caregiver, called *Kanhuren* ("the person who watches and protects") or *Zhaoliao zhe* ("one who cares, manages, or attends to someone's needs"), is defined as someone who has intimate knowledge of the impaired elderly and who helps with activities of daily living. Such a person is considered a *zhiqingren* in Chinese, which means "the person who knows one's emotions or situations well," because the word *qing* can mean both *gan-qing* (emotion) or *qing-kuang* (situation or circumstances). The caregivers' characteristics examined in this chapter are: gender, age, education, marital status, occupational status, relationship to the elderly sampled in our study, and self-perceived health. A Memory and Behavior Problems Checklist consisting of 28 items was used (Zarit, Orr, & Zarit, 1985; Zarit & Zarit, 1982). The caregiver was asked to identify on a 5-point scale the presence and frequency of memory problems, personality change, irritating behaviors, destructiveness, self-care problems, and difficulties with household chores. The range of values include 0 (never occurred), 1 (has occurred once in the past week), 2 (has occurred once or twice in the past week), 3 (has occurred 3 to 6 times in the past week), and 4 (occurred daily or more often in the past week). The maximum score is 112.

A Caregiver Tolerance Scale (Zarit, Reever, & Back-Peterson, 1980; Zarit et al., 1985) was also used to assess the caregiver's tolerance with each of the 28 items on the Memory and Behavioral Checklist. Responses were recorded on a 5-point scale, which consists of 0 (I can tolerate this behavior when it occurs), 1 (I can tolerate this behavior though it bothers me a little), 2 (I can tolerate this behavior though it bothers me a lot), 3 (I don't know how much longer I can tolerate this behavior), and 4 (I can no longer tolerate this behavior and have to do something about it). The major difference between 2 and 3 is whether the caregiver feels that he or she can handle the behavior even if it is upsetting (score 2), or if they are beginning to question whether or not they can handle it (score 3). The possible maximum score is also 112. The higher the score, the less tolerable is the behavior.

The burden of care was assessed using a newly created Burden Scale (Montgomery & Borgatta, personal communication, 1986) developed from an earlier scale (Montgomery, Gonyea, & Hooyman, 1985). It requires the caregiver to compare his or her situation between now (time of interview) and a year ago on the following dimensions: time to oneself, stress in relationship with care recipient, personal privacy, attempts by care recipient to manipulate caregiver, time to spend in recreational activities, vacation activities and trips taken, nervousness and depression concerning relationship with care recipient, time to do own work and daily chores, demands by care recipient over and above needs, and time for own friends and other relatives. Responses range from a possible rating of 1 (a lot less) to 5 (a lot more), with 3 representing "the same."

In addition to the burden scale, we also constructed a simple binary scale (yes or no) in order to explore 10 possible changes in daily living that the caregiver might have had to make in taking care of the impaired elderly. The idea to examine these changes or "sacrifices" resulted from our effort to expand the burden-of-care concept and to obtain a preliminary grasp of the specificity of the concept of cost of caring itself. The items included in the scale were those perceived to be salient to caregiving situations in Shanghai.

RESULTS

Table 1.1 shows the sociodemographic characteristics of the cognitively and physically impaired persons found in our probability sample survey of 5,055 noninstitutionalized adults, 55 years and older, living in Jing-An District of Shanghai. As stated in our earlier articles (Yu et al., 1989; Levy et al., 1988, 1989), the sampling procedure was designed to produce nearly equal numbers of persons in the following three age groups: 55–64 years, 65–74 years, and 75 years and older.

In Tables 1.1 and 1.2, the unweighted columns represent sample characteristics, and the weighted columns are population estimates. Chi-square tests of significance are performed only for the unweighted data. The results show that a significantly higher percentage of women in our sample (i.e., the unweighted data) had "severe" cognitive impairment (81%), compared with those classified as physically disabled (74%). Likewise, differences in education, living arrangement, and income exists between the two groups of care recipients. However, no significant differences in age, marital status, and number of wage earners were found in the sample between the two groups of impaired older adults (Table 1.1).

If we shift our attention to the weighted columns in Table 1.1, we note that women tend to outnumber men by a ratio of at least 3:1, and more women fall into the severe cognitive impairment group than the disabled. The percentage of the severe cognitive impairment cases who do not have any education is also quite high (66%). As we have reported elsewhere (Katzman et al., 1988; Yu et al., 1989), severe cognitive impairment may be associated with lack of education in more complex ways than we had previously thought. Its relevance to caregiving is addressed in the Discussion section.

In addition, the weighted data show that the percentage of impaired persons is about the same (13%) for both the disabled and the cognitively impaired groups in the 55–64 years age range. That percentage increases with each older age group until the oldest cohort, where it appears that the survivors are largely unimpaired. An estimated 53% of the disabled and 57% of those who scored severe in cognitive impairment are spouseless (i.e., widowed or divorced). The dominant pattern of living arrangement is not the nuclear family, but one characterized by the presence of other relatives besides the nuclear family members. Some 12% of the physically disabled and 6% of the cognitively impaired are living only with nonrelatives. In 2.4% of the disabled, and in almost 6% of the cognitively impaired in Jing-An, the care recipient is living alone. Most of the households of these impaired older adults are characterized by the presence of at least one wage earner. Indeed, in almost 40% of each of the two impaired groups, at least three wage earners are present to provide financial support to the care recipient. Insofar as income is concerned, some 17% of the cognitively impaired older adults in Jing-An, compared with about 6% of the disabled, are living below the poverty line of 35 yuan a month or less (1 U.S. dollar equaled 3.71 yuan at that time). Most of the impaired are in the lower income range, a distribution not unlike those obtained for the entire population of 55 years and older in general (see Yu et al., 1989, for data on the overall income distribution of the population).

The caregivers' characteristics are presented in Table 1.2. Again, both weighted and unweighted data are shown. The *unweighted* data indicate that, in the survey sample as a whole, there was no statistically significant differences in gender, mean age, marital status, and self-perceived health between the caregivers of the two groups of impaired older adults. When age is broken down into two categories (those less than 55 compared with those 55 years and older), a significantly larger percentage of those caring for the disabled are in the older age group (64%), whereas a large percentage of those taking care of the cognitively impaired are less than 55 years of age (49%).

There are also significant differences in the educational level of these two types of caregivers, with those attending to the disabled having a smaller percentage of no education or only elementary education, compared to the caregivers of the cognitively impaired older adults. There are also significant

TABLE 1.1

Sociodemographic Characteristics of the Disabled and the Severe Cognitive Impairment Cases: Shanghai Epidemiologic Survey of Dementia

Care Recipient's Sociodemographic Characteristics	Disabled				Severe Cognitive Impairment[5]				χ^2
	Unweighted		Weighted		Unweighted		Weighted		
	(n)	Percent		Percent	(n)	Percent		Percent	
Sex									
Male	(55)	25.9		24.6	(55)	18.6		17.3	3.87*
Female	(157)	74.1		75.4	(240)	81.4		82.7	
Age in years									
55–64 years	(11)	5.2		12.9	(16)	5.4		12.9	N.S.
65–74 years	(37)	17.5		21.3	(76)	25.8		30.5	
75–84 years	(101)	47.6		40.0	(160)	54.2		44.3	
85 yrs. & older	(63)	29.7		25.9	(43)	14.6		12.3	
Mean age		79.19 ± 8.56		76.83 ± 10.17		76.90 ± 7.21		74.92 ± 8.20	
Median age	80			79	78			76	
Education									
None (= illiterate)	(99)	46.9		44.3	(200)	68.0		66.6	36.64**
Elementary or less	(71)	33.6		35.2	(81)	27.6		29.7	
High school or more	(41)	19.4		20.5	(13)	4.4		3.7	
Marital status									
Married	(83)	39.2		41.5	(110)	37.4		41.1	N.S.
Spouseless	(120)	56.6		53.1	(180)	61.2		56.9	
Never married	(9)	4.2		5.4	(4)	1.4		2.0	

Living arrangement[1]							
Nuclear family[1]	(40)	18.9	20.8	(56)	19.0	19.9	
Nuclear + relatives[2]	(119)	56.1	53.6	(183)	62.0	62.0	
Other relatives[3] only	(24)	11.3	11.7	(22)	7.5	6.4	
Nonrelatives[4]/others	(25)	11.8	11.5	(15)	5.1	5.7	
Alone	(4)	1.9	2.4	(19)	6.4	5.9	15.43*
No. of wage earners							
None	(30)	14.4	14.5	(45)	15.6	14.7	
1 person	(26)	12.5	11.8	(49)	17.0	17.0	
2 persons	(66)	31.7	33.4	(81)	28.1	28.5	
3 + persons	(86)	41.3	40.3	(113)	39.2	39.8	N.S.
Income per capita							
0–35 yuan/mon.	(10)	6.5	5.9	(37)	16.0	16.7	
36–55 yuan/mon.	(42)	27.1	25.0	(44)	18.6	18.2	
56–85 yuan/mon.	(77)	49.7	52.5	(110)	48.1	46.9	
86–115 yuan/mon.	(17)	11.0	11.2	(26)	11.3	12.2	
116 or more yuan/mon.	(9)	5.8	5.5	(14)	6.1	6.0	9.77*

*$p \leq .05$
**$p \leq .01$

[1]The family structure consists of the older person, his or her spouse and/or their offspring only.
[2]Co-residence of at least one relative with the nuclear family members.
[3]Co-residence with relatives other than the older person's spouse or children.
[4]Presence of at least one person in the household who is not related to the older person at all, e.g., a housemaid or nurse.
[5]These are codes 3 and 4 in the ECA Computer Scoring Program.

TABLE 1.2

**Sociodemographic Characteristics of the Caregivers of the Disabled and Severe Cognitive Impairment Cases:
Shanghai Epidemiologic Survey of Dementia**

Caregiver's Characteristics	Disabled			Severe Cognitive Impairment			χ^2
	Unweighted		Weighted	Unweighted		Weighted	
	(n)	Percent	Percent	(n)	Percent	Percent	
Sex							
Male	(85)	40.1	38.6	(140)	47.5	50.9	N.S.
Female	(127)	59.9	61.4	(155)	52.5	49.1	
Age in years							
< 55 years	(75)	35.4	36.6	(143)	48.5	48.9	8.59**
55 years and older	(137)	64.6	63.4	(152)	51.5	51.1	
mean age	(212)	57.85 ± 16.70	57.22 ± 17.21	(295)	54.04 ± 17.29	53.51 ± 17.62	
median age	60[a]			55[a]			
range	20–87			15–88			
Education							
None (= illiterate)	(38)	17.9	17.5	(30)	10.2	9.1	6.80*
Elementary or less	(49)	23.1	23.7	(83)	28.3	27.8	
High school or more	(125)	59.0	58.8	(180)	61.4	63.0	

Marital Status							
Married	(166)	78.3	75.9	(235)	79.7	78.8	
Spouseless	(25)	11.8	13.0	(25)	8.5	8.2	
Never married	(21)	9.9	11.0	(35)	11.9	13.0	N.S.
Occupational Status							
Caregiver	(37)	17.5	16.8	(21)	7.1	7.4	
Employed elsewhere	(66)	31.1	32.1	(139)	47.1	47.5	
Retired	(92)	43.4	43.2	(117)	39.7	39.2	
Housewife (never employed)	(17)	8.0	7.9	(18)	6.1	5.9	20.39**
Relationship to Older Person							
Spouse	(61)	28.8	29.9	(76)	25.8	27.8	
Children and/or their spouse	(98)	46.2	44.8	(167)	56.6	55.9	
Parents, sibs, or other relatives	(39)	18.4	18.6	(32)	10.8	9.4	
Other	(14)	6.6	6.7	(20)	6.8	6.9	8.57*
Perceived Health							
Poor	(10)	4.7	4.2	(25)	8.5	7.9	
Fair	(64)	30.2	30.2	(72)	24.4	23.9	
Good	(99)	46.7	47.0	(142)	48.1	47.4	
Excellent	(39)	18.4	18.6	(56)	19.0	20.9	N.S.

*$p \leq .05$
**$p \leq .01$
aThe median age is the same for both weighted and unweighted data.

differences in the work roles of these two types of caregivers. Some 17% of the caregivers of the disabled have caregiving as their main occupational role, compared to only 7% of the caregivers of the cognitively impaired. And, a larger percentage of those caring for the cognitively impaired, compared to those caring for the disabled, are employed elsewhere.

Insofar as relationship to the care recipient is concerned, some 57% of the caregivers of the cognitively impaired are children and/or in-laws, compared with 46% among the caregivers of the disabled. A larger percentage of those caring for the disabled are parents, siblings, and other relatives (18%), compared with those caring for the cognitively impaired (11%).

If we examine the *weighted* columns and evaluate the sociodemographic characteristics of the caregivers, we observe that in Jing-An, the caregivers of the cognitively impaired are evenly distributed by gender. The same is not so for the caregivers of the disabled (Table 1.2). A large percentage of the caregivers in both groups of impaired persons tend to be older adults; about 60% or so in each group of caregivers have had middle or high school education; more than 75% in each type of caregivers are married. In terms of occupation, some 17% of the caregivers of the disabled are working exclusively as caregivers, compared to only 7% of those caring for the cognitively impaired. About 48% of those caring for the cognitively impaired have a regular job besides caregiving, compared to only 32% among caregivers of the disabled. As much as 43% of the caregivers of the disabled are retired, compared to 39% among the caregivers of the cognitively impaired; only a small percentage of the caregivers in both groups are housewives who had never worked before. The weighted data also show that nearly 3 out of 10 caregivers are the spouses of the impaired older adults. The largest majority of caregivers are children and/or in-laws. Other relatives account for 19% of the caregivers of the disabled but only 9% of those caring for the cognitively impaired. Significant differences in self-ratings of health between the two groups of caregivers are not found.

By and large, both weighted and unweighted data in Tables 1.1 and 1.2 have provided essentially similar information. Hence, for the sake of parsimony, in what follows only unweighted data are presented on the caregiver's tolerance score, estimated mean score on frequency of behavioral problems occurring in the care recipients, and self-assessment of the burden of care. Table 1.3 shows the caregivers' estimated mean score on frequency, in the past week, of behavioral problems occurring in the care recipients grouped according to types of impairment. The entire 28-item Memory and Behavioral Checklist was regrouped into the following subscales or subtypes of problems:

1. **Memory problems** (wandering or getting lost, having difficulty remembering how to do simple tasks, losing or misplacing things, not recognizing familiar people, and forgetting what day it is).

TABLE 1.3
Mean Score on Frequency of Specific Problems Exhibited by the Disabled and the Severe Cognitive Impairment Cases: Shanghai Epidemiologic Survey of Dementia

	Mean Frequency of Specific Problems			
		Severe Cognitive		
	Disabled	Impairment		
Types of Behavior	(N = 212)	(N = 295)	Ratio	t-test
Memory problems	3.2925	3.8847	0.85	1.42*
Personality change	1.3160	0.6712	1.96	3.60**
Irritating behaviors	3.3255	2.1178	1.57	1.65**
Destructiveness	0.5613	0.1525	3.68	7.42**
Self-care problems	3.9953	2.8339	1.41	2.07**
Housekeeping chores	7.5802	6.1051	1.24	N.S.

Note: The higher the score, the greater the frequency.
*$p \leq .05$
**$p \leq .01$

2. **Personality change** (being suspicious and accusative, hearing voices from the past, reliving situations from the past, seeing or hearing things that are not there).

3. **Irritating behavior** (asking repetitive questions, not completing tasks, waking you up at night, being constantly restless or talkative, and packing up special items).

4. **Destructiveness** (destroying property; having objectionable, rude, or embarrassing behavior; engaging in behavior potentially dangerous to others; engaging in behavior potentially dangerous to self).

5. **Self care problems** (unable to dress oneself, feed oneself, bathe or shower, groom or shave, incontinent of bowel or bladder).

6. **Inability to perform housekeeping chores** (unable to prepare meals, clean house, use the phone, handle money, and shop).

In order to facilitate comparison across subtypes of behavioral problems, we adjusted the total score of the two subscales (destructiveness and personality change) that consisted of only four, instead of five, items. Among the six types of problems examined, the most frequent (i.e., occurred most frequently in the week preceding the interview) was inability to sustain housekeeping chores, according to caregivers of both the disabled and the cognitively impaired elderly (Table 1.3). For the disabled, the next most frequent set of problems was self-care, followed by irritating behavior, memory problems, personality changes, and destructiveness. For the cognitively impaired, the order of frequency is memory problems, self-care, irritating behavior, personality changes, and destructiveness.

Next, we examined the caregiver's mean tolerance score for specific types of problems (Table 1.4). We noted that, in general, caregivers of the disabled

TABLE 1.4
Caregiver's Mean Tolerance Score (× 100) for Specific Problems Exhibited by the Disabled and the Severe Cognitive Impairment Cases: Shanghai Epidemiologic Survey of Dementia

	Mean Tolerance Score (× 100)			
Types of Problems	Disabled (N = 212)	Severe Cognitive Impairment (N = 295)	Ratio	t-test
Memory Problems	66.51	49.49	1.34	1.97**
Personality Change	38.21	26.44	1.45	3.60**
Irritating Behaviors	81.60	48.47	1.68	3.58**
Destructiveness	25.00	7.46	3.35	5.81**
Self-care problems	183.41	148.08	1.24	1.92**
Housekeeping chores	101.89	41.36	2.46	4.26**

Note: The higher the score, the less tolerable is the behavior. The original score is multiplied by 100 for convenience.
**$p \leq .01$

reported higher scores, indicative of greater intolerance, than caregivers of the cognitively impaired. This consistency is remarkable. Contrary to the American attitudes, symptoms of dementia appear to be more tolerable to Chinese caregivers than behavioral manifestations of physical disabilities.

Table 1.5 shows the correlation between frequency of, and tolerance for, each type of problem and for each group of caregivers. In all instances, the association is statistically significant, and the magnitude of the correlation coefficient is in the modest-to-good range. Among the caregivers of the severely impaired, the highest correlation coefficients are found in two subtypes of behavioral problems: personality change and irritating behaviors. Among the disabled, irritating behaviors, destructiveness, and personality change showed the highest correlations between frequency and tolerance score.

TABLE 1.5
Correlation between Frequency and Tolerance for Specific Disorders Exhibited by the Disabled and the Severe Cognitive Impairment Cases: Shanghai Epidemiologic Survey of Dementia

Types of Behavior	Disabled (N = 212)	Severe Cognitive Impairment (N = 295)
Memory problems	0.45931**	0.32805**
Personality change	0.56351**	0.71108**
Irritating behaviors	0.58400**	0.60511**
Destructiveness	0.57854**	0.41703**
Self-care problems	0.54720**	0.50572**
Housekeeping chores	0.36692**	0.26657**

**$p < .01$

Next, we evaluated the caregiver's tolerance score by the caregiver's characteristics (Table 1.6). In every group except for "Relationship to care recipient," the caregivers of the disabled reported significantly higher intolerance scores than the caregivers of the cognitively impaired persons. The results are less striking when we examine the care recipient's characteristics in Table 1.7. Higher intolerance scores among caregivers of the disabled, compared with those of the cognitively impaired, are found only among women, persons 65–74 years of age, without any education, and those who were married. Thus, it appears that a caregiver's tolerance scores are more

TABLE 1.6
**Caregiver's Mean Tolerance Score (× 100) by the Caregiver's Sociodemographic
Characteristics: Shanghai Epidemiologic Survey of Dementia**

	Caregiver's Tolerance Score (× 100)					
	Disabled		Severe Cognitive Impairment			
Caregiver's Characteristics	(n)	Mean	(n)	Mean	Ratio	t-test
Sex						
Male	(85)	241.18	(140)	167.86	1.44	2.10**
Female	(127)	522.83	(155)	251.67	2.08	4.85**
Age						
< 55 years	(75)	341.33	(143)	200.70	1.70	2.77**
55 years and older	(136)	450.74	(151)	223.84	2.01	4.57**
Education						
None	(38)	586.84	(30)	180.00	3.26	7.03**
Elementary or less	(49)	512.24	(83)	236.14	2.17	5.74**
High school or more	(125)	316.00	(180)	202.22	1.56	2.42**
Marital status						
Married	(166)	442.17	(235)	187.66	2.36	5.24**
Spouseless	(25)	204.00	(25)	256.00	0.80	N.S.
Never married	(21)	400.00	(35)	342.86	1.17	3.33*
Living with care recipient?						
No	(14)	207.14	(40)	130.00	1.59	3.19*
Yes	(198)	424.24	(255)	224.17	1.89	4.12**
Occupational status						
Caregiver	(37)	518.92	(21)	100.00	5.19	18.96**
Employed elsewhere	(66)	371.21	(139)	195.68	1.90	3.84**
Retired	(92)	382.61	(117)	264.96	1.44	3.09**
Housewife	(17)	470.59	(18)	122.22	3.85	7.52**
Relationship to care recipient						
Spouse	(61)	408.20	(76)	155.26	2.63	N.S.
Children and/or in-laws	(99)	374.75	(169)	240.24	1.56	N.S.
Parents, sibs, or kins	(38)	294.74	(30)	210.00	1.40	N.S.
Other	(14)	78.57	(20)	190.00	0.41	N.S.

*$p \leq .05$
**$p \leq .01$

TABLE 1.7
The Caregiver's Mean Tolerance Score by the Care Recipient's Sociodemographic Characteristics: Shanghai Epidemiologic Survey of Dementia

	Caregiver's Tolerance Score (× 100)					
	Disabled		*Severe Cognitive Impairment*			
Care Recipient's Characteristics	*(n)*	*Mean*	*(n)*	*Mean*	*Ratio*	*t-test*
Sex						
Male	(55)	452.73	(55)	260.00	1.74	N.S.
Female	(157)	394.90	(40)	200.83	1.97	2.05*
Age						
55–64 years	(11)	300.00	(16)	50.00	6.00	N.S.
65–74 years	(37)	367.57	(76)	84.21	4.36	2.14*
75 years and older	(164)	426.83	(203)	272.41	1.57	N.S.
Education						
None	(99)	552.53	(200)	200.00	2.76	2.49*
Elementary or less	(71)	297.18	(81)	200.00	1.49	N.S.
High school or more	(41)	270.73	(13)	361.54	0.75	N.S.
Marital status						
Married	(83)	430.12	(110)	168.18	2.56	2.32*
Spouseless	(120)	388.33	(180)	241.11	1.61	N.S.
Never married	(9)	511.11	(4)	150.00	3.41	N.S.

*p ≤ .05
**p ≤ .01

closely associated with the caregiver's characteristics than those of the care recipient. Additional analyses are underway to explore this issue and will be published separately.

The caregivers' self-reports of the burden of care are presented in Table 1.8. In all but one dimension of the Burden Scale, significant differences exist between the caregivers of the disabled and of the cognitively impaired. A larger percentage of those caring for the disabled indicated that, compared to a year ago, they had less time for themselves, more stress in their relationship with the care recipient, less personal privacy, less time for recreation, vacation, or trips, and less time to do their own work or be with their own friends. Altogether, 55% of the caregivers of the disabled and 40% of those caring for the cognitively impaired reported any burden of care. The mean scores for those reporting any burden of care between the two groups of caregivers are fairly similar.

To obtain a preliminary insight as to the costs of caregiving, we inquired about certain changes that might have been made by the caregiver in order to adapt to the demands of caregiving (Table 1.9). Specifically, we asked if there had been any of the following changes as a result of caring for the impaired

TABLE 1.8
The Caregiver's Self-Report of the Burden of Care: Shanghai Epidemiologic Survey of Dementia

Self-Report of the Burden of Care	Disabled		Severe Cognitive Impairment		χ^2
	(n)	%	(n)	%	
Time to oneself					
a lot less time	(19)	9.0	(20)	6.8	
a little less time	(79)	37.3	(68)	23.1	
the same as before	(109)	51.4	(204)	69.2	
more than before	(5)	2.4	(3)	1.0	17.05**
Strain in relationship with the care recipient					
a lot less stress	(18)	8.5	(27)	9.2	
a little less stress	(22)	10.4	(7)	2.4	
the same as before	(153)	72.2	(245)	83.1	
more than before	(19)	9.0	(16)	5.4	17.98*
Personal privacy					
a lot less privacy	(20)	9.4	(18)	6.1	
a little less privacy	(74)	34.9	(16)	20.7	
the same as before	(113)	53.3	(210)	71.2	
more than before	(5)	2.4	(6)	2.0	17.46*
Being manipulated					
a lot less	(57)	26.9	(68)	23.1	
a little less	(16)	7.5	(8)	2.7	
the same as before	(131)	61.8	(208)	70.7	
more than before	(8)	3.8	(10)	3.4	8.28*
Time for recreation					
a lot less	(23)	10.8	(28)	9.5	
a little less	(68)	32.1	(49)	16.6	
the same as before	(114)	53.8	(215)	72.9	
more than before	(7)	3.3	(3)	1.0	23.22**
Took vacation or trips					
a lot less	(71)	14.6	(28)	9.5	
a little less	(49)	23.1	(30)	10.2	
the same as before	(126)	59.4	(236)	80.0	
more than before	(6)	2.8	(1)	0.3	28.91**
Feeling nervous or depressed					
a lot less	(54)	25.5	(56)	19.0	
a little less	(19)	9.0	(10)	3.4	
the same as before	(122)	57.5	(210)	71.2	
more than before	(17)	8.0	(19)	6.5	13.03**
Time to do own work					
a lot less	(19)	9.0	(14)	4.7	
a little less	(64)	30.2	(51)	17.3	
the same as before	(121)	57.1	(225)	76.3	
more than before	(8)	3.8	(5)	1.7	21.16**

(continued)

TABLE 1.8 (*continued*)

Self-Report of the Burden of Care	Disabled		Severe Cognitive Impairment		χ^2
	(n)	%	(n)	%	
Unrealistic demands					
a lot less	(54)	25.5	(67)	22.7	
a little less	(13)	6.1	(7)	2.4	
the same as before	(137)	64.6	(214)	72.5	
more than before	(8)	3.8	(7)	2.4	N.S.
Time for own friends					
a lot less	(22)	10.4	(25)	8.5	
a little less	(57)	26.9	(37)	12.5	
the same as before	(130)	61.3	(231)	78.3	
more than before	(3)	1.4	(2)	0.7	19.85**
Mean score for those reporting any burden of care	28.52 ± 4.09		29.26 ± 3.59		
Total number of caregivers reporting any burden of care	(117)	55.2%	(117)	39.7%	

*$p \leq .05$
**$p \leq .01$

TABLE 1.9
Percentage of Caregivers Reporting Having Had to Change Their Lifestyle as a Result of Being a Caregiver: Shanghai Epidemiologic Survey of Dementia

Types of Change	Disabled		Severe Cognitive Impairment		χ^2
	(n)	%	(n)	%	
Change job	(18)	8.5	(12)	4.1	4.33*
Quit job completely	(8)	3.8	(5)	1.7	N.S.
Shorten work hours	(7)	3.3	(6)	2.0	N.S.
Change work hours	(10)	4.7	(9)	3.1	N.S.
Change residence	(16)	7.5	(17)	5.8	N.S.
Change place of sleep	(18)	8.5	(18)	6.1	N.S.
Change in diet	(18)	8.5	(16)	5.4	N.S.
Modify the house	(10)	4.7	(9)	3.1	N.S.
Hire someone to help	(14)	6.6	(12)	4.1	N.S.
Pinch pennies	(10)	4.7	(13)	4.4	N.S.
Mean number of changes for those reporting any change	2.19		2.34		
Total number of caregivers who reported any change	59 or 27.8%		50 or 16.9%		

Note: For the sake of parsimony, only the number and percent responding "yes" to type of change are shown.
*$p \leq .05$, $df = 1$.

elderly: change of jobs, quit job completely, shorten work hours, change work hours, change residence, change place of sleep, change in diet, modify the house, hire someone to help, and pinch pennies. A statistically significant difference was reported only for job change. Proportionally more caregivers of the disabled than the cognitively impaired reported that they had had to change jobs in order to meet the needs of the care recipient. It is important to note that about 28% of the caregivers of the disabled reported any change in life-style, compared to only 17% among the caregivers of the cognitively impaired.

DISCUSSION

Although several descriptive studies of caregivers have been conducted in the United States since the 1970s (Stephens & Christianson, 1986; Stone et al., 1987), few have specifically compared the experience of caring for the cognitively impaired with those of other types of impairment or disability. To the best of our knowledge, this is the first descriptive survey of caregivers in China that is based on a representative probability sample of noninstitutionalized community residents, 55 years of age and older. It is also the first study, as far as we know, that compares caregivers of the cognitively impaired with those of the disabled. The results highlight the importance of culture in caregiving and in caregiving research.

First, it is taken for granted in the U.S. that caring for the elderly with dementia is probably the most stressful caregiving role to undertake. In Shanghai, China, caregivers for the disabled appear to experience more stress than caregivers for the cognitively impaired. Proportionally more caregivers of the disabled than those of the cognitively impaired reported that they had experienced stress in the preceding 2 weeks and that stress had affected their health. Regardless of their gender, age, education, occupational roles, and marital status, caregivers of the disabled, compared to those of the cognitively impaired, uniformly reported a greater intolerance for the behavior of the care recipient. Their intolerance cuts across different types of memory and behavioral problems as well.

Second, there are significant cross-cultural differences between China and the U.S. in terms of caregivers' sociodemographic profiles. Whereas 61% of the disabled were taken care of by females, the cognitively impaired were as likely to be taken care of by males as by females. Less than 33% of all caregivers in Shanghai are spouses. Our population estimates suggest that spouses represent only 30% of the caregivers of the disabled and 28% of the caregivers of the cognitively impaired. By far, the largest category of caregivers in Shanghai, China, are children and in-laws. Nonkin caregivers are rare, accounting for only 7% of the caregivers in Shanghai.

Third, in the United States, being without a spouse is almost always associated with singlehood in old age and a higher probability for institutionalization in the face of disability or chronic illness. But in Shanghai, China, being without a spouse does not confine the elderly to a life alone nor to institutionalization; very few elderly actually live alone. Among those classified as being cognitively impaired by the CMMSE screening test, only 6% live alone, and among the disabled, only about 2% live alone. Nearly 75% of the disabled in Shanghai, compared to 82% of the cognitively impaired, were living with at least one of their own children at the time of our study. Another 12% of the disabled, and 6% of the cognitively impaired, were living with a relative other than one's nuclear family member. The general lack of institutionalized care facilities for the aged and the pervasiveness of inter- as well as intra-generational co-living arrangements in Shanghai have resulted in the availability of a large amount of informal social support to the elderly. That is quite impressive, compared to what one might find in the United States. Only 28% of the caregivers of the disabled, compared to 17% of those caring for the cognitively impaired, reported having had to change their life-style in order to perform their caregiving role. Forty-seven percent of the caregivers of the cognitively impaired are employed outside of the home, compared to 31% of the caregivers of the disabled.

Fourth, there are some cross-cultural commonalities in caregiving as well. The mean and median ages of caregivers in Shanghai do not appear to be significantly different from those reported in the United States. By and large, caregivers tend to be the "middle-aged" group sandwiched between two generations. Here is where the similarities end, however. In Shanghai, the age range of caregivers (20 to 87 years old for the disabled vs. 15 to 88 years old for the cognitively impaired) appears to be much wider than that reported in the U.S. literature. Chinese living in Shanghai take on the responsibility of caring for the aged at relatively young ages.

Fifth, our study in Shanghai also calls attention to the cultural assumptions hidden in our conceptualization of caregiving as social scientists. In the United States, caregiving as a concept implies a *dyadic* relationship—which may not necessarily hold in other countries where the nuclear household is not the dominant type of family structure and husband–wife relationship is not the predominant relationship in the family.

Sixth, in all cultures, caregiving implies both dependency and deviance on the part of the care recipient; but the extent to which dependency is viewed as part of the "expected" behavior of the aging population, and the extent to which the memory and behavioral problems associated with cognitive impairment and dementia are perceived as *deviant* may differ across cultures. Furthermore, such differences may underline the variations in tolerance exhibited by caregivers. We hypothesize that in Shanghai, probably a large majority of lay people associate the memory and behavioral problems of cognitive impairment and dementia with normal, rather than abnormal, aging processes. Because dependency in old age is the expected behavior in China, family members may experience less stress in the elderly's declining ability to perform household functions and self-care than in the United States.

Seventh, China and the U.S. differ greatly in the ways in which society adapts to the needs of the physical disabled. The relative scarcity in China of modern conveniences, prosthesis, and aides to facilitate the mobility of persons with disabilities is probably an important factor in explaining why Chinese in Shanghai find it more stressful to care for a disabled than a cognitively impaired elderly. For many Chinese, taking a shower may require fetching the water from outside the house, rather than just turning on the faucets; cooking a meal may require stooping to start a fire with the use of charcoal and wood or paper, rather than just turning a knob on the gas stove; and going to the toilet may entail daily emptying of the "pot" into a public waste collection system outside the house. Likewise, transporting a disabled person demands heavy exertion of energy in the absence of inexpensive mechanized locomotives for private use.

Eighth, the relationship between the care recipient's educational level and the caregiver's burden of care, as well as the effect of caregivers' education on their subjective burden, need to be better understood. Data from Shanghai indicate that one out of every five disabled had middle or high school education, compared to only 4% among those classified as cognitively impaired. Is it less stressful to care for a less-educated impaired elderly than a better educated one? Do highly educated caregivers experience more stress if they work exclusively as caregivers than less-educated caregivers? Would the highly educated caregivers feel less stress if they were not working exclusively as caregivers? A larger sample size is necessary to answer these questions adequately.

Finally, we wish to emphasize that this chapter is only the first of a series of analyses planned for the Shanghai caregivers' study. It is aimed at providing a preliminary descriptive profile of caregivers in Jing-An, Shanghai and to generate, rather than to test, hypotheses. Hence, it is important to acknowledge certain limitations in this chapter. As a preliminary analysis, cognitive impairment is defined tentatively by the application of a uniform cutoff score on the CMMSE rather than clinicians' diagnosis or education-adjusted cutoff scores. By choosing the lowest possible cutoff score reported in the literature, we have ensured that the uneducated are not likely to be misclassified as having cognitive impairment. But, by the same reasoning, it is possible that an undetermined portion of the educated whom we tentatively classify as not cognitively impaired — using the Yale-New Haven computer procedure — should in fact be classified as cognitively impaired if other criteria (such as education-adjusted cutoff scores) were used for caseness. Both issues — the lack of clinical diagnosis and the choice of a uniform cutoff score in determining caseness — will be addressed in greater detail in our future analyses.

Furthermore, the disabled in our study were those who were so obviously impaired physically as to be unable to perform on certain items of the CMMSE. For instance, those who were deaf simply could not hear the questions asked, and those who were blind simply could not see the objects being presented to them. In this context, should one consider their impairment to be more "severe" than those who were classified as cognitively impaired after taking the CMMSE? In our future work, we hope to examine more carefully the level of functioning in daily living among the disabled compared with the cognitively impaired. Perhaps, too, this is the time to begin planning a systematic community survey of caregiving *per se* in China, taking into account the type of impairment, disability, and chronic illness.

ACKNOWLEDGMENTS

The study described herein was funded by the Pacific/Asian American Mental Health Research Center housed formerly at the University of Illinois at Chicago through a grant from the National Institute of Mental Health (MH 36408-07), the Alzheimer's Disease Research Center at the University of California, San Diego, and the Shanghai Department of Health through a grant to the Shanghai Mental Health Center. Preparation of this chapter was made possible by a grant from the National Institute on Aging (1 RO1 AG10327-01). The authors are grateful to Yin-Ming Kean for her clerical assistance.

APPENDIX A

The SAS-Mainframe program called "ORGBRAIN" is based on:

Current syndrome of cognitive impairment based on Mini-Mental State Exam. The complex scoring arises because we do not know whether unanswered questions should be constructed as if they were errors (example: respondent is demented), or as if they were correct (example: a competent respondent says, "I do not like to take exams"). To understand the scoring, imagine that there are two parallel scoring systems of the MMSE: one based on the number of errors (OBSTOT) and the other based on the number of errors plus the number of unanswered questions (TOTWRNG). Each system classifies the respondent as having a severe disorder if the score is 13 or more and mild disorder for scores 7–12. When the two scoring systems agree with each other, we use the term *Definite* to define our level of certainty of the classification. When the two scoring systems disagree, we say the disorder may *Possibly* be present.

Meaning	OBSTOT	TOTWRNG	CORRECT	Value
Absent	0–6	0–6	24–30	1
Definite, Mild	7–12	7–12	18–23	2
Definite, Severe	13+	13+	0–17	3
Possibly severe, definitely mild	7–12	13+	0–17	4
Possibly mild, or none	0–6	7–12	18–23	6
Possibly severe, or none	0–6	13+	0–17	7
Missing diagnosis	0–6	–	–	.

REFERENCES

Branch, L., & Jette, A. (1983). Elders' use of informal long-term care assistance. *The Gerontologist, 23,* 51–56.

Brody, E. M. (1981). Women in the middle and family help to older people. *The Gerontologist, 25,* 19–29.

Brody, S., Poulshock, S. W., & Masciocchi, C. (1978). The family caring unit: A major consideration in the long-term support system. *The Gerontologist, 18,* 556–561.

Cantor, M. H. (1975). Life space and social support system of the inner city elderly of New York. *The Gerontologist, 15,* 23–24.

Cantor, M. H. (1980). The informal support system, its relevance in the lives of the elderly. In E. Borgatta and N. McCloskey (Eds.), *Aging and society* (pp. 131–144). Beverly Hills: Sage Publications.

Cantor, M. H. (1983). Strain among caregivers: A study of experience in the United States. *The Gerontologist, 23,* 597–604.

Dobrof, R., & Litwak, E. (1977). *Maintenance of family ties of long-term care patients.* Rockville, MD: National Institute of Mental Health.

Folstein, M. F., Folstein, S. E., & McHugh, P. R. (1975). Mini-Mental State: A practical method for grading the cognitive state of patients for the clinician. *Journal of Psychiatric Research, 12,* 189–198.

Horowitz, A. (1985a). Family caregiving in the frail elderly. In C. Eisdorfer (Ed.), *Annual Review of Gerontology and Geriatrics* (Vol. 5, pp. 194–246). New York: Springer.

Horowitz, A. (1985b). Sons and daughters as caregivers to older parents: Differences in role performance and consequences. *The Gerontologist, 25,* 612–617.

Katzman, R., Zhang, M. Y., Qu, G. Y., Wang, Z. Y., Liu, W. T., Yu, E., Wong, S. C., Salmon, D., & Grant, I. (1988). A Chinese version of the Mini-Mental State Examination: Impact of illiteracy in a Shanghai dementia survey. *Journal of Clinical Epidemiology, 41,* 971–978.

Kovar, M. G. (1986). *Aging in the eighties: Preliminary data from the supplement on aging to the National Health Interview Survey, United States, January–June 1984.* Advance Data from Vital and Health Statistics (115 DHHS Publication No. PHS 86–1250). Hyattsville, MD: Public Health Service.

Lee, G. R., & Ellithorpe, E. (1982). Intergenerational exchange and subjective well-being among the elderly. *Journal of Marriage and the Family, 44,* 217–224.

Levy, P. S., Yu, E. S. H., Liu, W. T., Wong, S. C., Zhang, M. Y., Wang, Z. Y., & Katzman R. (1989). Single-stage cluster sampling with a telescopic respondent rule: A variation motivated by a survey of dementia in elderly residents of Shanghai. *Statistics in Medicine, 8,* 1537–1544.

Levy, P. S., Yu, E. S. H., Liu, W. T., Zhang, M., Wang, Z., Wong, S., & Katzman, R. A. (1988). Sample design of the Shanghai elderly survey: A variation of single-stage cluster sampling. *International Journal of Epidemiology, 17,* 931–933.

Litwak, E. (1985). *Helping the Elderly: The complementary roles of informal networks and formal systems.* New York: Guilford Press.

Litwak, E., & Figueira, J. (1970). Technological innovation and ideal forms of family structure in an industrial society. In R. Hill, & R. Konig (Eds.), *Families in east and west: Socialization process and kinship ties.* Paris: Moulton.

Martin, L. G. (1988). The aging of Asia. *Journal of Gerontology: Social Sciences, 43*(4), S99-113.

Montgomery, R. J. V., Gonyea, J. G., & Hooyman, N. R. (1985). Caregiving and the experience of subjective and objective burden. *Family Relations. 34.* 19-26.

Rosenmayr, L. (1977). The family—a source of hope for the elderly. In E. Shanas & M. Sussman (Eds.), *Family Bureaucracy and the Elderly.* Durham, NC: Duke University Press.

Shanas, E. (1979a). Social myth as hypothesis: The case of the family relations of old people. *The Gerontologist, 19,* 3-9.

Shanas, E. (1979b). The family as a social support system in old age. *The Gerontologist, 19,* 169-174.

Shanas, E., Townsend, P., Wedderburn, D., Frills, H., Mihoj, P., & Stehouwer, J. (1968). *Old people in three industrial societies.* New York: Atherton Press.

Stephens, S. A., & Christianson, J. B. (1986). *Informal care of the elderly.* Lexington, MA: D. C. Heath.

Stone, R., Cafferata, G. L., & Sangl, J. (1987). Caregivers of the frail elderly: A national profile. *The Gerontologist, 27*(5), 616-626.

Weissman, M. M., Myers, J. K., Tischler, G. L., Holzer, C. E., Leaf, P. J., Orvaschel, J., & Brody, J. (1985). Psychiatric disorders (DSM-III) and cognitive impairment among the elderly in a U.S. urban community. *Acta Psychiatrica Scandinavica, 71,* 366-379.

Yu, E. S. H., Liu, W. T., Levy, P., Zhang, M. Y., Katzman, R., Lung, C. T., Wong, S. C., Wang, Z. Y., & Qu, G. Y. (1989). Cognitive impairment among elderly adults in Shanghai, China. *Journal of Gerontology: Social Sciences, 44*(3), S97-106.

Zarit, J. M., & Zarit, S. H. (1982). *Measuring burden and support in families with Alzheimer's disease elders.* Paper presented at the 35th Annual Scientific Meeting of the Gerontological Society of America, Boston, MA.

Zarit, S. H., Reever, K. E., & Back-Peterson, J. (1980). Relatives of the impaired elderly: Correlates of feelings of burden. *The Gerontologist, 20,* 649-655.

Zarit, S. H., Orr, N. K., & Zarit, J. M. (1985). *The hidden victims of Alzheimer's: Families under stress.* New York: New York University Press.

Intergenerational Transfer of Resources Within Policy and Cultural Contexts

Lucy C. Yu
The Pennsylvania State University

The demographic shifts occurring in American and Chinese populations are having a variety of effects on family interaction, thereby stimulating a great deal of interest in family-related issues, such as the care of aged parents. Numerous articles in the gerontological literature concerning caregiving burden underscore the problems and solutions that relate to the care of aged parents. However, their care requires more than family commitment. Cultural values and public policy also exert an influence on the care provided by families to their elderly.

Cross-national comparisons that put aging in cultural and policy contexts can help to elaborate general behavioral laws. This chapter examines support of aged parents as part of the continuum of the intergenerational transfer of resources in two populations—the Chinese in the People's Republic of China and the Chinese-Americans in the United States. By exploring this issue within cultural and policy contexts, readers can gain a deeper understanding of the dynamics of the intergenerational exchange of resources, a sharpened sensitivity to the effects of structural and cultural constraints, and a look at the varying possibilities for action within these constraints. Furthermore, the support of aged parents has economic consequences for the family as well as policy implications for society.

Cultural values provide a form of conduct that members consider ideal; it provides a special status to those who fulfill the desired behavioral pattern, and rewards the ideal behavior with honors, possessions, or special privileges (Goldschmidt, 1971). Subcultures protect different ethnic groups by providing continuity. Yet at the same time, the different cultural values held by these subgroups often create conflicting demands on the people whose cultural values differ from those in the social mainstream. Thus, a cultural value may produce normative behavior for society at large, but can act as either a positive or negative force in shaping immigrants' and their descendants' behavior in the United States. Filial piety is just such a cultural value shared by Chinese in the People's Republic of China and Chinese-Americans in the United States. Regardless of ethnic and cultural background, individuals have to practice their cultural values within the social structure (public and social policy) of the country in which they reside. This chapter examines how a cultural value, filial piety, evolves within (Chinese) and between (Chinese and American) cultures in the context of public policies in the People's Republic of China and the United States.

Some of these answers may be found in evolutionary theory, which suggests that in developing, high-fertility societies, such as China, families obtain help from the extended kin network. The care of kinfolk is a familial responsibility. In developed, low-fertility societies, such as the United States, social and economic aid is partially provided by public policy and obtained from social agencies outside the family. In low-fertility societies, the children in the nuclear family are the focus of the parents' reproductive heritage; investments in the children often continue into adulthood; care of and dependence on extended kin are not the intensive activities found in high-fertility societies (Turke, 1989).

China traditionally has been an agrarian, high-fertility society that encouraged large families with strong ties to the extended family. From its feudal, agrarian past, Confucius emerged to develop the concept of filial piety which then was incorporated into social policy. In contemporary China, government policy encourages low fertility (one child per family), but its policy toward the aged resembles that of earlier times (i.e., aged parents are the responsibility of their children).

The investigator focused on two salient components of filial piety, financial support to aged parents and coresidence with aged parents, to examine the intergenerational transfer of resources within the societal and cultural contexts of China and the United States. The objectives were (a) to explore the effect of government policies on the practice of filial piety among Chinese-Americans in the United States and among the Chinese in China; (b) to examine, in the absence of structural and institutional support in the United States, the manifestations of filial piety in America among Chinese immigrants and their descendants in this country; and (c) to explore the effect of cultural expectations (differences) on the expression of filial piety in the United States and in China. The specific aim was to use data taken from two earlier studies of Chinese Americans in the United States (Yu, 1983) and Chinese in the People's Republic of China (Yu, Yu, & Mansfield, 1990) to examine the treatment of aged parents in the context of filial obligation in two different countries. The two sets of data were collected in the same year, but the Chinese data were not analyzed until recently.

The theoretical basis for this study is rooted in the Confucian Doctrine of Filial Piety. Confucius was the most influential and respected philosopher in Chinese history. From 400 B.C. to 1900 A.D., his ideas served as the single strongest influence on Chinese society. His philosophy, called Confucianism, stressed the need to develop individual moral character and responsibilities; one of the primary emphases among the responsibilities is the care of aged parents (Sih, 1961). Translating the Confucian doctrine into everyday life meant loyalty, respect, fidelity, devotion, sacrifices, and absolute obedience to one's parents. Filial piety was held to be the highest ideal in traditional China. The goal of filial piety is to promote harmony within the family; the ultimate goal is to provide old age security for aged parents.

Within this cultural context, sons traditionally inherited their fathers' wealth or in the absence of wealth, supposedly paid their fathers' debts; sons were expected to take care of their aged parents while the parents were alive. Until the establishment of the People's Republic of China, there was no official policy to set aside retirement funds. Although public policy lacked specific legislation mandating old age security for the individual, the Confucian ethic emphasized social mores and conventions that expected adult sons to provide old age security for aged parents (i.e., sons were expected to fulfill their filial obligations). The support of aged parents came before all other obligations. Ideally, when there was competition for resources between the grandparent and the grandchild, filial obligation was fulfilled, even at the expense of the grandchild.

Both traditional and contemporary Chinese emphasize interdependence. The young depend on their parents and family connections, while the old depend on their adult children and children's connections. A person who did not fulfill his filial obligation would be sanctioned by friends, neighbors, and society at large. Hsu (1970) stated:

> The son not only had to follow the Confucian dictum that parents were always right but at all times, and in all circumstances, he must try to satisfy their wishes and look after their safety. If the parents were indisposed, the son would spare no trouble in obtaining a cure for them. Formerly, if a parent was sentenced to prison, the son might arrange to take that parent's place. If the parents were displeased with their daughter-in-law, the good son did not hesitate to think about divorce. (p. 78)

In the service of the elders, no effort was too extraordinary or too great. Folk tales contain many examples of filial duty. One story describes a man who gave up his hard-won official post in order to walk many miles in search of his long-lost mother. In another, a 14-year old boy jumped on and strangled a tiger when the beast was about to devour his father. In a third story, a man cut a piece of flesh from his arm and boiled it in the pot with his father's medicine, believing the soup would help the father to recover from illness. Chinese people have been known to copy these folk heroes in trying to fulfill their filial obligations (Hsu, 1970). Remember however, that these stories portray ideal extremes of filial piety that act as illustrations for the education of Chinese children.

On the other hand, Americans are concerned with what parents can do for their children. Young adults are encouraged to be independent and the elderly are proud not to be a burden to their children. Independence rather than interdependence is encouraged between the generations. Wake and Sporakowski (1972) have identified several factors that may have contributed to intergenerational independence, including: increased urbanization, increased cultural diversity between generations, increased national mobility, increased standard of living, social welfare programs, and cultural values which stress independence, decrease in the support of filial responsibility. In spite of these trends, Van Meter and Johnson (1985) found that the majority of frail elderly in the United States were cared for by their families and within the community. Although older cohorts of Chinese expect to live with their children, Americans have no such expectations. In general, the number of elderly persons in this country who live with their adult children has declined over the past 35 years.

METHOD

Sample

Detailed descriptions of the sample, procedures, and measurements are available elsewhere (Yu, 1983; Yu, Yu, & Mansfield, 1990). Brief summaries are provided below. The United States sample consisted of 510 (59% return rate) Chinese-Americans, 18 years and older, from a midwestern university town. It included an American-born Chinese group and three first-generation immigrant groups (the three groups were categorized by their length of stay in the United States). Table 2.1 presents respondents' length of stay in the United States and ages. The rationale to divide the immigrant group into three categories is based on the assumption that those who had lived in the United States for shorter lengths of time were less acculturated to American values than those who had lived here longer. Thus, the investigator expected to find that among the four groups, the American-born Chinese would profess the lowest level of filial belief and filial behavior, and that long-time residents (Chinese-Americans) would report the strongest beliefs and behavior in support of aged parents.

TABLE 2.1
Length of Stay in the U.S. and Age of Respondents
$n = 510$

	Age Groups								
	18–25		26–35		36–55		56+		Total
Years lived in the U.S.	n	%	n	%	n	%	n	%	n
1–5	(49)	31	(76)	54	(4)	3	(7)	12	(136)
6–15	(24)	15	(43)	31	(51)	34	(14)	23	(132)
16+	(6)	4	(6)	4	(72)	48	(33)	55	(117)
U.S. Born*	(80)	50	(16)	11	(23)	15	(6)	10	(125)
Total	(159)	100	(141)	100	(150)	100	(60)	100	(510)

*Lived in the U.S. their entire lives.

Fifty-three percent of the sample were male and 47% were female. Seventy-five percent were first-generation immigrants: 64% were born in China, 25% were born in the United States, and 10% were born elsewhere. Fifty-nine percent were married and 38% were single. Eighteen percent had some college education; 27% had graduated from college; 34.2% finished their master's degrees; 13% had PhDs; 51.2% of the sample had graduate degrees. Occupationally, 54% of the respondents classified themselves as professional and technical personnel. Only 1% was employed in health sciences (five physicians and one dentist); there were no lawyers; 40% were students; 7% were not in the labor force (excluding students and housewives without incomes). The fact that medical, dental, and law schools did not accept Chinese-Americans until recently probably accounted for the small number in health care and legal professions and the many physical scientists and engineers among them. This sample's educational attainment was higher than the national average for the United States. However, a university town would probably contain a larger percentage of college-educated individuals than would nonuniversity towns. Characteristics of nonrespondents indicated that the sample was representative of Chinese-Americans in a university town.

The Chinese sample consisted of 48 Chinese (96% return rate) who participated in a pilot study on a university campus in the People's Republic of China (PRC). Most respondents were physicists or engineers. Most scientists were assigned to university jobs based on their technical training. Respondents' ages ranged from 20 to 75. More than half were 36 or older. Eighty percent were married, 11% were single, and 6% were widowed. Fifty-six percent were males, and 44% were females. Eighty percent of males and 48% of females had finished college. All of the males and 86% of the females were employed. This sample's educational attainment was higher than the national average in the People's Republic of China. Again, one would expect this to be the case on a university campus. The participants in both studies shared a common cultural value (filial piety) and social position (faculty, university students, staff and their families).

Although these samples are not representative of the general populations, findings should suggest the extent to which filial piety exists today among two groups of Chinese living in very different social and economic spheres. Furthermore, these samples provided an opportunity to compare the articulation of a cultural value within and between cultures and within the policy contexts of two different countries.

Measurements and Procedure

Bilingual questionnaires were developed and pre-tested to ensure that the items were culturally relevant and linguistically correct. The purpose of the questionnaires was to examine respondents' beliefs and behaviors vis-a-vis financial support of and coresidence with aged parents in the context of filial obligation. In the American study, leaders of the Chinese-American community, student leaders, and the Dean of the School of Public Health were enlisted to support the Chinese-American project in the United States. The questionnaires were mailed after the project was announced by the investigator and key community and student leaders. Stamped, self-addressed envelopes were provided for the respondents' convenience. Three follow-ups, including a letter from the Dean and a postcard, were subsequently sent to nonrespondents. Respondents could request the assistance of a researcher to complete the questionnaire (Yu, 1983).

In the Chinese study, university officials were enlisted to help recruit respondents, and to distribute and collect questionnaires (Yu et al., 1990). Without university assistance and permission, the data would have been impossible to obtain. Although the letter of explanation and informed consent explicitly guaranteed anonymity, whether respondents seriously believed the guarantee due to official involvement is not known.

FINDINGS

Financial Support.   First, respondents were asked whether they believed in providing financial support to aged parents (yes or no). They then were asked how strong their belief was (low, medium, or high). Table 2.2 shows that overall, 70.2% of Chinese-Americans reported believing in giving financial support to aged parents, whereas 89% of the Chinese in the PRC reported the same belief. More Chinese-Americans (29.2%) in the United States than Chinese (11%) in the PRC reported that their filial belief depended on the family situation.

TABLE 2.2
Filial Relief (financial)

	Chinese-Americans in the U.S.		Chinese in the PRC	
	n	%	n	%
Yes	(358)	70.2	(42)	89
No	(3)	.6	–	–
Depends on Situation	(149)	29.2	(6)	11
Total	(510)	100.0	(48)	100.0

Table 2.3 shows that among Chinese-American men (87%) and women (80%), the most recent immigrants reported the largest percentage of high levels of filial belief. Newly immigrated men, x^2 $(3df)$ = 14.05; p < .002 and women, x^2 $(9df)$ = 6.51; p = n.s., had stronger filial belief levels than those of long-time Chinese-American residents in the United States.

TABLE 2.3
U.S. STUDY
Percent of Filial Belief/Financial Support Given to Parents and
Length of Stay in the U.S. by Gender

	Men Length of Stay (Yrs. in the U.S.)								
Filial Belief/	1–5		6–15		16 +		U.S. Born		Total
Financial Support	n	%	n	%	n	%	n	%	n
Low	–	–	–	–	–	–	–	–	–
Medium	(11)	13	(16)	23	(24)	40	(14)	23	(65)
High	(73)	87	(53)	77	(36)	60	(47)	77	(209)
Total n	(84)		(69)		(60)		(61)		(274)
Total %		100		100		100		100	

X^2 $(3df)$ = 14.05; p < .002

	Women Length of Stay (Yrs. in the U.S.)								
Filial Belief/	1–5		6–15		16 +		U.S. Born		Total
Financial Support	n	%	n	%	n	%	n	%	n
Low	–	–	(1)	2	(2)	4	–	–	(3)
Medium	(10)	20	(20)	32	(30)	55	(24)	38	(84)
High	(41)	80	(42)	66	(23)	42	(40)	62	(146)
Total n	(51)		(62)		(55)		(64)		(233)
Total %		100		100		100		100	

X^2 $(9df)$ = 6.51; p N.S.

In general, within immigrant groups, the shorter the stay in the United States had been, the stronger was the filial belief. This probably reflects the effects of acculturation: the newest immigrants who were the least acculturated reported the strongest filial belief among all groups. Older immigrants (not older in age, but older in having been in the United States longer than other groups) who were more acculturated reported lower levels of filial belief than the new immigrants. Filial belief as reported by American-born Chinese (the most acculturated group) was somewhere between the new immigrants and the older immigrants.

Financial Behavior.   Respondents were asked whether they gave money and gifts to their parents. If they answered affirmatively, they were asked how often and how much they gave. Table 2.4 shows that 86.5% of Chinese-Americans and 90% of Chinese gave financial support and/or gifts to their aged parents. Among those who gave, 65.9% of Chinese-Americans and 41% of Chinese gave on a regular basis; 20.6% of Chinese-Americans and 49% of Chinese gave on special occasions.

Next, Chinese-American respondents' length of stay in the United States and their filial behavior levels were examined. Table 2.5 shows that, again, among Chinese-American immigrants, the pattern of giving varied. Men, x^2 $(9df) = 28.91$; $p < .001$ and women, x^2 $(9df) = 28.72$; $p < .001$ who had lived in the United States longer gave more money and gifts to their parents than the American-born Chinese (some immigrants lived longer in the United States than the American-born Chinese, most of whom were 25 years of age or younger), and the newer immigrants.

Table 2.6 shows that for Chinese-Americans, marital status and employment were important factors affecting the provision of financial support: 90% of married, employed respondents gave to their parents, as compared to 78% of married unemployed respondents who gave to their parents, x^2 $(1df)$ $= 5.42$, $p = .02$, x^2 $(1df) = 12.11$, $p = .001$. However, these differences, although significant, are trivial compared to the high percentage of "givers" in all groups. In the PRC, public policy assigns each adult a job; therefore,

TABLE 2.4
Financial Behavior: Support Given to Aged Parents

Frequency	Chinese-Americans in the U.S.		Chinese in the PRC	
	n	%	*n*	%
Never	(67)	13.1	(5)	10
Weekly or Monthly	(336)	65.9	(20)	41
Birthdays, Holidays, and Special Occasions	(105)	20.6	(23)	49
Irregularly	(2)	.4	–	–
Total	(510)	100.0	(48)	100.0

TABLE 2.5
U.S. STUDY
Percent of Filial Behavior/Financial Support Given to Parents and
Length of Stay in the U.S. by Gender

	Men Length of Stay (Yrs. in the U.S.)								
	1–5		6–15		16+		U.S. Born		Total
Filial Behavior/ Financial Support	n	%	n	%	n	%	n	%	n
Low	(27)	32	(24)	37	(14)	25	(15)	25	(80)
Med. low	(10)	12	(7)	11	(12)	21	(5)	9	(34)
Med. high	(37)	45	(17)	26	(10)	18	(29)	49	(93)
High	(9)	11	(17)	26	(20)	36	(10)	17	(56)
Total n	(83)		(65)		(56)		(59)		(263)
Total %		100		100		100		100	

X^2 (9df) = 28.91; p < .001

	Women Length of Stay (Yrs. in the U.S.)								
	1–5		6–15		16+		U.S. Born		Total
Filial Behavior/ Financial Support	n	%	n	%	n	%	n	%	n
Low	(8)	16	(18)	31	(18)	34	(19)	30	(63)
Med. low	(8)	17	(8)	14	(6)	12	(1)	2	(23)
Med. high	(29)	59	(18)	32	(14)	27	(36)	57	(97)
High	(4)	8	(13)	23	(14)	27	(7)	11	(38)
Total n	(49)		(57)		(52)		(63)		(221)
Total %		100		100		100		100	

X^2 (9df) = 28.72; p < .001

theoretically, all adult Chinese were supposed to be employed. For that reason, we did not do this analysis for the Chinese.

Although it appears that many Chinese-Americans in the United States and Chinese in the PRC fulfilled their filial obligations by providing financial support to their parents, their behavior was stressful. Table 2.7 shows that 11.2% of Chinese-Americans and 9% of Chinese reported great difficulty in providing support (they provided it anyway); 27.3% of Chinese-Americans and 14% of Chinese reported difficulty in providing support.

At this point it seems logical to ascertain the level of discomfort experienced by Chinese-American respondents if unemployed and thus unable to provide financial support to their parents. Analysis of variance was computed. Table 2.8 shows that unemployed men who did not give financial support to their parents reported the highest discomfort level ($\bar{x}$ = 1.48); men who were employed but who did not give financial support to parents reported higher discomfort levels ($\bar{x}$ = 1.40) than both employed and unemployed women.

Culturally, Chinese men were expected to provide for aged parents. Failure to do so may have contributed to their discomfort.

TABLE 2.6
Percentage of Respondents Giving Financial Support to Parents by Marital Status and Employment[a]

	Yes		No		
Financial Support Given	n	%	n	%	
		Employed			
Yes	(277)	88	(138)	80	$p = .02$[b]
No	(39)	12	(35)	20	
		Married			
Yes	(257)	90	(148)	78	$p = .001$[c]
No	(0)	10	(42)	22	

[a]Among 72 married couples, 58 couples including both husband and wife gave something to parents (81%); for 6 couples, only one spouse gave to parents (8%); 8 couples supplied incomplete information (11%).
[b]$x^2(1df) = 5.42$.
[c]$x^2(1df) = 12.11$.

TABLE 2.7
Difficulty in Giving Financial Support to Parents

	Chinese Americans in the U.S.		Chinese in the PRC	
	n	%	n	%
Not Difficult	(314)	61.6	(37)	77
Sometimes Difficult	(138)	27.3	(7)	14
Very Difficult	(57)	11.2	(4)	9
Total	(510)	100.0	(48)	100

TABLE 2.8
One-Way Analysis of Variance of Employment by Gender and Discomfort in Providing Financial Support for Aged Parents*

	n	Stratum Mean	S.D.
Male, Work	(112)	1.40	.33
Female, Work	(80)	1.32	.28
Male, No Work	(35)	1.48	.41
Female, No Work	(53)	1.36	.35
Total	(280)	p Value = .0456	

*Significant Level = .05.

Coresidence. Traditionally, Chinese fulfilled their filial obligation by either living in their parents' household after they (the respondents) were married or by bringing their aged parents to live with them after the respondents established their own households. Respondents were asked if they believed in fulfilling their filial obligation by coresiding with aged parents. Fifty-four percent of Chinese-Americans and 84% of Chinese believed in having their aged parents live with them. Our data (not presented here) also shows that men whose parents did not coreside with them reported higher discomfort levels than men whose parents lived with them. Table 2.9 shows that among Chinese-American immigrants in the United States, the shorter the stay in the United States was, the stronger was the respondents' belief in fulfilling their filial obligation by establishing coresidence with aged parents.

TABLE 2.9
U.S. STUDY
Percent of Filial Belief/Housing and Length of Stay in the U.S. by Gender

	\<br\>*Men*\<br\>*Length of Stay (Yrs. in the U.S.)*								
Filial Belief/	*1–5*		*6–15*		*16+*		*U.S. Born*		*Total*
Housing	*n*	*%*	*n*	*%*	*n*	*%*	*n*	*%*	*n*
Low	(16)	19	(12)	17	(20)	32	(16)	26	(64)
Med. low	(18)	21	(22)	32	(15)	24	(18)	20	(73)
Med. high	(24)	28	(18)	26	(12)	20	(14)	23	(68)
High	(27)	32	(17)	25	(15)	24	(13)	21	(72)
Total *n*	(85)		(67)		(62)		(61)		(277)
Total %		100		100		100		100	

X^2 (9*df*) = 9.17; *p* < .427

	\<br\>*Women*\<br\>*Length of Stay (Yrs. in the U.S.)*								
Filial Belief/	*1–5*		*6–15*		*16+*		*U.S. Born*		*Total*
Housing	*n*	*%*	*n*	*%*	*n*	*%*	*n*	*%*	*n*
Low	(6)	12	(11)	18	(25)	45	(24)	37	(66)
Med. low	(9)	18	(19)	30	(18)	33	(23)	36	(69)
Med. high	(20)	39	(17)	27	(8)	15	(14)	22	(59)
High	(16)	31	(16)	25	(4)	7	(3)	5	(39)
Total *n*	(51)		(63)		(57)		(64)		(233)
Total %		100		100		100		100	

X^2 (9*df*) = 43.30; *p* < .001

In Table 2.10, within groups of immigrant men and women among Chinese-Americans, the longer the stay in the United States was, the greater was the possibility that their parents lived with them. These Chinese-Americans were older and more financially established than younger groups;

TABLE 2.10
U.S. STUDY
Percent of Filial Behavior/Housing and Length of Stay in the U.S. by Gender

Filial Behavior/ Housing	Men Length of Stay (Yrs. in the U.S.)								Total
	1–5		6–15		16+		U.S. Born		
	n	%	n	%	n	%	n	%	n
Low	–	–	(1)	1	(1)	2	–	–	(2)
Med. low	(52)	61	(32)	47	(24)	39	(50)	82	(158)
Med. high	(19)	22	(15)	22	(14)	23	(5)	8	(53)
High	(14)	17	(21)	30	(22)	36	(6)	10	(63)
Total n	(85)		(69)		(61)		(61)		(276)
Total %		100		100		100		100	

Filial Behavior/ Housing	Women Length of Stay (Yrs. in the U.S.)								Total
	1–5		6–15		16+		U.S. Born		
	n	%	n	%	n	%	n	%	n
Low	(2)	4	(3)	5	(1)	2	–	–	(6)
Med. low	(27)	55	(32)	51	(21)	38	(55)	86	(135)
Med. high	(14)	29	(11)	18	(14)	26	(5)	8	(44)
High	(6)	12	(16)	26	(19)	34	(4)	6	(45)
Total n	(49)		(62)		(55)		(64)		(230)
Total %		100		100		100		100	

the older group was also more likely to live in larger houses. Their parents came to live with them not because of illness, disability, or being less affluent than the children (although some children were more affluent than their parents), but because it is a Chinese tradition. Tradition and filial obligation not withstanding, the data indicated coresidence with parents did not last as long among Chinese-Americans as it did among Chinese in the PRC. Most American-born Chinese in the sample were still financially dependent on their parents while they were in school; therefore, the parents did not live with them. If they had a choice, a greater proportion of Chinese-Americans than Chinese (in the PRC) preferred to live by themselves in their own homes. A greater proportion of Chinese preferred to live with their children.

When respondents were asked if their parents actually lived with them, only about 20% of the Chinese-Americans (106 out of 510 respondents) responded affirmatively, whereas 50% of Chinese in the PRC had had a parent live with them. Table 2.11 shows that in general PRC parents live with their children longer than Chinese-American parents in the United States: Fifty-four percent of Chinese-Americans had their parents live with them for up to one year. Most reported that these were temporary arrangements. Few (n = 9) Chinese-Americans had their parents live with them up to 10 years; fewer (n

TABLE 2.11
Actual Number of Years Aged Parents Lived with Respondents

	Chinese Americans in the U.S. n = 106		Chinese in the PRC n = 48	
	n	%	n	%
Up to 1 Year	(57)	53.7	–	–
2–5 Years	(32)	30.3	(12)	26
6–10 Years	(9)	8.5	(6)	12
11–12 Years	(8)	7.5	–	–
12–20 Years	–	–	(4)	8
More than 20 Years	–	–	(2)	4
Parents Never Lived in My Home	N/A	N/A	(24)	50

= 8) had their parents live with them for up to 12 years. However, Chinese in the PRC were more likely than the Chinese-Americans to have a parent live with them for more than 6 years; 8% of Chinese had a parent live with them for 12 to 20 years; and 4% had a parent live with them for more than 20 years.

DISCUSSION

This study found that Chinese-Americans and Chinese have similar filial beliefs but different behaviors regarding financial support and coresidence with aged parents. These differences cannot be explained only by variations in tradition and culture in the United States and in China. A plausible explanation lies in the interaction of multiple factors that affect intergenerational relations and the transfer of resources from one generation to another. Chinese-Americans in this country and Chinese in the PRC still share the Confucian belief that children should care for their parents in old age. But there are discrepancies in their filial behavior. Factors that may have been responsible for these differences are varying government policies, cultural values, societal expectations, and individual circumstances in the United States and the People's Republic of China. The 1982 Chinese Constitution mandates that "children who have come of age have the duty to support and assist their parents and grandparents" (Sher, 1984, p. 49). Retired workers have the right to stay in their preretirement housing. Because of scarce housing, the aged in the PRC do not normally live alone; three or four generations commonly live under the same roof in the elderly's household. If the elderly were not employed and did not have assigned housing, they were expected to live with their children. In the extended family, more than one income is common. The pensions of the elderly are often pooled with the wages of the working adults, who in turn fulfill their filial duties by caring for and living with the elderly. This mutual support among the generations is reinforced by public policy that requires adult children to care for their parents and uphold the traditional value of filial piety. Furthermore, because everyone in the PRC is assigned jobs, married adult children have routinely turned to their retired mothers (women retire at age 50) to provide full-time, live-in child care. The Chinese emphasize the interdependence rather than the independence of the generations.

In the United States, different generations of the same family are often separated geographically, making coresidence unlikely. Americans encourage the independence rather than the dependence of the aged. Chinese-American behavior in particular is also confounded by geographic separation of aged parents and adult children who left home to pursue graduate education in the United States. Many Chinese-Americans in this study said that their parents were either in Taiwan, China, or deceased. Some reported that their parents did not need financial support and were still living in their own homes. Also in this country, although the care of the elderly is still a family affair, the care of aged parents is not mandated by law and the tradition is not strongly reinforced by societal mores or social structure. Because their length of stay in this country seemed to affect Chinese-Americans' filial behavior, this investigator speculates that acculturation may have contributed to the irreg- ular record of financial support and the living patterns of the Chinese- Americans in this country. Although the Chinese-American sample had evidently maintained this cultural value, their behavior was more similar to that of other American adults. Eggebeen and Hogan (1990) found that "during the 1980s American adults were in frequent contact with their non-coresident parents, but these contacts were not characterized by a high level of regular exchange. Instead, support tends to be episodic and to be concentrated in periods of need." Among Americans, only 4% give money to their parents. Large numbers of non-coresident American adults are not regularly involved in any exchange of support with their living parents (41% of the sample neither give nor receive aid on any of the four dimensions: gift or loan to parents of at least $200 in the past 5 years; gave advice, encouragement, moral or emotional support to parent in past month; gave help with childcare or babysitting to parent in past month; gave help with transportation, repairs to house or car, or work around the house). The Chinese-Americans in this sample did support their parents more often than was reported for the aged in the Hogan and Eggebeen study, but did not support their parents to the extent that the Chinese in the PRC did.

Regarding coresidence, for many elderly who can no longer live indepen- dently, Van Meter and Johnson (1985) found that in 1940, approximately 15% of the elderly males resided with adult children versus 4% in 1975; 45% of the single elderly women were living with family in 1950 as compared to 25% in 1977 (Mindel, 1980). In the United States, a stable percentage of approximately 20%-25% of those over 75 years of age reside in a family setting (Mindel, 1980). In contrast, 72% of Chinese elderly live with their children (*Hsin Hwa News,* 1991). Single elderly women tend to live by themselves and single elderly men tend to remarry and live with their new spouse. Most of the elderly in the United States prefer to retain their independence in their own homes, although some will move in with their children to avoid institutionalization (Mindel, 1980). No figures are available on institutionalization among Chinese-Americans in the United States and Chinese in the PRC. Institutionalization of a parent because of old age or infirmity was not acceptable in traditional Chinese society. In 1979, when this investigator visited China, the authorities searched for five weeks before finding a small nursing home for her to visit. This home was located outside a major metropolitan seaport. However, a number of nursing homes exist in the PRC today. A survey has not yet been carried out to determine who would place their parents in nursing homes.

In conclusion, by reexamining two previous studies carried out in the same year, one in the United States and the other in the People's Republic of China, this chapter explored the intergenerational transfer of resources as one way to support aged parents. Seventy percent of Chinese-Americans believed in providing financial support to aged parents but not all of them gave this support on a regular basis. Ninety percent of Chinese in the PRC believed in providing financial support to aged parents; a larger proportion gave on a regular basis than did Chinese-Americans in the United States. A larger proportion of the Chinese believed in coresiding with aged parents; most Chinese-Americans felt that aged parents should maintain separate living quarters from their adult children. Few Chinese-Americans ever had their parents live with them for an extended period but 50% of the Chinese in the PRC in our sample had one or both parents live with them for an extended period of time. Because the length of stay in the United States among Chinese-Americans seemed to affect their filial belief and behavior, this investigator suggests that acculturation has contributed to the irregular financial support record and the living patterns of the Chinese-Americans in this country. However, differences in belief and behavior between Chinese-Americans in the United States and Chinese in the PRC cannot be attributed to acculturation alone. Factors that may have been responsible for the differences are government policies, cultural values, societal expectations, and individual circumstances in the United States and the People's Republic of China. Although the Chinese traditionally expect children to care for their aged parents, it is useful to view the PRC group against the background of the 20th-century Chinese social and intellectual revolutions, which included a rebellion against the traditional power structure of the family. That so many adult children still profess or practice filial piety may be partly a result of the lack of alternative measures, and only partly ideological. In the PRC, job mobility is limited; people are not allowed to move from one job to another or from one city to another. Chinese law and social policy, plus the reality of pooled family income across the generations and severe housing shortages, made coresidence necessary. In the United States, occupational mobility is characteristic of certain segments of the population. Social Security, Medicaid, and Medicare, however inadequate, provide some financial assistance for the aged. In regard to living quarters, Van Meter and Johnson (1985) found that in the United States, "most older people live less than an hour from at least one of their children. Most older people want to be as independent as possible but when they cannot manage for themselves, they may expect some help from their children." No law requires children to care for their parents. The lack of social structure and government policies to reinforce filial piety in the United States, and perhaps acculturation, led Chinese-Americans to exhibit beliefs and behaviors toward aged parents similar to those of the host country. However, the Chinese in the PRC still fulfill their filial obligations by providing financial support to aged parents and by living with their parents in the same household.

ACKNOWLEDGMENT

The author is indebted to Drs. Gretchen Cornwell and E-tu Sun for their critical reading of the manuscript.

REFERENCES

Eggebeen, D. J., & Hogan, D. P. (1990). Giving between generations in American families. *Human Nature, 1(3),* 211–232.

Elderly in The People's Republic of China. *Hsin Hwa News* (1991, May 11).

Goldschmidt, W. (1971). The comparative study of values. In W. Goldschmidt (Ed.), *Exploring the ways of mankind* (2nd ed.). New York: Holt, Rinehart, & Winston, Inc.

Hsu, F. (1970). *Americans and Chinese.* Garden City, NY: Doubleday & Company, Inc.

Mindel, C. H. (1980). Extended familism among urban Mexican Americans, Anglos and Blacks. *Hispanic Journal of Behavioral Sciences, 2,* 21–34.

Sher, E. A. (1984). *Aging in post-Mao China.* Boulder and London: Westview Press.

Sih, P. (1961). *The Hsaio Ching.* New York: St. John's University Press.

Turke, P. W. (1989). Evolution and the demand for children. *Population and Development Review, 15,* 61–90.

Van Meter, M. J. S., & Johnson, P. (1985). Family decision making and long-term care for the elderly, Part II: a review. *Journal of Religion & Aging, 1(4),* 59–88.

Wake, S. B., & Sporakowski, M. J. (1972). An intergenerational comparison of attitudes toward supporting aged parents. *Journal of Marriage and the Family, 34(1),* 42–47.

Yu, L. C. (1983). Patterns of filial belief and behavior within the contemporary Chinese-American family. *International Journal of Sociology of the Family, 13,* 17–36.

Yu, L. C., Yu, Y. J., & Mansfield, P. K. (1990). Gender and changes in support of aged parents in China. *Gender and Society, 4,* 83–89.

3

Temporal Context and the Caregiver Role: Perspectives from Ethnographic Studies of Multigeneration African-American Families

Linda M. Burton
Silvia Sörensen
The Pennsylvania State University

The role of caregivers in the lives of dependent elders has received considerable attention in the gerontological literature since the 1970s (Gatz, Bengtson, & Blum, 1990; MaloneBeach & Zarit, 1991). Currently, there exist a plethora of conceptual and empirically based discussions on such topics as: the personal attributes of caregivers (e.g., Fitting, Rabins, Lucas, & Eastman, 1986; Horowitz, 1985; Zarit, Birkel, & MaloneBeach, in press); patterns of well-being, stress, and coping among caregivers (Brody, 1985; Cantor, 1983; George & Gwyther, 1986; Haley, Levine, Brown, & Bartolucci, 1987; Pearlin, Mullan, Semple, & Skaff, 1989; Quayhagen & Quayhagen, 1988); and the effectiveness of intervention programs and community services on relieving caregiver burden (Gallagher, Lovett, & Zeiss, in press; Niederehe & Fruge, 1984). Although these discussions have contributed significantly to our understanding of the caregiver role from psychological, clinical, and policy/ programs perspectives, critical gaps in knowledge prevail with regard to contextual perspectives on caregiving. In particular, the impact of temporal context, or dimensions of time, on the caregiver role have rarely been addressed in existing literature.

This chapter examines the relationship between temporal context and the caregiver role and suggests ways to think about this relationship in a manner that has not been previously addressed in the literature. Traditionally, in discussions of caregiving, the concept of time refers to either the number of hours per day spent in caregiving activities (time allocation studies) or the length of time one has been a caregiver (caregiver duration studies) (e.g., Birkel, 1987; Brody & Schoonover, 1986; Matthews & Rosner, 1988). Time allocation and caregiver duration studies are not the central focus of this chapter. Rather, this chapter highlights the social and psychological dimensions of temporal context that influence both the role perceptions and performances of individuals and families who are principally responsible for providing care to elderly dependents.

Temporal context is defined according to five dimensions of time—historical time, social service time, kin time, peer time, and intergenerational developmental time. *Historical time* focuses on both the demographic changes in family structures and the cohort or "generational" attitudes about caregiving that are related to a distinct time period or era (Elder 1987; Hareven, 1978; Kertzer 1983; Mannheim, 1952). *Social service time* involves the schedule or clock hours during the day or night when social service agencies offer support to care providers (Burton, 1991). *Kin time* encompasses shared understandings among family members concerning expectations and designations about who and when certain family members assume the caregiver role (Plath, 1980; Stack & Burton, in press). *Peer time* involves the patterns of temporal synchronicity in which the age-mates, colleagues, or friends of the caregiver assume caregiving roles in their own families (Hagestad & Burton, 1986). *Intergenerational developmental time* concerns: (a) The effects of timing of entry to the caregiver and care recipient roles on individual development, and (b) the compatibility of developmental life stages between the caregiver and the care recipient (Kivnick, 1985).

Role perceptions are defined as the caregiver's attitudes and beliefs about their position or status as a care provider (Rosow, 1985). *Role performances* are the specific duties and behaviors involved in giving assistance to older relatives or friends who are physically or cognitively impaired and who are unable to provide for themselves (Biddle, 1979; Gatz et al., 1990; Malone-Beach & Zarit, 1991).

In exploring the relationship between dimensions of time and the caregiver role, we address three themes. First, a conceptual framework linking temporal context and roles is presented. Second, we discuss the relationship between specific dimensions of time and the caregiver role. Case-history data from ethnographic studies of multigeneration African-American families are used to illustrate the relationship between temporal context and the caregiver role. Third, we highlight the implications of exploring dimensions of time and the caregiver role for future research.

TEMPORAL CONTEXT AND SOCIAL ROLES

Notions of time as it relates to social and psychological phenomena have been of interest to philosophers and social scientists for centuries (Frank, 1939; Hendricks & Hendricks, 1975; Nydegger, 1986; Roth, 1963; Seltzer &

Hendricks, 1986; Shostrom, 1968). Early conceptualizations of time, such as those defined by Aristotle and Newton, focus on its physical dimensions — namely, those quantitative indicators, such as age, hours, days, and weeks, that are "unilinear, infinitely divisible, continuous, measurable units" (Sorokin & Merton, 1937, p. 618). Notions of time, however, also have qualitative dimensions. The meaning of time is not only derived from calendric measures, but from people's cultural construction and personal definitions as well (Lewin, 1948; Nuttin, 1985; Rakowski, 1979; Zerubavel, 1981).

Since the 1960s, definitions of time and the impact of time on social roles and interactions has received considerable attention from social scientists interested in the life course perspective (Bengtson & Allen, in press; Clausen, 1986; Elder, 1985; Hagestad & Neugarten, 1985; Hogan, 1987; Kertzer, 1983; Plath, 1980; Rossi, 1980). Studies of the life course "trace individuals as social personas and their pathways along an age-differentiated, socially marked sequence of transitions" (Hagestad, 1990, p. 151). The life course perspective, while inherently based on a quantitative dimension of time — age — incorporates qualitative dimensions of time as well. This perspective considers how societies and individuals give meaning to the passage of time.

Elder (1984, 1987) noted that there are four dimensions of time that influence the flow of individuals through the life course: life time, social time, family time, and historical time. Life time is delineated by chronological age and represents an individual's stage in the aging process. Social time defines the set of norms that "specify when particular life transitions or accomplishments are expected to occur in a particular society or social milieu" (Clausen, 1986, p. 2). Family time refers to the ordering of family events and roles by age-linked expectations, sanctions, and options. Historical time anchors an individual or a family in a social and cultural era.

In understanding temporal context in the life course, the issue of timing, that is, sequencing and synchronization of major life role transitions such as marriage and parenthood, is also important (see review by Hagestad, 1990). The timing of these role transitions, in some societies, are gauged by social timetables. Social timetables are shared ideas of when key life changes ought to happen. They serve as guides to individuals about what the appropriate and inappropriate times are to enter and exit specific roles over the course of life (Hogan, 1978; Neugarten, Moore, & Lowe, 1965; Wood, 1971).

Traditionally, statistical norms derived from aggregate data on, for example, age at first marriage, have been used as indicators of normative social timetables. Recent research, however, has questioned both the meaning and generalizability of timetables derived from quantitative indicators of time such as age. Timetables for role transitions across social groups may be more variable and more closely linked to contextually defined dimensions of time than statistically derived notions indicate. For example, Nydegger (1973) investigated the presence of timetables regarding the timing of fatherhood and found that respondents either formulated age-linked timetables for their role transition that were extremely vague, or they tended to resist the notion of parenthood as an age-dependent transition. Instead, their decisions concerning when to become fathers were based on their involvement with other social roles, processes, and events (i.e., the attainment of maturity, completion of education, or getting a good job). Similarly, Burton's research (1985, 1990a) indicates that the timing, or age-appropriateness of the transition to grandmotherhood is not determined singularly by age, but by the prevailing contextually defined norms of the group to which the individual belongs and by the synchronization of the grandmother role with social roles that the individual already occupies. These studies are examples of how the social construction of time affects perceptions of social roles.

Quantitative and qualitative notions of time and the life course designations of life time, historical time, social time, family time, and social timetables are concepts that provide the foundation for our discussion of temporal context and the caregiver role (Elder, 1985). Each of these aspects of time create the parameters of social roles. Biddle (1979, p. 53) noted that "time exists, and that events, including human beings, behaviors, and features, are laid within it." Thus building on the life course perspective and the linkage between temporal context and social roles, we suggest that specific dimensions of time, both in their construction and meaning, can shape the role perceptions and performances of caregivers.

Dimensions of Time and the Caregiver Role

Five dimensions of time as they relate to the role perceptions and performances of caregivers are discussed—historical time, social service time, kin time, peer time, and intergenerational developmental time. These dimensions are rooted in the life course perspective, but also reflect the social constructions and meanings of time observed in four ethnographic studies of multigeneration African-American families. Although the conceptual definitions of these dimensions of time emerged, in part, from studies of African-Americans, the concepts may also be applicable to the study of caregiving in families from a variety of racial, ethnic, socioeconomic, and cultural backgrounds.

Case history data from several families involved in the four studies are used here to illustrate the relationship between temporal context and the caregiver role. Study 1 was conducted from December 1982 to June 1984 and involved a sample of 41 four-, five-, and six-generation, working-class female lineages living in the south central Los Angeles area (Burton 1985; Burton & Bengtson, 1985; Burton & Martin, 1987). The sample for Study 2 comprised

20 multigeneration families living in a small semi-rural African-American community in the northeast portion of the United States. These families were studied for a period of 3 years, from January 1985 to March 1988 (Burton, 1990a; Stack & Burton, in press). Study 3 was conducted in a Northwestern urban community from December 1988 to June 1989 with a sample of 15 grandmothers and great-grandmothers (Burton, 1990b). Study 4 is a 5-year community-based study of 150 multigeneration families residing in a Northeastern urban community. This study began in December 1989 (Burton, 1991; Sörensen, Burton, & Dilworth-Anderson, 1991).

Historical Time

There are two aspects of historical time that we suggest influence the role perceptions and performances of caregivers — the changing demography of families (Bengtson, Rosenthal, & Burton, 1990; Hagestad, 1988; Preston, 1984; Treas & Bengtson, 1987); and cohort or "generational" membership (Kertzer, 1983; Mannheim, 1952).

Demographic Change, Families, and Caregiving. The changing demography of families in any society is an artifact of events that occur within the context of historical time. For example, the recent "one child per family" policy adopted in China in response to historically high patterns of fertility within its population, will drastically alter the structure of families residing in that country. The families will become structurally "top-heavy," meaning that there will be more older adults in families than children. This alteration in family structure has salient implications for caregiving. Specifically, the concern is that because of the mandated decrease in fertility, future generations of aging parents and grandparents will have fewer adult children available to care for them (Schulz & Davis-Friedman, 1987).

Similarly, in contemporary industrialized societies, recent changes in patterns of mortality and fertility (due to advances in health technology) and divorce and remarriage (due to changing social attitudes concerning marital relationships) have produced a variety of family structures, which also have distinct implications for the caregiver role. Declines in mortality and fertility, for example, have produced the *bean pole* family structure (Bengtson, Rosenthal, & Burton, 1990). Also called *the verticalized family,* this structure is characterized by intergenerational extension, which means that the number of living generations within lineages has increased, and intragenerational contraction, which means that there has been a decrease in the number of members within each generation (Bengtson & Dannefer, 1987; Hagestad, 1986; Knipscheer, 1988).

Although not as dramatic as the predicted family situation in China, patterns of decreased mortality and fertility within the beanpole family may have a similar impact on caregiving. Individuals within these families are living to "an advanced old age," but their increased longevity puts them at greater risk for experiencing physical and mental frailty and for becoming "dependent aged parents." At a time when family members are living longer and subsequently are more susceptible to dependency at older ages, concurrent declines in fertility within these families decreases the size of the potential caregiver pool within the younger generations. Intragenerationally "slimmer" families means that there are fewer siblings within the younger generations to share the sometimes considerable burden of dependent elderly parents. Again, we see that having fewer children to share caregiving is a recent historical trend in conflict with the longer survival of aging parents (Treas & Bengtson, 1987).

Another family structure that has emerged in contemporary industrialized societies and has implications for the caregiver role is the reconstituted family form. This family form is a product of increased rates of divorce and remarriage. The implications of this family structure for caregiving are profound, particularly as they relate to allegiances individuals have to former and current elderly in-laws. Jackie, a 45-year-old recently remarried divorcee, who participated in one of our ethnographic studies, explained:

> My God in heaven, I am so torn now. I was always very close to my ex-husband's mother, even after the divorce. I promised her I would take care of her. Now she needs me. I must do it, I promised. But what am I going to do if my father gets sick, and even worse, if my (current) husband's mother gets sick too? Will I have to choose who I will care for? I can't choose. I love them all.

The top-heavy, beanpole, and reconstituted families are but three examples of the variety of family structures that exist in contemporary societies. What is important to note here is that these structures are a product of a historical era — an era marked by changing policies concerning fertility, by advances in health technology that increase longevity, and by changing attitudes and practices concerning marriage and divorce. These historical events may indirectly affect the parameters of the caregiver role via demographic changes in family structure. Thus, it becomes particularly important in studies of caregiving to examine this role in the context of historical time — more specifically, how the events within an era affect the family structures within which older people are cared for.

Generational Membership and the Caregiver Role. The second aspect of historical time hypothesized as influencing perceptions and performances in the caregiver role is generational membership. Generation, discussed in the context of historical time, is not defined as a lineage position within a family, but rather as a person's membership in a particular birth cohort (Mannheim, 1952). Because members of a birth cohort age together through history, they sometimes share a common "generational" experience which shapes their lives (Kertzer, 1983). This common generational experience could be an event, like the Civil Rights movement, or a prevailing societal attitude, such as a strong sense of filial piety. Whether it be an event or an attitude, a cohort's collective experience can both limit and shape individual development, thoughts, feelings, and actions. Mannheim (1952) wrote:

> The fact of belonging to the same class, and that of belonging to the same generation or age group, have this in common, that both endow the individuals sharing in them with a common location in the social and historical process, and thereby limit them to a specific range of potential experience, predisposing them for a certain characteristic mode of thought and experience, and a characteristic type of historically relevant action. Any given location, then, excludes a large number of possible modes of thought, experience, feeling, and action, and restricts the range of self-expression open to the individual to certain circumscribed possibilities. This *negative* delimitation, however, does not exhaust the matter. Inherent in a *positive* sense in every location is a tendency pointing towards certain modes of behaviour, feeling, and thought. (p. 291)

If common generational experiences influence an individual's attitudes and behaviors, how might those experiences manifest themselves in role perceptions and performances of caregivers? The caregiving attitudes of three women — Ida, age 64, Delores, age 40, and Yvonne, age 22 — provide valuable insights on this issue. Ida currently provides care for her 87-year-old aunt, two grandchildren, and three great-grandchildren. When asked about her caregiver role, Ida stated:

> Why are you asking me about this [providing care]? I do it without thinking. This is what I am suppose to do. My kin, my friends, all the people my age know this is what they should do. We were all raised this way. You never question it, you just do it. I wish my kids were more like this.

Delores, who provides care for her 63 year-old-mother offered this perspective:

> I came along between the "we" generation and the "me" generation. I learned the rules of my parents' generation . . . you must take care of old people in your family . . . but I also know the rules of my son's generation . . . every man or woman for themselves. . . . Sometimes I feel pulled in several directions, wanting to have the free spirit of my son, but most of the time I feel committed because I believe in the message of my parents' generation . . . I think we are

probably the last in a long line of generations who believe in caring for our old people.

Yvonne, in discussing her caregiving plans concerning her parents noted:

> I have options and I know it. I have talked to my friends about this. Times are different than they were for my parents and grandparents. They were expected to take care of everybody. Now, we have too many things facing us. We have to work and deal with the pressures of our kids and living in this crazy world. I will do the best I can to help my parents if they ever get sick, but I am gonna need some help. You better believe I'm gonna *get* some help . . . some respite care.

These three women, all members of different "generations" and also at different stages in the caregiver role, provided perspectives on their roles that were indicative of their perception of certain prevailing attitudes at distinct points in historical time. Ida grew up in a family context and during a social era when assuming responsibility for the care of kin was a normative, unquestioned obligation in the life course. Delores speaks of the confusion she sometimes experiences in her caregiving role because she is a member of the "transition generation"—the generation between the "we" generation of her parents and grandparents and the "me" generation of her son. Yvonne, in contrast, indicates that the demands of contemporary life, and the respite care options she perceives are available through social services, have provided her with a different set of guidelines for her duties as a potential care provider.

Although, most assuredly, there are a number of factors that influence these three women's role perceptions and performances as caregivers, the focus on their generational membership highlights an important point. Caregivers can associate their beliefs and duties regarding caregiving with a specific group's ideology and norms. These groups may vary by composition (i.e., the caregivers family, community, or broader societal age peers), but are often described as having distinct temporal or historical anchors. For example, in our ethnographic research, older generations of caregivers are quick to distinguish themselves from younger generations of caregivers with such statements as: "Back in our day, we knew what taking care of our elders meant. Young people today don't know how to do it right," or "My grandmother's generation is too serious about taking care of people. People need to know how to take care of themselves." Whether such historically based distinctions in caregiving behaviors are perceived or real, they have implications for policy and programs concerning caregivers.

Understanding the historical anchoring of caregivers' perceptions of their roles may help those who offer services for caregivers to provide "generationally relevant" assistance. Ida, for example, is part of the "we" generation and would "not take kindly" to a caregiver assistance program in which the philosophy was to strongly encourage her to deal with her own developmental needs first, and secondly, the needs of her care recipients. Yvonne, in contrast, would benefit from a program that had clearly articulated objectives about meeting her personal developmental needs as well as the needs of the individual she provided care for. In both cases a generationally relevant caregiver assistance program would attend to the current needs of these caregivers based on an appreciation of the historical basis of their belief systems about providing care.

Social Service Time

The temporal availability of services has in a number of cultures served as a point of reference that people organize their lives by. For example, in a number of simple agricultural societies, people may organize their daily lives around the scheduled opening and closing of markets where they obtain daily necessities (Sorokin & Merton, 1937). In such societies there is typically a shared understanding among people that appointments and commitments are not made according to particular hours in the day, but rather around communally determined cycles of market operation.

In industrialized societies, particularly in American culture, services are available to individuals at circumscribed times of the day and week — usually 9:00 a.m. to 5:00 p.m., Monday through Friday. The scheduling of services, which is usually defined by the service providers, is typically inflexible. The time that services are available is frequently not compatible with the temporal needs of those who could best use them. For example, a common theme that has emerged in our ethnographic research of multigeneration African-American families concerns temporal incongruences between the availability of services designed to assist caregivers, (i.e., adult daycare) and the schedule needs of caregivers. The life situation of John, a 54-year-old caregiver, illustrated the dilemma. John, who works the 3:00 p.m. to 11:00 p.m. shift in a factory in his community, takes care of his 70-year-old sister who has dementia, his 84-year-old aunt who suffers from major physical impairments, and his 86-year-old aunt who says that she is "just too old to get around." John commented on the temporal conflicts between his work schedule and adult day care services in his community:

> These people just don't understand. I need to be able to at least take my aunt and sister somewhere while I work. I don't have no one to watch them while I'm at work and the day care is closed in the evening. They qualify for the services but the time is wrong. This is too much for me because I have to trust my oldest

aunt to take care of things while I'm at work. I also have to keep calling home
to check on them and come home on my lunch.

John also noted how the temporal incongruencies between his needs and
available services affect his role:

> Because I can't get the services when I need them I end up doing more than I
> should, I think. I could send them during the day but between me trying get
> some sleep and getting them back home and settled before I go to work, it's too
> much of a problem. Then on top of that I feel sometimes like a begging social
> coordinator. I spend a lot of time on the phone trying to get my friends and
> some of my family to help out.

Although it is difficult to determine from existing discussions of caregiving
how prevalent John's situation is, his temporal dilemma draws attention to an
issue our society may face in the future. Demographic projections suggest that
the "oldest old" or "frail elderly" is one of the fastest growing subpopulations
in industrialized societies (Manton, 1990). The growth of this subpopulation
is of special concern because of its relatively high rates of illness and disability
(Kane & Kane, 1990). Providing care for family members in this subpopulation may create particular difficulties for working-class and working-poor
caregivers whose employers require them to work evening and night shifts.
The emerging question is: Will there be social services available to assist these
caregivers during the time of *day or night* that they need them?

Kin Time

Kin time represents the temporal scripts of multigeneration families. It is an
expanded conceptualization of the life course perspective's family time. Kin
time reflects the shared understanding among family members of the timing
and sequencing of role transitions. It also encompasses family norms and
expectations concerning familial duties and roles. For example, kin time may
include temporal guides and designations for the assumption of family
leadership roles and caregiving responsibilities. The norms comprising kin
time are the consequence of culturally constructed family obligations defined
by economic, social, physical, and psychological family needs. Consequently,
the normative structure of kin time may vary from family to family.

Henry Evans, a 38-year-old resident in a northeastern African-American
community provided a very clear profile on how kin time affected the
caregiver role for him. Henry is the only surviving son in his family. His
mother had given birth to eleven other sons, all of whom were stillborn or died
shortly after birth. At the time of his interview, Henry was providing care for

his 72-year-old father who had recently suffered a heart attack, his 36-year-old sister who was suffering from a chronic neuromuscular disease, and his 40-year-old sister and her four children. When asked about his family duties, he remarked:

> I was designated by my family as a child to provide care for all my family members. My duties read just like a job description. The job description says the following: (a) you will never marry; (b) you will have no children of your own; (c) you will take care of your sisters, their children, your mother and your father in old age; and (d) you will be happy doing it.

Henry went on to discuss how the kin time designation of his role affected his perceptions and performance as a care provider:

> I honestly have never thought about doing anything else with my life other than working and providing care for others in my family. All my choices about life revolve around my responsibilities to provide care. I feel good about what I do and I do it well. That is my family's expectation of me.

Valerie, a 35-year-old mother of four children provided a contrasting view of kin time:

> Normally what happens, the person that needs the help, everybody kinda just ends up at that person's house and it just evolves. Everybody finds out what's needed and everybody . . . does what they can. It's easier when people wanna do something instead of being told: this is what you have to do. You just let everybody know what's needed and then everybody does what they can do. Then you don't feel like, oh I can't do that because I have to be here by 2 o'clock . . . you don't have to change your life. It's like OK, I'll go at this time and do whatever, and if you happen to be there at the same time somebody else is there it doesn't matter, because there's always something to do. There are no assignments. If something didn't get done . . . whoever comes in next and realizes it will do it.

Henry's and Valerie's caregiving perceptions and behaviors reflect familial diversity in the notion of kin time. Henry's family has well-defined scripts concerning the designation of caregiving responsibilities and the temporal organization of individual lives, whereas Valerie's does not. This diversity in temporal scripts may have implications for the role performances and perceptions of caregivers. As the family therapy literature indicates, scripts prescribe patterns of family interactions—they are mental representations that guide the role performances of family members within and across contexts (Byng-Hall, 1988). Life stresses and tensions are produced and negotiated between individuals in families in response to scripts. With respect to variation in the temporal scripts of kin as it relates to caregiving, a potentially important implication to examine in future research would be how delineations of kin time within families affect stress outcomes for caregivers. Are there differential outcomes in the levels of stress experienced by caregivers in families with well-defined temporal scripts compared to those in families with flexible notions of kin time?

Peer Time

Peer time is the temporal spacing of role acquisitions among age-mates, friends, or colleagues. The relationship between peer time and the caregiver role is hypothesized as follows: When a group of age-mates, friends, or colleagues assume caregiving roles at about the same time, they are more likely to view their roles more positively than those individuals who do not have peers that are also caregivers. Peers who are caregivers are more likely to foster feelings of group solidarity and be supportive to one another because of their "common life experience." Ethel, a 57-year-old caregiver, described the importance of peer caregivers in her life:

> Right now I have about five of my friends from church who are all taking care of their mommas or somebody in their family. Even though we don't have a lot of time to socialize, whenever we do get together we have a lot to talk about. We talk about how tired we are from what we do. Sometimes, one of us knows about something that can help the others. That's a good thing. I always feel better when I talk to my friends. We all know what each other is going through.

Marie, a 26-year-old caregiver, had a different experience to share:

> None of my friends are taking care of old people. I'm the only one. It's such a strange thing to be the only one doing this. Actually I resent this sometimes. All my friends are enjoying their lives. They don't too much want to be bothered with me because they don't understand what I do. I don't have much to talk about to my friends anymore.

There are two themes that emerge in comparing the caregiving situations of Ethel and Marie in relation to peer support — the timing of their role entries and feelings of isolation. Ethel, because of her age is more likely than Marie to have age-peers who are caregivers. As such, Marie can be considered an "off-time" caregiver, meaning that she has assumed a social role that is "out of sync" with the social roles of her age-mates. As a product of this off-time role transition Marie, as compared to Ethel, experiences a strong sense of isolation because she does not have friends who are doing the same thing she is doing.

Feelings of isolation are attributes that are often associated with the caregiver role (Zarit, Birkel, & MaloneBeach, in press). However, what becomes important for those who develop programs for caregivers to determine is the source of isolation. Often, feelings of isolation for the caregiver emerge from the lack of support received by relatives (Zarit, Reever, & Bach-Peterson, 1980). What the notion of peer time suggests is that not having age-mates who are also caregivers, may be an equally important source of isolation.

Intergenerational Developmental Time

Intergenerational developmental time refers to: (a) the effects of timing of entry to the caregiver and care recipient roles on individual development; and (b) the compatibility of developmental stages between the caregiver and the care recipient. To explore this dimension of time, we draw upon themes in developmental psychology and the life course perspective.

Authors from both developmental psychology and the life course perspective discuss notions of "the normal expectable life"—a set of seasons, with characteristic preoccupations, changes, challenges, and rewards (Levinson, 1978). In psychodynamic approaches to individual life time, the emphasis is on how developmental changes and the social context in combination present individuals with a series of *developmental tasks* (Erikson, 1982; Havighurst, 1972). Erikson (1963, 1980), for example, described late adolescence and young adulthood as a period in which personal identity and intimacy must be achieved, whereas the central theme in middle age is attaining a sense of generativity. Havighurst (1972) described the developmental tasks of young adulthood as involving the differentiation from one's family of origin and the establishment of a new family of one's own. In contrast, the developmental tasks for late life involve attaining integrity (Erikson, 1980), and adjusting to the limitations created by diminished physical strength, shrinking social networks, and reduced income (Havighurst, 1972). Inherent in each of these developmental tasks is the process of negotiating and resolving psychosocial tensions at each stage of life.

Within the life course perspective, the emphasis in examining developmental stages is on role transitions. As discussed earlier, role transitions often follow timetables and established sequences. Individuals build expectations about what life will bring, and crises are often presented by events that represent breaches of such expectations. Events that occur out of sequence, later or earlier than expected, are considered "off-time."

The timing of taking on caregiving responsibilities and receiving care has implications for the psychosocial development of both the caregiver and the care recipient. The timing of giving or receiving care may in some cases interfere with, and in others facilitate, the immediate developmental tasks individuals face in different periods of their lives. The process of negotiating developmental tasks is also affected by the individual's involvement with other people, with institutions, and with the society at large (Kivnick, 1985). The assumption of an off-time caregiving role can conflict with some of these involvements and thereby hinder the achievement of developmental tasks. For example, the main tasks of young adulthood involve establishing an identity, differentiating from the family, and achieving intimacy. Being responsible for elder care as a young adult may restrict opportunities to experiment with identities or build intimate non-family relationships. Beverly, a 22-year-old caregiver for her 73-year-old grandmother commented on this point:

> I am so busy taking care of my grandmom that I don't have no kind of social life. I don't have a boyfriend and probably won't get one 'til I'm too old to do anything with him.

In other situations, however, assuming the caregiver role as a young-adult or even adolescent may be viewed as an opportunity to develop closeness, intimacy, and mutuality across generations. The perspective of Joshua, a 17-year-old high school student who takes care of his grandmother illustrated this:

> My grandma took care of me before she got sick. I've been with her since I was six. I don't mind doing for her because she has taught me so much. In her own way she has taught me how to be a man. A man does for old people [as well as] for his wife and children.

Kivnick (1985) suggested that although the focus of each phase of the life course may be on particular tasks or psychosocial tensions, individuals often preview and revisit the tasks of other stages of the life cycle simultaneously. As such, extensive contact with older generations through caregiving may provide an opportunity for young and middle-aged adults to preview the process of coming to terms with old age and learning to, for example, balance ego integrity and despair (Kivnick, 1985). Without ego integrity, the older person fears death. The resolution of this task has ramifications for the young in family, according to Erickson (1963), because they may fear life if their elders fear death. Charles Anderson, a 37-year-old former caregiver had this to say on the topic:

> You asked me what I learned from taking care of my grandmother? I learned how to die with dignity. I'm not afraid to live or die. My grandmother was in great pain and you would never know it. I am grateful to her for teaching me these things. In her suffering and death, I found life.

Constraints and opportunities for previewing and revisiting developmental tasks exist for the care recipient as well, especially when the care is primarily necessary because of physical disabilities. For example, being dependent on other people makes it possible to revisit struggles of childhood related to trust and mistrust, balance feelings regarding industry and inferiority, which are likely to reemerge with increasing inability to contribute to one's own upkeep and care, and renew an age-appropriate balance between intimacy and isolation (Kivnick, 1985).

The second aspect of intergenerational developmental time we explore is the compatibility of developmental stages between the caregiver and care recipient. Although the opportunity to revisit developmental tasks of earlier life stages can be a positive force in resolving present tensions, it can also intensify the internal conflicts of the care recipient as well as the caregiver. Just as middle-aged parents, who are concerned with developing and maintaining a sense of creativity and productiveness in the face of gradually narrowing opportunities, can feel especially challenged by the increasing opportunities available to their adolescent children, care recipients may feel threatened by the industriousness and efficiency of their young adult caregivers in the face of their own decreasing ability. Alternately, a middle-aged caregiver might find the focus of the older generation on finding meaning in a life already lived, or on resigning to not having accomplished what they wanted, as a threat to their own attempt to surpass stagnation and contribute to society (McAdams, Ruetzel, & Foley, 1986). The comments of Earlene, a 57-year-old caregiver underscore this point:

> After five years of taking care of my father, I realized my life was going to turn out like his. All my chances for making something out of myself are gone. I will never be what I wanted to be. . . . He never will be either.

In summary, intergenerational developmental time focuses on (a) issues of congruency between the caregiver's and care recipient's developmental stages and the temporal assumption of their respective roles, and (b) the opportunities for individual growth that are created for caregivers and care recipients given the compatibility of their developmental stages. Three questions for future research emerge from this discussion: (a) How does *when* one assumes the caregiver or care recipient roles affect the resolution of developmental tasks?, (b) What opportunities for previewing and revisiting developmental tasks are created by the respective life stages of caregivers and care recipients?, (c) How does the degree of compatibility between the developmental life stages of caregivers and care recepients promote or hinder individual growth?

CONCLUSION

The purpose of this chapter was to explore the relationship between temporal context and the caregiver role. Building on the scholarship of life-course, developmental, and role theorists we examined five dimensions of time as they relate to caregiving—historical time, social service time, kin time, peer time, and intergenerational developmental time. A central focus in examining these dimensions was on the qualitative aspects of time—that is, how caregivers assign meaning to certain social and psychological domains of temporal context.

Our objective here was to suggest additional ways of thinking about the relationship between temporal context and caregiving. The ideas presented are, indeed, preliminary and have emerged principally from our ethnographic research on multigeneration African-American families. Nonetheless, they raise a number of important issues that should be considered in future research.

First, it is important that research on caregiving evaluate the caregiver role in the context of historical time. Caregivers' role performances and perceptions may be indirectly shaped by emerging changes in family structure and also by the caregivers' "generational memberships." How do changes in family structure affect the available pool of caregivers? What implications do these changes have for who assumes the caregiving role in families? How does a caregiver's "generational" experiences affect their role? Are there cohort differences in caregiver role perceptions and performances across historical time?

Second, the focus on social service time highlights the temporal rigidity that exists in organizations designed to assist caregivers. As we look toward projections of familial caregiver responsibilities in the 21st century and the employment obligations of caregivers, we must begin to question whether the current schedules for providing services will be amenable to the future needs of caregivers.

Third, the notion of kin time draws attention to the potential power of temporal scripts in families as it relates to the caregiving role. Additional research is needed to determine (a) how pervasive temporal family scripts concerning caregiving are in the general population, and (b) what impact these scripts have on caregiver role perceptions and performances.

Fourth, peer time suggests that it is important to assess the degree of peer support and the synchronicity of entry to the caregiving role by peers as it affects feelings of isolation among caregivers. An emerging question is: Are there differences in the role perceptions and performances of caregivers who have peers that are also caregivers as compared to those who do not?

Fifth, the discussion of intergenerational developmental time underscores the complexity of psychosocial developmental issues between caregivers and care recipients. With the exception of Kivnick's (1985) notable work on cross-generational relationships and psychosocial development of grandparents, we know very little about how the temporal interweaving of developmental stages between individuals from different generations and in different familial roles affects personal growth. Theoretical discussion and empirical research are needed to address this issue.

In conclusion, the dimensions of time discussed here are not mutually exclusive concepts. Rather, they represent interrelated themes that may have variable meanings based on the type of caregiving being explored and the cultural ethnic, racial, and socioeconomic contexts caregiving is explored within. Further theoretical discussions are needed to refine the conceptual definitions of historical time, social service time, kin time, peer time, and intergenerational developmental time offered here. Moreover, empirical research that test the applicability of these concepts to the role perceptions and performances of caregivers in varied cultures is also needed.

ACKNOWLEDGMENT

The research reported in this chapter was supported by grants to the first author from the Brookdale Foundation, the National Institute of Mental Health (No. R29MH46057-01), and the William T. Grant Foundation. The authors wish to thank Leonard Pearlin and Steven Zarit for their helpful comments on an earlier draft of this chapter.

REFERENCES

Bengtson, V. L., & Allen, K. R. (in press). Life course perspectives applied to the family. In P. G. Boss, W. Doherty, R. LaRossa, W. Schumm, & S. Steinmetz (Eds.), *Sourcebook of family theories and methods: A contextual approach.* New York: Plenum.

Bengtson, V. L., & Dannefer, D. (1987). Families, work, and aging: Implications of disordered cohort flow for the 21st century. In R. A. Ward & S. S. Tobin (Eds.), *Health in aging: Sociological issues and policy directions* (pp. 256–289). New York: Springer-Verlag.

Bengtson, V., Rosenthal, C., Burton, L. (1990). Families and aging: Diversity and heterogeneity. In R. H. Binstock & L. K. George (Eds.), *Handbook of aging and the social sciences* (3rd ed., pp. 151–168). New York: Academic Press.

Biddle, B. J. (1979). *Role theory: Expectations, identities, and behaviors.* New York: Academic Press.

Birkel, R. C. (1987). Toward a social ecology of the home-care household. *Psychology and Aging, 2*(3), 294–301.

Brody, E. M. (1985). Parent care as normative family stress. *The Gerontologist, 25,* 19–29.

Brody, E. M., & Schoonover, C. B. (1986). Patterns of parent-care when daughters work and when they do not. *The Gerontologist, 26,* 372–381.

Burton, L. M. (1985). *Early and on-time grandmotherhood in multigeneration Black families.* Unpublished doctoral dissertation, University of Southern California.

Burton, L. M. (1990a). Teenage childbearing as an alternative life-course strategy in multigenerational Black families. *Human Nature, 1,* 123–143.

Burton, L. M. (1990b, November). *Grandparents as parents in drug-addicted families.* Paper presented at the annual meeting of the Gerontological Society of America, Boston, MA.

Burton, L. M. (1991). Drug trafficking schedules and child-care strategies in a high-risk neighborhood. *American Enterprise, 2*(3), 34–47.

Burton, L. M., & Bengtson, V. L. (1985). Black grandmothers: Issues of timing and meaning in roles. In V. L. Bengtson & J. Robertson (Eds.), *Grandparenthood: Research and policy perspectives* (pp. 61-67). Beverly Hills, CA: Sage.

Burton, L. M., & Martin, P. (1987). Thematik in der Mehrgenerationenfamilie: Ein Beispiel. *German Journal of Gerontology, 21,* 275-282.

Byng-Hall, J. (1988). Scripts and legends in families and family therapy. *Family Process, 27,* 167-179.

Cantor, M. H. (1983). Strain among caregivers: A study of experience in the United States. *The Gerontologist, 23,* 597-604.

Clausen, J. A. (1986). *The life course.* Englewood Cliffs, NJ: Prentice-Hall.

Elder, G. H., Jr. (1984). Families, kin, and the life course: A sociological perspective. In R. D. Parke (Ed.), *Advances in child development research: The family* (pp. 80-135). Chicago, IL: University of Chicago Press.

Elder, G. H., Jr. (1985). Perspectives on the life course. In G. H. Elder, Jr. (Ed.), *Life course dynamics, trajectories, and transitions, 1968-1980* (pp. 23-49). Ithaca, NY: Cornell University Press.

Elder, G. H., Jr. (1987). Families and lives: Some developments in life-course studies. *Journal of Family History, 12,* 179-199.

Erikson, E. H. (1963). *Childhood and society* (2nd ed.). New York: Norton.

Erikson, E. H. (1980). On the generational cycle: An address. *International Journal of Psycho-Analysis, 61,* 213-233.

Erikson, E. H. (1982). *The life cycle completed.* New York: Norton.

Fitting, M., Rabins, P., Lucas, M. J., & Eastman, J. (1986). Caregivers for dementia patients: A comparison of husbands and wives. *The Gerontologist, 26,* 248-252.

Frank, L. K. (1939). Time perspectives. *Journal of Social Philosophy, 4,* 293-312.

Gallagher, D., Lovett, S., & Zeiss, A. (in press). Interventions with caregivers of frail and elderly persons. In M. Ory & K. Bond (Eds.), *Aging and health care: Social science and policy perspectives.* New York: Tavistock Publications.

Gatz, M., Bengtson, V. L., & Blum, M. J. (1990). Caregiving families. In J. Birren & K. Schaie (Eds.), *Handbook of the psychology of aging* (3rd ed., pp. 46-57). New York: Academic Press.

George, L. K., & Gwyther, L. P. (1986). Caregiver well-being. A multidimensional examination of family caregivers of demented adults. *The Gerontologist, 26,* 253-259.

Hagestad, G. O. (1986). The aging society as a context for family life. *Daedalus, 115,* 119-139.

Hagestad, G. O. (1988). Demographic change and the life course: Some emerging trends in the family realm. *Family Relations, 37,* 405-414.

Hagestad, G. O. (1990). Social perspectives on the life course. In R. Binstock & L. George (Eds.), *Handbook of aging and the social sciences* (3rd ed., pp. 35-61). New York: Van Nostrand Reinhold.

Hagestad, G. O., & Burton, L. M. (1986). Grandparenthood, life context, and family development. *American Behavioral Scientist, 29,* 471-484.

Hagestad, G. O., & Neugarten, B. O. (1985). Age and the life course. In R. Binstock & E. Shanas (Eds.), *Handbook of aging and the social sciences* (2nd ed., pp. 35-61). New York: Van Nostrand Reinhold.

Haley, W. E., Levine, E. G., Brown, S. L., & Bartolucci, A. A. (1987). Stress, appraisal, coping, and social support as predictors of adaptational outcome among dementia caregivers. *Psychology and Aging, 2,* 323-330.

Hareven, T. K. (Ed.). (1978). *Transitions: The family and the life course in historical perspective.* New York: Academic Press.

Havighurst, R. J. (1972). *Developmental tasks and education* (3rd ed.). New York: D. McKay.

Hendricks, C. D., & Hendricks, J. (1975). Historical development of the multiplicity of times and implications for the analysis of aging. *Human Context, 2,* 117-129.

Hogan, D. P. (1978). The variable order of life events in the life course. *American Sociological Review, 43,* 573–586.

Hogan, D. P. (1987). The demography of life-span transitions: Temporal and gender comparisons. In A. Rossi (Ed.), *Gender and the life course* (pp. 65–78). New York: Aldine.

Horowitz, A. (1985). Sons and daughters as caregivers to older parents. *The Gerontologist, 25*(6), 613–617.

Kane, R. L., & Kane, R. A. (1990). Health care for older people: Organizational and policy issues. In R. H. Binstock & L. K. George (Eds.), *Handbook of aging and the social sciences* (pp. 415–437). New York: Academic Press.

Kertzer, D. I. (1983). Generation as a sociological problem. *Annual Review of Sociology, 9,* 125–149.

Kivnick, H. Q. (1985). Intergenerational relationships: Personal meaning in the life cycle. In J. A. Meacham (Ed.) *Contributions to Human Development,* (Vol. 14, pp. 93–109). New York: Krager.

Knipscheer, K. (1988). Temporal embeddedness and aging within the multigenerational family: The case of grandparenting. In J. E. Birren & V. L. Bengtson (Eds.) *Emergent theories of aging,* (pp. 426–446). New York: Springer.

Levinson, D. J. (1978). *The seasons of a man's life.* New York: Ballantine Books.

Lewin, K. (1948). Time perspective and morale. In K. Lewin (Ed.), *Resolving social conflicts* (pp. 103–124). New York: Harper & Row.

MaloneBeach, E. E., & Zarit S. H. (1991). Current research issues in caregiving to the elderly. *International Journal of Aging and Human Development, 32*(2), 103–114.

Mannheim, K. (1952). The problem of generations. In D. Kecskemeti (Ed.), *Essays on the sociology of knowledge* (pp. 276–322). London: Routledge & Kegan Paul.

Manton, K. G. (1990). Mortality and morbidity. In R. H. Binstock & L. K. George (Eds.), *Handbook of aging and the social sciences* (pp. 68–90). New York: Academic Press.

Matthews, S. H., & Rosner, T. (1988). Shared filial responsibility: The family as the primary caregiver. *Journal of Marriage and the Family, 50,* 185–195.

McAdams, D. P., Ruetzel, K., & Foley, J. M. (1986). Complexity and generativity at mid-life: Relations among social motives, ego development, and adults' plans for the future. *Journal of Personality and Social Psychology, 50,* 800–807.

Neugarten, B. L., Moore, J. W., & Lowe, J. C. (1965). Age norms, age constraints, and adult socialization. *American Journal of Sociology, 70,* 710–717.

Niederehe, G., & Fruge, E. (1984). Dementia and family dynamics: Clinical research issues. *Journal of Geriatric Psychiatry, 17,* 21–56.

Nuttin, J. (1985). *Future perspective and motivation.* Hillsdale, NJ: Lawrence Erlbaum Associates.

Nydegger, C. N. (1973, November). *Late and early fathers.* Paper presented at the annual meeting of the Gerontological Society of America, Miami Beach, FL.

Nydegger, C. N. (1986). Timetables and implicit theory. *American Behavioral Scientist, 29*(6), 710–729.

Pearlin, L. I., Mullan, J. T., Semple, S. J., & Skaff, M. M. (1989). Caregiving and the stress process: An overview of concepts and their measures. *The Gerontologist, 30,* 583–594.

Plath, D. W. (1980). *Long engagements.* Stanford, CA: Stanford University Press.

Preston, S. (1984). Children and the elderly: Divergent paths for America's dependents. *Demography, 21,* 435–457.

Quayhagen, M. P., & Quayhagen, M. (1988). Alzheimer's stress: Coping with the caregiving role. *The Gerontologist, 28,* 391–396.

Rakowski, W. (1979). Future time perspective in later adulthood: Review and research directions. *Experimental Aging Research, 5,* 43–88.

Rosow, I. (1985). Status and role change through the life cycle. In R. H. Binstock & E. Shanas

(Eds.), *Handbook of aging and the social sciences* (2nd ed., pp. 62–93). New York: Van Nostrand Reinhold.

Rossi, A. S. (1980). Life-span theories and women's lives. *Signs: Journal of Women in Culture and Society, 6,* 4–32.

Roth, J. A. (1963). *Timetables: Structuring the passage of time in hospital treatment and other careers.* New York: Bobbs-Merrill.

Seltzer, M. M., & Hendricks, J. (1986). Explorations in time. *American Behavioral Scientist, 29*(6), 653–661.

Shostrom, E. L. (1968). Time as an integrating factor. In C. Buhler & F. Massavik (Eds.), *The course of human life* (pp. 351–359). New York: Springer.

Schulz, J. H., & Davis-Friedman, D. (Eds.). (1987). *Aging China: Families, economics, and government policies in transition.* Washington, DC: Gerontological Society of America.

Sörensen, S., Burton, L. M., & Dilworth-Anderson, P. (1991, November). *Preparation and planning for caregiving: The dimensions, antecedents, and consequences of thinking ahead.* Paper presented at the annual meeting of the Gerontological Society of America, San Francisco, CA.

Sorokin, P. A., & Merton, R. K. (1937). Social time: A methodological and functional analysis. *The American Journal of Sociology, 42*(5), 615–629.

Stack, C. S., & Burton, L. M. (in press). Kinscripts. *Journal of Comparative Family Studies.*

Treas, J., & Bengtson, V. L. (1987). The family in later years. In M. B. Sussman & S. K. Steinmetz (Eds.), *Handbook of marriage and the family* (pp. 625–648). New York: Plenum.

Wood, V. (1971). Age-appropriate behavior for older persons. *The Gerontologist, 11,* 74–78.

Zarit, S. H., Birkel, R. C., & MaloneBeach, E. E. (in press). Spouses as caregivers: Stresses and interventions. In M. Z. Goldstein (Ed.), *Family involvement in the treatment of the frail elderly.* Washington, DC: American Psychiatric Association.

Zarit, S. H., Reever, K. E., & Bach-Peterson, J. (1980). Relatives of the impaired elderly: correlates of feelings of burden. *The Gerontologist, 20,* 649–655.

Zerubavel, E. (1981). Hidden rhythms: Schedules and calendars in social life. Chicago, IL: University of Chicago Press.

Caregiving Families and Cross-Cultural Perspectives

Richard Morycz
University of Pittsburgh

THE CULTURAL AND TEMPORAL CONTEXT OF CAREGIVING

The chapters by Lucy Yu and Linda Burton address the cultural and temporal context of caregiving. Cultural and ethnic issues in family caregiving create an often neglected context for focusing on the differential impact on caregiving. How the current caregiver is perceived within a particular cultural or ethnic tradition is essential for both clinical and research questions. Not only is the history of relationships between care givers and care receivers important, but expectations within a particular cultural-ethnic tradition are also not trivial.

This is demonstrated by Yu's chapter and its discussion of the Chinese legal and moral expectation regarding filial maturity and financial support. Yu concludes that, although Chinese within the People's Republic of China still fulfill particular filial obligations by providing money to aged parents and by living in the same household as their parents, Chinese Americans seem to hold beliefs and behavior toward aged parents similar to those of other caregivers within the United States. This does not change the fact, however, that Chinese Americans must diverge (consciously or unconsciously) from a particular tradition, and that the expectations of this tradition enter into their decision making, their beliefs, and their behaviors toward their parents.

For Asian immigrants and refugees, filial piety is still an important norm in caring for aged parents; this norm includes issues of respect, responsibility, family harmony, and sacrifice (Sung, 1990). This cultural standard of filial piety still becomes a moral benchmark to judge caregiving attitudes and behaviors. If Asian families cannot successfully retain traditional values of filial piety while in a different culture, reactions to the caregiving situation can range from frustration to indifference. The fact that there are not legalistic expectations to realize filial piety does not deter from its inherent cultural value to be accepted, adapted, or rejected by caregiving children.

Asian immigrants and refugees clearly have special problems in adjusting to life within the United States. They may come here when they are already elderly; they may have never intended to come to this country. As such, they have experienced a tremendous series of losses. Support networks have been shattered; there has been a change in status within both family and society, and there has been cultural and fiscal change. Many of these elderly immigrants are dependent on adult children before they become physically or mentally disabled. They may experience loss of control over their day-to-day lives and no longer maintain the position of authority within the home. There can be indifference to their wisdom; their decision making may be limited or nonexistent; and they can be a financial drain because of lack of health insurance. There may be family caregiving conflicts, especially when living with daughters-in-law.

Within the family context, each ethnic and minority group retains its own individual meaning of family structure and family caregiving. Hispanics, for example, have traditionally retained strong family ties; the same is true of Italians, Japanese, and Poles (see Gelfand, 1982, 1986; Kalish, 1986). However, as Mindel (1983) noted:

> Mexican Americans are not Mexicans, Cuban Americans are not Cubans, Puerto Ricans in the mainland are not Puerto Ricans living in Puerto Rico. Culture is not static and social change based on cultural contact and assimilation has occurred. (p. 208)

The interaction of ethnicity and culture with the caregiving situation can be a central dynamic in the adaptation to the family caregiving response.

In the conceptual model of caregiving stress developed by Pearlin, Mullan, Semple, and Skaff (1990), cultural and temporal issues in caregiving are considered within the domains of background and context, and, to a lesser extent, the mediators of stress. On a simpler level, it is possible to think about family burden as being influenced by particular characteristics of the patient, the caregiver, and the environment (Morycz, 1985).

The physical and social environment can include living arrangements of the patient and caregiver, income, formal and informal support services, family issues, cultural tradition, and the temporal context of caregiving. Burton notes that there is little in the literature regarding these types of issues in caregiving, and she is correct. Other researchers have tried to address temporal issues as control variables: How long one has been in the caregiving role and how much time per day or per week is spent on caregiving tasks.

Burton extends the temporal concept to include how time affects the actual perception of and performance in the caregiving role.

Burton briefly reviews the literature on the notions of time, including social time. It is unclear whether her five dimensions of time, as they relate to caregiver role perceptions and performance, are meant to encompass and be a model for the concepts presented in the literature review. For instance, is Alder's description of life time and social time similar to Burton's description of historical time?

Burton describes the temporal context of caregiving within five dimensions: first, *historical time* relates to sociodemographic change and generational membership. Next, *social service time* underscores that when services are available, they become an organizing point for routine in caregivers' lives; sometimes the scheduling of services is mismatched with actual caregiver need. *Kin time,* Burton maintains, is a temporal script for multigenerational families; it is an expanded concept of family time within a life course perspective. There is a shared conception within the family of who are designated as caregivers, as well as when they are designated as caregivers. These family norms and expectations help to define caregiving roles and delineate family obligations. Burton maintains that these are culturally constructed and defined by particular needs in the family; thus, norms vary from family to family. *Peer time* is the temporal spacing of role acquisitions among same-age peers, other family members, friends, and colleagues. Burton rightly believes that when there is solidarity with others who share common life experiences and who are involved in similar roles, then caregiving can be viewed more positively. However, one would suspect that when these roles are not shared, it leads to even further constriction of caregivers' social life, and to increased isolation. Finally, Burton describes *intergenerational developmental time* as the timing of caregiving responsibilities as it affects particular developmental tasks that an individual caregiver may be facing in this particular period of his or her life. Hence, one can assume that caregiving can impede or enhance the challenge of these developmental tasks. Burton maintains that caregiving taken up at a non-normative time may cause role and developmental conflicts, but that these conflicts may be buffered when caregiving is culturally normative.

Although historical time and kin time appear to be more related to past literature, social service time, peer time, and intergenerational developmental time are not as well linked. There also appears to be considerable overlap among Burton's five dimensions. For instance, caregiving taken up at a non-normative time is discussed under intergenerational developmental time, but it also relates to historical time and generational membership. When one assumes the caregiver role, other roles may disappear and one becomes only a caregiver; this is role contraction. Other times, however, the caregiving role is just one of many other roles; these other roles compete or conflict with the role of caregiver. The consequences of these role transitions can actually be related to both of Burton's conceptions of kin-time and intergenerational developmental time.

Although Burton does not fully link and develop her dimensions of time as they specifically relate to past literature, I believe that she nevertheless builds upon and extends these concepts. This is an important contribution to further understanding the caregiving process. It is especially important to note her point that the specific timing for role transitions can differ across social groups and be culturally and temporally bound. Thus, issues in caregiving can be based not only on specific and normative social time tables; caregiving may also be shaped by the physical and social environment, including the cultural context of caregiving. Burton correctly contends that these dimensions of time and culture can influence and shape the caregiving role.

However, it should also be noted that the process is reciprocal: Caregiving roles can actually shape and influence further dimensions of social time. Never before have so many adults cared for so many functionally disabled older relatives, who may range in age from their fifth to ninth decade. Although there may be caregiving models in specific families and cultural-ethnic groups, the delivery of family care to the old and very old now occurs more often and at different times in the life course for various family members. The roles of this generation of caregivers will shape the beliefs, expectations, and perceptions of those who will provide family care to the aged in the future. Current caregiving role transitions will modify indicators of time and will emphasize the importance of shared beliefs and customs of caregiving within particular ethnic and cultural groups.

RACIAL DIFFERENCES IN FAMILY BURDEN

Burton uses the dimensions of time to better understand the caregiving role, and she applies these concepts to a variety of caregiving situations in Black families. There has actually been little work on studying caregivers with diverse racial and ethnic backgrounds. Parsons, Cox, and Kimboko (1989) looked at Hispanic, Black, and White caregivers but did not show statistically significant differences between the three groups. The study sample was quite small ($n = 33$), but all three groups of elders viewed themselves as a burden when they lived in the same household. A continuing question, as Jackson (1980) posed it, is to assess if racial differences are differences of degree rather than kind. Although Henderson (1984) attempted to focus attention on developing culturally relevant intervention strategies for elderly people of racial and ethnic minorities coping with Alzheimer's disease, there has been a dearth of data exploring differential approaches to interventions. A variety of research has emphasized Black families as being a kinship group where there is a strong support system that provides a whole range of services to the family (Gelfand, 1982; Jackson, 1980; Mindel, 1983). Caregiving within this context frequently goes beyond the nuclear family; it involves other extended families and non-kin helpers in the care network (Bengston, 1979; Devore, 1983; Hareven, 1980).

One previous study (Morycz, Malloy, Bozich, & Martz, 1987) concluded that there was no essential difference, based on race, in the experience of family burden as a social problem. Race, education, and income appeared to make little difference in the human response to the stress of caring for an older disabled family member. However, in this study, there was a difference within the intersection of race and caring for an elderly person with Alzheimer's disease; there was more perceived strain, felt stress, for family burden in caregivers who were White.

Black caregivers had less problems with the amount of vigilance required in caring for an Alzheimer's disease patient; they were not as burdened by patients who needed supervision or reminded to do a variety of self-maintenance activities or instrumental adult daily living (ADL) tasks such as cooking, cleaning, taking medicine, shopping, and so on. When Black caregivers did experience burden, it was due to the more labor-intensive help needed for patients to dress themselves, toilet themselves, and bathe themselves. On the other hand, White families were more burdened by Alzheimer's disease patients who required more step-by-step reminders to perform ADL tasks. Thus, this sense of constant vigilance may be more difficult for White families to handle. As Wiley (1971), Hareven (1980), and Devore (1983) have suggested, Black families rely on extended kin more heavily than White families in times of strain. Black caregivers may thus utilize available extended family supports more often because they are more used to doing so throughout the life cycle and because they have had more experience in mastering stress (see Jackson, Bacon, & Peterson, 1977–1978).

The actual experience of burden was perceived in much the same manner by Blacks and Whites, especially within the context of change in living patterns and altered living states. This was especially true in the subjective description of affect. Despair and embarrassment about the patient's condition were the least experienced difficulties for caregiving families of both races. For changes in particular living patterns, however, Whites reported more difficulties with decreased socialization and activities, whereas these were indicated as less frequent difficulties for Black caregivers. This difference may again manifest the elasticity of the extended family network; Black caregivers may perceive little change in their own level of activities and social interaction as they more easily use available social support in times of strain.

An additional explanation in this particular study of racial differences in caring for family members with Alzheimer's disease may be that Blacks continue to handle multiple roles more comfortably and, because of the flexibility of the extended family, may not have as many difficulties with role overload, conflict, and exhaustion within the context of caregiving burden.

SUMMARY

Cultural values about aging vary, and they make a difference in the acceptance of and accommodation to the aging process in caregivers and their kin (see Nydegger, 1986). Comparison of cross-cultural caregiving experiences can be problematic. For example, do research questions actually mean the same thing in different cultures, and how do you control for such built-in compounds as economic differences? More complex analyses of racial, ethnic, and cultural factors need to be conducted on caregiving well-being and caregiver burden, as well as caregiver intervention. Lucy Yu and Linda Burton make valuable research contributions in these areas. Future studies need to consider ethnic and cultural determinants and contexts of caregiving, so that differential models of impact and outcome can be suggested and more effective clinical interventions can be introduced. Coping with caregiving stress can vary from culture to culture and within various ethnic backgrounds. This has implications not only for understanding the levels and dynamics of caregiving, but also for the creation of relevant service delivery systems and responsive social policies.

REFERENCES

Bengtson, V. (1979). Ethnicity and aging: Problems and issues in current social sciences inquiry. In D. Gelfand & A. Kutzik (Eds.), *Ethnicity and aging: Theory, research and policy.* (pp. 9-31). New York: Springer.

Devore, W. (1983). Ethnic reality: The life model and work with black families. *Social Casework, November,* 525-531.

Gelfand, D. E. (1982). *Aging: The ethnic factor.* Boston: Little, Brown.

Gelfand, D. E. (1986). Families, assistance, and the Euro-American elderly. In C. L. Hayes, R. A. Kalish, & D. Guttmann (Eds.), *Euro-American elderly: A guide for practice* (pp. 79-93). New York: Springer.

Hareven, T. (1980). *Main themes of the mini-conference from historical perspective in the social welfare forum, 1979.* Proceedings from the 106th annual forum of the National Conference on Social Welfare. New York: Columbia University Press.

Henderson, J. (1984). *Creating culturally relevant Alzheimer's support groups for racial and ethnic minorities.* Symposium presented at the 37th annual meeting of the Gerontological Society of America,

Jackson, J. J. (1980). *Minorities in aging.* Belmont, CA: Wadsworth.

Jackson, J. J., Bacon, J., & Peterson, J. (1977-1978). Life satisfaction among Black urban elderly. *International Journal of Aging and Human Development, 8,* 169-180.

Kalish, R. A. (1986). The meanings of ethnicity. In C. L. Hayes, R. A. Kalish, & D. Guttmann (Eds.), *Euro-American elderly: A guide for practice.* (pp. 16-34) New York: Springer.

Mindel, C. H. (1983). The elderly in minority families. In T. H. Brubaker (Ed.), *Family relationships in late life.* (pp. 193-208). Beverly Hills: Sage Publications.

Morycz, R. K. (1985). Caregiving strain and the desire to institutionalize family members with Alzheimer's disease: Possible predictors and model development. *Research on Aging, 7,* 321–361.

Morycz, R. K., Malloy, J., Bozich, M., & Martz, P. (1987). Racial differences in family burden: Clinical implications for social work. *Journal of Gerontological Social Work, 10,* 133–154.

Nydegger, C. N. (1986). Family ties of the aged and cross-cultural perspective. In L. E. Troll (Ed.), *Family issues in current gerontology* (pp. 145–161). New York: Springer.

Parsons, R. J., Cox, E. O., & Kimboko, P. J. (1989). Satisfaction, communication, and affection in caregiving. *Journal of Gerontological Social Work, 13,* 9–19.

Pearlin, L. I., Mullan, J. T., Semple, S. J., & Skaff, M. M. (1990). Caregiving and the stress process: An overview of concepts and their measures. *The Gerontologist, 30,* 583–594.

Sung, K. T. (1990). A new look at filial piety. *The Gerontologist, 30,* 610–617.

Wiley, F. M. (1971). Attitudes towards aging and the aged among Black Americans: Some historical perspectives. *Aging and Human Development, 2,* 66–70.

4

The Impact of Caregiving: Comparisons of Different Family Contexts and Experiences

William R. Avison
The University of Western Ontario

R. Jay Turner
The University of Toronto

Samuel Noh
Kathy Nixon Speechley
The University of Western Ontario

A substantial body of research in the areas of health and aging has examined the burdens and strains experienced by individuals in caring for family members with various illnesses, disabilities, or other problems. Indeed, it may be accurate to suggest that the study of informal caregiving has represented a veritable growth industry since the 1960s.

The increased number of cases of Alzheimer's disease and other senile dementias has stimulated substantial research activity on informal caregiving and it is clear that gerontologists have made progress in documenting the problems associated with caregiving to family members with this disease. To some extent, however, advances in research on this topic appear to have occurred in relative isolation from work on caregiving to individuals with other types of illnesses or impairments. This absence of linkages to other caregiving experiences is hardly peculiar to studies of Alzheimer's disease. Most investigations of caregiving have tended to focus solely on single disease entities or impairments. The very nature of the particular illness or disease often means that studies of caregiving are largely restricted to family providers within a relatively narrow age span and to strains or burdens that are often thought to be unique to that specific illness. In this chapter, we examine the lives of caregivers in different settings and in different stages of the life course. In so doing, we suggest that the comparative study of different caregiving experiences might assist us in better understanding the key elements that shape caregivers' lives: Those factors that assist family members in shouldering the burden of care and those that may exacerbate the negative consequences of providing such care.

CAREGIVING CONTEXTS ACROSS THE LIFE COURSE

To some extent, one of the responsibilities of every family is the provision of care for children and other family members. Beyond these "normative" caregiving experiences, there appears to be a substantial increase in the number of individuals who must assume responsibility for caring for family members under extenuating circumstances. Most recently, the growing number of cases of Alzheimer's disease and senile dementias and the epidemic nature of AIDS have meant that more and more individuals have had to assume the responsibilities of informal care of family members.

These are relatively recent trends that are only now being systematically investigated by social scientists. There are, however, other developments in North American society that have contributed to the numbers of caregivers who provide for family members under somewhat exceptional circumstances: (a) policies related to the deinstitutionalization of adults and children with mental illnesses or disabilities; (b) advances in the treatment of life-threatening and chronic pediatric illnesses such as cancer, cystic fibrosis, and diabetes; and (c) the growing number of single-parent families in which parents assume sole responsibility for the care of their children without the assistance of a partner.

Since the early 1980s, we have conducted studies of families that have assumed these exceptional caregiving responsibilities as a result of each of these developments. We begin by reviewing the social context of each of these caregiving circumstances and then summarize some of the results of our own work. Our goal is to identify potentially important aspects of the caregiving process that may have implications for future studies of caregiving in a variety of different circumstances.

Care of Children With Developmental Disabilities

Children with developmental disabilities were once routinely cared for in institutions for most of their lives, whereas it is now more often the rule than the exception that these children live with their families and receive treatment on an outpatient basis and through home visitation programs. Research on the parents of mentally handicapped children has paid particular attention to differences between families of autistic children and those of children with

Down syndrome (Cummings, Bayley, & Rie, 1966; De Myer, 1979; Holroyd & McArthur, 1976; Noh, Dumas, Wolf, & Fisman, 1989). Although children with these developmental problems exhibit cognitive deficits, the handicaps or disabilities typically associated with these two conditions vary considerably.

Rutter (1985) identified three major handicaps associated with autism. First, these children experience developmental difficulties related to language, cognitive abilities, and problems of socialization and interpersonal relationships. Second, they tend to engage in rigid, repetitive behaviors that lack creativity and flexibility. Third, autistic children exhibit a variety of other problem behaviors including self-destructive actions, temper tantrums, and aggression. Given these problems and the poor prognosis of autism (Wing, 1985; Wolf & Goldberg, 1986), the responsibilities of caring for an autistic child impose emotional and physical burdens on parents (Bristol & Schopler, 1984; Crnic, Friedrich, & Greenberg, 1983; Korn, Chess, & Fernandez, 1978; Noh et al., 1989).

The circumstances surrounding the care of children with Down syndrome may be considerably different. Although mothers of children with Down syndrome report problems associated with their child's mental retardation, there is some indication that these children are easier to care for (Noh et al., 1989). Indeed, despite the difficulties associated with Down syndrome, it appears that mother–child attachments are likely to proceed through the same stages as normal children, but at a slower pace (Berry, Gunn, & Andrews, 1980; Cicchetti & Serafica, 1981). In contrast, difficulties in relations between autistic children and their parents are frequent because these children often have problems in communicating and sharing feelings (Hobson, 1983).

Down syndrome children appear to be less disruptive than are autistic children and present fewer behavioral problems that parents must manage (Holroyd & McArthur, 1976). Nevertheless, Holroyd and McArthur found that caring for these children often constitutes a burden: Mothers of children with Down syndrome or autism must cope with demands on their time and often experience health problems.

Thus, providing care to an autistic child may be more burdensome than caring for a child with Down syndrome. Both caregiving situations generate chronic strains, but the behavioral problems of autistic children may make it more onerous for parents to care for them.

Care of Children With Life-Threatening Illnesses

Advances in the treatment of life-threatening pediatric illnesses have resulted in longer life expectancies for these children. In many cases, however, the improved prognoses for these children do not necessarily mean that the patterns of family life are the same for them as for healthy children. Rather, parents are often faced with demanding therapeutic responsibilities, concerns about the course of their children's illness, and worries about their children's future.

Pless and Satterwhite (1975) conducted a survey of the parents of children with various chronic illnesses and a comparison sample of parents of healthy children. Their results reveal that the childhood illnesses have a substantial impact on family life. Caring for a chronically ill child significantly alters parents' lives; these alterations increase in frequency and disruptiveness with the severity of the child's illness. Studies of the onset of diabetes among children report similar findings (Garner & Thompson, 1978; Kovacs & Feinberg, 1982) as do investigations of chronic physical disabilities (Breslau & Davis, 1986; Breslau, Staruch, & Mortimer, 1982).

Childhood cancer is another disease that appears to have important consequences for the family. Parents typically experience feelings of doubt, despair, and detachment following initial diagnosis of their child's illness (Friedman, Chodoff, Mason, & Hamburg, 1963; Kubler-Ross; 1969). During the first year of oncological treatment, many parents exhibit elevated levels of anxiety and depression (Powazek, Payne, Goff, Paulson, & Stagner, 1980) and report a variety of somatic problems (Lascari & Stebbins, 1973) and an erosion of self-esteem (Chodoff, Friedman, & Hamburg, 1964; Futterman & Hoffman, 1973; Schulman, 1976). Each stage of the illness is accompanied by a variety of negative effects on family members (Evans, 1975; Kagen-Goodheart, 1977; Kubler-Ross, 1969; Powazek et al., 1980).

Although childhood cancer is no longer an inevitably fatal disease, patients and their families are now faced with longer phases of treatment, an inability to predict the future, and thus a set of new and complex emotional and practical problems (Johnson, Rudolph, & Hartmann, 1979; Kagen-Goodheart, 1977). Even when chemotherapy is successfully concluded, the level of anxiety experienced by some parents remains high (Lewis & LaBarbera, 1983). The elective cessation of treatment can be stressful because it is often difficult for patients and their families to believe that the child will continue in health without active treatment (Kagen-Goodheart, 1977; Lewis & LaBarbera, 1983). Little is known, however, about these families during periods of remission. Parents are faced with the possibility that childhood cancer may result in some serious complications for the child, including physical defects and abnormalities (Jaffe, O'Malley, & Koocher, 1981; Jaffe et al., 1984; Li & Stone, 1976), the development of second primary neoplasms (Holmes & Holmes, 1975; Li & Stone, 1976), as well as psychological and social problems (Koocher, 1981; Links & Stockwell, 1985). Thus, the uncertainties attached to childhood cancer are likely to constitute continuing emotional strain for these parents.

Other stressful life events may simultaneously occur in these families;

however, little research has systematically assessed the impact of these stressors. Such efforts seem crucial for understanding the impact of childhood cancer on families across every stage of the illness, but especially for the increasing number who have entered the stage where they may prepare themselves for the child's normal development while coping with long-term uncertainty.

Single-Parent Families

Several studies have documented the substantial increase in the number of single-parent families in North America since the early 1970s (Glick, 1979; Hetherington, Cox, & Cox, 1979a, 1979b; National Center for Health Statistics, 1984; Statistics Canada, 1984; U.S. Bureau of the Census, 1982a, 1982b, 1984). This increase has been largely due to the rising rates of marital separation and divorce, although the proportion of never-married single parents has also increased significantly.

Reviews of the literature on separated and divorced parents have concluded that married persons report higher levels of both physical and psychological well-being than do the unmarried, especially the divorced (Bloom, Asher, & White, 1978; Gove, Hughes, & Style, 1983; Kessler & Essex, 1982; Tcheng-Larouche & Prince, 1983). In their longitudinal investigation, Menaghan and Lieberman (1986) argued that divorce leads to elevated levels of depression because of a decline in living standard, economic difficulties, and a reduction in social support. They concluded that ". . . even when marital termination provides some escape from a distressing relationship, the transition to divorce brings a change in life conditions that has depressive consequences" (Menaghan & Lieberman, 1986, p. 326). These findings are consistent with cross-sectional studies that have concluded that marital dissolution generates various stresses and strains, both economic and social, that impair one's psychological well-being (Bachrach, 1975; Pearlin & Johnson, 1977; Weiss, 1975).

There is also substantial research documenting the socioeconomic difficulties experienced by unwed mothers. Numerous studies find that unwed mothers tend to be very young, poorly educated, and from more economically disadvantaged backgrounds (Grindstaff & Turner, 1989; Madge, 1983; Rutter & Madge, 1976). Furstenburg and Brooks-Gunn (1986) argued that early pregnancy represents a major obstacle to further education. Thus, the unwed mother is likely to possess few resources for coping with her situation. Lacking such resources, these young women experience considerable deprivation and report numerous difficulties in finding employment, meeting financial needs, and arranging for suitable living accommodations. Such problems frequently result in unmarried mothers residing in disadvantaged neighborhoods where informal and formal support networks are less developed and where services are less available (Furstenburg & Brooks-Gunn, 1986). When such pervasive socioeconomic disadvantages are aggravated by perceptions of isolation, role strains associated with being the prime income provider and child caregiver, and a lack of emotional and instrumental support, elevated levels of distress are common consequences (Bachrach, 1975; Guttentag, Salasin, & Belle, 1980; Pearlin & Johnson, 1977; Ross & Sawhill, 1975).

Care of Mentally Ill Adults

Since the 1960s, governments have systematically adopted health care and social policies of de-institutionalization of individuals with chronic mental illnesses. Individuals who at one time might have spent large parts of their lives in hospitals or institutional treatment centers have been discharged in large numbers to the care of their families or to community-based group homes. These changes in patterns of treatment of serious mental illness have meant that discharged psychiatric patients are no longer a rarity in the community, however visible or invisible they may be. Indeed, Freeman and Simmons' (1963) assertion of almost three decades ago remains appropriate: "At the present time, it is no exaggeration to observe that the major problem in the field of mental illness is not the hospitalized but the formerly hospitalized patient" (p. 1).

Research on the families of these individuals has a long and rich history, and a variety of familial factors have been found to affect the community adjustment of discharged psychiatric patients (Avison & Speechley, 1987). A smaller body of knowledge documents how living with a formerly hospitalized patient constitutes a burden for family members. Early studies documented the stressful experiences that characterize the lives of these family members (Clausen & Yarrow, 1955; Clausen, Yarrow, Deasy, & Schwartz, 1955; Grad & Sainsbury, 1968; Pasamanick, Scarpitti, & Dinitz, 1967). More recently, investigators have examined the extent to which the discharged patient in the home is a source of strain to other family members that results in elevated levels of distress and social isolation (Arey & Warheit, 1980; Creer & Wing, 1974; Doll, 1976; Hatfield, 1978; Hertz, Endicott, & Spitzer, 1976; Noh & Turner, 1987). It now seems clear that caring for a discharged psychiatric patient exacts a "price" or burden from family members (cf. Freedman & Moran, 1984, for a review).

Until recently, however, little systematic research has focused on the correlates of such burdens. Little is known about the extent to which the experience of burden is conditioned by social and family environments, the patient's psychiatric status or history, or personal characteristics of family members.

QUESTIONS ABOUT CAREGIVING EXPERIENCES

One of the most significant contributions to the study of stress and strain in families has been the well-known work of Pearlin and his colleagues (Pearlin & Lieberman, 1979; Pearlin, Lieberman, Menaghan, & Mullan, 1981; Pearlin, Mullan, Semple, & Skaff, 1990; Pearlin & Schooler, 1978). Briefly, their model describes the interplay among three major components: sources of stress, mediators of stress, and manifestations of stress. Multiple sources of stress are thought to interact to produce elevated levels of emotional problems. Pearlin and others have suggested that stress arises out of two broad circumstances: the occurrence of discrete stressful life events and the presence of relatively continuous problems or strains. According to this formulation, the co-occurrence of eventful life experiences and chronic strains may produce stress in two ways. First, the experience of eventful stress may generate new strains or magnify existing ones; second, life events may change the meanings of existing strains. In these ways, then, eventful stressors and chronic strains are said to have stress amplifying effects.

The model also postulates the existence of factors that mediate the experience of stressors and the expression of symptoms of illness or dysfunction. Social resources or social supports, psychosocial resources, and coping behaviors are three critical groups of mediating factors. These factors are thought to either intervene between stress and illness, or to have interactive or stress buffering effects.

In the following sections of this chapter, we address four questions concerning the utility of the stress process model for studies of caregiving. First, is there consistent evidence across a range of caregiving circumstances that supports any of the major contentions of the stress process model? Second, does an examination of various caregiving experiences at different stages of family life provide any insights into the life course trajectories of caregivers? Third, do these studies suggest any new directions for research that might be useful to pursue? Finally, what kinds of caregiving studies hold the most promise for future research?

STUDIES OF CAREGIVING

Table 4.1 summarizes the sample characteristics of the four studies we address. With the exception of our study of the families of psychiatric patients, these investigations are all case-comparison designs.

The Child Developmental Problems Study (CDPS)

This study (Noh et al., 1989; Wolf, Noh, Fisman, & Speechley, 1989) included parents of 31 autistic children and 31 children with Down syndrome.

TABLE 4.1
Characteristics of Samples from Four Studies of Family Caregiving

	CDPS	CCS	SPFS	MICS
Receivers of Care	31 children with autism 31 children with Down syndrome	63 children with cancer	100 children	211 patients
Caregivers	Autism: 30 mothers 27 fathers Down: 31 mothers 29 fathers	63 mothers 49 fathers	100 single mothers	163 spouses 48 parents
Comparison Families	31	64	91	NA
Comparison Caregivers	31 mothers 30 fathers	64 mothers 62 fathers	91 married mothers	NA NA
Measures				
Psychological Distress	BDI	CES-D	CES-D DIS	GHQ
Chronic Strain	PSI	–	Financial Strains	Patient as Problem PARS
Life Events	19 events 12 months	30 events 6 months	31 events 12 months	21 events 6 months
Social Support	Kaplan	PSR	Kaplan	Kaplan
Mastery	–	Pearlin & Schooler	Pearlin & Schooler	Pearlin & Schooler

All autistic children were receiving services from a regional assessment and developmental center in London, Canada and had been diagnosed according to DSM-III (American Psychiatric Association, 1980) criteria. All Down syndrome children had been seen at this same center for assessment or treatment. Of the 31 families of autistic children, 30 mothers and 27 fathers participated in the study; 31 mothers and 29 fathers from families with a Down syndrome child took part.

A comparison group of 31 families of developmentally normal children was recruited from the case loads of family practice clinics, pediatricians, and a public health center. These families were matched with case families on the child's chronological age and gender. For this group, 31 mothers and 30 fathers participated. In addition, a sample of 31 families of normal children were matched with case families on the child's developmental age; however, for our purposes, we focus only on the former comparison sample.

The Childhood Cancer Study (CCS)

Speechley (1986) studied 80 families of children who had been treated for cancer at Children's Hospital of Western Ontario in London, Canada, before December 1, 1984. Families were included in the study if their child had not received any treatment for cancer for at least 6 months prior to the study and if the child's illness was in remission at the time of interview. A comparison sample of 79 families with healthy children was also selected to match the case families on area of residence, age of the child, and ages of the parents. For the purposes of this chapter, we excluded children who were 18 years of age or older so that the samples described here consist of 63 case mothers, 49 case fathers, 64 comparison mothers, and 62 comparison fathers.

The Single-Parent Family Study (SPFS)

Preliminary to a longitudinal investigation of single parents, a pilot study of single mothers was conducted to test elements of the proposed research design (Avison, 1989, 1990; Avison & McAlpine, 1989). Using provincial tax assessment lists for London, Ontario, we were able to draw a random sample of 100 female-headed single-parent households with at least one child under age 18 at home. A comparison sample of 91 married women with at least one child under age 18 at home was selected from a sample of respondents who were surveyed as part of a larger study on physical disability and psychological adjustment (Avison & Turner, 1988; Turner & Avison, 1989; Turner & Noh, 1988). These women were selected from the nondisabled comparison sample that was part of this case-comparison study (cf. Avison & Turner, 1988, for a detailed description of this sample).

The Mentally Ill in the Community Study (MICS)

As part of a larger study of 523 discharged psychiatric patients residing in the community in southwestern Ontario (Turner & Avison, 1983), we interviewed family members who were living with these patients (Noh & Avison, 1988; Noh & Turner, 1987). A total of 314 patients were living with significant others of whom we successfully interviewed 211 (67%). Approximately 77% were spouses of patients and the remaining 23% were parents, children, or relatives of the patient. Unlike the other studies described in this chapter, no comparison group was included in this investigation. Caregivers in this survey were predominantly spouses rather than parents.

MEASUREMENT STRATEGIES

In all four studies, our selection of constructs was significantly influenced by our interest in assessing the utility of the stress process model to understand caregiving experiences among these different families. In each study, we attempted to collect information on caregivers' levels of psychological distress, measures of chronic strains within the family, stressful life experiences of caregivers, various dimensions of psychosocial resources, as well as information on sociodemographic factors. Although identical measures were not employed in all studies, the indexes that we employed are comparable to one another. The lower portion of Table 4.1 displays the specific measures used in each study.

Distress Among Caregivers

Psychological distress in the CDPS was assessed with the Beck Depression Inventory (BDI) (Beck, Ward, Mendelson, Mock, & Erbaugh, 1961). The BDI is perhaps the most widely used measure of depressive symptoms and substantial evidence has been presented on its reliability and validity (Gotlib & Cane, 1989). Some authors suggest that scores of 16 or above are indicative of clinically significant depression (Shaw, Vallis, & McCabe, 1988).

For both the CCS and SPFS, psychological distress was measured with the Centre for Epidemiologic Studies Depression Scale (CES-D) (Radloff, 1977), a 20-item scale designed to measure an individual's current level of depressive symptoms. The CES-D also exhibits excellent discriminant and convergent validity and reliability (Husaini, Neff, Harrington, Hughes, & Stone, 1980; Radloff, 1977; Weissman & Klerman, 1977).

We also employed the depression section of the Diagnostic Interview Schedule (DIS) in the SPFS to generate DSM-III-R diagnoses of major depression and dysthymia for various time periods, including 6 months and lifetime. The reliability of the DIS has been demonstrated (Anthony et al., 1985; Robins, Helzer, Croughan, & Ratcliff, 1981) and it appears that it converges with other assessment techniques in identifying more severe disorders (Anthony et al., 1985; Helzer et al., 1985; Robins, 1985).

In the MICS, caregivers responded to a 30-item subset of the General Health Questionnaire (GHQ) (Goldberg, 1972). This instrument is widely used to measure mental health problems and has been validated in samples of patients from general medical practices (Goldberg, Rickels, Downing, & Hesbacher, 1976). Huppert, Gore, and Elliott (1988) presented additional information on the reliability and validity of the GHQ.

Chronic Strains

In each study except the CCS, we attempted to measure dimensions of strain that could be expected to be especially significant to the particular caregiving experience that was studied. In the CDPS, parents completed the Parenting Stress Index Form 6 (PSI) (Loyd & Abidin, 1985), a multi-item measure of strain in the parent–child system.

Although we have been interested in several dimensions of chronic strain in the SPFS, we limit our focus in this chapter to economic strains experienced by the women in both samples. This seven-item index included questions concerning difficulties in meeting financial needs related to child care, dental expenses, and other such needs.

In the MICS, we assessed two dimensions of chronic strain. To assess *subjective family burden,* we employed a nine-item modified version of the "patient as problem" scale developed by Pasamanick et al. (1967) to measure family members' perceptions of the patient as a source of worry within the family. *Objective burden* refers to difficulties and problems that patients present in terms of their role performance. This was measured with a subset of items from Ellsworth's (1975a, 1975b) Personal Adjustment and Role Skills Scale (PARS).

In the CCS, chronic strain was not directly measured. Instead, membership in the sample of parents with children surviving cancer as opposed to the comparison sample of parents of healthy children was considered to represent a proxy measure for these caregivers' experience of chronic strain.

Stressful Life Events

Parents in the CDPS were administered a checklist of 19 events abstracted from the Parenting Stress Index Form 6 (Loyd & Abidin, 1985). Subjects were asked to indicate which events had happened to them or to their family over the past 12 months.

Parents in the CCS responded to a life events checklist containing 30 events drawn from a scale employed in a study of adjustment to physical disability (Avison & Turner, 1988; Turner & Noh, 1988). Respondents indicated which events had occurred to them or to their families or close friends over the preceding 6 months to produce a count of events that was relatively unconfounded with events resulting from childhood cancer itself.

In the SPFS, a 31-item life events checklist that included events common to many life events measures was administered to case and comparison samples. Respondents were asked to indicate which events they had personally experienced during the 12 months preceding the interview. For specified events, respondents also indicated if other relatives experienced the event.

This checklist has been shown to address problems of inter- and intra-event variability (Avison & Turner, 1988; Turner & Avison, 1992).

Family members of psychiatric patients responded to a 21-item life events checklist previously employed in the Canada Health Survey. Respondents were asked whether they had personally experienced any of these events over the 6 months preceding the interview.

Psychosocial Resources

Our investigation of the impact of psychosocial resource variables focuses primarily on perceived social support. In all four studies, we employed one of two such measures: the Provisions of Social Relations Scale (PSR) or the Revised Kaplan Scale (Turner, Frankel, & Levin, 1983). The PSR is a 15-item scale in which subjects are asked to rate how closely each item corresponds to a description of his or her social relationships. Respondents use a 5-point scale ranging from *very much like my experience* to *not at all like my experience.* Across several studies, this index exhibits good measurement properties (Turner et al., 1983). This scale was administered in the CCS where Cronbach's alpha was .84.

The Revised Kaplan Scale (Turner et al., 1983) is composed of a series of vignettes, each scored from one to five with high scores indicating greater support. The scale has been used in several studies (Turner & Avison, 1985; Turner & Noh, 1988) of diverse populations and exhibits substantial internal reliability with Cronbach's alphas ranging from .79 to .83. This instrument was used in the CDPS, the SPFS, and the MICS.

For comparative purposes across studies, these two measures appear to be reasonably similar. Indeed, Turner et al. (1983) reported that the two scales are strongly correlated ($r = .62$).

In the CCS, SPFS, and MICS, we also assessed levels of mastery, the degree to which individuals believe that they control their own actions and manage the outcomes of life circumstances. In all three studies, we employed Pearlin and Schooler's (1978) seven-item scale which has been widely used in stress-process research and has good measurement properties (Noh & Turner, 1987; Turner & Noh, 1988).

A SYNOPSIS OF RESULTS

Given the number of studies to be reviewed and the wealth of information collected, it is impossible to present a detailed summary of our results. Rather, we have chosen to describe the variations in psychological distress and then summarize case-comparison and gender differences in the major variables of interest.

Psychological Distress

Table 4.2 presents scores on the measures of psychological distress for each of the three studies that included comparison samples (CDPS, CCS, and SPFS). Where possible, differences of means between case and comparison samples for each study have been calculated separately by gender of the caregiver. In the CDPS, mothers with Down syndrome or autistic children have significantly higher scores on the BDI than do comparison mothers, but no such

TABLE 4.2
Depressive Symptomatology in Case and Control Groups from Three Studies of Parental Caregiving

		Children with Developmental Problems Study				
		Autism		Control		Down
BECK	Mothers	10.47 (7.95) 30	*	5.00 (3.80) 31	*	8.03 (6.77) 31
	Fathers	* 4.58 (5.81) 27		4.30 (5.54) 31		* 3.76 (3.59) 39

		Childhood Cancer Study	
		Cancer	Control
CES-D	Mothers	9.14 (9.33) 63	8.76 (7.60) 64
	Fathers	8.06 (9.25) 49	7.57 (6.54) 62

	Single-Parent Family Study		
	Single Mothers		Married Mothers
CES-D	12.47 (13.09) 100	*	7.86 (9.07) 91
Major Depression:			
Lifetime	52.0%	*	11.0%
6 Months	35.0%	*	4.4%
2 Weeks	17.0%	*	1.1%
Dysthymia	10.0%	*	2.2%

*$p \leq .05$

differences were obtained for fathers. There is also some indication that mothers of autistic children suffer from higher levels of psychological distress than mothers of children with Down syndrome or comparison mothers. An examination of gender differences revealed that case mothers have significantly higher mean BDI scores than do case fathers. No difference is observed between comparison mothers and fathers.

In the second panel, we see that neither mothers nor fathers of children with cancer differ from comparisons in CES-D scores. While mothers report higher CES-D scores than fathers in both samples, these differences are not statistically significant. The bottom segment of Table 4.2 displays differences between single-parent mothers and the comparison sample of married women in levels of psychological distress and in rates of depressive disorders. These differences are striking. Single-parent mothers have CES-D scores that are almost 60% higher than their married counterparts. With regard to depressive disorder, the results are even more pronounced. Whereas 11.0% of the comparison sample met criteria for at least one lifetime depressive episode, more than half of the single mothers had experienced an episode of major depression. Furthermore, 17.0% of all single parents met criteria for major depression in the 2 weeks prior to interview as compared to only 1.1% of married women. Additionally, 10.0% of single mothers appeared to suffer from dysthymia; among married women, the comparable figure is only 2.2%.

Because no comparison sample was available for the MICS, mean distress scores have not been presented. It is worth noting, however, that female caregivers reported higher scores on the GHQ than did males.

Taken together, it appears that case-comparison differences in reported symptoms of distress appear to vary substantially by the caregiving experience. These results do not provide clear insights into the factors associated with caregiving that contribute to elevated levels of distress. Furthermore, whereas there is some evidence that the burden of caring for family members has greater effects on mothers than fathers, this pattern is by no means uniform. Whatever the explanations for the variability in these differences in distress, it seems clear that the costs of caregiving are by no means identical across different family circumstances.

Exposure to Stress and Strain

One potential explanation for elevated levels of distress among some caregivers may be their greater exposure to stressful life events or to the burden of strains associated with the provision of care to family members. We examined all four studies to determine whether observed significant case-comparison or gender differences in distress were reflected in parallel differences in either stressful life events or measures of strain.

Briefly, it appears that differential exposure to strain is a more plausible explanation of case-comparison differences in distress than is any variation in exposure to stressful life events. For both the CDPS and SPFS, case parents report higher levels of strain than do comparison parents. Interestingly, patterns of gender differences in stressful life events appear to correspond to differences in psychological distress across all four studies involving men and women. We observe significant gender differences in both distress and the number of reported stressful life events in the CDPS and the MICS. In the CCS, where there is no significant variation in distress by gender, neither is there a significant difference in eventful stressors. It seems, then, that caregiver distress is more closely associated with the burden of strain, whereas gender differences may be more strongly related to women's elevated exposure to life events.

Levels of Psychosocial Resources

No clear patterns are observed with respect to perceived social support. With only one exception, no case-comparison differences in levels of social support are found in any of the studies except that mothers of Down syndrome children have higher support scores than do mothers of autistic children or comparison mothers. There is also little evidence that gender differences in distress are attributable to variations between females and males on social support. The only instance of this pattern is to be found among spouses of discharged psychiatric patients. In summary, there is little evidence to suggest that observed case-comparison differences in distress can be attributed to deficits in perceived social support.

Any inferences concerning the role of levels of mastery in accounting for distress differences are difficult to make. In the CCS, there are no significant case-comparison differences among mothers or fathers. A modest gender difference occurs among the comparison families where fathers have slightly higher mastery scores than do mothers. In the SPFS, single-parent and married mothers do not differ from one another on mastery. Among spouses of discharged psychiatric patients in the MICS, males (husbands) have significantly higher levels of mastery; this is consistent with their lower levels of psychological distress.

STRESS PROCESS ANALYSES

In all four studies, we attempted to assess the utility of the stress process for understanding variations in psychological distress among caregivers. In general, these analyses involved a number of steps. First, we estimated the impact of social stressors (stressful life events and chronic strain, where measured) on psychological distress. Second, we determined whether psychosocial resources (social support and mastery) had significant, independent effects on psychological distress. Third, we tested for the stress buffering effects of psychosocial resources and estimated stress amplifying influences, chronic strains, and eventful stressors by computing appropriate interaction terms. Because any detailed presentation of these results for all four studies would require numerous tables and diagrams, a brief summary of our major findings from these studies is displayed in Table 4.3. A detailed presentation of these results can be found in our work that has been published or presented elsewhere (Avison, 1989, 1990; Avison & McAlpine, 1989; Noh & Avison, 1988; Noh et al., 1989; Noh & Turner, 1987; Speechley, 1986; Turner & Avison, 1983).

TABLE 4.3
Summary of Stress Process Analyses Across Four Studies[a]

Study/Sample	Main Effect[b]				Interaction Effects[c]		
	Life Events	Chronic Strain	Social Support	Mastery	Resources × Life Events	Resources × Strain	Life Events × Strain
CDPS							
Mothers of Down Children	0	0	0	NA	0^s	$0^s (0)^s$	0 (0)
Mothers of Autistic Children	0	0	0	NA	0^s	$0^s (0)^s$	0 (0)
Fathers of Down Children	+	0	−	NA	$-^s$	$0^s (0)^s$	0 (0)
Fathers of Autistic Children	0	+	−	NA	$-^s$	$0^s (0)^s$	0 (0)
CCS							
Mothers	+	NA	−	−	0^s 0^m	NA $(-)^s$ NA $(0)^m$	NA (0)
Fathers	+	NA	−	−	0^s 0^m	NA $(-)^s$ NA $(-)^m$	NA (0)
SPFS							
Single-Parent Mothers	+	+	−	−	$-^s$ $-^m$	$-^s (-)^s$ $-^m (-)^m$	(0)
MICS							
Spouses/ Children	+	+	0	−	NA	0^s $-^m$	0

[a]Results are presented only for case groups
[b]For main effects: + = significant positive effect; − = significant negative effect; 0 = no significant effect; NA = no available measure of strain.
[c]For interactions involving psychosocial resources: − = buffering effect; s = support and m = mastery. Tests in parentheses represent case-control membership as a proxy measure of strain.

Main Effects

It is clear that the effects of eventful stressors vary substantially across these four studies. We observed only weak stress-distress associations among parents of children with developmental problems; this association is significant only among fathers of children with Down syndrome. In contrast, among families in the CCS, the number of life events is a strong predictor of depression among both mothers and fathers whose children had cancer. Similarly, stressful events are strongly related to distress scores among single-parent mothers in the SPFS. Finally, among family members in the MICS, the association between eventful stressors and GHQ scores is significant but modest.

Turning to the impact of chronic strain on distress, we observed no effects of parenting problems on distress among parents in the CDPS except for fathers of autistic children. In contrast, financial strains contributed substantially to elevated levels of distress among single-parent mothers. Similarly, measures of the burden of caring for a psychiatric patient are significantly related to distress among family members in the MICS.

Although social support is only weakly related to distress among mothers of autistic children and has no effect among mothers of Down children, its effects are strong among fathers in both of these groups. In the CCS, both perceived social support and mastery are extremely important predictors of distress for both fathers and mothers. For single-parent mothers in the SPFS and family members in the MICS, both perceived support and mastery are significant, inverse correlates of psychological distress. In the MICS, however, the effect of social support disappears when mastery is also included in the analysis.

Three conclusions about these main effects seem warranted. First, the impact of stressful life experiences varies substantially according to which caregivers we examine. It is interesting to note that these correlations are weakest among those individuals who provide care to individuals with psychiatric or developmental problems. Second, with the exception of the CDPS, there seems to be a consistent impact of chronic strains on levels of distress. Third, with the exception of mothers in the CDPS, psychosocial resources have strong main effects on psychological distress. Among those caregivers whose levels of stress or strain exerted significant effects on distress, controlling for these psychosocial resources only marginally reduced the stress-distress relationship. Thus, it appears that the contribution of psychosocial resources to better mental health is largely independent of the stresses and strains that contribute to distress.

Stress Buffering Effects

An important component of the stress process formulation is the notion that psychosocial resources may moderate the effects of stress or strain on measures of psychological distress. There are essentially two ways in which these stress buffering effects can be assessed in case-comparison analyses. The first involves the regression of distress scores on stress-by-resource interaction terms. The second entails assessing whether the effects of psychosocial resources on distress are stronger among cases than among comparison subjects. This latter approach assumes that caregivers in the case group are experiencing more chronic strains than are their comparison counterparts.

Among mothers in the CDPS, we found little evidence that social support buffers the effects of eventful stressors or parenting strain on psychological distress. In contrast, the impact of stressful life events among fathers of children with autism or Down syndrome is moderated substantially by social support.

In the CCS, we found no evidence of buffering effects of social support or mastery on stressful life events among mothers or fathers. There are, however, indications that the social support / distress relationship is stronger for case mothers and fathers than for comparisons. It also appears that the magnitude of the correlation between mastery and distress is greater among case than comparison fathers. If we assume that parents of children with cancer constitute a group that experiences greater strain than the group of comparison mothers, these results support a buffering explanation. Thus, whereas social support and mastery do not appear to moderate eventful stress, these resources do seem to play some role in reducing the effects of the chronic strains associated with giving care to children with cancer.

Results from the SPFS strongly support the stress buffering hypothesis. Among both single-parent and married mothers, perceived social support and mastery both moderate the effects of stressful life events and reduce the impact of chronic financial strain on psychological distress.

Similarly, our analyses of these interaction effects among family members in the MICS reveal that caregivers with higher levels of mastery are less likely to be distressed by the burden of caring for a family member with mental health problems. No such buffering effects of social support could be identified.

To summarize, the evidence for stress buffering effects of perceived social support and mastery is relatively strong. For all samples except the mothers of children with developmental disabilities, there is some indication that these resource factors moderate the impact of at least one dimension of stress or strain.

Stress Amplification

What evidence is there that chronic strains and stressful life events amplify one another to elevate distress scores among caregivers? Across these four studies, we found few indications that the experience of chronic strains is associated with elevated relationships between eventful stressors and psychological distress. There is some evidence that parents of children with cancer are more vulnerable to stressful events than are comparison mothers and fathers but these effects are modest.

DISCUSSION

Any attempt to synthesize the results of these studies requires caution. Nevertheless, we believe that the patterns we have observed provide us with some insights into the factors associated with distress among individuals who care for family members under exceptional circumstances. They also suggest some important directions that further research might take.

The Burden of Caregiving

Our results indicate that family caregiving is associated with elevated levels of psychological distress only in certain circumstances. It seems clear that the burden of care affects female caregivers' psychological well-being more than males'. This pattern appears to be consistent with the "cost of caring" hypothesis that has been explored by Kessler and McLeod (1984) and Turner and Avison (1989).

In the studies reviewed here, distress among female caregivers seems to be associated with two types of circumstances. The first appears to occur when women must provide care to individuals with psychiatric problems or developmental disabilities (as is the case in the MICS and the CDPS). The second situation occurs in the SPFS where single parents must provide nurturance to their children in the face of a number of other disadvantages.

Regardless of their child's health, there is little doubt that all mothers experience concerns and anxieties about their children's well-being. It seems, however, that what distinguishes families of children with developmental problems from those of children with cancer is the additional strain associated with the day to day care of the child. Children with developmental problems frequently require greater attention on a daily basis than children whose development is normal. We have also described how parents of autistic children appear to face many more problems associated with the management of their child's behavior, especially those that are self-injurious or aggressive. Parents of Down syndrome children are more likely to encounter difficulties with the child's dependency and slower development — serious problems, but ones that may not be as stress-provoking as those experienced by parents of autistic children.

Family members of discharged psychiatric patients often make considerable efforts to cope with the symptomatic behaviors of the patient. Some patients engage in disruptive behaviors that create interpersonal tensions in the household; others become withdrawn to the point that normal interactions among family members are difficult. Elsewhere (Noh & Avison, 1988), we reported that working wives of psychiatric patients experience greater strains in the caregiving role than wives who do not work. We attributed this to role overload — the responsibilities of child care, work, and support of a psychiatrically ill spouse may add substantially to their daily burden (Noh & Avison, 1988).

Among single-parent mothers, the operant burden of stress is likely to include balancing work and parenting demands in the absence of a spouse who might share these responsibilities. This may be further exacerbated by these single parents' sense of isolation and by their relatively difficult socioeconomic circumstances. Thus, the theme of role overload once again emerges.

For mothers of children whose cancer is in remission, there are few instances in which daily care is likely to differ substantially from care of healthy children. Indeed, from a caregiver's perspective, the most difficult times and crises for these parents are more likely to have occurred during the child's initial diagnosis and treatment when parents and children must deal with chemotherapy, surgery, and extended hospitalization. Mothers of children with cancer may be more likely to worry about the possible recurrence of the disease and their child's life expectancy than issues of daily care.

These differences in the type and quality of chronic strains associated with the caregiving role appear to be reflected in our analyses. Thus, the elevated levels of distress exhibited by mothers of developmentally handicapped children, families of discharged psychiatric patients, and single-parent mothers appear to be associated with the daily burden of strain experienced in these family environments. These responsibilities and concerns may be continuous and may require a repertoire of coping skills on a daily basis.

This interpretation is consistent with our work on the effects of chronic strain on depressive symptoms. Avison and Turner (1988) have argued that more enduring strains contribute to distress because they add substantially to the burden of operant stress experienced by the individual at any one point in time. For parents of children with developmental problems and caregivers of psychiatric patients, the added burden of strain associated with the special needs of these individuals may be more persistent and, therefore, more likely to affect levels of depression at any point in time than is the case for parents of children with cancer. Thus, at the time these respondents were interviewed, the operant strains related to the health problem may have been more prevalent among caregivers in the CDPS and MICS. Among single parents, the operant burden of stress may have less to do with their children's behavior than with the role overload associated with being a sole caregiver.

These considerations suggest that there might be value in a system for classifying salient differences and similarities among caregiving circumstances. Rolland (1984) argued that chronic and life-threatening illnesses can be categorized according to (a) gradual versus sudden onset; (b) progressive, episodic, or constant course; (c) fatal, possibly fatal, or non-fatal outcome; and (d) absence versus presence of incapacitation. Cross-cutting these is the specification of the phase of the illness: whether the illness is in a crisis phase, a more chronic period of activity, or a terminal, life-threatening phase.

In our view, this typology might be relevant to a range of caregiving experiences and need not be restricted to chronic and life-threatening illnesses. Rolland's conceptualization might enable stress researchers to identify more clearly the salient characteristics of a particular caregiving situation and to categorize the types of burdens and strains that are likely to be experienced by caregivers. Attending to variations across these dimensions may provide stress researchers with a stronger theoretical basis for predicting how various illnesses or problems experienced by family members are likely to affect the mental health of their caregivers.

A second issue arises out of Rolland's (1984) recognition that health problems have different courses and sequelae. In the CCS, we focused on parents at a time when their child's illness was in remission. It is likely that a study of these families at crisis points might have produced different findings. Thus, the need for prospective research is apparent; however, given the difficulties in conducting such studies, it may be that synthetic cohort designs are more practical and would at least enable us to determine whether different strains arise in the course of the child's health problem.

Beyond the need for a more systematic means for classifying different illnesses, our findings suggest the need for more detailed information about the nature of strains associated with caregiving. Attempts should be made to measure the different sources of strain in these families. It seems clear that problems directly associated with treatment of the family member's illness or impairment and management of behavioral problems need to be assessed. It may also be important to design measures that index the extent to which less concrete strains such as worries about the family's future and concerns about making correct decisions about care constitute a psychological burden for caregivers. Some strategy is required for examining the role that other family members play in terms of alleviating or exacerbating the costs of caregiving as well.

Finally, little is known about the ways in which interactions among family members may add to or ameliorate levels of strain. For example, given the behavioral problems that are often associated with childhood autism or with adult psychiatric illnesses, the quality of interpersonal relationships between caregivers and care recipients may further contribute to experienced burden in these families. Conversely, the frequently reported positive relationships between Down syndrome children and their parents may alleviate some of the strains associated with the care of these children. Studies that attend to these differences in family interaction patterns might advance our understanding of caregiving experiences by taking these patterns into consideration.

A promising first step in better understanding the nature and dynamics of strains in these families might be the use of diary studies. This approach is being used in a variety of research settings to collect detailed information about specific problems arising in households and the ways in which family members respond to such difficulties. This strategy might provide a richer source of information about the most significant problems that confront caregivers in various situations.

Although the use of diaries has become popular in recent years, we suggest that such methods will have greater informational value when they are imbedded in longitudinal studies of caregiving. In this way, it might be possible to use measures derived from diaries to explain differences over time that have been captured in panel analyses.

The Role of Psychosocial Resources

Across these four studies, we consistently found that psychosocial resources play an important role in reducing psychological distress among caregivers. Regardless of whether these factors have direct or buffering effects, it seems incontestable that the enhancement of psychosocial resources among caregivers is likely to have positive consequences for them. This conclusion is by no means new. The wealth of evidence on the beneficial effects of being part of a supportive network or perceiving oneself to be in control of one's life have been amply demonstrated in the research literature across a broad array of life circumstances. Cross-sectional studies, retrospective, and prospective studies all tend to converge on this same conclusion: psychosocial resources provide substantial mental health benefits.

If there is agreement on this point, then there is merit in seriously considering a somewhat new direction for stress process research. This may be the opportune time to consider the implementation of intervention studies of caregiving. Because the stress process model specifies a number of points of intervention, we have a theoretical basis for designing programs that might enhance the social support of caregivers or increase their sense of mastery. In addition, there are a number of examples of intervention techniques that are applicable to the caregiving situation. Intervention programs with demonstrable efficacy exist in other areas that might well be tailored to the needs of specific groups of caregivers. For example, Dunst, Trivette, and Deal (1988) provided a detailed approach to the development of interventions that focus on the family as a dynamic system. They describe a number of strategies that emphasize the enhancement of families' supportive systems and the encouragement of a greater sense of control or empowerment among family members. Gottlieb and Selby (1989) presented one of the most comprehensive reviews of social support interventions. They developed a typology of interventions, review the evidence on the outcomes of such interventions, specify guidelines for developing support interventions, and discuss problems and pitfalls of intervention projects. There are now a number of edited collections describing effective interventions that focus on enhancing social support, mastery, and competence in a variety of family circumstances (Albee, Joffe, & Dusenbury, 1988; Bond & Wagner, 1988; Price, Cowen, Lorion, & Ramos-McKay, 1988).

Beyond the public health benefits that may accrue from these interventions, such initiatives may make important theoretical contributions to our understanding of social stress and its consequences. Although longitudinal studies provide a reasonably strong design for estimating the causal impact of psychosocial resources on mental health, interventions that are experimental or quasi-experimental in design have the capacity to resolve many of the doubts and objections that have been raised about the causal power of social support and mastery.

Of course, intervention research is fraught with difficulty. In developing interventions among family caregivers, a number of principles need to be underscored. First, such programs need to be focused; that is, the content of the program of intervention needs to be carefully specified similarly to the ways in which treatment plans are developed in primary care situations. Second, random assignment of caregivers to intervention and control groups must not be compromised. Third, appropriate outcomes that can be measured must be specified prior to the intervention. In our view, such outcomes should go beyond measures of the caregiver's well-being to include some assessment of the quality of care delivered to the family member and an evaluation of the potential savings to the health care delivery system. In this way, the value of successful psychosocial interventions will be more apparent to those individuals responsible for program and policy development.

Such initiatives in intervention research need not be large scale programs that are expensive and risky. Rather, the development of small, focused interventions that show promise may lead the way for future initiatives designed to address the needs of caregivers and their family members.

Life Course Trajectories Among Caregivers

As with all individuals, the life histories of caregivers can be expected to be marked by important role transitions and significant stressors. What may distinguish those who provide care under exceptional circumstances from those who assume more normative family caregiving responsibilities is the frequency and timing of such experiences as well as their predictability. For some problems, the trajectories of caregiving may be measured in terms of a number of years; for others, the provision of care may encompass a lifetime.

Parents of children with developmental problems may be faced with life-long responsibilities for care and support of their child. To be sure, a substantial proportion of children with such health problems make substantial gains in independent living as they grow older; however, it is rarely the case that autistic children or those with Down syndrome can assume complete independence. Consequently, the trajectory of caregiving for these parents typically involves a significantly extended period of continued exposure to strains associated with the burden of care.

For parents of a child whose cancer is in remission, the course of caregiving may be marked by continuing anxieties about their child's health that become allayed with time. The longer the child's disease is in remission, the more likely is it that caregiving responsibilities may revert to a pattern of experiences that approaches those of families of healthy children. Thus, for those children who return to good health, the special burdens experienced by their parents may decline over time.

Among single mothers, the transition into parenthood among never-married women often cuts short their education, preempts their entry into the labor force, and limits opportunities for social relationships and finding a partner. Subsequent attempts at educational upgrading or obtaining a job are made extremely difficult by child care responsibilities. The social and economic strains arising from these circumstances make such transitions all the more difficult. Separated or divorced mothers also experience transitions that often depart significantly from those of married parents. The change from marriage to single parenthood is frequently characterized by interpersonal conflict that has consequences for the health of parents and children alike. For many women, separation or divorce involves role transitions that require them to be the sole caregiver and breadwinner. The consequences of assuming almost total responsibility for these roles include the experience of overload and a sense of isolation. Many single parents report that working and parenting leaves them with little time or energy for social activities or involvement in new relationships. For some women, these strains are alleviated by subsequent marriage or remarriage although there may be other strains associated with so-called "blended" families. Among those single-parent mothers who do not enter into a subsequent marriage, their caregiving responsibilities, like those of married mothers, ultimately decrease as their children grow up and assume independence as adults.

Families of discharged psychiatric patients may be more likely to experience particularly unpredictable caregiving trajectories. Some patients experience no subsequent episodes of their illness and their family life may return to relatively normal conditions. Others may endure several additional periods of psychiatric illness that create additional strains for family members. The somewhat unpredictable recurrence of psychiatric problems that generate problems in family relationships may heighten feelings of apprehension or anxiety among family caregivers over relatively long time periods.

These variations in trajectories have not yet been carefully investigated by social scientists. To date, most studies have been restricted to cross-sectional "snapshots" of caregiving experiences or, at best, longitudinal studies that examine changes over a few years' time. There is a pressing need for studies that compare the experiences of caregivers who have assumed these responsibilities for a relatively short period of time with those who have devoted several years to a family member in need of assistance.

We know even less about the experiences of family members when their exceptional caregiving responsibilities are finally over. To our knowledge, there are almost no studies that examine how family members adapt to life once they have been relieved of these duties. Of course, these outcomes will vary dramatically according to the circumstances under which care no longer needs to be provided. Moreover, it seems likely that the effects of these reductions in caregiving responsibilities will differ according to the life stage of the care provider. In our view, these are long-term outcomes that require attention by researchers who are interested in the life course of caregiving experiences.

CONCLUSION

The study of caregivers is exceedingly complex given the wide range of health problems, disabilities, and impairments that exist. We have employed a stress process framework to explore the burden of very different caregiving experiences. In doing so, we have drawn attention to a number of important substantive and methodological issues that need to be addressed further by researchers in this field.

First, it appears that variations in the levels of distress experienced by caregivers may be linked closely to the nature of chronic strains that confront them. The elevated levels of distress exhibited by mothers of developmentally handicapped children and psychiatric patients' families suggest that strains related to behavioral problems are of particular significance. It seems, therefore, that attempts to better measure these kinds of strains may be particularly fruitful in understanding the costs of caregiving.

Second, there is good reason to believe that the stress process formulation is useful for understanding how these strains, other eventful stressors, and psychosocial resources affect the mental health of caregivers. In particular, this model has assisted us in showing that the operant burden of stress and strain may be a crucial determinant of caregiver distress. It also suggests that any understanding of the caregiving experience needs to take into account the beneficial effects of psychosocial resources.

The stress process model also assists us in thinking about crucial aspects of research designs that will better enable us to answer some key questions about the ways in which caregivers adjust and respond to their special responsibilities. We have outlined a number of these design features that might be usefully incorporated into studies of caregiving. In our view, future research that employs a stress process model as a conceptual framework and that includes some of these methodological features is likely to generate new insights into the dynamics of family caregiving.

ACKNOWLEDGMENTS

An earlier version of this chapter was presented at the Penn State Gerontology Center Conference on Social Structure and Caregiving: Family and Cross-National Perspectives, The Pennsylvania State University, University Park, PA, October, 1990. The studies reported in this chapter were supported by grants from the Ontario Ministry of Health and Health and Welfare Canada to R. Jay Turner and William R. Avison, by grants from the Laidlaw Foundation and the Dean of Social Science, The University of Western Ontario, to William R. Avison, and by a Doctoral Student Award from the Ontario Ministry of Health to Kathy Nixon Speechley.

REFERENCES

Albee, G. W., Joffe, J. M., & Dusenbury, L. A. (1988). *Prevention, powerlessness, and politics: Readings on social change.* Beverly Hills, CA: Sage Publications.

American Psychiatric Association. (1980). *Diagnostic and statistical manual of disorders* (3rd ed.). Washington, DC: Author.

Anthony, J. C., Folstein, M., Romanoski, A. J., Von Korff, M. R., Nestadt, G. R., Chahal, R., Merchant, A., Brown, H., Shapiro, S., Kramer, M., & Gruenberg, E. M. (1985). Comparison of the lay diagnostic interview schedule and a standardized psychiatric diagnosis. *Archives of General Psychiatry, 42,* 667–675.

Arey, S., & Warheit, G. J. (1980). Psychosocial costs of living with psychologically disturbed family members. In L. N. Robins, P. J. Clayton, & J. K. Wing (Eds.), *The social consequences of psychiatric illness* (pp. 158–175). New York: Brunner/Mazel.

Avison, W. R. (1989, August). *Mental and physical health of single parents and their children.* Paper presented at the Family Structure and Health Conference, University of California — San Francisco.

Avison, W. R. (1990, August). *Family structure and distress: Understanding elevated levels of depression among single-parent mothers.* Paper presented at the annual meeting of the Society for the Study of Social Problems, Washington, DC.

Avison, W. R., & McAlpine, D. D. (1989). *Assessing the mental and physical health of parents and children in single-parent families: A pilot study.* Toronto, Ontario: The Laidlaw Foundation.

Avison, W. R., & Speechley, K. N. (1987). The discharged psychiatric patient: A review of social, social psychological, and psychiatric correlates of outcome. *American Journal of Psychiatry, 114,* 10-18.

Avison, W. R., & Turner, R. J. (1988). Stressful life events and depressive symptoms: Disaggregating the effects of acute stressors and chronic strains. *Journal of Health and Social Behavior, 29,* 253-264.

Bachrach, L. L. (1975). Marital status and mental disorder: An analytical review (DHEW Publication No. ADM 75-217). Washington, DC: U.S. Government Printing Office.

Beck, A. T., Ward, C. H., Mendelson, M., Mock, J., & Erbaugh, J. (1961). An inventory for measuring depression. *Archives of General Psychiatry, 4,* 561-571.

Berry, P., Gunn, P., & Andrews, R. (1980). Behavior of Down's syndrome infants in a strange situation. *American Journal of Mental Deficiency, 85,* 213-218.

Bloom, B. L., Asher, S. J., & White, S. W. (1978). Marital disruption as a stressor: A review and analysis. *Psychological Bulletin, 85,* 867-894.

Bond, L. A., & Wagner, B. M. (1988). *Families in transition: Primary prevention programs that work.* Beverly Hills, CA: Sage Publications.

Breslau, N., & Davis, G. C. (1986). Chronic stress and major depression. *Archives of General Psychiatry, 43,* 309-314.

Breslau, N., Staruch, K. S., & Mortimer, Jr., E. A. (1982). Psychological distress in mothers of disabled children. *American Journal of Disabled Children, 136,* 682-686.

Bristol, M. M., & Schopler., E. (1984). A developmental perspective on stress and coping in families of autistic children. In J. Blancher (Ed.), *Severely handicapped children and their families* (pp. 91-141). New York: Academic Press.

Chodoff, P., Friedman, S., & Hamburg, D. A. (1964). Stresses, defenses and coping behavior: Some observations in parents of children with malignant disease. *American Journal of Psychiatry, 120,* 743-749.

Cicchetti, D., & Serafica, F. C. (1981). Interplay among behavioral systems: Illustrations from the study of attachment, affiliation, and wariness in young children with Down's syndrome. *Developmental Psychology, 17,* 36-49.

Clausen, J., & Yarrow, M. (1955). Introduction: Mental illness and the family. *Journal of Social Issues, 11,* 3-5.

Clausen, J., Yarrow, M., Deasy, L., & Schwartz, C. (1955). The impact of mental illness: Research formulation. *Journal of Social Issues, 11,* 6-11.

Creer, C., & Wing, J. (1974). *Schizophrenia at home.* London: Institute of Psychiatry.

Crnic, K. A., Friedrich, W. N., & Greenberg, M. T. (1983). Adaptation of families with a mentally retarded child: A model of stress, coping, and family ecology. *American Journal of Mental Deficiency, 88,* 125-138.

Cummings, S. T., Bayley, H. C., & Rie, H. E. (1966). Effects of the child's deficiency on the mother: A study of mothers of mentally retarded, chronically ill, and neurotic children. *American Journal of Orthopsychiatry, 36,* 595-608.

De Myer, M. K. (1979). *Parents and children with autism.* Washington, DC: V. H. Winston and Sons.

Doll, W. (1976). Family coping with the mentally ill: An unanticipated problem of deinstitutionalization. *Hospital and Community Psychiatry, 27,* 183-185.

Dunst, C., Trivette, C., & Deal, A. (1988). *Enabling and empowering families: Principles and guidelines for practice.* New York: Brookline Books.

Ellsworth, R. B. (1975a). Consumer feedback in measuring the effectiveness of mental health programs. In M. Guttentag & E. L. Struening (Eds.), *Handbook of evaluation research* (Vol. 2, pp. 239-274). Beverly Hills, CA: Sage Publications.

Ellsworth, R. B. (1975b). *PARS scale manual.* Roanoke, VA: Institute for Program Evaluation.

Evans, A. E. (1975). Practical care for the family of a child with cancer. *Cancer, 35,* 871-875.

Freedman, R. I., & Moran, A. (1984). Wanderers in a promised land: The chronically mentally ill and deinstitutionalization. *Medical Care, 22,* S1-S59.

Freeman, H. E., & Simmons, O. G. (1963). *The mental patient comes home.* New York: Wiley.

Friedman, S. B., Chodoff, P., Mason, J., & Hamburg, D. (1963). Behavioral observations of parents anticipating the death of a child. *Pediatrics, 32,* 610-625.

Furstenburg, F. F., Jr., & Brooks-Gunn, J. (1986). Teenage childbearing: Causes, consequences, and remedies. In L. H. Aiken & D. Mechanic (Eds.), *Applications of social science to clinical medicine and health policy* (pp. 307-334). New Brunswick, NJ: Rutgers University Press.

Futterman, E. H., & Hoffman, I. (1973). Crisis and adaptation in the families of fatally ill children. In E. J. Anthony & C. Koupernik (Eds.), *The child in his family* (pp. 127-143). New York: Krieger.

Garner, A. M., & Thompson, C. W. (1978). Juvenile diabetes. In P. R. Magrab (Ed.), *Psychological management of pediatric problems* (Vol. 1, pp. 221-258). Baltimore: University Park Press.

Glick, P. C. (1979). Children of divorced parents in demographic perspective. *Journal of Social Issues, 35,* 170-181.

Goldberg, D. P. (1972). *The detection of psychiatric illness by questionnaire: A technique for the identification and assessment of non-psychotic illness.* New York: Oxford University.

Goldberg, D. P., Rickels, K., Downing, R., & Hesbacher, P. (1976). A comparison of the psychiatric screening tests. *British Journal of Psychiatry, 129,* 61-67.

Gotlib, I. H., & Cane, D. B. (1989). Self report assessment of depression and anxiety. In P. C. Kendall & D. Watson (Eds.), *Anxiety and depression: Distinctive and overlapping features* (pp. 131-169). New York: Academic Press.

Gottlieb, B. H., & Selby, P. (1989). *Social support and mental health: A review of the literature.* Final unpublished report to National Health Research and Development Program, Health and Welfare Canada, Ottawa, Ontario.

Gove, W. R., Hughes, M., & Style, C. B. (1983). Does marriage have positive effects on the psychological well-being of the individual? *Journal of Health and Social Behavior, 24,* 122-131.

Grad, J., & Sainsbury, P. (1968). The effects that patients have on their families in a community care and a control psychiatric service: A two year follow-up. *British Journal of Psychiatry, 114,* 265-278.

Grindstaff, C. F., & Turner, R. J. (1989). Structural factors associated with birth complications in adolescent fertility. *Canadian Journal of Public Health, 80,* 214-220.

Guttentag, M., Salasin, S., & Belle, D. (1980). *The mental health of women.* New York: Academic Press.

Hatfield, A. B. (1978). Psychological costs of schizophrenia to the family. *Social Work, 23,* 355-359.

Helzer, J. E., Robins, L. N., McEvoy, L. T., Spitznagel, E. L., Stoltzman, R. K., Farmer, E. A., & Brockington, I. F. (1985). A comparison of clinical and diagnostic interview schedule diagnoses. *Archives of General Psychiatry, 42,* 657-666.

Hertz, M., Endicott, J., & Spitzer, R. (1976). Brief versus standard hospitalization: The families. *American Journal of Psychiatry, 133,* 795-801.

Hetherington, M. E., Cox, M. E., & Cox, R. (1979a). Family interaction and the social, emotional, and cognitive development of children following divorce. In V. Vaughn & T. Brazelton (Eds.), *The family: Setting priorities* (pp. 71-87). New York: Science and Medicine.

Hetherington, M. E., Cox, M. E., & Cox, R. (1979b). Play and social interaction in children following divorce. *Journal of Social Issues, 35,* 26-49.

Hobson, R. P. (1983). *Origins of the personal relation, and the unique case of autism.* Paper presented at the annual meeting of the Association for Child Psychology and Psychiatry, London, Canada.

Holmes, A. H., & Holmes, F. F. (1975). After ten years, what are the handicaps and lifestyles of children treated for cancer? *Clinical Pediatrics, 14,* 819–823.

Holroyd, J., & McArthur, D. (1976). Mental retardation and stress on the parents: A contrast between Down's syndrome and childhood autism. *American Journal of Mental Deficiency, 80,* 431–436.

Huppert, F. A., Gore, M., & Elliott, B. J. (1988). The value of an improved scoring system (CGHQ) for the general health questionnaire in a representative community sample. *Psychological Medicine, 18,* 1001–1006.

Husaini, B. A., Neff, J. A., Harrington, S. B., Hughes, M. D., & Stone, R. H. (1980). Depression in rural communities: Validating the CES-D scale. *Journal of Community Psychology, 8,* 20–27.

Jaffe, N., O'Malley, J. E., & Koocher, G. P. (1981). Late medical consequences of childhood cancer. In G. P. Koocher & J. E. O'Malley (Eds.), *The Damocles syndrome* (pp. 51–59). New York: McGraw-Hill.

Jaffe, N., Toth, B. B., Hoar, R. E., Ried, H. L., Sullivan, M. P., & McNeese, M. D. (1984). Dental and maxillofacial abnormalities in long-term survivors of childhood cancer: Effects of treatment with chemotherapy and radiation to the head and neck. *Pediatrics, 73,* 816–823.

Johnson, F. L., Rudolph, L. A., & Hartmann, J. R. (1979). Helping the family cope with childhood cancer. *Psychosomastics, 20,* 241–251.

Kagen-Goodheart, L. (1977). Re-entry: Living with childhood cancer. *American Journal of Orthopsychiatry, 47,* 651–658.

Kessler, R. C., & Essex, M. (1982). Marital status and depression: The importance of coping resources. *Social Forces, 61,* 484–506.

Kessler, R. C., & McLeod, J. D. (1984). Sex differences in vulnerability to undesirable life events. *American Sociological Review, 49,* 620–631.

Koocher, G. P. (1981). Psychological adaptation. In G. P. Koocher & J. E. O'Malley (Eds.), *The Damocles syndrome* (pp. 60–73). New York: McGraw-Hill.

Korn, S. J., Chess, S., & Fernandez, P. (1978). The impact of children's physical handicap on marital quality and family integration. In R. M. Lerner & G. B. Spanier (Eds.), *Influences on marital and family interaction: A life-span perspective* (chap. 11). New York: Academic Press.

Kovacs, M., & Feinberg, T. L. (1982). Coping with juvenile onset diabetes mellitus. In A. Baum & J. E. Singer (Eds.), *Handbook of psychology and health* (Vol. 2, pp. 165–212). Hillsdale, NJ: Lawrence Erlbaum Associates.

Kubler-Ross, E. (1969). *On death and dying.* New York: MacMillan.

Lascari, A. D., & Stebbins, J. A. (1973). The reactions of families to childhood leukemia. *Clinical Paediatrics, 12,* 210–214.

Lewis, S., & LaBarbera, J. (1983). Terminating chemotherapy: Another stage in coping with childhood leukemia. *American Journal of Pediatric Hematology/Oncology, 5,* 33–37.

Li, F. P., & Stone, R. (1976). Survivors of cancer in childhood. *Annals of Internal Medicine, 84,* 551–553.

Links, P. S., & Stockwell, M. L. (1985). Obstacles in the prevention of psychological sequelae in survivors of childhood cancer. *American Journal of Pediatric Hematology/Oncology, 7,* 132–140.

Loyd, B. H., & Abidin, R. R. (1985). Revision of the parenting stress index. *Journal of Pediatric Psychology, 10,* 169–177.

Madge, N. (1983). *Families at risk.* London: Heinemann.

Mcnaghan, E. G., & Lieberman, M. A. (1986). Changes in depression following divorce: A panel study. *Journal of Marriage and the Family, 48,* 319–328.

National Center for Health Statistics. (1984). *Births, marriages, divorces, and deaths for 1983.* (Monthly Vital Statistics Report No. 23, March 26, PHS-84-112.) Washington, DC: Author.

Noh, S., & Avison, W. R. (1988). Spouses of discharged psychiatric patients: Factors associated with their experience of burden. *Journal of Marriage and the Family, 50,* 377–389.

Noh, S., Dumas, J., Wolf, L., & Fisman, S. (1989). Delineating sources of stress in parents of exceptional children. *Family Relations, 38,* 456–461.

Noh, S., & Turner, R. J. (1987). Living with psychiatric patients: Implications for the mental health of family members. *Social Science and Medicine, 25,* 263–271.

Pasamanick, B., Scarpitti, F. R., & Dinitz, S. (1967). *Schizophrenics in the community.* New York: Appleton-Century-Crofts.

Pearlin, L. I., & Johnson, J. S. (1977). Marital status, life strains, and depression. *American Sociological Review, 42,* 704–715.

Pearlin, L. I., & Lieberman, M. A. (1979). Social sources of emotional distress. *Research in Community and Mental Health, 1,* 217–248.

Pearlin, L. I., Lieberman, M. A., Menaghan, E. G., & Mullan, J. T. (1981). The stress process. *Journal of Health and Social Behavior, 22,* 337–356.

Pearlin, L. I., Mullan, J. T., Semple, S. J., & Skaff, M. M. (1990). Caregiving and the stress process: An overview of concepts and their measures. *The Gerontologist, 30,* 583–594.

Pearlin, L. I., & Schooler, C. (1978). The structure of coping. *Journal of Health and Social Behavior, 19,* 2–21.

Pless, I. B., & Satterwhite, B. B. (1975). Family functioning and family problems. In R. J. Haggerty, K. J. Rioghmann, & I. B. Pless (Eds.), *Child health and the community* (pp. 41–54). New York: Wiley.

Powazek, M., Payne, J. S., Goff, J. R., Paulson, M. A., & Stagner, S. (1980). Psychosocial ramifications of childhood leukemia: One-year post-diagnosis. In J. L. Schulman & M. J. Kupst (Eds.), *The child with cancer: Clinical approaches to psychosocial care* (pp. 143–155). Springfield, IL: Charles C. Thomas.

Price, R. H., Cowen, E. L., Lorion, R. P., & Ramos-McKay, J. (1988). *14 ounces of prevention: A casebook for practitioners.* Washington, DC: American Psychological Association.

Radloff, L. S. (1977). The CES-D scale: A self-reported depression scale for research in the general population. *Applied Psychological Measurement, 1,* 385–401.

Robins, L. N. (1985). Epidemiology: Reflections on testing the validity of psychiatric interviews. *Archives of General Psychiatry, 42,* 916–924.

Robins, L. N., Helzer, J. E., Croughan, L., & Ratcliff, K. (1981). *The NIMH diagnostic interview schedule, version III.* Washington, DC: Public Health Service.

Rolland, J. S. (1984). Toward a psychosocial typology of chronic and life-threatening illness. *Family Systems Medicine, 2,* 245–262.

Ross, H. L., & Sawhill, I. V. (1975). *Time of transition: The growth of families headed by women.* Washington, DC: The Urban Institute.

Rutter, M. (1985). The treatment of autistic children. *Journal of Child Psychology and Psychiatry, 26,* 193–214.

Rutter, M., & Madge, N. (1976). *Cycles of disadvantage.* London: Heinemann.

Schulman, J. L. (1976). *Coping with tragedy: Successfully facing the problem of a seriously ill child.* Chicago, IL: Follett Publishing.

Shaw, B. F., Vallis, T. M., & McCabe, S. B. (1988). The assessment of the severity and symptom patterns in depression. In E. E. Beckham & W. R. Leber (Eds.), *Handbook of depression: Treatment, assessment, and research* (pp. 372–407). Homewood, IL: Dorsey Press.

Speechley, K. N. (1986). *Surviving childhood cancer: The psychosocial impact on parents.* Unpublished doctoral dissertation, The University of Western Ontario, London, Ontario.

Statistics Canada. (1984). *Canada's lone-parent families.* Publication 8-5200-738. Ottawa: Minister of Supply and Services Canada.

Tcheng-Larouche, F., & Prince, R. (1983). Separated and divorced women compared with married controls. *Social Science and Medicine, 17,* 95–105.

Turner, R. J., & Avison, W. R. (1983). *The mentally ill in the community.* Final report to the Ontario Ministry of Health, Toronto, Ontario.

Turner, R. J., & Avison, W. R. (1985). Assessing risk factors for maladaptive parenting: The significance of social support. *Journal of Marriage and the Family, 47,* 881–892.

Turner, R. J., & Avison, W. R. (1989). Gender and depression: Assessing exposure and vulnerability to life events in a chronically strained population. *Journal of Nervous and Mental Disease, 177,* 443–455.

Turner, R. J., & Avison, W. R. (1992). Sources of attenuation in the stress–distress relationship: An evaluation of modest innovations in the application of event checklists. In J. R. Greenley & Philip Leaf (Eds.), *Research in Community and Mental Health* (Vol. 7, pp. 259–294). Grenwich, CT: JAI Press.

Turner, R. J., Frankel, B. G., & Levin, B. M. (1983). Social support: Conceptualization, measurement and implications for mental health. In J. Greenley (Ed.), *Research in Community and Mental Health* (Vol. 3, pp. 105–155). Greenwich, CT: JAI Press.

Turner, R. J., & Noh, S. (1988). Physical disability and depression: A longitudinal analysis. *Journal of Health and Social Behavior, 29,* 23–37.

United States Bureau of the Census. (1982a). *Household and family characteristics: March 1981* (Current Population Reports, Series P-20, No. 372). Washington, DC: U.S. Government Printing Office.

United States Bureau of the Census. (1982b). *Marital status and living arrangements: March 1981* (Current Population Reports Series P-20, No. 372). Washington, DC: U.S. Government Printing Office.

United States Bureau of the Census. (1984). *Marital status and living arrangements: March 1983* (Current Population Reports Series P-20). Washington, DC: U.S. Government Printing Office.

Weiss, R. S. (1975). *Marital separation.* New York: Basic Books.

Weissman, M. M., & Klerman, G. L. (1977). Sex differences in the epidemiology of depression. *Archives of General Psychiatry, 34,* 98–111.

Wing, L. (1985). *Autistic children: A guide for parents and professionals.* New York: Brunner/Mazel.

Wolf, L. C., & Goldberg, B. D. (1986). Autistic children grow up: An eight to twenty-four year follow-up study. *Canadian Journal of Psychiatry, 31,* 550–556.

Wolf, L., Noh, S., Fisman, S., & Speechley, M. (1989). Psychological effects of parenting stress on parents of autistic children. *Journal of Autism and Developmental Disorders, 19,* 157–166.

Issues in the Examination of the Caregiving Relationship

Anne Martin Matthews
University of Guelph

Within the context of a conference where most of the papers and the majority of the researchers present focus on issues of caregiving for an aged relative, the chapter by Avison, Turner, Noh and Speechly provides a unique opportunity to consider how a discussion of parental caregiving (caregiving provided by parents) in a variety of non-normative situations can contribute to our understanding of the issues both generic to the caregiving experience across the life course and unique to the caregiving experience at different points in the life course. The Avison et al. chapter raises the question of how inherently different the contexts and circumstances of elder care and parental care are.

In discussing issues raised by Avison et al., I consider: (a) selected characteristics of the caregiver role, such as its expectability as a life event, its anticipated duration, and its apparently individualistic nature; (b) caregiving in the context of other potentially competing role demands and life circumstances such as work and family relationships; (c) conceptual and methodological issues in the study of caregiving in general and of social support in particular; and (d) the challenges that yet face the design and evaluation of interventions related to caregiving.

CHARACTERISTICS OF THE CAREGIVER ROLE

Avison et al. lauded the progress that gerontologists have made in documenting the problems associated with caregiving to family members with Alzheimer's disease, but they noted that "advances in research on this topic have occurred in relative isolation from work on caregiving to individuals with other types of illnesses or impairments." They observed that many studies of caregiving have focused only on "single disease entities or impairments," and that, consequently, caregiving research is "largely restricted to family providers within a relatively narrow age span and to strains or burdens that are often thought to be unique to that specific illness." Although gerontological research has certainly attempted to determine the association between caregiver burden and the level of functioning of the elderly care recipient, it is the case that many of the better-known measures of caregiver burden have been developed for use with caregivers to individuals with dementia (Vitaliano, Young, & Russo, 1991). Thus, the comparative analysis of different kinds of caregiving experiences undertaken by Avison et al. is not only timely but long overdue.

This comparative analysis yields several important findings about the characteristics of the caregiver role. The first is that "the impact of stressful life events varies substantially according to which caregiver we examine." The case-control methodology employed by Avison et al. is rare indeed in studies of caregiving to the elderly; equally rare is the collection of data from more than one caregiver. Although gerontological research has typically viewed caregiving as essentially an individual activity (see Marshall, Rosenthal, & Sulman, 1990, for further discussion of this point), Avison et al. collected data from two caregivers in most of their case and comparison groups. (It is worth noting, however, that the studies of caregivers to mentally ill adults obtained information from only one caregiver and contained no comparison group. This is the sample most similar to survey populations of caregivers to the elderly in that [a] the care recipient is not a minor, and [b] the careprovider is typically a spouse or adult child).

Although some gerontological research does distinguish between primary and secondary caregivers (Tennstedt, McKinlay, & Sullivan, 1989), "most articles focus on a single individual who fulfills the caregiving role, so there is no analysis of the total support network" (Barer & Johnson, 1990, p. 26). This is in spite of the fact that no less than 75% of caregiving situations described by Tennstedt et al. contained both primary and secondary caregivers. The findings of Avison et al. document well how the effects of eventful stressors vary substantially for male and female caregivers in the same caregiving situations. Research findings will therefore be very much influenced by whether data are obtained from one or multiple caregivers; this is a potential source of bias that must be overcome in gerontological studies of caregiving.

The findings of Avison et al. also point to significant variability in reported symptoms of distress across the family circumstances and caregiving relationships they describe. In summary, "the costs of caregivers are by no means identical across different family circumstances." There are several implications of this finding. Despite the prevalence of studies of caregiving to the elderly with dementia, these research findings can only provide a limited understanding of the challenges and rewards of caregiving for frail elderly suffering from stroke, emphysema, or other health problem. In a similar vein, Avison et al. noted that little is known about the role that other family members play in alleviating or exacerbating the costs of caregiving. Family circumstances can vary in terms of whether, for example, the primary caregiver is an only child assuming the full responsibility of care, or one of several siblings who are generally nonsupportive of the caregiver role, or whether there are multiple caregivers supportive of one another's responsibilities toward the care recipient.

The variability in the family circumstances of caregiving is not well understood. Most studies focus on spousal or adult child caregivers to the elderly. However, as Gee (1987) indicated, rates of childlessness among women who have ever been married were particularly high for Canadian women born between 1902 and 1921 (ranging between 12 and 16%). Fertility rates were also very low for ever married women in the 1907–1921 cohorts (Gee, 1987). It is very likely that these now very old mothers have outlived that child, especially for those women whose one child was a son. As a consequence of both these factors, it is likely that substantial proportions of the very aged do not even have child caregivers available to them. In my own current study of caregivers to frail elderly receiving home help services, I found that fully 56% of the elderly identify someone other than a child as their primary caregiver; fully 15% identified a nonrelative as their primary caregiver. We know very little about how the experience of caregiving differs for the niece who must unexpectedly assume the care of her elderly aunt, as compared with the dutiful daughter who has devoted herself to the care of her parents. Largely because of the way caregiving research has focused on particular types of impairments, comparative research remains to be done on the caregiving role under conditions of quite distinct illnesses and variable family circumstances.

Avison et al. also make an important distinction between caregiving in exceptional versus normative circumstances. Although their own research is of families who have assumed exceptional caregiving responsibilities, their discussion of this point raises several issues in relation to caregiving to the elderly. Rosenthal, Matthews, and Marshall (1989) and Spitze and Logan (1990) have presented compelling evidence for the non-normative nature of care to elderly parents, but it is nevertheless the case that the definition of parent care as normative will vary considerably across caregivers. Avison et al. cite the frequency, timing, and predictability of caregiving as the features distinguishing exceptional from normative care. We understand little about how the experience of caregiving differs for those who report, "I hadn't anticipated any of this" (a 23-year old single female caring for her frail mother and developmentally handicapped sister in a separate household) versus those who say, "I had made the offer a long time ago, that we would expect to help her when she needed it" (a 52-year old woman, married 18 years, with two adolescent children). Through the process of anticipatory socialization, of course, individuals play at roles that they will one day play for real (Himmelfarb & Richardson, 1982). The process of anticipatory socialization is particularly important in relation to caregiving, although it has been virtually ignored in the caregiving literature. It lies at the heart of whether caregiving for an aged parent or spouse is considered an expectable role or an exceptional circumstance. This distinction is important for, as Pearlin (1980) noted, "as far as the transitional events are concerned, coping does not begin with the emergence of the event, but with its advance anticipation" (p. 355). The role of anticipatory socialization in easing or exacerbating the stresses and strains of caregiving is not well understood, and it relates to the methodology of caregiving research, which is discussed later in this chapter.

This raises the question of the extent to which the temporal expectation of amount of time likely to be spent in the caregiving role affects the experience of the role itself. The anticipated duration of the caregiving experience can, of course, vary enormously: Caregiving may last potentially a lifetime, as in the case of the developmentally handicapped children described by Avison et al.; maybe 5–10 years for the children of an 82-year-old frail mother; it will likely be shorter, but perhaps more intense, for the caregivers to an AIDS patient. Largely because of the cross-sectional nature of most caregiving research, the implications of these temporal expectations and ensuing temporal realities remain largely unknown in relation to the caregiving experience.

CONTEXTUAL FACTORS IN CAREGIVING

The examination of the characteristics, circumstances, and temporal nature of caregiving must also take into consideration the broader social context within which caregiving occurs. Avison et al. observed that there is "little research on the impact of other stressful life events that may simultaneously occur in families caring for a child with cancer." This lack of research on concurrent events or contextual factors is by no means exclusive to the caregiving situations that Avison et al. describe. This lack of understanding of the broad social context within which the caregiving relationship occurs (ranging from cultural and societal norms, to community resources that facilitate or hinder caregiving, to the historical context of the family's structure and interaction patterns, to the competing role demands and responsibilities of primary and secondary caregivers) remains a serious omission in caregiving research overall.

The emerging body of research on the interface between work and family responsibilities suggests some recognition of the potential for "spillover" of stressors and strains from one domain to another. It is now estimated that about one third of caregivers are employed in the paid labor force (Select Committee on Aging, 1990; Scharlach, Lowe, & Schneider, 1991), and issues of work and eldercare are now emerging as significant social and corporate policy issues in both Canada and the United States (MacBride-King, 1990; Scharlach, Lowe, & Schneider, 1991). Canadian data suggest that employed caregivers report substantial difficulty in satisfactorily balancing these competing role demands (MacBride-King, 1990), but it is also important to recognize that, for some caregivers, employment may represent not a strain but rather a respite from caregiving responsibilities (Brody, 1990).

Among the measures of stressful life events and chronic strain studied by Avison et al., the only situation where the presenting problem had an effect on stress was the financial strain experienced by single mothers. This may be because of the particular potency of financial insecurity as a chronic strain and its potential for spillover into so many other domains. As Lopata (1979) observed in relation to the widowed, "Poverty impoverishes all of life including the emotional level" (p. 345). Given the universal health care system operating in Canada, and the fairly broad base of publicly funded community-based services (although this varies provincially), one might speculate that, despite high rates of taxation, caregiving is associated with fewer financial strains in Canada—a point worthy of investigation in future cross-national comparisons.

Several other points relevant to the consideration of the context of caregiving are also raised in the Avison et al. chapter. They used a measure of life events experienced personally by the caregiver and, for specified events, respondents also indicated if other relatives had experienced the event. This recognizes the potential impact on caregivers of events occurring to others. This is a promising technique for use in examining the broader social and family context of the caregiving experience.

Avison et al. also raised the important point that the quality of the care giver–care receiver relationship is vital to the understanding of the caregiving experience. Of particular interest, I would stress, is the nature of the relationship before the assumption of the caregiver role. In their recent article on caregiving and the stress process, Pearlin, Mullan, Semple, and Skaff (1990) noted the importance of gathering information about "conflict and distance that might have existed in the past caregiver–patient relationship" (p. 586). I would also argue that our understanding nevertheless remains limited if the focus of all our research is exclusively on the caregiving relationship after the role is assumed. There remains much to be learned about how the caregiver role is approached and entered. One research strategy may be to examine the roles and responsibilities of caregivers relative to those family situations where individuals do not yet consider their supportive activities worthy of the appellation caregiver. To conduct such an analysis requires conceptual clarity as to what constitutes the caregiver role, and, as Zarit (1989) noted, our research has not yet reached this point. To this end, we can learn much about what is unique about caregiving by also examining relationships that are not-quite caregiving but are nevertheless supportive.

CONCEPTUALIZATION AND MEASUREMENT ISSUES

This section of the contribution considers issues of conceptualization and measurement of the caregiving experience in general and of perceived social support in particular. As Avison et al. quite correctly pointed out, most studies of caregiving represent cross-sectional "snapshots" or longitudinal studies across a few years only. Their call for prospective research designs that follow caregiving over a period of years and even beyond the relinquishing of the role itself is echoed throughout the field and must be addressed. Particularly insightful is their suggestion for the application to caregiving of Rolland's typology for classifying chronic and life-threatening illnesses. Many situations of caregiving to the elderly can be readily depicted in terms of gradual or sudden onset of ailments precipitating the need for care; the progressive, episodic, or constant course of the need for care; the nature of the anticipated outcome; and the absence or presence of incapacitation across a variety of spheres. Such an application could potentially contribute a conceptual rigor noted earlier as yet lacking in the field as a whole.

The conceptualization and measurement of social support is also an issue in this section, as it is in caregiving research in general. Typically, social support is measured in terms of perceived or enacted support. The most popular measures of support focus primarily on perceptions of support, and involve respondent's assessments of the adequacy of the support that they receive (Gottlieb, 1991).

Several authors have argued, however, that measures of perceived support defy ready interpretation and may be far more complex than originally believed. Krause (1989), for example, observed the difficulty in determining how perceptions of social support in fact arise. He cited research findings that suggest "that, to a large extent, perceptions of support are determined by something other than support that has actually been provided" (Krause, 1989, p. 48). Gottlieb (1991) also expressed reservations about measurements of perceived social support, noting that "these judgements of support are likely to be coloured by many factors . . . [such as] the respondent's present mood, by the overall quality of the relationship with the provider of support, by the respondent's expectations of different associates, and by the attributions made about why certain parties rendered as much or as little support as they did" (pp. 363–364). Rather than self-reported rating scales for determining perceived social support, Gottlieb (1991) called for "intensive interviews . . . to probe how the interactions that occurred with different parties gain or lose their supportive meaning" (p. 364). Such statements suggest that issues of conceptualization and measurement remain to be resolved in the examination of social support as a psychosocial resource in the stress process model.

It is difficult to ascertain the extent to which the measurement of social support may be influencing our research findings, but we must recall Avison et al.'s conclusion on that: "In summary, there is little evidence to suggest that observed case-comparison differences in distress can be attributed to deficits in perceived social support." Although they do not focus on the potential reasons for such a finding, it may well reflect the measurement of perceived social support. As someone who has used measures of perceived social support on numerous occasions (Martin Matthews, 1988, 1991), I am convinced that they have a place in caregiving research. But we do need to consider multiple measurement approaches as Krause has attempted to do. This will better enable us to specify the relationship between different types and sources of support and the stresses, strains, and rewards of the caregiving experience. Such an approach will permit the determination of "whether and how life stressors affect people's appraisals of or cognitions about . . . support . . . [and] whether or not these appraisals . . . affect feelings of self-worth and control . . ." (Gottlieb, 1991, p. 363).

As important as the conceptualization of social support, however, is its measurement. Avison et al. suggested that the application of their measure of perceived social support across a variety of research settings and with rather disparate survey populations worked well for them. I, however, had a somewhat different research experience in measuring perceived social support.

In my research, the perception of social support was measured by means of the Interpersonal Support Evaluation List (Cohen, Mermelstein, Kamarck, & Hoberman, 1985). This instrument (ISEL) provides an overall measure of perceived support, as well as scores on four subscales that measure self-esteem, appraisal, belonging, and tangible support. The self-esteem subscale measures the availability of someone to promote a sense of self-worth; appraisal assesses the availability of a confidant and advisor; belonging measures the perceived availability of companionship; and the measure of tangible support includes the availability of material aid and service support.

I utilized several versions of the ISEL in a number of research projects. The general population form of the ISEL was used with a sample of 203 couples interviewed in the process of treatment for infertility; a slightly modified ISEL was used in five studies with elderly samples ranging in age from 60 to 96 years: 152 widowed men and women; 19 separated/divorced men and women; 62 never-married men and women; 132 low-income men and women participating in a study of nutrition behavior; and 60 rural elderly participating in a different nutrition study. A brief discussion of the research findings based on these projects helps to illustrate my point concerning the difficulties in using standardized instruments across a range of age cohorts.

For example, the measure of self-esteem support, which worked quite well with the younger sample in the infertility study, did not fare well with the older samples. In addition to the problems of face validity and internal reliability of the instrument, the elderly respondents consistently expressed difficulty in answering questions involving esteem support. In responding to such statements as, "Most people I know think highly of me" or "I have someone who takes pride in my accomplishments," many of the elderly respondents expressed strong discomfort about that kind of statement, frequently speculating that they would have "no way of knowing such things." Factor analysis failed to yield a four-item solution for any of the elderly groups, whereas it worked as Cohen et al. predicted for the younger infertile couples.

Such findings are important in identifying the psychometric properties of scales such as the ISEL and the need to enhance their internal reliability and face validity among elderly samples. But the fact that there was such variability across samples is not only a methodological point; it is also relevant to the conceptualization of social support. A self-esteem component characterizes many measures of perceived social support and, although Avison et al. did not find this problematic in their research on young and midlife parental caregivers, I certainly found it so among a more elderly cohort. Cohort differences in level of comfort in reporting self-esteem support was clearly a factor in my research (although all the subscales of the ISEL also had much lower internal reliability among the elderly than among the younger sample). It is evident that if we are to achieve the objective of attempting to understand the life course trajectories of caregivers, we need research instruments that are sensitive to age-related (and cohort-specific) differences in response patterns.

IMPLICATIONS FOR INTERVENTION

A final point raised by the Avison et al. chapter involves the challenges that yet face the design and evaluation of interventions related to caregiving. They suggest that it is time to consider the implementation of small, focused intervention studies of caregivers. The stress process model does indeed provide the theoretical basis for designing programs that may enhance the social support of caregivers or increase their sense of mastery. One must, however, question the adequacy of our current research findings on the caregiving experience, especially in relation to social support, as a sufficient basis for the move to intervention research.

In order to address this issue, one must recall the previous discussion of the measurement of perceived versus experienced or enacted support. Although there is empirical evidence that "perceived rather than objective support affects outcomes" (Graney, 1985, p. 303), I would argue, as have others (Gottlieb, 1991), that we cannot base interventions on individual perceptions of how well supportive needs are being met, because there are so many contextual factors potentially influencing that assessment. The relationship between perceived and enacted support has been found to be weak (Wethington & Kessler, 1986). Therefore, a requisite first step, prior to the consideration of any intervention strategy, is to develop a fuller appreciation of the relationship between the type and source of the support received and what caregivers perceive as supportive in a variety of contexts. In order to provide interventions, we have to be able to hypothesize the nature and type of enacted support most appropriate to the caregiving situation. I do not believe that we are at that point yet.

These outstanding questions about the conceptualization and measurement of social support represent significant obstacles to the implementation of caregiver interventions at this time. As Pearlin (1985) noted, "One of the serious (but not obvious) obstacles in the assessment of the effects of supports is that often the nature of the problems whose effects the supports are supposed to buffer is insufficiently understood" (p. 55). This is true of caregiving. The fact that we know comparatively little about the trajectory of caregiving speaks also to the prematurity of large-scale interventions. Despite the breadth and depth of research on caregiving as reflected in this volume, there is much that is not well understood in terms of the process of the caregiving career. Just as research on widowhood has focused primarily on the characteristics of those who currently hold the status of widowed person, rather than on the way in which social relationships and support networks are changed by the process of becoming widowed (Martin Matthews, 1987), so has caregiver research focused almost exclusively on correlates of status rather than issues of process. The importance of the temporal aspects of caregiving, of the circumstances under which the caregiver role is assumed, are briefly considered in the Avison et al. chapter but are not well understood in the caregiving literature overall. Knowledge of the temporal aspects of the caregiver experience — the "courses and sequelae" in the terminology used by Avison et al. — is essential to the development and implementation of interventions. Interventions must be sensitive to the context of caregiving as determined at the time of assumption of the role. The timing as much as the nature of intervention may be critical, and yet the determination of appropriate timing will be extra-ordinarily difficult if we continue to know little about the relationship between sources, mediators, and manifestations of stress in the caregiver role at different points in time, points not just arbitrarily selected but carefully identified.

Extant research does not enable us to know, for example, whether the potentially most promising interval for intervention with caregivers is at the very beginning of the caregiver career when the caregiver role is assumed. Indeed, this may be true of many transitional life events. Previous research with mid-life women, for example, has led me to speculate that the real stress for parents is frequently not the completion of the process of coming to live in an empty nest, but rather its onset—the emptying nest, particularly if the initiation of the transition is precipitous or "off-time" in some way. The analogy here to the caregiving experience may, for some circumstances, be an appropriate one.

To ruminate on what the process of becoming a caregiver might involve (and its impact on the subsequent caregiving experience) is to speculate on what is a caregiver—how does one become a caregiver as distinct from simply being a family member? What is involved in having a person come to define herself no longer as just a mother but as a parental caregiver to a handicapped child? As a daughter as compared to being a caregiver to a frail parent? Are interventions more potentially beneficial at this point (the point of assumption of the role) rather than later when the patterns have been laid down, the expectations (of caregiver, care receiver, and their web of family members, friends and formal service providers) have been set, when informal social supports may already have been exhausted or the issue of mastery long since abandoned? It is not just an issue of what works in intervention, but what works best at what point in time in the process.

Concern about the advisability of intervention studies has also recently been expressed by Zarit (1989) and George (1990). There is strong pressure on many of us funded to do intervention studies to provide evidence for the efficacy of interventions in caregiving and yet the current state of knowledge—and measurement—in the field may complicate or even doom our efforts irrespective of the utility of the interventions themselves. In terms of intervention studies we need, as suggested by George (1990), to proceed cautiously lest we promise more than we can presently deliver.

CONCLUSIONS

In its focus on issues of caregiving provided by parents in exceptional circumstances, the chapter by Avison et al. informed the study of caregiving to the elderly through a discussion of the characteristics of the caregiver role, contextual factors influencing caregiving, conceptual and methodological issues in the study of caregiving and perceived social support, and the challenges in designing and evaluating caregiver interventions. Through this comparison, we are able to make several generalizations to the experiences of both parental care (caregiving provided by parents) and elder care. Family caregiving is associated with higher levels of stress for female caregivers more than male, especially in circumstances of psychiatric or developmental disabilities, when caregiving responsibilities are continuous and demanding on a day-to-day basis, and when caregiving occurs within the context of such chronic strains as financial insecurities and role overload.

ACKNOWLEDGMENT

Selected data reported in this chapter were collected as part of a project funded by the Ministry of Community and Social Services, Government of Ontario, Canada.

REFERENCES

Barer, B. M., & Johnson, C. L. (1990). A critique of the caregiving literature. *The Gerontologist*, *30*(1), 26–29.

Brody, E. M. (1990). *Women in the middle: Their parent-care years.* New York: Springer.

Cohen, S., Mermelstein, R., Kamarck, T., & Hoberman, H. M. (1985). Measuring the functional components of social support. In I. G. Sarason & B. R. Sarason (Eds.), *Social support: Theory, research, and applications* (pp. 74–94). Hingham, MA: Kluwer Boston Inc.

Gee, E. M. (1987). Historical change in the family life course of Canadian men and women. In V. Marshall (Ed.), *Aging in Canada: social perspectives* (2nd ed., pp. 265–287). Toronto: Fitzhenry and Whiteside.

George, L. K. (1990). Caregiver stress studies—there really is more to learn. *The Gerontologist*, *30*(5), 580–581.

Gottlieb, B. (1991). Social support and family care of the elderly. *Canadian Journal on Aging, 10*(4), 359–375.

Graney, M. J. (1985). Interpersonal support and health of older people. In W. A. Peterson & J. Quadagno (Eds.), *Social bonds in later life*, (pp. 287–304). Beverly Hills, CA: Sage.

Himmelfarb, A., & Richardson, C. J. (1982). *Sociology for Canadians: Images of society.* Toronto: McGraw-Hill Ryerson.

Krause, N. (1989). Issues of measurement and analysis in studies of social support, aging, and health. In K. S. Markides & C. L. Cooper (Eds.), *Aging, stress, and health*, (pp. 43–66). Chichester: Wiley and Sons.

Lopata, H. Z. (1979). *Women as widows: Support systems.* New York: Elsevier.

MacBride-King, J. L. (1990). *Work and family: Employment challenge of the 90's* (Report 59–90). Ottawa: The Conference Board of Canada, Compensation Research Centre.

Marshall, V. W., Rosenthal, C., & Sulman, J. (1990, July). *Caring for the carers: A study of resiliency in support networks.* Paper presented at The Future of Adult life: Second International Conference, Leeuwenhorst, Netherlands.

Martin Matthews, A. (1987). Widowhood as an expectable life event. In V. W. Marshall (Ed.), *Aging in Canada: Social Perspectives* (2nd ed., pp. 343–366). Toronto: Fitzhenry and Whiteside.

Martin Matthews, A. (1988). Social supports of the rural widowed elderly. *Journal of Rural Health*, *4*(3), 57–70.

Martin Matthews, A. (1991). *Widowhood in later life.* Toronto: Butterworths.

Pearlin, L. I. (1980). The life cycle and life strains. In H. M. Blalock Jr. (Ed.), *Sociological theory and research: A critical approach* (pp. 349–360). New York: The Free Press.

Pearlin, L. I. (1985). Social structure and processes of social support. In S. Cohen & S. L. Syme (Eds.), *Social support and health* (pp. 43–60). Orlando, FL: Academic Press.

Pearlin, L. I., Mullan, J. T., Semple, S. J., & Skaff, M. M. (1990). Caregiving and the stress process: An overview of concepts and their measures. *The Gerontologist, 30*(5), 583–594.

Rosenthal, C. J., Matthews, S. H., & Marshall, V. (1989). Is parent care normative? The experiences of a sample of middle-aged women. *Research on Aging, 11*(3), 44–60.

Scharlach, A. E., Lowe, B. F., & Schneider, E. L. (1991). *Elder care and the work force: Blueprint for action.* Lexington, MA: Lexington Books.

Select Committee on Aging. (1990, March). *Sharing the caring: Options for the 90's and beyond* (Committee Publication No. 101–750). Washington, DC: U.S. Government Printing Office.

Spitze, G., & Logan, J. (1990). More evidence on women (and men) in the middle. *Research on Aging, 12*(2), 182–198.

Tennstedt, S. L., McKinlay, J. B., & Sullivan, L. M. (1989). Informal care for frail elders: The role of secondary caregivers. *The Gerontologist, 29*(5), 677–683.

Vitaliano, P. P., Young, H. M., & Russo, J. (1991). Burden: A review of measures used among caregivers of individuals with dementia. *The Gerontologist, 3*(1), 67–75.

Wethington, E., & Kessler, R. C. (1986). Perceived support, received support, and adjustment to stressful life events. *Journal of Health and Social Behaviour, 27,* 78–89.

Zarit, S. H. (1989). Do we need another "stress and caregiving" study? *The Gerontologist, 29,* 147–148.

5

Changes in Depression Among Men and Women Caring for an Alzheimer's Patient

Richard Schulz
University of Pittsburgh
Gail M. Williamson
University of Georgia
Richard Morycz
University of Pittsburgh
David E. Biegel
Case-Western Reserve University

Caregiving continues to hold center stage among gerontological researchers in the United States (George, 1990). Hundreds of studies have been published since the early 1980s (Biegel, Sales, & Schulz, 1991) and the next decade will likely yield at least an equivalent number. Much of the early research in this area has been criticized for its lack of attention to important methodological and conceptual issues (e.g., Barer & Johnson, 1990; Schulz, Visintainer, & Williamson, 1990) but recent work promises to address some of these shortcomings (e.g., Pearlin, Mullan, Semple, & Skaff, 1990).

One of the hallmarks of the maturation of a research area in the social sciences is a shift from cross-sectional strategies to increased numbers of studies using longitudinal or prospective designs. Although prospective caregiving studies are still non-existent, the number of longitudinal studies recently published and currently underway is on the rise. These studies are particularly important in that they potentially provide important information about the dynamics of caregiving.

In this chapter, we report results of a four wave longitudinal study of caregivers of Alzheimer's patients and interpret these data in the context of existing similar studies (Haley & Pardo, 1989; Pagel, Becker, & Coppel, 1985; Pruchno, Kleban, Michaels, & Dempsey, 1990; Zarit, Todd, & Zarit,

119

1986). Because longitudinal studies on Alzheimer caregivers are still quite rare, we draw on longitudinal data reported for caregivers of diverse patient populations, including patients discharged from an acute care hospital (Johnson & Catalano, 1983), the frail elderly (Townsend, Noelker, Deimling, & Bass, 1989) and stroke patients (Scannell, 1988; Schulz & Tompkins, 1990; Schulz, Tompkins, & Rau, 1988; Tompkins, Schulz, & Rau, 1988).

BACKGROUND

One of the fundamental questions about the effects of caregiving is, what happens to caregivers over time? Providing support to an Alzheimer's patient has been likened to exposure to multiple and severe long-term stressors (Pearlin et al., 1990). It would seem reasonable, therefore, to expect that caregivers' physical and psychological stamina are depleted over time, compromising their physical and psychological health. This basic idea has been described as the downward trajectory or *wear-and-tear model* of caregiving (Haley & Pardo, 1989; Townsend et al., 1989) and is partially supported by a large number of cross-sectional studies showing increased prevalence of psychiatric and physical symptomatology among caregivers when compared to control groups or to age- and gender-based population norms (see Schulz et al., 1990). However, longitudinal data, which bear more directly on this hypothesis, are equivocal. As shown in Fig. 5.1, studies reporting health-related outcomes such as depression, show stability over time among caregivers rather than decline or improvement.

Taken together, the data provide little support for a downward trajectory or the wear-and-tear model of caregiving impact. Instead, the dominant

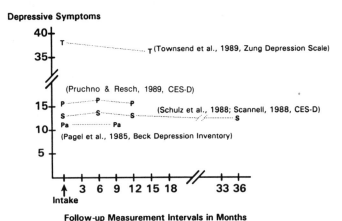

FIG. 5.1. Comparison of depression scores in longitudinal studies of caregiving.

pattern is one of stability, which is difficult to interpret because we do not know the status of caregivers prior to taking on the caregiving role. If pre- and post-caregiving levels of functioning are identical at least two explanations might account for such a result: (a) affective functioning among caregivers is a reflection of well-established traits that render the individual relatively impervious to major life stressors, (b) the availability of stable social support and/or economic resources enable the caregiver to weather the storms of caregiving with relative equanimity. On the other hand, if there is discontinuity in caregiver functioning such that levels of depressive symptomatology are significantly higher before taking on the role than after, then we must look to another explanation. Such an effect would suggest that individual coping skills and social resources of the caregiver are insufficient to maintain prior levels of functioning but are sufficient to maintain a new but somewhat lower level of functioning. Whether or not such a response pattern is deemed adaptive would depend on the level of functioning maintained. Finally, it is possible that an initial decrement in functioning is followed by a recovery to prior levels, although current data do not support this alternative on major outcome variables.

The models we have presented do not encompass all possibilities. For instance, we have omitted models that predict increased well-being, because most data argue against this—at least at the aggregate level (see Fig. 5.2).

The present study builds on the existing longitudinal research by attempting to address some of the limitations found in prior work. First, patients in at least two earlier studies (Schulz et al., 1988; Townsend et al., 1989) were only mildly disabled, a limitation that raises questions about the magnitude of stress experienced by caregivers. In the present work, partici-

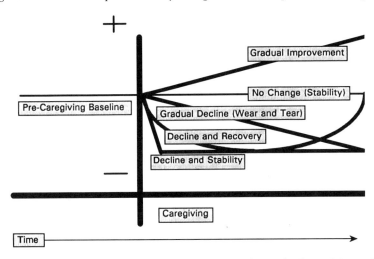

FIG. 5.2 Models of possible outcomes developed from longitudinal caregiving studies.

pants were limited to caregivers of patients in the mild to moderate stages (at intake) of Alzheimer's disease — patients whose condition could be predicted to gradually decline over time. Second, inferences that can be drawn from earlier research are limited by the length of time encompassed by the study and by the number of measurement points. For instance, it is difficult to derive individual growth curves from data collected at only two points in time (Rogosa, 1988). In our study, data were collected at four measurement points (intake, and 6, 18, and 24 months post-intake). A third limitation is that existing studies provide little information about the role that various types of attrition (e.g., patient death or institutionalization vs. subject drop out) might play in constructing an accurate picture of the long-term effects of caregiving. We carefully monitored patient and caregiver status throughout this 2-year period of study, allowing us to assess caregiver well-being in relation to patient functional and residential status and to conduct extensive attrition analyses. A final limitation is that aggregate data (e.g., means) may obscure substantial individual change. We analyzed our data at both the aggregate and individual levels. In order to capture individual change among caregivers, we used an approach developed by Aneshensel (1985), which classifies individuals into those who remain stable in levels of depressive symptomatology over time ("stayers") and those who do not ("movers").

METHOD

Sample and Procedure

Participants were identified from sources of Alzheimer's disease (AD) and related diseases diagnostic centers in the Pittsburgh and Cleveland metropolitan areas. Individuals were eligible if they were primary caregivers of family members diagnosed with possible or probable Alzheimer's dementia. Diagnoses were based on clinical symptoms, psychological testing, and laboratory studies as outlined in the NINCDS/ADRDA criteria (McKann et al., 1984). Only caregivers of noninstitutionalized patients scoring between 12 and 27 on the Folstein Mini-Mental Status Exam (MMSE) (Folstein, Folstein, & McHugh, 1975) were eligible for inclusion in the study. The MMSE assesses orientation, memory, and attention with questions requiring verbal responses (e.g., What is the date? Where are we?) as well as ability to name objects, follow commands, write a sentence, and copy a figure. Highest possible score on the MMSE is 30, with lower scores reflecting greater cognitive impairment.

Individuals who met these criteria ($N = 244$) received a letter describing the project and inviting them to participate. Of these, 174 (71%) agreed.

Those who agreed did not differ from those who refused in gender, familial relationship to the patient, age of the patient, or patient MMSE scores. Participants were usually interviewed in their own homes. Initial interviews were conducted in 1986 and 1987, and on average, 27 months had elapsed since AD was first diagnosed. Each interview took approximately 90 minutes to complete and included questions eliciting information about demographic characteristics, problem behaviors exhibited by patients, amount and type of help provided by caregivers, support received by caregivers from others, and caregiver symptoms of depression. These interviews were repeated at Time 2 (6 months after the initial interview), Time 3 (12 months after Time 2), and Time 4 (6 months after Time 3). Interviewers requested that patients not be present during interviews. Two participants did not give enough data at Time 1 to be included in the analyses, leaving $N = 172$ at intake.

Descriptive Analysis of Patients and Caregivers

Patients. Patients were predominantly female (70%). Average age was 76 years (range = 56–98). The mean MMSE score for this sample was 19.9 (out of 30), indicating moderate levels of cognitive impairment at intake. A typical patient required some assistance with 9 of 18 Activities of Daily Living and Instrumental Activities of Daily Living.

Caregivers. Mean caregiver age was 57.8 years. Most (71.0%) were female. About one third (33.1%) of the women were spouses of the patient and slightly more than half (56.2%) were daughters. Male caregivers were older than females ($Ms = 62.7$ and 55.7 years, respectively; $F[1,171] = 9.03$, $p < .003$) and were more likely to be spouses than adult children of the patient (58.8% vs. 37.2%). This population is similar in age, gender, and type of relationship to national estimates of caregivers of demented elderly (Select Committee on Aging, 1987; Stone, Cafferata, & Sangl, 1987). Modal yearly household income was between \$20,000 and \$25,000.

Measures

Analyses focused on three categories of quantitative data thought to be important in understanding stress-related outcomes:

1. indicators of patient functional status (objective stressors),
2. demographic characteristics of patients and caregivers, quality of relationship between caregiver and patient prior to AD onset, social support, and caregiver health (conditioning variables), and

3. caregiver depression (enduring outcome). Specific topics covered within each category are briefly described below.

Objective Stressors: Patient Status Indicators

Patient cognitive function was assessed using the Folstein Mini-Mental Status Exam (Folstein et al., 1975) described previously. Amount of help patients received from their caregivers was assessed with 18 items from the Older Americans Resource and Services scales (OARS) (Center for the Study of Aging and Human Development, 1978) measuring 7 Activities of Daily Living (ADL) such as bathing, dressing, and eating and 11 Instrumental Activities of Daily Living (IADL) such as managing money, doing laundry, and shopping for personal items. Each item was rated on a 5-point scale, with 0 indicating no help given and 4 indicating complete help given. Scores could range from 0 to 28 for ADL and 0 to 44 for IADL. Cronbach's alphas for internal reliability based on T1 data were .89 and .87 for the ADL and IADL measures, respectively.

Caregivers were also asked to indicate to what extent patients exhibited 40 different behavioral problems associated with Alzheimer's disease (e.g., wandering, asking repetitive questions, losing things, trouble dressing, failing to recognize familiar people). Frequency of problem behavior occurrence was rated on a 5-point scale of 0 (never) to 4 (almost always). Scores could range from 0 to 160. Cronbach's alpha on T1 ratings was .89.

Conditioning Variables

Demographic Characteristics. Traditional demographic data collected included caregiver age, gender, household income, and number of people living in caregiver's household. Caregivers were also asked how they were related to the patient (e.g., husband, wife, daughter-in-law, friend) and whether the patient lived in their household. Additional questions included perceived adequacy of caregiver's household income (scored 1 = much more than adequate to 5 = not at all adequate) and number of people who helped care for the patient.

Social Support. Perceived social support was measured using a 6-item version of the Interpersonal Support Evaluation List (ISEL) (Cohen, Mermelstein, Kamarck, & Hoberman, 1985). On a scale of 0 (definitely true) to 3 (definitely false), respondents rated these statements: (a) When I feel lonely, there are several people I can talk to, (b) I often meet or talk with family or friends, (c) If I were sick, I could easily find someone to help me with my daily chores, (d) When I need suggestions on how to deal with a personal problem, I know someone I can turn to, (e) If I had to go out of town for a few weeks, it would be difficult to find someone who would look after my house or apartment (reverse scored), and (f) There is at least one person I know whose advice I really trust. Higher scores indicated lower levels of perceived support. Cronbach's alpha for T1 responses was .44 in this sample, although alphas of .73 or greater have been obtained with samples of elderly persons (Schulz & Williamson, 1990).

Responses to three items were summed to yield an index of satisfaction with social contact: (a) How satisfied would you say you have been with the amount of social contacts you've had in the past 6 months? (b) What about the quality or closeness of the contacts you have had? and (c) Compared to 6 months ago, has the number of people you feel close to increased, stayed about the same, or decreased? Responses to items (a) and (b) were scored on a scale of 1 (very dissatisfied) to 5 (very satisfied); scores on item (c) were reversed. Higher scores indicated greater satisfaction with social contact. Cronbach's alpha for T1 scores on this measure was .57.

Negative support was assessed by summing responses to five questions asking caregivers the number of network members who (a) criticize your handling of things, (b) don't [help] as much as [you] thought they would, (c) try to help but wind up making things worse, (d) seem to be out to make problems for you, and (e) have withdrawn from you or (patient). Higher scores represented more negative social support. Cronbach's alpha at T1 was .65.

Prior Relationship.   To measure quality of caregiver/patient relationship before AD, 14 items were selected from the Communication, Affective Expression, and Involvement subscales of the Dyadic Relationship component of the Family Assessment Measure (Skinner, Steinhauer, & Santa-Barbara, 1983). Items selected measured quality of prior relationship in terms of communication (e.g., "I knew what this person meant when he or she said something"), affect expression (e.g., "When I was upset, this person usually knew why"), and involvement (e.g., "This person and I weren't close to each other"—reverse scored). Scores could range from 14 to 56 with lower ratings indicating closer relationships. Cronbach's alpha for the 14-item instrument employed in the present study was .87. Prior relationship quality was assessed only at Time 1.

Depressive Symptomatology

The primary outcome measure was the Center for Epidemiologic Studies Depression Scale (CES-D) (Radloff, 1977). The CES-D is a 20-item self-report scale designed to identify individuals at risk for depression. This instrument measures current levels of symptoms by asking respondents to indicate on a 4-point scale (0 to 3) how often they experienced each symptom during the previous week. Scores could range from 0 to 60, with higher scores reflecting more depressive symptoms. Individuals scoring 16 or above on the CES-D are generally considered to be "at risk" for developing clinical depression. Internal consistency in this sample was .90.

RESULTS

Preliminary Analyses: Gender Differences

One-way ANOVAs (men vs. women) revealed several important gender differences. The results of these analyses are presented in Table 5.1. As can be seen, women reported significantly more symptoms of depression than did men, $F(1,167) = 13.89$, $p < .0001$, with mean level of depression for women (14.6) very close to the cutoff score (16.0) for being at risk for clinical depression. At intake, 38.7% of the women and 16.0% of the men qualified as being at risk for clinical depression. Levels of depression for both male and female caregivers were substantially higher than population means for similarly aged individuals (men = 6.7; women = 8.82) reported by Berkman et al. (1986).

Men and women caregivers reported providing equal amounts of ADL and IADL assistance and identified about equal numbers of problem behaviors in their patients, all Fs < 0.48, ns. There were no gender differences at T1 in patients' cognitive status (MMSE scores), $F(1,161) = 0.29$, ns. Nor did male and female caregivers differ in number of people who helped care for the

TABLE 5.1
Gender Differences in Patient Status and Caregiver Variable Means at Time 1

	Caregivers	
	Male	Female
CES-D	8.7	14.6**
Patient MMS	19.6	20.0
ADL	4.3	4.9
IADL	24.3	23.3
Problem behaviors	59.0	61.9
Number of people helping with patient care	0.9	0.9
Satisfaction with social contacts	10.4	9.6*
Perceived social support	4.9	4.8
Negative social support	3.6	3.4
Prior relationship[a]	21.8	25.6**
Number in household	1.4	2.1**

*males and females differ, $p < .05$
**males and females differ, $p < .01$
[a]higher scores = less close relationship

patient, perceptions of social support available, or reports of negative social support, all Fs < 0.16, ns. However, men rated their relationship with the patient prior to illness onset more favorably than did women, $F(1,166) = 7.23$, $p < .008$, and also reported more satisfaction with social contacts, $F(1,170) = 5.15$, $p < .02$. Women reported that more people lived in their household than did men, $F(1,170) = 6.27$, $p < .01$.

Attrition from Time 1 to Time 4

Thirty-one caregivers (18.0%) were lost to attrition, leaving $n = 141$. The attrition group included 23 caregivers who could not be located or who refused to participate during the course of the study without giving a reason. Six others refused to continue because their patient had died ($n = 4$) or had been placed in an institution ($n = 2$). One caregiver became terminally ill and another died during the study. Of the 31, 21 (68.0%) were women, primarily daughters of the patient. Of the 10 men lost to attrition, the majority were husbands.

An additional 26 subjects continued to participate in the study even though they were no longer acting as caregivers at Time 3 or Time 4, either because their patient was deceased ($n = 19$) or institutionalized ($n = 7$). The majority (77.0%) of these were children of the patient (11 daughters, 4 sons) or other relatives (4 daughters-in-law, 1 sister) rather than spouses (5 wives, 1 husband). A third group of caregivers was comprised of caregivers ($n = 35$) whose patient was institutionalized but who continued to provide some assistance with ADL or IADL. The largest group ($n = 79$) consisted of continuing caregivers. These were individuals who provided care to a patient living in a noninstitutional setting throughout the study.

To summarize, a total of four groups can be differentiated, based on patient and caregiver status: (a) those who were lost to various types of attrition ($n = 31$), (b) those who relinquished their caregiving role because of institutionalization or death of the patient but remained in the study ($n = 26$), (c) those who continued to provide care but to a patient who had been institutionalized ($n = 36$), and (d) those who were caregivers of a patient living at home throughout the study ($n = 79$).

Two types of analyses were carried out to assess differences between these groups. First, oneway ANOVAs (attrition group vs. all others combined) revealed only one significant difference when patient status variables (MMSE, ADL, IADL, frequency of disturbing behavior) and caregiver variables (CES-D, age, income, social support measures, quality of prior relationship) were examined. CES-D scores for the attrition group ($M = 16.32$) were significantly higher than scores for those subjects who remained in the study ($M = 12.04$), $F(1,167) = 4.99$, $p < .03$, all other Fs < 2.50, ns.

Chi square analyses for the effects of gender and kinship revealed no significant differences between the two groups, both chi-squares < 0.08, ns.

A second set of oneway ANOVAs (attrition group vs. no longer caregivers group vs. caregivers of institutionalized patients vs. continuous caregivers) was carried out using the same measures identified above. Results of these analyses are summarized in Table 5.2. A number of reliable differences in patient status indicators were found. At T1, the groups differed in patient MMS scores ($F[3,159] = 3.52$, $p < .02$), ADL ($F[3,168] = 3.90$, $p < .01$), and IADL, ($F[3,168] = 4.21$, $p < .007$). Compared to the other groups, individuals whose patient subsequently died or was institutionalized (and no longer received any direct assistance from the former caregiver) were caring for more cognitively impaired AD victims and were providing more ADL and IADL assistance at T1. As would be expected, over time this pattern changed. At T4, continuous caregivers were providing significantly more ADL assistance, $F(2,108) = 7.95$, $p < .001$, and more IADL assistance, $F(2,108) = 28.76$, $p < .0001$. At T1, T2, and T3, continuous caregivers reported significantly less frequent incidence of disruptive patient behaviors than the other groups (all $Fs > 2.83$, all $p < .04$ or better).

Some differences in social support between the caregiver groups were also apparent in our attrition analyses. At T1, continuous caregivers reported reliably greater perceived social support than those in the attrition group and those in the caregivers of institutionalized patients group, $F(3,165) = 3.01$, $p < .03$. Additionally, at T2, continuous caregivers were more satisfied with their social contacts than individuals in the other groups, $F(3,148) = 2.87$, $p < .04$.

To summarize, these findings are consistent with the caregiver groupings that emerged over time. For example, data from the earlier panels indicate that patients with high care needs were more likely to be institutionalized or to die, and T4 data indicate that only continuous caregivers were still heavily involved in providing patient care. More interestingly, however, was the evidence that when compared to the other groups, continuous caregivers had relatively greater social support resources and were more content with the quality and quantity of their social interactions.

Effects of Patient Institutionalization and Death on Caregiver Depression

A total of 39 patients (22.7%) were institutionalized and 31 patients (18.0%) died during the course of the study. Repeated measures ANOVAs revealed no significant differences between depression scores prior to the event and scores after the event, all $Fs < 2.20$, ns. Analyses including caregiver gender also did not yield statistically reliable effects, all $Fs < 0.96$, ns.

TABLE 5.2
Attrition Group Analysis: Patient Status and Caregiver Variables

	(1) Attrition	(2) No care	(3) Some care	(4) Full care
CES-D				
Time 1	16.32	11.88	12.37	11.94
Time 2	17.89	12.65	14.55	13.48
Time 3	11.27	10.35	12.26	12.55
Time 4	–	9.38	12.06	13.72
ADL				
Time 1**	3.97	8.54	4.06	4.08
Time 2	5.83	8.83	4.85	4.96
Time 3	5.09	7.67	5.63	6.14
Time 4	–	0.00	2.25	7.45
IADL				
Time 1**	24.13	29.92	23.42	21.38
Time 2	23.33	28.50	20.48	24.00
Time 3**	26.00	26.61	18.63	26.71
Time 4**	–	6.33	13.46	28.34
Problem behaviors				
Time 1*	65.68	66.54	66.86	54.64
Time 2*	66.12	67.04	70.94	56.89
Time 3**	73.27	72.00	80.26	61.47
Time 4	–	75.00	71.67	66.13
MMS*	19.72	17.43	19.80	20.68
Caregiver age	55.60	59.69	53.83	59.82
Household income[a]	5.53	5.04	5.69	5.55
Satisfaction with social contacts				
Time 1	9.74	9.92	9.31	10.04
Time 2*	9.83	9.50	9.24	10.44
Time 3	10.55	10.00	10.26	10.33
Time 4	–	10.69	10.44	10.23
Negative support				
Time 1	4.06	2.38	4.39	3.18
Time 2	2.39	2.64	3.45	2.18
Time 3	3.82	2.47	3.67	2.75
Time 4	–	2.43	5.69	4.64
Perceived support				
Time 1*	4.29	5.08	4.06	5.27
Time 2	3.00	3.65	2.88	3.85
Time 3	4.27	5.19	5.17	5.20
Time 4	–	4.77	4.14	5.00

*groups differ, $p < .05$
**groups differ, $p < .01$
[a]5 = $20–25,000/year

Analyses of Continuous Caregivers

As noted previously, 79 of the original sample of 172 caregivers remained in the study and continued as their relative's primary caregiver for the full 2-year period. Analyses reported in subsequent sections are based on data from this group of continuous caregivers.

Correlates and Predictors of Depression

Zero-order correlations were calculated between known correlates of depression (see Williamson & Schulz, in press) and CES-D at Times 1, 3, and 4. Because CES-D scores were missing for a substantial number of subjects at Time 2 (due primarily to participants delaying second interviews too far beyond the initial 6-month follow-up period), this data point was not examined in these analyses. As shown in Table 5.3, four variables were significantly related to depression at each of the three measurement points: (a) frequency of patient problem behaviors, (b) satisfaction with social support, (c) negative support, and (d) perceived social support. Caregivers were less likely to be depressed if they reported greater satisfaction with their social contacts, greater perceived availability of support, and lower levels of negative support and if the patient exhibited fewer problem behaviors. Three additional variables were significantly related to depression at two of the three measurement points. Correlations between gender and depression indicate

TABLE 5.3
Cross-sectional Correlates of Symptoms of Depression among Continuous Caregivers

	Time 1	Time 3	Time 4
Caregiver gender[a]	−.34***	−.24*	−.18
Caregiver age	−.16	−.03	.02
Household income	−.15	−.11	−.18
Income adequacy[b]	.33**	.23*	.13
ADL	.12	.07	.03
IADL	.04	.00	−.09
Patient problem behaviors	.26**	.39***	.35***
Satisfaction with social contacts	−.28**	−.35***	−.20*
Negative support	.22*	.25*	.26**
Perceived social support[c]	.24*	.27**	.31**
Prior relationship[d]	.18	.31**	.27**

[a]1 = female; 2 = male
[b]Higher scores = less adequate income
[c]Higher scores = less perceived support
[d]Higher scores = less close relationship
*p < .05
**p < .01
***p < .001

that women were more depressed than men at T1 and T3. Individuals more concerned about adequacy of their income reported higher levels of depression at T1 and T3. Closeness of the relationship between caregiver and patient prior to illness onset was related to depression at T3 and T4; the closer the prior relationship, the lower the level of depression.

Hierarchical multiple linear regression analyses examined the effects of these variables on caregiver depression. First, two sociodemographic variables, gender and income adequacy, were entered. This was followed by frequency of problem behaviors, quality of prior relationship, negative support, satisfaction with social contacts, and perceived social support.

Together, these variables explained 32% of the variance in depression at T1, 35% at T3, and 27% at T4. Overall, frequency of patient problem behavior explained the most variance (5%, 16%, and 12% at T1, T3, and T4, respectively), followed by gender (11%, 5%, and 4%), perceived support (4%, 4%, and 7%), income adequacy (6%, 3%, and 0%) and satisfaction with social contact (5%, 5%, and 0%). The effects of prior relationship and negative support were negligible in the context of these other variables.

In summary, these data indicate that patient problem behaviors were important contributors to caregiver depression; the more often such behaviors occurred, the more depressed caregivers were. Perceived availability of supportive resources was also important throughout the caregiving period; the more caregivers perceived that support was available, the less their depression. Caregiver gender and concern about financial resources appeared to be important early in the caregiving process. The impact of problem behaviors increased over time, reflecting patients' changing status.

Changes from Time 1 to Time 4

Repeated measures ANOVAs were calculated for men and women separately. As shown in Table 5.4, both women and men reported significant increases in amount of ADL assistance provided ($Fs = 5.87$, $p < .004$, and 13.29, $p < .00001$, respectively) IADL assistance provided ($Fs = 15.47$, $p < .00001$, and 12.54, $p < .00001$, respectively) and in number of problem behaviors exhibited by patients ($Fs = 9.87$, $p < .0001$, and 10.74, $p < .001$, respectively). Men also reported increases in depression ($F = 8.82$, $p < .001$) and declines in the adequacy of their income ($F = 4.19$, $p < .02$). In contrast, changes in depression and adequacy of income were not significant among women, both $Fs < 1.04$, ns. Women reported a significant increase in the amount of negative support received ($F = 6.75$, $p < .001$); reported negative support did not change significantly among men, $F = 0.18$, ns. Neither men nor women reported reliable changes in satisfaction with social contacts or perceived social support, all $Fs < 2.87$, ns.

To investigate correlates of change in depression, we calculated difference

TABLE 5.4
Changes Over Time by Gender of Caregiver

	Females	Males
CES-D		
Time 1	13.98	6.91
Time 3	13.94	9.77
Time 4	14.73	11.32***
Income adequacy		
Time 1	3.23	2.70
Time 3	3.34	3.09
Time 4	3.28	3.09*
Negative behaviors		
Time 1	55.52	48.57
Time 3	62.12	58.87
Time 4	66.65***	62.52***
ADL		
Time 1	4.23	3.48
Time 3	5.45	7.74
Time 4	6.17**	10.22***
IADL		
Time 1	21.02	21.78
Time 3	25.40	29.74
Time 4	27.23***	30.39***
Satisfaction with social contacts		
Time 1	9.98	10.26
Time 3	10.34	10.30
Time 4	10.17	10.70
Negative support		
Time 1	3.58	2.43
Time 3	2.75	2.74
Time 4	5.19***	2.91
Perceived social support		
Time 1	5.52	4.91
Time 3	4.83	5.82
Time 4	4.73	5.45

*change over time, $p < .05$
**change over time, $p < .01$
***change over time, $p < .001$

scores by subtracting T1 CES-D values from T4 CES-D values. T1–T4 changes in depression were then regressed onto gender, age, depression at T1, prior relationship, and T1–T4 changes in income adequacy, ADL, IADL, negative behaviors, satisfaction with social contacts, negative support, and perceived social support. Together these variables explained 45% of the variance in depression change scores. As expected, depression at T1 accounted for a substantial portion of depression change variance (20%). Beta for depression at T1 was negative, indicating that lower CES-D at T1 was related to greater increase in depression over time. Gender explained an additional 6% of the variance; men were more likely than women to experience increases in symptoms of depression over time. The only other important individual contributor was change in perceived social support (8%). As perceptions of available support declined, depression increased. Other variables in the equation each accounted for less than 4% of the variance in T1–T4 change in depression.

Patterns of Depressive Symptoms Over Time

A second approach to the analysis of change was more qualitative in nature. In order to examine patterns of depressive symptoms over time, individuals were classified as being *symptomatic* or at risk for depression if they scored 16 or above on the CES-D scale, or *asymptomatic* if they scored below 16. All individuals were classified in this manner at each of the four measurement points. This cross-classification of subjects as symptomatic or asymptomatic across time yields 16 possible combinations that fall into three general categories: (a) individuals who are consistently symptomatic at all measurement points, (b) individuals who are consistently asymptomatic at all measurement points, and (c) individuals who are both asymptomatic and symptomatic; that is, persons who have at least one depressive episode and at least one nondepressive episode during the follow-up period.

As shown in Table 5.5, 45% of our sample was consistently asymptomatic, and another 41% was both asymptomatic and symptomatic. A smaller percentage (13.7%) was consistently symptomatic. As expected for this chronically stressed group, the prevalence of consistently symptomatic individuals is considerably higher (11.7% vs. 2%) in this population when compared to others (Aneshensel, 1985). Moreover, if we examine separately the percentage of the sample that is symptomatic at each of the four measurement points, we find a substantial increase from Time 1 to Time 4 (T1 = 26.0%, T2 = 31.4%, T3 = 34.2%, T4 = 37%), suggesting a gradual erosion over time in the ability of our sample to cope with caregiving.

Table 5.5 further shows that the three groups identified above differ significantly on three of the predictor variables examined. Consistent with findings reported earlier, females were more likely to be symptomatic at Time 1 than males (17.6% vs. 4.5%). Furthermore, the consistently depressed group reported its income to be less adequate than the other two groups, and the consistently nondepressed group felt that they had significantly closer relationships with the patient prior to the illness.

We can also examine stability and change within those initially classified as depressed and within those initially classified as not depressed. Aneshensel (1985) described this as a movers–stayers analysis. As shown in Table 5.6, the results of this analysis are essentially identical to those reported above. Individuals who are symptomatic at Time 1 and who have at least one

TABLE 5.5
Asymptomatic and Symptomatic Caregivers at Time 1 Through Time 4

		Depressive Symptom Status Time 1 Through Time 4					
	N	Consistently Asymptomatic	Consistently Symptomatic	Both Asymptomatic and Symptomatic	Chi-square	F	p
Total	73	45.2%	13.7%	41.1%			
Gender					(2) 7.07		<.03
Male	22	68.2%	4.5%	27.3%			
Female	51	35.3%	17.6%	47.1%			
Kinship					(4) 3.19		ns
Spouse	40	40.0%	12.5%	47.5%			
Child	30	53.3%	16.7%	30.0%			
Other	3	33.3%	—	66.7%			
Means at Time 1							
Caregiver age		60.0	53.5	61.3		(2,70) 1.21	ns
Household income[a]		5.9	4.6	5.5		(2,68) 1.43	ns
Income adequacy[b]		2.9	3.8	3.0		(2,70) 5.98	<.004
ADL		3.3	5.8	4.2		(2,70) 0.69	ns
IADL		21.3	23.7	24.8		(2,54) 0.65	ns
Patient MMS		20.0	21.0	21.4		(2,68) 1.07	ns
Patient problem behaviors		47.1	62.4	59.7		(2,67) 2.47	<.09
Number of people helping with patient care		0.8	0.9	0.8		(2,69) 0.04	ns
Satisfaction with social contacts		10.3	9.5	9.9		(2,70) 0.81	ns
Perceived social support		4.8	5.4	5.8		(2,70) 1.46	ns
Negative social support		2.6	4.7	3.7		(2,69) 0.94	ns
Prior relationship[c]		21.4	28.6	26.0		(2,69) 4.62	<.01
Number in household		1.8	1.9	1.7		(2,70) 0.08	ns

[a]5 = $20–25,000/year
[b]Higher scores = less adequate income
[c]Higher scores = less close relationship

TABLE 5.6
Movers and Stayers by Depressive Symptom Status at Time 1

	N	Prevalence of Symptoms at Time 1	Depressive Symptom Status Time 2 Through Time 4				Chi-square	F	p
			Asymptomatic at Time 1		Symptomatic at Time 1				
			Stays Asymptomatic	Moves to Symptomatic	Stays Symptomatic	Moves to Asymptomatic			
Total	73	26.0%	61.1%	38.9%	52.6%	47.4%			
Gender							(3) 9.51		<.02
Male	22	4.5%	71.4%	28.6%	100.0%	—			
Female	51	35.3%	54.5%	45.5%	50.0%	50.0%			
Kinship							(6) 11.09		<.09
Spouse	40	25.0%	53.3%	46.7%	50.0%	50.0%			
Child	30	23.3%	69.6%	30.4%	71.4%	28.6%			
Other	3	66.7%	100.0%	—	—	100.0%			
Means at Time 1									
Caregiver age			60.0	61.7	53.5	60.2		(3,69) 0.82	ns
Household income[a]			5.9	5.4	4.6	5.8		(3,67) 1.00	ns
Income adequacy[b]			2.9	3.0	3.8	3.1		(3,69) 3.96	<.01
ADL			3.3	4.2	5.8	4.2		(3,69) 0.45	ns
IADL			21.3	26.7	23.7	21.0		(3,53) 0.87	ns
Patient MMS			20.0	21.1	21.0	22.3		(3,67) 0.90	ns
Patient problem behaviors			47.1	58.8	62.4	62.0		(3,66) 1.66	ns
Number of people helping with patient care			0.8	0.5	0.9	1.6		(3,68) 1.46	ns
Satisfaction with social contacts			10.3	10.2	9.5	9.1		(3,69) 1.39	ns
Perceived social support			4.8	5.6	5.4	6.3		(3,69) 1.18	ns
Negative social support			2.6	3.0	4.7	5.6		(3,68) 1.29	ns
Prior relationship[c]			21.4	26.6	28.6	24.7		(3,68) 3.18	<.03
Number in household			1.8	1.9	1.9	1.3		(3,69) 0.51	ns

[a]5 = $20–25,000/year
[b]Higher scores = less adequate income
[c]Higher scores = less close relationship

symptomatic episode at a subsequent measurement point report lower levels of income adequacy when compared to all other groups. Individuals who start out as asymptomatic and who stay asymptomatic report a closer prior relationship compared to all other groups. All males who are symptomatic at Time 1 remained symptomatic at all subsequent measurement points. Females exhibited more variable patterns over time.

In summary, these analyses indicate that 59% of our continuous caregivers exhibit stable patterns of depressive symptomatology over a 2-year period. About three quarters of these stable individuals are consistently asymptomatic and the remaining quarter is consistently symptomatic. Forty-one percent of the continuous caregivers exhibited fluctuating patterns of depressive symptomatology. Overall, higher rates of depressive symptomatology were reported at the end of the 2-year follow-up than at the beginning of that period. These results should be viewed as suggestive rather than conclusive given the small number of subjects available for this analysis.

DISCUSSION

The major findings of this study show that the mean level of depressive symptomatology among continuous caregivers is consistently higher among females when compared to non-caregiving females of similar age. Male caregivers exhibited normative levels of depressive symptomatology at the outset of the study but became significantly more depressed over time. These findings are generally consistent with existing data showing increased risk of psychiatric morbidity among caregivers (Schulz et al., 1990).

When individuals were classified as being either above or below the threshold for being at risk of clinical depression, analyses of individual patterns of change over time showed that the majority of caregivers (59%) exhibited stable patterns of depressive symptomatology. Seventy-five percent of these stable individuals were consistently asymptomatic whereas 25% (11.7% of the total sample) were consistently symptomatic. These rates of symptomatology are likely to be underestimates because our attrition analyses showed that individuals lost to follow-up were significantly more depressed than individuals who remained in the study. Pruchno et al. (1990) reported similar results. One interpretation of these data is that caregivers who are at highest risk for becoming dysfunctional are lost to attrition in longitudinal studies.

Being symptomatic was related to being concerned over the adequacy of one's income at Time 1, whereas being asymptomatic was related to having a close personal relationship with the patient prior to the illness. Females were more likely to be symptomatic than males. These findings are consistent with existing longitudinal studies showing stability over time in levels of depressive symptomatology (Pagel et al., 1985; Pruchno, & Resch, 1989; Schulz et al., 1988; Townsend, et al., 1989). Although it is tempting to conclude that the chronic depression characteristic of the consistently symptomatic group is attributable to the stress of caregiving, we must be cautious in making this claim. Because we have no data available concerning affective states prior to caregiving, we cannot conclude with certainty that the observed high levels of symptomatology are attributable to caregiving. A possible alternative explanation is that these individuals were just as depressed prior to taking on the caregiving role because of inadequate social and economic resources or because of well-established life-long traits.

The remaining continuous caregivers (41%) exhibited fluctuating patterns of depressive symptomatology with a tendency toward increased depression over time. This response pattern is consistent with wear-and-tear models predicting a downward trajectory of caregiver functioning, suggesting that over time individuals' capacity to cope with the demands of caregiving is eroded. Because we have strong evidence that levels of patient disability and care demands increased over time, this study represents a stronger test of the wear-and-tear hypothesis than previous studies (e.g., Townsend et al., 1989; Schulz et al., 1988). Our data suggest that this hypothesis is worth pursuing in future longitudinal studies of caregiving.

Predictors of Depression and Depression Change

Multivariate analyses of variance were carried out to identify predictors of depression cross-sectionally as well as changes in depression longitudinally. Cross-sectional analyses showed that patient problem behaviors were important contributors to caregiver depression; the more often such behaviors occurred, the more depressed caregivers were. The negative impact of problem behaviors increased over time, reflecting the declining status of patients. Perceived availability of social support was also an independent predictor of caregiver depression at all measurement points; the more caregivers perceived that support was available, the less their depression. Caregiver gender and concern about financial resources appeared to be important early in the caregiving process.

Three variables were significant predictors of change in depression from T1 to T4. First, lower depression scores at T1 were related to greater increases in depression over time. Second, men were more likely than women to experience increases in symptoms of depression over time; and third, as perceptions of available social support declined, depression increased.

The composite picture that emerges from these analyses is that women experience higher levels distress than men, although over time, men who remain in the caregiving role also report high levels of depressive symptomatology. For both men and women, the primary patient characteristic that determines caregiver coping is not the functional status of the patient but rather the number of problem behaviors (e.g., wandering, asking repetitive questions, losing things) exhibited by the patient. Finally, the perceived availability of social support from relatives and friends is an important determinant of caregiver functioning.

On the whole, these findings are consistent with much of the existing literature on Alzheimer's caregiving. They go beyond the existing literature by showing that patient problem behaviors, social support, financial concerns, and gender are independent predictors of caregiver well-being. Moreover, our data suggest that the impact of these variables varies as a function of where the individual is located in a caregiving trajectory. Gender and concern about financial resources are important early in the caregiving process but less so later on. Problem behaviors and social support are important determinants of caregiver well-being throughout the caregiving process. Finally, our data represent the first longitudinal evidence that the capacity of some caregivers to cope with the demands of caregiving is gradually eroded over time.

Limitations

A major limitation of this study is the relatively small group sizes that resulted as the population of caregivers differentiated itself into various subgroups. Although the initial sample size of 172 caregivers was large enough to test complex multivariate models of caregiving outcomes, this group quickly separated into a number of subgroups as patients died or were institutionalized. We feel it is important to examine these subgroups separately. Because a number of currently ongoing caregiving studies are quite similar to each other, it may be feasible to combine data from multiple studies for analytic purposes.

A second limitation characteristic of all caregiving studies — including this one — is the absence of data on caregiver status prior to taking on the caregiving role. Without such data, it is impossible to construct a complete picture of the temporal impact of caregiving. A prospective study of caregiving, although difficult to carry out, should receive high priority in the future.

Finally, although this study is important in providing a fairly detailed descriptive picture of patterns of change among caregivers over time, it is limited in its ability to point to specific underlying causes of change. We have identified a number of variables likely to be related to increased levels of depression over time, but our limited sample size precludes causal modeling of these relationships.

ACKNOWLEDGMENT

This research was supported by Grant AGO-5444 from the National Institute on Aging. Gail Williamson's participation in the preparation of this manuscript was also supported by a NIMH postdoctoral fellowship (MH17184) in Clinical Services Research.

Portions of this manuscript were previously published in *Psychology and Aging.* Permission obtained from the American Psychological Association.

REFERENCES

Aneshensel, C. S. (1985). The natural history of depressive symptoms: Implications for psychiatric epidemiology. In J. R. Greenley (Ed.), *Research in community and mental health* (Vol. 5, pp. 45-75). Greenwich, CT: JAI Press.

Barer, B. M., & Johnson, C. L. (1990). A critique of the caregiving literature. *The Gerontologist, 30,* pp. 26-29.

Berkman, L. F., Berkman, C. S., Kasl, S. V., Freeman, D. H., Leo, L., Ostfeld, A. M., Cornoni-Huntley, J., & Brody, J. A. (1986). Depressive symptoms in relation to physical health and functioning in the elderly. *American Journal of Epidemiology, 124,* 372-388.

Biegel, D. E., Sales, E., & Schulz, R. (1991). *Family caregiving in chronic illness.* Newburg Park, CA: Sage.

Center for the Study of Aging and Human Development (1978). *Multidimensional functional assessment, the OARS methodology: A manual* (2nd ed.). Durham, NC: Duke University.

Cohen, S., Mermelstein, R., Kamarck, T., & Hoberman, H. M. (1985). Measuring the functional components of social support. In I. G. Sarason & B. R. Sarason (Eds.), *Social support: Theory, research, and application* (pp. 73-94). The Hague: Martines Niijhoff.

Folstein, M. F., Folstein, S., & McHugh, P. R. (1975). "Mini-Mental State": A practical method for grading the cognitive state of patients for the clinician. *Journal of Psychiatric Research, 12,* 189-198.

George, L. K. (1990). Caregiver stress studies—There really is more to learn. *The Gerontologist, 30,* 580-581.

Haley, W. E., & Pardo, K. M. (1989). Relationship of severity of dementia to caregiving stressors. *Psychology and Aging, 4,* 389-392.

Johnson, C. L., & Catalano, D. J. (1983). A longitudinal study of family supports to impaired elderly. *The Gerontologist, 23,* 612-618.

McKann, D., Drachman, D., Folstein, M., Katzman, R., Price, D., & Standlan, E. M. (1984). Clinical diagnosis of Alzheimer's disease: Report of the NINCDS-ADRDA Work Group under the auspices of the Department of Health and Human Services Task Force on Alzheimer's disease. *Neurology, 34,* 939-944.

Pagel, M. D., Becker, J., & Coppel, D. B. (1985). Loss of control, self-blame, and depression: An investigation of spouse caregivers of Alzheimer's disease patients. *Journal of Abnormal Psychology, 94,* 169-182.

Pearlin, L. I., Mullan, J. T., Semple, S. J., & Skaff, M. M. (1990). Caregiving and the stress process: An overview of concepts and their measures. *The Gerontologist, 30,* 583-595.

Pruchno, R. A., Kleban, M. H., Michaels, J. E., & Dempsey, N. P. (1990). Mental and physical health of caregiving spouses: Development of a causal model. *Journal of Gerontology: Psychological Sciences, 45,* pp. 192-199.

Pruchno, R. A., & Resch, N. L. (1989). Aberrant behavior and Alzheimer's disease: Mental health effects on spouse caregivers. *Journal of Gerontology: Social Sciences,* S177–182.

Radloff, L. (1977). The CES-D Scale: A self-report depression scale for research in the general population. *Applied Psychological Measurement, 1,* 385–401.

Rogosa, D. (1988). Myths about longitudinal research. In K. W. Schaie, R. T. Campbell, W. Meredith, & S. C. Rawlings (Eds.), *Methodological issues in aging research* (pp. 171–210). New York: Springer.

Scannell, A. U. (1988). The long-term psychosocial impacts of caregiving on caregivers for persons with stroke. *Dissertation Abstracts International, 50,* 1052A.

Schulz, R., & Tompkins, C. A. (1990). Life events and changes in social relationships: Examples, mechanisms, and measurement. *Journal of Social and Clinical Psychology, 9,* 69–77.

Schulz, R., Tompkins, C. A., & Rau, M. T. (1988). A longitudinal study of the psychosocial impact of stroke on primary support persons. *Psychology and Aging, 3,* 131–141.

Schulz, R., Visintainer, P., & Williamson, G. M. (1990). Psychiatric and physical morbidity effects of caregiving. *Journals of Gerontology: Psychological Sciences, 45,* 181–191.

Schulz, R., & Williamson, G. M. (1990). *Depression and physical illness in the elderly.* Unpublished manuscript, University of Pittsburgh, Pittsburgh, PA.

Select Committee on Aging, U.S. House of Representatives. (1987). *Exploding the myths: Caregiving in America* (Committee Publication No. 99-611). Washington, DC: U.S. Government Printing Office.

Skinner, H. A., Steinhauer, P. D., & Santa-Barbara, J. (1983). The Family Assessment Measure. *Canadian Journal of Community Mental Health, 2,* 91–105.

Stone, R., Cafferata, G. L., & Sangl, J. (1987). Caregivers of the frail elderly: A national profile. *The Gerontologist, 27,* 616–626.

Tompkins, C. A., Schulz, R., & Rau, M. T. (1988). Post-stroke depression in primary support persons: Predicting those at risk. *Journal of Consulting and Clinical Psychology, 56,* 502–508.

Townsend, A., Noelker, L., Deimling, G., & Bass, D. (1989). Longitudinal impact of interhousehold caregiving on adult children's mental health. *Psychology and Aging, 4,* 393–401.

Williamson, G. M., & Schulz, R. (in press). Physical illness and symptoms of depression among elderly outpatients. *Psychology and Aging.*

Zarit, S. H., Todd, P. A., & Zarit, J. M. (1986). Subjective burden of husbands and wives as caregivers: A longitudinal study. *The Gerontologist, 26,* 260–266.

Caregiving Research: Juggling While Walking

Michael A. Smyer
The Pennsylvania State University

As I prepared this section, I struggled with the appropriate metaphor to capture the task of researchers focusing on adaptation among caregivers of Alzheimer's patients. Eventually, I settled on the image of juggling while walking. Let me fill in the details of the metaphor and its applicability to caregiving research. The consummate juggler must simultaneously keep track of and control for a variety of influences (e.g., weight differences, size differences, wind, audience distraction, etc.). The seasoned professional, however, knows that stationary juggling is less appealing and represents an earlier stage of competence than juggling while walking.

In a similar fashion, the task of the caregiving researcher is to simultaneously assess and account for a variety of influences on the caregiver and the care recipient (e.g., history of the disability, history of the relationship prior to and subsequent to the disability, the social structure of the caregiver, age and gender of caregivers, etc.). Consider, for example, the helpful conceptual model that Pearlin and his colleagues (Pearlin, Mullan, Semple, & Skaff, 1990) presented recently. As George (1990) commented, their contribution is a "conceptual tour de force." Pursuing the juggling metaphor, from Pearlin et al.'s perspective, an appropriate study of the caregiving process would focus on four domains: the background and context of stress; the stressors; the mediators of stress; and the outcomes of stress. The most adequate studies, then, require a simultaneous consideration (juggling?) of these elements.

Like the seasoned juggler, however, seasoned researchers in the caregiving area understand that a static view of these issues is not adequate. Longitudinal studies that assess patterns of stability and change are essential for a comprehensive understanding of the complexity of caregiving for all involved. The Pearlin et al. (1990) framework implies temporal causality but still represents a cross-sectional view.

This section is designed to assist those who are working at both the basic process of juggling, as well as those, like Schulz and colleagues, who have taken on the more ambitious task of juggling while walking. I want to acknowledge the thoughtful presentation that Schulz, Williamson, Morycz, and Biegel have provided. I use their work as a counterpoint to focus attention on more general issues of studying stability and change within the caregiving relationship. In doing so, however, I want to begin by underscoring the clarity of design and presentation of their work.

This contribution focuses on four major themes: Measurement strategies to capture stability and change; the importance of intraindividual differences; the importance of interindividual differences in intraindividual differences; and the salience of inter- and intrafamilial differences.

Measurement of Stability and Change

In their discussion, Schulz et al. highlight one of the most striking findings of their study: Forty-one percent of the continuous caregivers exhibited fluctuating patterns of depressive symptomatology. Finding substantial fluctuation is important to note. It raises several basic questions regarding measurement and design strategies to adequately reflect fluctuation.

Measurement of Depression

The first issue focuses on the outcome domain itself: depression. Depression among caregivers is a frequent area of concern. Indeed, Pearlin et al. (1990) listed it first among their outcome variables. Thus, it is not surprising that Schulz et al. have assessed depression among caregivers.

In terms of measurement strategy, Boyle (1985) reviewed self-report measures of depression, focusing on psychometric aspects of the measures: the importance of assessing at both the "surface syndrome" level (e.g., symptoms) and the more fundamental source/trait level. Boyle (1985) noted that measures like the CES-D, which Schulz et al. used, focus on both symptoms and mood of depression. Boyle suggested that researchers either use multiple measures or that multivariate approaches be used. As he put it:

> In order to measure adequately the surface syndrome of depression, self-report instruments such as the CES-D need to index the full-range of components which are the source states or traits underlying the overall syndrome. Measure

ment of these several components needs to be representative of the relative
importance of each in the composition of the depression syndrome. This
psychometric requirement is clearly a task for future research as the current
instruments do not adequately assess the depression syndrome in terms of the
whole range of its underlying components. (p. 47)

Blazer and his colleagues (Blazer, Hughes, & George, 1987) offered
suggestions on what might constitute the whole range of components underlying depression. They reported on the prevalence of depressive symptomatology in a community sample of adults 60 years of age or older. Their work
drew upon the Epidemiological Catchment Area (ECA) data. The ECA
studies used the Diagnostic Interview Survey (DIS) to elicit the presence or
absence of symptoms, their severity, frequency, and relationship to other
potential causes (e.g., physical illness, drug or alcohol use, or other psychiatric diagnoses). Blazer et al. (1987) reported that 27% of the 1,304 adults 60
years of age and over reported depressive symptoms. Importantly, however,
the majority were not classified within the traditional DSM-III depressive
categories of major depression (0.8%) and dysthymia (2%). In contrast, two
other subgroups emerged that are not captured by the traditional DSM-III
nosology: those with a mixed anxiety and depression set of symptoms (1.2%)
and those with symptomatic depression (4%). In addition, 19% were
diagnosed as suffering mild dysphoria. These findings are consistent with
earlier reports that depressive symptoms are more common among the elderly
than are DSM-III diagnoses of depression (e.g., Blazer & Williams, 1980).
For our purposes, however, it is important to stress that we must differentiate
clinical depression from depressive symptoms when we discuss depression as
an outcome.

The implications for those involved in caregiving research are clear: If
depression is an outcome of major concern (and it should be), then
appropriate measurement strategies probably include attention to both symptoms and underlying state or trait elements of depression.

However, realistically, studies usually rely on one measure, such as the
CES-D, which focuses on symptoms of depression. Such measures, however,
are unlikely to represent only a single, pure component of depressive
symptoms. Gatz and Karel (1990), for example, assessed change in positive
and negative mood structure, using the CES-D. (This work is part of a larger
study of intergenerational relationships and, therefore, includes members of
several adult generations.) They identified four subscales: depressed mood;
psychomotor retardation; lack of well-being; and interpersonal difficulty (see
Table 1). Gatz and Karel reported that these factors are consistent with earlier
efforts at factor analysis of the CES-D (e.g., Clark, Aneshensel, Frerichs, &
Morgan, 1981; Hertzog, Van Alstine, Usala, Hultsch, & Dixon, 1990; Liang,

TABLE 1
CES-D Items

Depressed Mood
  3. I felt that I could not shake the blues . . .
  5. I felt depressed.
  9. I thought my life had been a failure.
10. I felt fearful.
14. I felt lonely.
17. I had crying spells.
18. I felt sad.

Psychomotor Retardation
  1. I was bothered by things that usually don't bother me.
  2. I did not feel like eating . . .
  5. I had trouble keeping my mind on what I was doing.
  7. . . . everything I did was an effort.
11. My sleep was restless.
13. I talked less than usual.
20. I could not "get going."

Lack of Well-being
  4. I felt . . . just as good as other people.
  8. I felt hopeful about the future.
12. I was happy.
16. I enjoyed life.

Interpersonal Difficulties
15. People were unfriendly.
19. I felt that people disliked me.

Tran, Krause, & Markides, 1989). Because the interpersonal difficulties subscale included only two items, Gatz and Karel dropped this area from further analysis.

For our purposes, it is important to consider whether or not these subareas are likely to exhibit different patterns of functioning across the life span and across time. Again, Gatz and Karel's work offer helpful clues.

In a cross-sectional view, Gatz and Karel reported different patterns of age differences for the three subareas and for the overall CES-D score (see Figs. 1 and 2). These figures are drawn from waves of data collection in 1984–1985 and in 1988.

Gatz and Karel's work is also helpful in assessing patterns of change across the life span and across time. For example, in Schulz et al.'s work, the age structure of the sample (of both those who dropped out and those who continued) is unclear. However, because both spouses and children were caregivers, it is safe to assume that a range of ages are represented in the caregivers. Gatz and Karel (1990) presented change information on four different age groups, using the overall CES-D score (as Schulz et al. did).

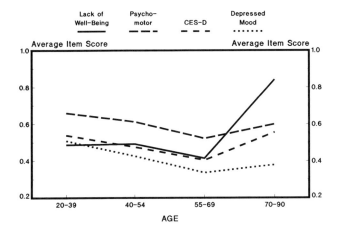

FIG. 1. Time 2 cross-sectional (from Gatz & Karel, 1990).

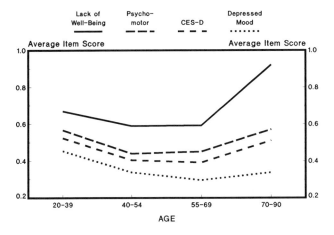

FIG. 2. Time 3 cross-sectional (from Gatz & Karel, 1990).

Gatz and Karel (1990) used the following age groups: young adults (20–39), younger middle-aged (40–54), older middle-aged (55–69), and older adults (70–90). They presented the patterns of change over 3 years for the four age groups (see Fig. 3). It is important to note that the patterns of change are different for the four age groups, as are the relative standings.

Finally, we again draw on Gatz and Karel's work to assess patterns of change across the sub-areas of the CES-D. Collapsing across the sample, Gatz and Karel (1990) tracked three of the factor areas: lack of well-being; psychomotor retardation; and depressed mood (see Fig. 4). It is important to note that the factors have different patterns of change over the 3-year period.

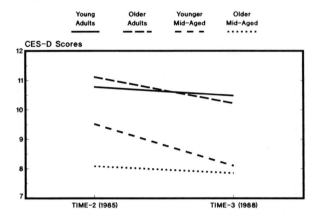

FIG. 3. Longitudinal CES-D scores (from Gatz & Karel, 1990).

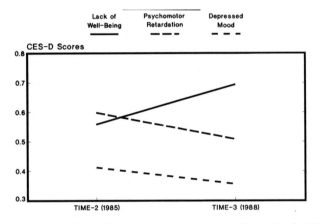

FIG. 4. Longitudinal subscale scores (all ages) (from Gatz & Karel, 1990).

Obviously, we must be cautious in comparing these results with those presented by Schulz et al. The samples are different (caregivers/others), the scores are different (higher for caregiving sample), and the time frames are different (18 months/3 years). However, Gatz and Karel's data remind us of the importance of considering the underlying domains within a single measure. Their data should also alert us to the difficulty of collapsing across age and generations to come up with a composite picture of caregivers.

Intraindividual Change

Schulz et al.'s emphasis on fluctuation also raises another issue: What are the most effective strategies for charting change both within and across individuals? Recent work at The Pennsylvania State University has highlighted alternative strategies for considering these issues (e.g., Nesselroade & Ford, 1985). In the next two sections, I draw on this work to illustrate these alternative strategies. Consider for a moment a simple question: If you assume that fluctuation or change is an essential element of the mood of caregivers, how frequently should you assess mood? Schulz et al.'s work represents an advance, because they are using a longitudinal approach with 4 times of measurement over 18 months. This strategy is consistent with traditional r-technique approaches to the study of change (i.e., many individuals measured over a few times of measurement). In contrast, the p-technique focuses on one individual over extensive repeated measurements. Therefore, each subject constitutes an independent study replication. By factor analyzing data across occasions of measurement rather than individuals (as with cross-sectional research design), this methodology is able to identify intraindividual patterns of covarying behaviors or symptoms over time.

The data in the next few figures are drawn from a recent dissertation by Adam Garfein. Dr. Garfein focused on patterns of intraindividual variability in depressive symptoms. I report on two aspects of his work. First, some of the details: The data were collected from October, 1988, through January, 1989. Demographic, social resources, physical health, cognitive functioning, and affective status information was collected at pre- and post-test. A second questionnaire, which included measures of medicine use, physical health, social contact, sleep disturbances, affect, and daily hassles was completed on a daily basis for approximately 100 days.

In terms of affect, a revised 60-item version of the Multiple Affect Check List (MACL) (Zuckerman & Lubin, 1965) assessed daily variation in mood. The state of today's version of the MACL has five subscales: Anxiety, Depression, Hostility, Positive Affect, and Sensation Seeking.

In the following illustrative figures, data are drawn from a single subject:

> The subject was a 72-year-old widow. She had seen her doctor seven times in the past 6 months and suffered from multiple chronic conditions, including arthritis, high blood pressure, diabetes, and urinary tract problem, anemia, a hiatal hernia, numbness, and fatigue. More recently, she suffered a staph infection. She used crutches when walking outside her apartment building. She had no children and almost never felt lonely. She consumed 726 prescription and 901 nonprescription medications during the 101 days of the study (Total = 1,627) . . . These large numbers of prescription and nonprescription medicines increase the subject's risk for the possible deleterious effects of polymedicine. (See Garfein & Smyer, 1990, for more details.)

Figures 5 through 9 represent that person's data for the five subscale areas.

Two points are noteworthy here: There is substantial intraindividual

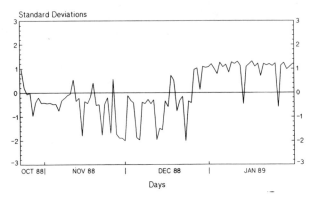

FIG. 5. Factor scores: positive affect

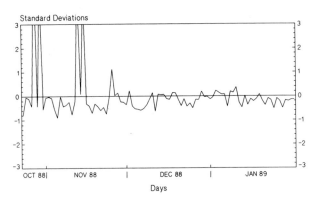

FIG. 6. Factor scores: annoyed

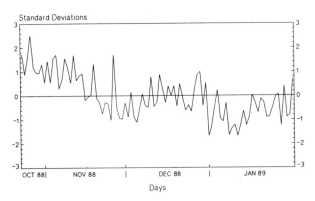

FIG. 7. Factor scores: "passive" sensation seeking.

148

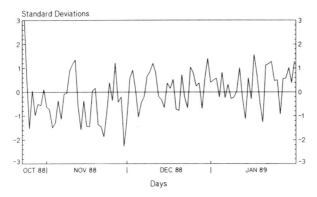

FIG. 8. Factor scores: "active" sensation seeking.

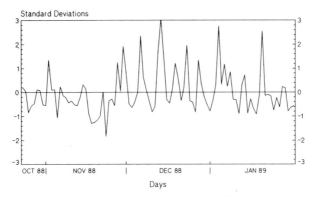

FIG. 9. Factor scores: shopping problems.

fluctuation over time within each subscale. There is also substantial variability across the five subscales. Thus, if one is interested in capturing the essential fluctuations of aspects of mood, a *p*-technique approach may be helpful.

Interindividual Differences in Change Patterns

Although the *p*-technique approach is useful for modeling patterns of intraindividual variability, it can also shed light on the patterns of interindividual differences in such variability. Again, Garfein's work is illustrative. As part of his larger study, Garfein reported on the factor structure of three women — having factor analyzed their data for more than 100 times of measurement (Garfein, Smyer, Nesselroade, Zarit, & Thayer, 1989). It is important to note that each factor analysis focused solely on the data of one

Respondent One's Factor Scores

Positive Affect

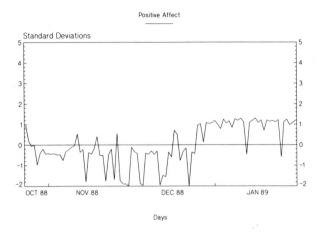

FIG. 10. Daily variability of Respondent 1.

Respondent Two's Factor Scores

Positive Affect and Sensation Seeking

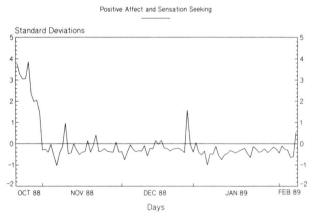

FIG. 11. Daily variability of Respondent 2.

person. Thus, each subject represented a replication. Their factor structures
and day-to-day variability are presented in Figs. 10, 11, and 12.

Again, several elements are important in reviewing these data: The datasets
suggest similarities in patterns of covariation over time. Secondly, there is
considerable lability in functioning over time—even among this sample of
women who were not in a caregiving situation. This has significant implica-

Respondent Three's Factor Scores

Positive Affect and Sensation Seeking

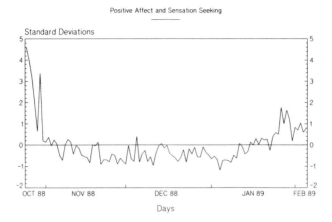

FIG. 12. Daily variability of Respondent 3.

tions for both our measurement and research design approaches. As Garfein and his colleagues (1989) noted:

> Assessment instruments that are sensitive enough to capture unique components of individual variability over time, as well as capable of representing groups of individuals for aggregate descriptive purposes (e.g., to permit the development of norms) are required. (p. 10)

Variety of Family Response

The final element that adds to the complexity of caregiving research is the variety of family response to the stress of caregiving. Here the emphasis is on two types of variability: intrafamilial and interfamilial variations. As we consider the element of family response, it is helpful to consider the similarities between Alzheimer's disease and other chronic illnesses, particularly chronic mental illness. Although those who are involved in Alzheimer advocacy have sought to distance themselves from the "taint" of mental illness (Gatz & Smyer, 1992), there are substantial reasons for considering the similarities of adaptive stresses and tasks for caregivers of Alzheimer patients and caregivers for other chronic groups. In a recent publication, my colleague Rick Birkel and I highlighted three types of adaptation a family must make in coping with chronic mental illness (CMI) in a relative (Smyer & Birkel, 1991) (See Table 2).

TABLE 2
Major Tasks of Family Coping and Adaptation

Interpersonal Adjustment
　Mourning the "lost" CMI relative
　Adjusting relationships within the household
　Maintaining relationships outside the household
　Establishing collaborative relations with professional providers

Instrumental Coping
　Managing day-to-day challenges
　Coordinating among formal and informal care options
　Adjusting household schedules
　Assigning responsibility for caregiving tasks

Life-Course Adaptation
　Planning the long-term family adaptation for intergenerational
　continuity
Reassessing individual developmental trajections—for the CMI relative and for other
　family members
Making adjustments in career and work commitments

Note: From Smyer and Birkel, 1991.

Our view is that adaptation to CMI involves three primary areas: interpersonal, instrumental, and life course. Families vary in the ease or difficulty they find in each adaptation. Moreover, some families may vacillate over or have difficulty with a specific set of concerns (e.g., managing the day-to-day challenges). Clearly, the instrumental coping domain has important salience for families, as evidenced by Schulz et al.'s finding that the frequency of patient problem behavior explained the most variance in caregiver depression.

Regardless of the specific adaptive challenges faced by a particular family or caregiver, however, it is important to note that there may be diversity within and across families as they struggle with these issues. The caregiving research community, however, often collapses across these tasks, without acknowledging the fluctuations in these elements, as well as in caregiving affect.

CONCLUSIONS

In these comments, I tried to highlight the challenges faced by researchers in the caregiving domain. Like the juggler trying to walk and juggle, the researcher must follow several simple steps.

1. Assemble to right objects to juggle: Make sure that the right measurement domains are included in your assessment battery.

2. Pick the right frequency of tosses: Select a research design that allows you to capture adequately the substantial fluctuation in mood and behavior among caregivers and patients.

3. Learn to juggle before you walk: Cross-sectional studies that allow refinement of the measurement battery and specific questions focused on change and stability can be an important first step. Pearlin et al.'s (1990) recent conceptualization helps point the way here, as does Schulz et al.'s contribution.

4. Once you can juggle, then add walking: Modeling stability and change over time involves attending to intra-and interindividual variability, as well as to inter-and intrafamilial variability over time. Research strategies may have to be modified to fully capitalize on the diversity of family form, rate of family adaption, and families' expectations for change or stability.

It is my hope that these comments assist current and future jugglers and researchers.

REFERENCES

Blazer, D. G., Hughes, D. C., & George, L. K. (1987). The epidemiology of depression in an elderly community population. *The Gerontologist, 27*(3), 281–287.

Blazer, D. G., & Williams, C. D. (1980). The epidemiology of dysphoria and depression in an elderly population. *American Journal of Psychiatry, 137*(4), 439–444.

Boyle, G. J. (1985). Self-report measures of depression: Some psychometric considerations. *British Journal of Clinical Psychology, 24,* 45–59.

Clark, V. A., Aneshensel, C. S., Frerichs, R. R., & Morgan, T. M. (1981). Analysis of effects of sex and age in response to items on the CES-D scale. *Psychiatry Research, 5,* 171–181.

Garfein, A. J., & Smyer, M. A. (1990, April). *A p-technique study of medicine use in an elderly woman.* Poster presented at a national conference on the impact of alcohol and other drug abuse affecting the aging population entitled, "Aging in the 1990s: Alcohol and Other Drug Abuse," Novi, MI.

Garfein, A. J., Smyer, M. A., Nesselroade, J. R., Zarit, S. H., & Thayer, J. F. (1989, November). *Patterns of intraindividual health variation.* Poster presented at the 42nd annual meeting of The Gerontological Society of America, Minneapolis, MN.

Gatz, M., & Karel, M. (1990, August). *Positive and negative mood factors on the CES-D over time.* Paper presented at the annual meeting of the American Psychological Association, Boston, MA.

Gatz, M., & Smyer, M. A. (1992). The mental health system and older adults in the 1990s. *American Psychologist, 47*(6), 741–751.

George, L. K. (1990). Caregiver stress studies—there really is more to learn. *The Gerontologist, 30*(5), 580–581.

Hertzog, C., Van Alstine, J., Usala, P. D., Hultsch, D. F., & Dixon, R. (1990). Measurement properties of the Center for Epidemiological Studies Depression Scale (CES-D) in older populations. *Psychological Assessment, 2,* 64–72.

Liang, J., Tran, T. V., Krause, N., & Markides, K. S. (1989). Generational differences in the structure of the CES-D scale in Mexican-Americans. *Journal of Gerontology: Social Sciences, 44,* S110–S120.

Nesselroade, J. R., & Ford, D. H., (1985). P-Technique comes of age: Multivariate, replicated, single-subject designs for research on older adults. *Research on Aging, 7,* 46–80.

Pearlin, L. I., Mullan, J. T., Semple, S. J., & Skaff M. M. (1990). Caregiving and the stress process. An overview of concepts and their measures. *Gerontologist, 30*(5), 583–591.

Smyer, M. A., & Birkel, R. C. (1991). Research focused on intervention with families of the chronically mentally ill elderly. In E. Light & B. Lebowitz (Eds.), *The chronically mentally ill elderly* (pp. 111–130). New York: Springer Publishing Company.

Zuckerman, M., & Lubin, B., (1965). *Manual for the multiple affect adjective checklist.* San Diego: Edits.

6

Research into Informal Caregiving: Current Perspectives and Future Directions

Leonard I. Pearlin
University of California, San Francisco
Steven H. Zarit
The Pennsylvania State University

For many reasons, family caregiving is a pivotal issue of later life. Indeed, caregiving to older members of a family is becoming an increasingly normative experience. Improved medical technology and extended longevity result in larger numbers of old people in the society and, unfortunately, also increase the chances that individuals will spend the last portions of their lives in an impaired and dependent state. Moreover, where the necessity for caregiving does arise, families are typically forced to define and redefine relationships, obligations, and capabilities. It is quite likely, too, that caregiving families will find it necessary to search for scarce time, money, and other resources to manage the formidable demands that are entailed.

Given the extensiveness and problematic character of family caregiving, it is understandable that there has been an explosion of interest in this activity over the past 10 or 12 years. In our view, the field is currently at a stage of consolidating what has been learned from past work and identifying what remains to be learned from future research. As with any new area of inquiry, the first wave of research needs to be followed by a critical examination of its assumptions and methods in the hope that new and productive paradigms will emerge to guide future work (see, e.g., George, 1990; Zarit, 1989). Although we are certainly not armed with crystal balls, we expect that future work will continue to be influenced by perspectives adapted from stress and coping research (e.g., Lazarus & Folkman, 1984; Pearlin & Schooler, 1978), and community mental health (Grad & Sainsbury, 1968; Kahn, 1975; Pasamanick, Scarpitti, & Dinitz, 1967). However, it is likely that these perspectives will be broadened in the next decade, bringing into consideration new substantive questions and developing methods that have either been ignored or given scant attention in the past. We can be sure that future work will not simply follow in the footsteps of the past but will become conceptually more elaborate and methodologically more sensitive.

The preceding chapters are highly suggestive of the agendas for future research into caregiving. Indeed, our goal in this chapter is to underscore and amplify in a selective way some of the theoretical and methodological issues threaded throughout the foregoing chapters. These issues combine to form a coherent picture of what is likely to be incorporated into caregiving research in the next decade. If our judgement is correct, the 1990s should be every bit as intellectually exciting as the 1980s and should yield a more sophisticated knowledge base. This base, in turn, should provide a much clearer guide to effective interventions.

COMPARATIVE PERSPECTIVES AND THEIR DIMENSIONS

It is evident from the preceding chapters that much can be gained by systematically adopting comparative strategies. In the absence of comparisons, it is easy to assume erroneously that what is observed of caregiving patterns in one group is also extant in other groups. Thus, comparisons are essential to identifying the limits to which research findings can be generalized. More than that, they enable us to identify the conditions that help to explain variations in patterns of family caregiving. For example, to recognize the circumstances that give rise to conflict in caregiving families, we need to compare families in conflict with those free of conflict. Or, to understand why some families are willing—even eager—to provide care and others loathe to do this, the conditions of life under which both live and the values and goals that guide their actions need to be systematically contrasted.

At some level, of course, strategies of comparison are built into most of the research that has been conducted in recent years. Thus, it is virtually standard to compare caregiving and its effects by the gender of the caregiver, by the relationship of the caregiver to the impaired person, and so on. These represent crucial social and economic characteristics of people whose importance in caregiving has been firmly established. However, several of the preceding chapters implicitly argue that our comparative perspectives need to be expanded to include at least three additional dimensions: (a) national, cultural, and ethnic groups; (b) the timing of caregiving as it involves different cohorts and generations and different locations on the life-course and; (c) the types of impairment or disability for which family care is provided.

Cultural Comparisons. Caregiving and its social and personal consequences do not take place in a cultural vacuum. The willingness and ability of
families to assume long-term responsibility for impaired and dependent aged
members depend on the traditions and values of the society, on the
composition of families and households, on general economic conditions, on
the availability of and access to alternative measures, and so on. One of the
best ways to discern the social and cultural circumstances that undergird
patterns of caregiving is to compare caregiving in different national, cultural,
and ethnic contexts. As we noted, such comparisons alert us both to the extent
of the variability of caregiving arrangements and to the factors that help
explain it. Chapters 1 and 2 help to highlight these issues.

The Yu et al. work, which presents data drawn in Shanghai, lays out an
epidemiological picture of caregiving in that city. It shows the distribution of
caregiver social and economic characteristics and those of the care recipients,
and of the kinds of problems that caregivers experience in providing
assistance to impaired relatives. Theirs is not an ordinary study. Although
other studies may describe the social and economic characteristics of their
samples, there are precious few, if any, that describe these characteristics as
they are distributed in a population. Because their sample is based on
procedures that make it representative of the population of the area, they are
able to provide a firm basis for comparisons with other societies. In this
regard, the reader will probably have noticed in their Table 1.8 that a large
majority of Shanghai caregivers to cognitively impaired relatives report that
the demands on their time, energies, and moods is "the same as before"
caregiving. We doubt that American families would judge their lives as being
so little disrupted by the need to provide assistance as do their Chinese
counterparts.

Some of the reasons for this apparently unruffled acceptance of the
caregiver role can be found in the chapter by Lucy Yu and, specifically, her
description of the value of filial piety. Filial piety in China does not simply
exist as an abstract value independently of the structure of parent–child
relations. Instead, it is deeply incorporated in the patterns of care that are
exchanged between parents and their adult children. Whereas the acceptance
of care by parents in the United States may represent a surrender to the
unwanted circumstances of old age and its dependencies, in China it is given
by children and accepted by their parents as a matter of unquestioned course.
There is a suggestion in Yu's data that commitment to the value weakens
among Chinese-Americans who become socialized to the very different
economic and social conditions in this country. Nevertheless, one has the
impression that even in this partly acculturated group, caregiving to impaired
older parents may not involve the radical restructuring of lives as often
happens in many American families.

As Morycz so aptly reminds us, elderly immigrants are often dependent on children long before they experience health problems. Forced from home-lands by harsh economic conditions or war, many immigrants have already depleted their adaptational resources earlier in life and may come to depend on the vigor of young children while they themselves are still young. How different this is from what we ordinarily see in the United States, where it is the parental generation that is often still engaged in assisting children long after the children have established their own households.

At any rate, the opportunity to explore the range of caregiving arrange-ments depends on cultural comparisons. These comparisons, we should emphasize, do not necessarily involve different societies but may also involve the comparison of different cultural groups within a society. In this regard, the differences in caregiving arrangements between Afro-Americans and Hispanic-Americans may be as instructive as those between, for example, the United States and China. In these comparisons, too, one can find cultural differences in definitions of family, expectations on the part of the recipients of care and internalized obligations on the part of the providers of care. We echo Morycz's view that informal caregiving to the aged needs to be understood within the context of social and ethnic cultural variations.

Life-Course Comparisons. The intriguing chapter by Burton and So-rensen suggests a comparative dimension that is somewhat new to caregiving research: the timing of the emergence and enactment of the caregiver role. In their chapter, the authors are primarily concerned with conceptually speci-fying the various aspects of timing, not with the differential effects of caregiving among those whose timing is different. Yet, the implications are clear. It is likely, for example, that just as being socialized to the values of different cultures shapes the meaning and impact of caregiving, so too does being socialized to caregiving within different historical eras. An older woman caring for an impaired spouse will probably experience caregiving differently from a younger wife engaged in the same activities. Although these differ-ences may be the consequence of many factors, the expectations and obligations each has internalized as members of distinct historical cohorts undoubtedly plays a part.

The Avison, Turner, Noh, and Speechley chapter also has some implica-tions for the matter of intergenerational developmental time. Thus, being a middle-aged caregiver to an old-aged parent is very different from being a middle-aged caregiver to an adolescent-aged child. In these instances, it is the developmental mix of caregiver and care recipient that influences caregiving and its consequences, not the life stage of the caregiver alone. Thus, it would be our guess that, other conditions being equal, the older family caregiver to the younger recipient experiences much more hardship than does the younger caregiver to an older relative. The reason, of course, is that a serious impairment or the threat of premature death among the young carries its own sense of horror. To illustrate from a study of AIDS caregivers in San Francisco, it has become evident that confronting death as a common occurrence in a population of young adults where death is ordinarily uncommon creates a somewhat unique stressor (Turner & Pearlin, 1989).

Caregiving and its effects, then, are probably quite sensitive to cohort differences and to the life-course locations of the caregiver and care recipient. And, as Burton and Sorensen discuss, the logistics of daily caregiving activities and their burdens are also sensitive to the ways in which the organization of the caregiver's time can be coordinated with that of significant others. Clearly, studies attempting to account for variations in caregiving and its impact should ideally allow for multiple temporal comparisons.

Comparisons by Type of Impairment. Do the stressful effects of caregiving vary with the illness or impairment for which care is given? That would appear to be the case from Yu et al.'s comparisons of caregivers' reactions to the disabled and the demented in Shanghai. Thus, the caregivers to disabled relatives report more dislocation in their lives than those caring for the demented. By and large, however, they also express greater tolerance for problems arising from the care of the disabled.

The chapter by Avison et al. also addresses the comparative effects of caregiving for different impairments. They find that whether or not one impairment has a greater impact than others largely depends on surrounding conditions. Specifically, although the adverse psychological consequences of caregiving do vary somewhat from one impairment to another, this variation is regulated by several conditions. Among these conditions are the external events and strains to which caregivers must adjust at the same time they are providing care. Caregiving is often stressful enough in its own right but when it is also embedded in the context of other stressors, it may become even more demanding. To use Matthews' term, there is a "spillover" of stressful effects from one role to another.

Most of Avison et al.'s comparisons involve parents giving care to children. It can be recognized, however, that parents caring for impaired and threatened children are likely to endow their caregiving roles with very different meanings than those found either among spousal caregivers or children caring for elderly relatives. Moreover, the particular generational mix that is involved must inevitably intersect with the issues of life-course timing raised in the Burton and Sorensen chapter and with the notion of normative versus exceptional circumstances described by Matthews. And, as Matthews also correctly emphasizes, the ease with which people undertake caregiving depends on their prior anticipation of and socialization for the role.

One of the interesting comparative dimensions found in Avison et al.'s work is that of mother–father. Fathers, it appears, tend to be less affected by caregiving to children than mothers, especially in the presence of other conditions. However, some caution is warranted where the impact of stressors on men and women is judged on the basis of depressive affect. There is some evidence that men and women may be equally affected by stressors but each may express the effects in different ways (Aneshensel, Rutter, & Lackenbruch, 1991). In particular, women are more disposed to manifest stress in depression, whereas men are more disposed to manifest stress in excessive drinking and aggressive behavior. Consequently, in comparing groups of people, it is best to employ a range of outcomes; otherwise, it is easy to misjudge the vulnerabilities of people to stressors.

CONCEPTUAL AND DESIGN PERSPECTIVES

In addition to comparative strategies, there are several other fundamental perspectives suggested by the foregoing chapters. Some of these, we believe, will be increasingly prominent in the next generation of caregiving research and, therefore, they deserve elaboration. One such perspective involves the treatment of caregiving and its stresses as a process.

Caregiver Stress: A State Versus a Process.   Caregiving and its surrounding conditions are typically in a state of change and flux. What might have been observed of caregiving in a household a month or a year ago is likely to be quite different from what can be observed in the present and, correspondingly, what can be observed in the present will be different from that which will exist a short time into the future. To understand caregiving, then, it is necessary to recognize that it encompasses a process comprised of many interrelated components such that a change in one of them results in a change in the others. In this respect, caregiving is not different from other situations of chronic stress (Pearlin, 1989). Wherever there are conditions imposing persistent or recurring demands on individuals, it is more appropriate to think of process than of stability.

The essential point to be underscored is that as the demands of caregiving continue over time, the mix of stressors impinging on caregivers may undergo profound restructuring. In the case of Alzheimer's disease, for example, there may be some easing of the need to monitor and control the impaired person as the disease progresses. But as this problem or stressor condition might diminish, others — those we refer to as secondary stressors — can arise de novo. These might involve a burgeoning economic hardship, the eruption of family conflicts, incompatibilities of occupational and caregiving activities, and so on. Once these secondary stressors surface, they may create at least as much distress as the stressors anchored more directly in caregiving activities (Pearlin, Mullan, Semple, & Skaff, 1990).

Paralleling the restructuring of stressors may be changes in coping behaviors and the uses and availability of social support. Under circumstances of enduring stress, it is chimerical to think of these mediating forces as constant. Coping repertoires change with trial and error and with changes in the configuration of stressors. Similarly, social support that once was available may no longer be appropriate to the changed needs, or the original donors of support may be burned out and replaced by others. Thus, available personal and social resources can be expected to change in response to changed stressors. And of course, these changes will be reflected in the impact of the stress process on caregivers and their ability to continue in the role.

Smyer, we might note, raises the interesting question of where we look for change. In the data he presents, the individual is the unit of analysis; that is, change is gauged by comparing individuals with themselves at different points in time. This yields a richly descriptive picture, one reflecting dramatic and volatile change. Yet, when we are searching not only for change but also for its causes and consequences, the comparisons we make are not at an intraindividual level but at a group level. For example, we might want to know if the use of respite facilities relieves the stressors to which one had been exposed and if this, in turn, eases psychological distress. For queries of this order, it is necessary to compare groups of individuals across time.

Whatever the unit taken for analysis, the kinds of dynamic changes that can occur in caregiving are amenable to study only with longitudinal data, although having longitudinal data does not by itself insure that there will be a conceptual sensitivity to such dynamic process. The issue to be recognized is that caregivers face a kaleidoscope of conditions and to understand how the well-being of caregivers changes over time, it is necessary to observe the changing mix of stressors and their mediators. To merely gauge the state of one's well-being or the demands they force at a single point in time will leave us short of our goals. By probing the basic processes driven by chronic stress, we have helped in fathoming what people experience in their continuing role as caregivers. It is by observing these experiences longitudinally that we are best able to understand them in a causal framework. And as we fathom this experience, we shall also learn about the stress process in general and how to form effective intervention programs.

Caregiver Stress Versus Caregiver Careers. Studies of caregiver stress are typically aimed at assessing the costs of caregiving, costs to psychological well-being, physical health, and material stability. Studies, including those that are longitudinal in design, tend to focus their attention on the period of active residential caregiving. It is usually assumed that once the impaired relative is institutionalized or deceased, the stress process is either terminated or radically altered. There is a different perspective that shows signs of emerging: Studies of caregiver stress are beginning to encompass the critical transition points of institutional placement (e.g., Pruchno, Michaels, &

Potashnik, 1990) and death (e.g., Bass, Bowman, & Noelker, 1991). The consideration of these transitions helps to cast the study of caregiving within the framework of careers. This observation, it is recognized, borrows from life-course research, where key transitions represent the important junctures that people move through. One of the features of life-course research is its efforts to ascertain whether the impact of a transition into a new stage is conditioned by the circumstances and experiences of an earlier stage. This kind of perspective offers the prospect of being able to capture the continuities and discontinuities one confronts over a considerable span of time.

An ignored phase of caregiving careers may emerge following the death of the impaired relative: It is the recovery from the stresses of active caregiving and the losses attendant upon death. Recovery may be observable only after the lapse of a lengthy period of time. By recovery we refer both to the diminishment of distress and to such things as the establishment or renewal of social ties, occupational life, and/or interests in organizations and leisure activities. Consequently, the longitudinal design of research must be suffi- cient not only to observe the transitions to institutionalization and death, but also the reintegration that may require well over a year to be discernible. In effect, inquiries only start with caregiving, branching out where relevant into inquiries about activities and experiences associated with the institutional placement of the impaired relative and/or the death of that person, and the bereavement and recovery process that follows. Linking later processes to earlier phases of the career is important; such linkage, we believe, can help shed light on why bereavement and recovery require more time for some former caregivers than others. Our long-range objectives are not simply to observe caregiver stress by itself or recovery alone, but to trace a career that embraces both processes.

Description Versus Explanation.   The growth and evolution of an area of psychosocial inquiry seems typically to follow an established pathway. It begins with description, moves to prediction, and then turns to interpretation and explanation. Research into caregiver stress appears to be proceeding along these lines and we can find ample evidence of its development in the chapters by Avison and his colleagues and by Schulz et al.

Initially, the main effort seemed to be directed toward establishing some phenomenological account of the demands and burdens of caregiving and the bearing of these on the well-being of family caregivers (e.g., Rabins, Mace, & Lucas, 1982). The establishment of these basic descriptions helped to provide the intellectual legitimation for more elaborate inquiry into care- giving, its stresses and consequences. It is fair to state that this legitimacy has been amply established.

It is interesting to note that much of the bed-rock descriptive knowledge of caregiving families and health costs of caregiving came from researchers who have clinical relationships with families. Clinical workers are direct witnesses to the profound effects that can be exerted by long-term caregiving. As the research progressed, it became increasingly concerned with issues of variability in the impact of caregiving on family members. People who appeared to be exposed to the same demands were differentially affected by them and the research questions turned more toward accounting for such differences. The search for explanations, in turn, called for increasingly elaborate research models. These models, first of all, disaggregated the stressors associated with caregiving (Lawton, Kleban, Moss, Ravine, & Glicksman, 1989; Romeis, 1989). That is, they attempt to measure caregiving stress not as a unitary global construct but in terms of its multiple dimensions. Second, they began to pay more attention to mediating conditions, coping, and social support, in particular.

Concomitantly with the conceptual and measurement refinement of caregiving stressors and the inclusion of these mediators, research is beginning to shift its attention from learning whether caregiving is on the whole stressful to the specific circumstances that explain why it is more or less stressful for different people at different times. These explanatory models, we believe, enrich research into caregiving and, in so doing, they help to move the field more into the mainstream of psychosocial stress studies.

Some Nuts and Bolts Choices. There are several methodological and procedural decision points in caregiver research that Schulz et al. allude to, and these deserve attention. Some of these concern sampling, including the sheer size of samples. A number of factors are driving the research toward increasingly large sample sizes. First of all, longitudinal studies demand relatively large samples. This is in part to compensate for sample attrition. Pearlin and his associates (Pearlin et al., 1990), for example, employ a multiwave survey of people, all of whom were originally caring for their relatives at home. Four waves have been completed at this time and at each of the successive waves there was an attrition of between 4% and 5% of the sample. This is a low rate by any standard; however, when it accumulates over multiple waves, the loss of sample can add up to a significant number.

A different pressure for large sample size stems from the career perspective we outlined earlier. Across time, there is a natural breakdown and division of an original sample of active caregivers into those who have placed their relatives and those whose relatives have died. If we continue to include these transition groups in our longitudinal research, rather than to treat them as attrited cases, then the original sample must be of sufficient magnitude so as to lead to eventual subsamples of a size that will permit analyses having a reasonable range of statistical power. Without such power, it would not be possible to place much confidence in the stability of our findings regarding the careers of caregivers.

The final consideration of sample size underlies multivariate analyses in general. We know that there is a broad array of experiences and conditions that influence the impact of caregiving on the well-being of caregivers. To begin to evaluate the contributions that each of these experiences and conditions makes to the outcomes of caregiving—to juggle all of the conditions simultaneously, to borrow Smyer's metaphor—requires a sample of substantial size. This is particularly the case if analyses require the systematic stratification of the sample. Thus, it may be necessary to build the differences between spousal caregivers and those who are adult children into an analysis. Similar analytic stratification might involve the giver–recipient gender mix (i.e., female–male, female–female, etc.). Before one is able to look at the part played by other factors, one must in effect make a multifold division of the sample if it is learned beforehand that such divisions are the bases of different stressful experiences and conditions.

Quite aside from sample size are serious limitations of sample composition and representativeness, the research of Yu and Liu in Shanghai being an outstanding exception. In most cases of studies of Alzheimer's caregivers, however, participants are recruited from the membership lists of organizations—usually the Alzheimer's Disease and Related Disorders Association—from diagnostic centers, from various treatment and service programs, or from some mix of these. The uncomfortable point about these recruitment channels is that each may be drawing people who do not represent the population of families in which there is a member with Alzheimer's disease. Even more at issue is that no estimate of sample bias can be made because the make-up of the population itself is unknown. To the extent that there are families in communities who are "going it alone," not seeking assistance or organizational affiliation, our research findings may not generalize to all caregiving families.

There is no easy or inexpensive way out of this dilemma. The kind of screening done in Shanghai, for example, would be prohibitively costly in the United States. Of course, studies usually do seek samples that are socially, ethnically, and economically diverse, albeit not necessarily representative of an unknown population. Although diversity is a desideratum, it too adds pressure for increased sample size. All in all, there is a good chance that any single study is likely to lack the resources needed to recruit a sample of adequate size and diversity, leave alone representativeness. As a way out of this impasse, we should perhaps begin to think of ways in which investigators might pool samples, to create a consortium of studies. Another strategy also deserves some consideration; this would involve the gathering of a large and representative sample through a nationwide screening effort. Although costly, this sample might then be tapped into by individual studies, thus reducing the sampling costs of a simple study while generally improving the quality of sampling. What can be asserted is that a problem exists that is awaiting a solution.

Turning now from sampling, there is another quandary faced by researchers into caregiving, this one concerning the spacing of interview waves in longitudinal research. We refer specifically to the point raised by Schulz et al. and Smyer about the length of the intervals between interviews or observations that are the data-gathering points in longitudinal research. What should these intervals be? No single answer to this query would satisfy all of the research questions that are likely to be guiding a study.

Ideally, one seeks intervals that are long enough to embrace significant antecedent changes in the conditions of caregiving and in the consequent manifestations of well-being, but not so long that their cause and effect relationships are obscured by the passage of time. The difficulty arises where the antecedents and consequences change at different paces. For example, there may be but a gradual and prolonged increment in the daily activities for which the patient becomes dependent on the caregiver, but the caregiver may experience a comparatively rapid increase in depressiveness with the first slight increment. Or, if the caregiver must give up or reduce outside employment to provide the care, the ensuing loss of income might be rapid but the consequences slow to emerge. A somewhat different problem exists where the antecedents and their consequences arise in close temporal proximity but the consequences are short-lived and, therefore, not likely to be discerned unless the intervals are short. Situations in which there are acute and ephemeral crises whose effects dissipate once the crises have passed would tend to compress cause and effect relationships in this manner.

There are key interrelated dilemmas underlying the selection of time intervals. First, antecedents and their consequences may surface and/or persist at different paces. Thus, antecedents and consequences may march to different drum beats such that their changes are best measured within different intervals of study; this, in turn, makes the establishment of causal relationships more difficult. Second, to the extent that we are not interested in simply observing the emergence of stressful conditions or changes in well-being but in observing the covariations between the two over time, we shall be tempted to expand the interval in order to insure that there will have been time for both changes in the conditions of caregiving and the well-being of the caregiver. However, the larger the interval the more difficult it is to identify with confidence the conditions that affected well-being.

A final brief and related note about design decisions is in order. How long should our longitudinal studies extend? Obviously, this depends on the goals of the study; however, we wish again to underscore that these goals may call for studies of considerable duration. As future studies look more closely at the long-term careers of caregivers—beginning with the early phases of caregiving, into placement and institutionalization, past death and immediate bereavement through recovery — the longer our studies will be extended and the more numerous will be the points of observation. The considerations that guide the design of current research are inadequate to the kinds of questions about caregiver careers that are beginning to surface.

Research and Intervention. Essentially, we have been arguing that to capture the realities of stress and recovery, caregiving inquiries require designs and methodologies that are complex and, unfortunately, costly. The knowledge yielded by such research about basic stress processes and their impact on well-being by itself justifies the effort and resources needed to conduct such elaborate studies. In addition, the utility of this new generation of research can be enhanced to the extent that it can be used as a guide to planned interventions. The next section of this volume deals with a variety of formal programs and we shall not discuss these here. We would argue, however, that much of what we learn about informal caregiving should be incorporated into the substance and range of formal programs.

First, we know that prolonged caregiving may bring one into encounters not only with stressors directly involving caregiving but also with secondary stressors. These involve problems that commonly emerge as a result of having a close relative impaired by Alzheimer's disease but are located in life domains outside of caregiving. As noted earlier, secondary stressors may include family conflicts, economic hardships, occupational cross-pressures, and the constriction of social and leisure life. Once established, these secondary stressors can be as stressful, if not more so, than those linked directly to caregiving activities. Moreover, evidence indicates that they may also painfully alter certain dimensions of self-concept, such as self-esteem.

Without belaboring the issue, it is evident that a worker charged with planning intervention programs could benefit from a mapping of the entire constellation of significant stressors that may be present in the lives of people. To direct efforts at helping people avoid secondary stressors, for example, may be a more effective long-term way to avoid or minimize depression than a program targeted directly and solely to therapies intended to manage depression. Although the latter may certainly be of some use, unless the range of problems leading to the depression are recognized and dealt with, depression and other disorders are likely to stubbornly persist or to resurge after brief relief.

The application of a career perspective also suggests the need for flexible and diverse interventions. Thus, deciding to institutionalize a relative, choosing the appropriate site, dealing with the staff and bureaucratic arrangements of the facility, and maintaining caregiving activities can each be a source of problems and difficulties. And by and large, caregivers are on their own in dealing with them, unable to count on programmatic help.

Similarly, caregivers may face a host of different challenges at the next transition, that which is initiated by the death of the relative. More is involved than ordinary bereavement processes. After many years of having caregiving as the central organizing activity of their lives, caregivers may find that the inevitable restructuring of their lives is threatening. Beyond adaptation to loss is an extended recovery process that includes a social as well as psychological reintegration. Interventions, we submit, might ideally be guided by a career perspective, extending their efforts through caregiving and bereavement and into the recovery process.

REFERENCES

Aneshensel, C. S., Rutter, C. M., & Lackenbruch, P. A. (1991). Social structure, stress, and mental health. *American Sociological Review, 56*(2), 167–178.

Bass, D. M., Bowman, K., & Noelker, L. S. (1991). The influence of caregiving and bereavement on adjusting to an older relative's death. *The Gerontologist, 31*(1), 32–42.

George, L. K. (1990). Caregiving stress studies—there really is more to learn. *The Gerontologist, 30,* 580–581.

Grad, J., & Sainsbury, P. (1968). The effects that patients have on their families in a community care and a control psychiatric service: A 2-year follow-up. *British Journal of Psychiatry, 114,* 265–278.

Kahn, R. L. (1975). The mental health system and the future age. *The Gerontologist, 15*(1), 15–34.

Lawton, M. P., Kleban, M. H., Moss, M., Ravine, M., & Glicksman, A. (1989). Measuring caregiver appraisal. *Journal of Gerontology: Psychological Sciences, 44*(3), 61–71.

Lazarus, R. S., & Folkman, S. (1984). *Stress, appraisal, and coping.* New York: Springer Publishing.

Pasamanick, B., Scarpitti, F., & Dinitz, S. (1967). *Schizophrenia in the community: An experimental study in the prevention of hospitalization.* New York: Appleton-Century-Crofts.

Pearlin, L. I. (1989). The sociological study of stress. *Journal of Health and Social Behavior, 30,* 241–256.

Pearlin, L. I., Mullan, J. T., Semple, S. J., & Skaff, M. M. (1990). Caregiving and the stress process: An overview of concepts and their measures. *The Gerontologist, 30,* 583–594.

Pearlin, L. I., & Schooler, C. (1978). The structure of coping. *Journal of Health and Social Behavior, 19,* 2–231.

Pruchno, R. A., Michaels, J. E., & Potashnik, S. L. (1990). Predictors of institutionalization among Alzheimer disease victims with caregiving spouses. *The Journals of Gerontology: Social Sciences, 45*(6), 259–266.

Rabins, P., Mace, N., & Lucas, M. J. (1982). The impact of dementia on the family. *Journal of American Medical Association, 248,* 333–335.

Romeis, J. C. (1989). Caregiving strain: Toward an enlarged perspective. *Journal of Aging and Health, 1,* 188–208.

Turner, H., & Pearlin, L. I. (1989, Fall). Issues of age, stress, and caregiving: The informal support of people with AIDS. *Generations,* 56–59.

Zarit, S. H. (1989). Do we need another "stress and caregiving" study? *The Gerontologist, 29,* 147.

II

FORMAL SYSTEMS
OF CARE

Introduction to Part II

For a comprehensive understanding of caregiving, we must look not only at informal care but at formal services and their synergistic relationship as well. Families complement the activities of the formal care system. With a larger number of elderly needing care than ever before and having more severe functional disabilities, families perform increasingly complex activities over long periods of time. A major theme in the caregiving literature has been how these activities interfere with other family, work, and social responsibilities. The interface of formal and informal systems of care is critical, because the formal system holds the potential for taking on a portion of responsibility and making the stress on families more manageable.

How formal care can best interact with informal systems is a major issue. A series of related, but sometimes contradictory, goals has guided the development of programs and policies. A prominent trend is to reduce the use of more costly in-patient services (acute hospitals and nursing homes), replacing them with home care. A compatible but different goal is to use community-based services to intervene earlier to reduce the strain on informal caregivers before it becomes overwhelming. As a practical matter, it is often difficult to differentiate between these target populations. Additionally, many factors besides severity of disability determine who is at risk for nursing home placement, including the strength of one's informal care network. Consequently, community programs find themselves serving a large, diverse population, even when their explicit goal is to divert people from nursing homes. When demand for services outstrips resources, programs have sometimes adopted complex formulas for eligibility and delivery of services. In doing so, they have had to make decisions about complicated issues concerning who should be served, what services are to be offered, and how to create efficiencies and reduce unnecessary costs in the delivery of services. The system is continually tugged between serving only the most needy (financially or in terms of disability) and addressing a wider group in the hope that earlier intervention will help families sustain their effort longer and with fewer negative effects on their own lives or the quality of care they give.

The chapters in this section examine innovative approaches to the provision of care and recent research on service utilization. Managed care approaches have been receiving considerable attention for their potential to control the costs of health and long-term care while providing adequate service. Harrington describes one of the most ambitious of recent demonstrations, the Social Health Maintenance Organization (SHMO), which uses a capitation approach for long-term care designed to be cost-effective while delivering a continuum of services. Brannon applies organizational theories in examining the SHMOs and other approaches to managed care, while Niederehe looks at policy and research issues raised by the SHMO demonstration and links them to initiatives specifically focused on Alzheimer's Disease. The chapter by Lévesque is a case study of the ambitious program of home care implemented in the province of Québec. While organized along different principles than the SHMOs, it has encountered some similar economic pressures. Whitlatch identifies several problems and issues that demonstrations such as the Québec program are likely to face.

Why caregivers underutilize available community services has been a major recurring question in service research. Mullan draws upon a theoretical model of adaptation to stress to explore how caregivers' feelings of depression and other factors may result in barriers to obtaining adequate help. Taking a somewhat different tact, Stephens applies a decision-making framework for examining families' use of formal services.

A major event in the care of disabled elders is discharge from an acute hospital. Pressures on hospitals from Medicare and other insurers have reduced inpatient stays and resulted in people being discharged sicker and quicker. Using a unique multimethod approach, Kane and Penrod explore the patterns of care that develop following an acute hospital stay and explore the impact on family caregivers. Townsend takes a broad perspective on service utilization research, examining basic conceptual issues that affect studies in this area.

In a concluding section, Zarit and Pearlin explore the points of junction between informal and formal systems. Basic assumptions about goals and objectives of services and policies as well as methodological issues for studying the relation of these care systems are discussed.

7

Social Health Maintenance Organizations: An Innovative Financing and Service Delivery Model

Charlene Harrington
University of California, San Francisco

Formal and/or informal services are necessities for many who are ill and disabled, particularly the elderly with chronic illnesses. Formal services needed by such individuals include acute and ambulatory care as well as long-term services such as homemakers, home health nurses, transportation, and other such services (Kane & Kane, 1987). Many individuals have difficulty in obtaining access to these services. Barriers to formal services include a fragmented delivery system with no central entry point, the lack of appropriate providers and services in some areas, inadequate or limited benefit coverage for services provided by many public and private insurers, and the inability of some individuals and families to purchase private insurance and/or to pay for services directly out-of-pocket (Harrington, Estes, & Newcomer, 1985; U.S. GAO, 1988).

Having access to basic health and long-term care services is critical in the detection, diagnoses, treatment, and management of illness/disability for individuals and their caregivers and families. Formal services can supplement and/or reduce the need for the provision of informal care services for those who are ill or disabled. Formal services may also serve as a mediator of stress for caregivers (Pearlin, Mullan, Semple, & Skaff 1990). Certainly, it is well recognized that the reverse situation also occurs, where the provision of informal care services can prevent the need for formal services and particularly institutionalization of the frail elderly. Thus, formal and informal services are intricately linked.

Many investigations and reports have criticized the system of financing and delivering health and long-term care in the United States (U.S. Senate, 1988). To address the inadequate formal care system in the United States, a number of demonstrations have been developed since the late 1970s by the Health Care Financing Administration (HCFA) to improve the financing and delivery of services to the frail elderly and their families (Hamm, Kickham, & Cutler, 1982; Kane & Kane, 1987; Kemper, Applebaum, & Harrington, 1987; Weissert, 1985, 1988; Zawadski, 1983). The outcomes of these demonstrations are difficult to evaluate, particularly because many of the individuals receiving services in these demonstrations are frail and have deteriorating conditions. Thus, improvements in health status or lower mortality rates are not necessarily appropriate outcome measures. In this situation, client and caregiver satisfaction and reports become important ways to evaluate the programs. Most of these models have been documented to provide services that are satisfying to clients and/or improve the quality of clients' lives and those of their informal caregivers.

Although the evaluations of these projects have generally been positive, unfortunately, the findings on cost effectiveness from these demonstrations have been mixed. This problem has led to a reluctance by public policy makers to expand the public availability of these programs because of the potentially high financial costs associated with delivering such care. The lack of demonstrated cost-effectiveness has led to the continued search for an improved financing and delivery system model in the United States.

All but two of the HCFA demonstrations have used standard fee-for-service reimbursement mechanisms for long-term care so that the projects had little incentive to control costs (Kemper et al., 1987). In contrast to this reimbursement approach, capitation models have obvious theoretical benefits for controlling costs. These models pay providers on a fixed prepaid monthly basis for each individual member regardless of the amount of services used and providers are placed at financial risk for costs beyond the basic capitation payment. Two capitation models for acute and long care services for the elderly have been developed to test the cost effectiveness of this alternative financing and delivery mechanism: the On Lok demonstration and the Social Health Maintenance Organizations (SHMOs) (Newcomer, Harrington, & Friedlob, 1989, 1990a; Zawadski, 1983). This chapter discusses the Social Health Maintenance Organization model and its experience after 5 years of operation. The SHMO model for formal service delivery has been successful in delivering a wide range of formal services, including case management and long-term care services. These services supplement the efforts of family members and caregivers, although the direct effects on caregivers are not examined in this chapter.

SOCIAL HMO MODEL

The SHMO model includes several unique organizational and financing features. First, a single organizational structure was established to provide a full range of acute and chronic care services to Medicare beneficiaries who enroll on a voluntary basis and pay a monthly premium for services. (The On Lok model also provides a full range of services, but is primarily targeted to individuals with a combination of Medicaid and Medicare coverage, rather than individuals who pay privately). Second, the SHMOs were designed to service a cross section of the elderly population including both the functionally impaired and the well elderly, unlike most demonstrations and On Lok, which were targeted only to the impaired or elderly at high-risk for institutional placement. In order to prevent adverse selection, the SHMOs were, however, allowed to limit their new enrollees to a maximum of 5% who were severely impaired (nursing home certifiable). The overall goal of the demonstration was to keep individuals healthy and perhaps reduce or slow the rate of impairment and disability.

Third, a coordinated case management system was established to approve service authorizations for long-term care for those members who met specified disability criteria (usually two limitations in activities of daily living) within a fixed budget amount of between $6,250-12,000 per year. (In contrast, On Lok provides full financial benefits for its Medicaid members without financial limits.) The SHMO case management system was also designed to improve access to and appropriateness of services delivered, while ensuring cost controls.

Fourth, financing was accomplished through prepaid capitation by pooled funds from Medicare, Medicaid, and member premiums. The initial financial risks were shared by the SHMOs and HCFA, whereas the SHMOs assumed full financing risk at the end of the first 30 months of the demonstration. This design feature was developed to provide an overall financial incentive to the SHMOs to control total program costs while allowing SHMOs greater flexibility in the services provided to members (Harrington & Newcomer, 1985; Leutz et al., 1985). This chapter reviews the SHMO experience in meeting each of the aforementioned objectives for providing services.

EVALUATION METHODS

The findings presented in this chapter are a part of a larger evaluation conducted by the University of California in collaboration with Berkeley Planning Associates, Duke University, and Westat, under a competitively bid contract with the Health Care Financing Administration. The evaluation has two components. The first was to examine the SHMOs as organizations in terms of the financing, management, enrollment, case management, and other features, which are reported on in this chapter. The second component was a large-scale comparison study of three groups of individual Medicare members: (a) those who received services in the traditional delivery system on a fee-for-service basis, (b) those who were enrolled in HMOs with capitated risk sharing contracts, and (c) those who elected to enroll in the SHMOs. This component of the evaluation involved collecting longitudinal data on health status, health service utilization, and expenditures over a 30 month period for each sample group. These data are currently in the analysis phase and are not discussed in this chapter.

Data for this chapter come from aggregate statistical data collected from each of the SHMOs, interviews with SHMO staff and key community informants, and documents collected by the HCFA program evaluators (Newcomer, Harrington, & Friedlob, 1989, 1990a). Respondents included: executive directors and key administrative staff, marketing directors, selected board members, and former staff. The interviews were conducted at the SHMO sites three times between January and December 1986, by telephone in spring 1987, and from on-site interviews during the summers of 1988 and 1989. Focused questions concerned key organization, management, and provider arrangements considered to be related to the financial success of prepaid health plans (Fox, Heinen, & Steele, 1986; Luft, 1987). Correspondence, contracts, board minutes, reports by the sites, audit reports, and other documents were also collected and analyzed to verify and supplement the interview data.

FINDINGS

Organization

The SHMOs were initially established by Brandeis University under a contract with the Health Care Financing Administration. After a delayed start, the SHMO demonstration projects became operational in 1985 (Leutz et al., 1985). The demonstration was tested by four different organizations in different market environments. These new organizational models were established by two types of sponsors: two health maintenance organizations (HMOs) and two long-term care organizations. Kaiser Permanente Northwest, an established HMO in Portland, Oregon, developed one project (Medicare Plus II). A partnership between a mature HMO and an experienced direct long-term care service provider (i.e., Group Health Inc. and Ebenezer Society) in Minneapolis-St. Paul, Minnesota developed Seniors Plus. The Metropolitan Jewish Geriatric Center Inc., a direct service provider in Brooklyn, New York, developed Elderplan. Senior Health Action Network (SCAN), a long-term care service broker in an informal partnership with a large medical center in Long Beach, California, became the sponsor of SCAN Health Plan (SHP).

Enrollment

The first issue was whether elderly individuals would voluntarily enroll in a SHMO organization that offered comprehensive benefits with some long-term care benefits delivered by a single organization. For the elderly, a decision to join an HMO or a SHMO is an important one, because in many cases it requires leaving existing providers or physicians to form new relationships and a willingness to use only the providers offered by the SHMO. This is in contrast to the Medicare fee-for-service program where individuals can chose to go to any provider or physician who accepts Medicare members.

The SHMO demonstration projects did confirm that individual elderly were willing to voluntarily enroll, but the initial enrollment response was disappointing. Although each site had expected to enroll about 4,000 individuals, all sites experienced initial difficulties in obtaining this target, and two sites were not able to reach their targets throughout the first 5 years of the demonstration (see Table 7.1). Elderplan and SHP had no previous Medicare HMO members, so all of their members were new health plan enrollees. In contrast, the two SHMOs sponsored by HMOs converted some of their Medicare members voluntarily from their existing HMO program to the SHMO demonstration (See also Newcomer et al., 1990a; Harrington, Newcomer, & Friedlob, 1989).

A number of factors affected the decisions of individuals regarding whether or not to join the SHMO. Probably the most important one was the HMO market competition in each SHMO area. In 1985, Brooklyn was a newly competitive market (with 7% Medicare enrollment in HMOs in the area); Portland was emerging as a competitive market (16% HMO penetration); and Los Angeles (24% penetration) and Minneapolis-St. Paul (60% penetration) were mature competitive markets. The lowest enrollment occurred at Seniors Plus and SHP in Minneapolis/St. Paul and Long Beach where competition was the greatest, both initially and throughout the 5-year period (Harrington et al., 1989).

Premium levels were also a key factor in consumer choice about enrollment. During the first year, monthly premium levels ranged from $29.50 to $49 (see Table 7.1). SHMO premiums were less than those of competing Medicare supplemental policies, but greater than competing Medicare HMO alternatives. Even though the SHMOs offered additional long-term care benefits beyond those of competing HMOs, the higher price of the SHMOs relative to competing HMOs led to lower enrollment than expected, which was most pronounced in Minneapolis and Long Beach where the competition was greatest (Harrington et al., 1989).

Consumer choice decisions are also greatly affected by public awareness. In a study of the SHMO joiners in comparison to a randomly selected

TABLE 7.1
Differences in Social HMO Enrollment, Premiums, Disability Levels, and Chronic Care Services Received

	1985	1986	1987	1988	1989
Net Enrollment					
Elderplan	770	2,502	4,205	5,000	5,082
Medicare Plus II	3,169	4,309	4,987	5,030	5,412
SCAN Health Plan	1,149	2,075	2,769	3,057	2,824
Seniors Plus	433	1,686	2,572	3,021	3,256
Monthly Premiums					
Elderplan	$29.89	$29.89	$29.89	$29.89	$29.89
Medicare Plus II	49.00	49.00	49.00	57.00	57.85
SCAN Health Plan	40.00	40.00	40.00	40.00	42.00
			24.95[a]	24.95[a]	24.95[a]
Seniors Plus	29.50	24.95	24.95	29.95	34.95
Percent Nursing Home Certified at Year End					
Elderplan	7.5%	4.1%	4.3%	4.8%	5.4%
Medicare Plus II	4.2%	6.7%	8.1%	10.5%	11.4%
SCAN Health Plan	4.0%	5.5%	8.7%	10.0%	7.9%
Seniors Plus	11.5%	7.2%	9.8%	8.1%	8.5%
Percent Receiving Chronic Care at Year End					
Elderplan	4.8%	2.9%	3.1%	2.1%	7.7%
Medicare Plus II	3.4%	4.5%	5.9%	7.3%	7.5%
SCAN Health Plan	8.7%	12.1%	10.0%	9.0%	8.5%
Seniors Plus	13.8%	11.0%	13.0%	12.7%	13.7%

[a]SCAN developed a low-option premium that excluded dental care for 1987.

comparison sample of nonjoiners in each SHMO geographical area, the awareness of the health plan options, including both the relative price and benefits among the competing options, was relatively high among both SHMO joiners and nonjoiners (Newcomer, Harrington, & Friedlob, 1990b). Because awareness of options did not appear to be a problem, local market competition and out-of-pocket cost appeared to be major factors in selection of the SHMOs.

Disability

Another key objective of the demonstration was to enroll a cross section of the elderly population in the SHMOs, including both the functionally impaired and the well elderly. A balanced mix between impaired and well elderly enrollees was needed to make the SHMO organizations financially viable. Each site had a different mix of members in terms of their age, gender, and disability levels. The Medicare rates to each SHMO for their members accounted for these differences by basing payment on the adjusted average per capita costs (AAPCC) for each region, by age, gender, welfare status, health status, and institutional status. Each SHMO received 100% of a modified AAPCC formula for all their Medicare members, subtracting out those community members who were in bed or at home most or all of the time because of a disability, or who needed the help of another person in getting around in the community (about 5% of the community sample). A separate capitation rate was used for the basis of payment for the frail members. Medicare paid 100% of the AAPCC institutional rate for all members living in the community who were determined to be nursing home certifiable according to predetermined state Medicaid criteria for disability. Although the SHMOs were open to Medicaid members and Medicaid would pay for the cost of membership, very few Medicaid recipients joined the SHMOs.

Although these payment adjustments were made for age and disability, the projects were anxious to avoid adverse selection at enrollment that could contribute to financial problems over time. Each SHMO was allowed to limit their new enrollees to a maximum of 5% who were severely impaired (i.e., were nursing home certifiable using state Medicaid criteria). The SHMOs could screen new applicants and place impaired applicants on a waiting list (queing) if they had already enrolled more than five % impaired. Three sites used some screening and queing at different points in the first 5 years (all except Medicare Plus II), to control entry and indirectly to prevent high utilization and costs. Seniors Plus reported that their enrolled population was older and more disabled than their enrollees in their basic Medicare plan (Seniors), and so they used queing throughout the demonstration period.

Table 7.1 shows the percentage of SHMO members who were severely impaired (and thus categorized as being certifiable for nursing home care even though the individuals may not have used nursing home care). Initially, the percentage certified for nursing home care ranged from 4% at Medicare Plus II and SHP to 7.5% at Elderplan and 11.5% at Seniors Plus. Therefore, two sites had less than the 5% expected to be severely impaired and two had more than expected. Although the percentage severely disabled increased gradually over the 5-year period at Medicare Plus II, the other SHMOs had varying levels of impairment over the same period. The issue of whether or not the plans had biased selection are being addressed in a separate publication where each SHMO impairment level is compared to the percentage impaired in the community (Manton, Tolley, Vertress, Newcomer, & Harrington, 1990).

Service Benefits

Each SHMO established a single organizational structure to provide a full range of acute and chronic care services to Medicare beneficiaries who enrolled on a voluntary basis and paid a monthly premium for services. The benefits included all those basic benefits required under Medicare including hospital, physician, nursing home, home health, hospice, and other related services. It also included an expanded care benefit package of nonemergency transportation, outpatient prescription drugs, hearing aides, eyeglasses, and other such services, as well as chronic care services. All sites included drugs benefits with minimal copayments ($1–$2 per prescription), except for SHP in 1989.

Chronic care services included custodial nursing home services, nonskilled home care services, homemaker, respite, and other such services. Chronic care benefits varied across demonstration sites and were limited to small, fixed benefit packages (ranging from $6,250–$12,000 per year) with copayments (see Table 7.2). Clients (or Medicaid) paid for any benefits required beyond the level allowed by the SHMO. Two sites retained their chronic care benefits throughout the 5-year period. SCAN Health Plan and Seniors Plus both changed their nursing home benefits in 1988 and 1989 in an effort to limit their chronic care nursing home utilization and costs. Thus, the SHMOs were able to retain the home and community benefits and the copayment levels, but limited nursing home services in the last 2 years in response to their nursing home utilization and cost experience.

Eligibility for Chronic Care Benefits

All SHMO members were eligible to receive benefits covered by Medicare (i.e., hospital, physician, skilled nursing home, skilled home health services, hospice, and durable medical equipment), so these benefits did not vary across sites. Each SHMO, however, established its own eligibility levels for chronic care services. Case managers conducted assessments on individuals to determine eligibility and reassessments on a periodic basis, authorized the use of chronic care services, and monitored service use and eligibility. Throughout the 5-year period, Medicare Plus II offered benefits only to severely impaired individuals (i.e., those who met the nursing home certification criteria of one limitation in activities of daily living (ADLs) or more). Elderplan and SHP initially offered chronic care benefits to those who were severely impaired and also to those with moderate impairments levels. After the first year, Elderplan restricted benefits to the severely impaired. SHP restricted its benefits to those with severe impairments beginning in 1988. Seniors Plus offered chronic care services to all its members based upon need and not disability levels; these included the moderately and severely impaired and others considered at risk of increasing disability. As a result, eligibility criteria at Seniors Plus were more generous at baseline and have continued to be so throughout the 5-year period.

TABLE 7.2
Differences in Social HMO Chronic Care Benefits

Chronic Care Benefit	1985	1986	1987	1988	1989
Elderplan					
Home & Community	$6,500/yr	no change	no change	no change	no change
Nursing Home	$6,500/yr	no change	no change	no change	no change
Overall Limit	$6,500/yr	no change	no change	no change	no change
Home Care Co-pay	10% of charges	no change	no change	no change	no change
Nursing Home Co-pay	20% of charges	no change	no change	no change	no change
Medicare Plus II					
Home & Community	$12,000/yr	no change	no change	no change	no change
Nursing Home	$12,000/yr or 100 days per stay	no change	no change	no change	30 days per spell of illness
Overall Limit	$12,000/yr	no change	no change	no change	no change
Home Care Co-pay	10% of charges	no change	no change	no change	no change
Nursing Home Co-pay	10% of charges	no change	no change	no change	no change
SCAN Health Plan					
Home & Community	$7,500/yr	no change	no change	$625/month	$625/month
Nursing Home	$7,500/yr	no change	no change	$1,000/mo. $9,400/lifetime	21 days per stay $7,500/lifetime
Overall Limit	$7,500/yr and 9,400/lifetime	no change	no change	no change	$7,500/year
Home Care Co-pay	$5.00/visit	no change	no change	$7.50/visit	$7.50/visit
Nursing Home Co-pay	15% of charges	no change	no change	20% of charges	20% of charges
Seniors Plus					
Home & Community	$6,250/yr	no change	no change	$7,200	$7,200
Nursing Home	$6,250/yr $7,800 lifetime	no change	no change	21 days per spell	21 days per spell
Overall Limit	$6,250/yr	no change	no change	$7,200/yr	7,200/yr
Home Care Co-pay	20% of charges	no change	no change	no change	no change
Nursing Home Co-pay	20% of charges	no change	no change	no change	no change

Service Use and Expenditures

Individuals enrolled in the SHMOs to receive a combination of acute and long-term care services through one coordinated delivery system. One primary goal of the demonstration projects was to deliver this range of services, while controlling overall service utilization and expenditures.

Acute and Ambulatory Care. The primary problem experienced by the SHMOs was managing and controlling hospital utilization and expenditures. The average hospital days per 1,000 members per year at the SHMOs was 1,780-2,270 and the average length of stay was 6-10 days in 1989. Although the SHMOs were able to stay below their target hospital utilization rates and close to the national averages for HMOs, the SHMOs considered utilization a problem (except Medicare Plus II) and invested considerable resources in tracking hospital use and attempting to reduce utilization. The two SHMOs sponsored by HMOs were generally able to keep days of care, length of stay, and admission rates lower than the other two SHMOs throughout the 5-year period. Hospital expenses represented a high proportion of the total SHMO budget (from 29%-40% in 1989) so that case managers and SHMO staff focused special attention on trying to reduce hospital utilization at most of the sites.

Ambulatory care utilization varied across sites, with the two HMO sponsored SHMOs generally having lower utilization in the first 3 years (see Table 7.3). In the fourth year, Elderplan and SHP were able to reduce the number of ambulatory care encounters and referrals, so that the utilization patterns across the sites were very similar. Ambulatory care expenditure patterns were similar at the projects (except for Seniors Plus, which was lower until 1989), ranging between $103-$126 per member per month for 1989 or from 26%-36% of total expenditures. The extent to which SHMOs substituted between ambulatory care and acute or long-term care services has not yet been analyzed.

Medicare Skilled Nursing Home and Home Health Care Services. Medicare skilled nursing utilization rates varied across sites (Table 7.3). These rates were lowest at Seniors Plus by half, even though it had a substantially higher proportion of its members eligible for chronic care services (Table 7.1). Elderplan also had low skilled nursing utilization, but had fewer members eligible for services. Interestingly, by 1989, all the plans had similar utilization patterns for skilled nursing homes, and sharp increases in the number of skilled nursing home days per 1,000 members. This increase was attributed by the SHMOs to a change in Medicare eligibility rules in 1988 and 1989.

Medicare home health care utilization tended to show a reverse pattern to

TABLE 7.3
Utilization of Chronic Care Services Across S/HMO Sites per 1,000 Members per Year

	1985	1986	1987	1988	1989
Elderplan					
Chronic Care SNF/ICF Days	199	835	1,012	425	1,636
Chronic Care Home Health Visits[a]	273	78	299	178	0
Chronic Care Respite, Homemaker Home Aide and Chore Hours[b]	40,165	21,154	18,926	15,923	40,277
Day Care Center Days[c]	151	224	146	20	15
Medicare Plus II[d]					
Chronic Care SNF/ICF Days	613	1,426	2,342	2,339	1,050
Chronic Care Home Health Visits[a]	–	100	99	83	38
Chronic Care Respite, Homemaker Home Aide and Chore Hours	4,180	7,849	11,927	14,400	16,090
Day Care Center Days	138	191	280	469	880
SCAN Health Plan					
Chronic Care SNF/ICF Days	1,487	1,852	5,551	5,100	831
Chronic Care Home Health Visits[a]	199	70	6	1	0
Chronic Care Respite, Homemaker Home Aide and Chore Hours	10,787	15,589	7,020	3,996	4,520
Day Care Center Days	145	633	129	447	279
Seniors Plus					
Chronic Care SNF/ICF Days	2,562	1,815	1,983	1,140	458
Chronic Care Home Health Visits[a]	608	588	4,807	1,470	377
Chronic Care Respite, Homemaker Home Aide and Chore Hours	17,364	12,157	4,369	9,226	8,907
Day Care Center Days	2,516	1,162	936	757	1,009

Source: S/HMO Demonstration projects; quarterly reports. Note: These are unaudited data. Elderplan and Medicare Plus II was based on authorizations. All other sites based on actual utilization.

[a]Includes all home health visits by registered nurse, physical, occupational, and speech therapists, hospice, and social worker.

[b]Elderplan reported a total of 385 private duty nursing hours during 1985, and 2,320 hours during 1986. Elderplan did not report any totals for chronic care nursing home health visits during July and August of 1986.

[c]Includes social day care and day treatment center days.

[d]Chronic care benefits were not offered to Medicaid members under the terms of the state Medicaid contract so that utilization is only calculated for Medicare member months at Medicare Plus II. Medicare Plus II reported a total of 1,741 home health aide visits and 363 homemaker visits in 1986.

that of nursing home use. Home health visits per 1,000 members were highest at Elderplan, Medicare Plus II, and Seniors Plus, suggesting that these sites may have been substituting home care for skilled nursing home care services. In contrast, SHP had high skilled nursing use and low home health care utilization. Medicare nursing home costs were $11–$19 per member per month (pmpm) and home health care costs were $3–$8 pmpm at the SHMOs in 1989.

Case Management. A coordinated case management system (entitled resource coordination at Medicare Plus II) was established at each SHMO. Case management services at the SHMOs covered a broad range of activities but reflected traditional case management functions of assessment, care planning, and service arrangement (Yordi, 1988, 1990). In addition, case managers approved service authorizations for long-term care for those members who met specified disability criteria within a pre-fixed annual budget of $6,250–$12,000 for each individual. The case management system was also designed to improve access and appropriateness of services delivered, while ensuring cost controls.

The SHMOs varied substantially in the amount of case management services provided (Yordi, 1988, 1990). The variations can be explained, in part, by the differences in eligibility for service and benefit levels discussed earlier, and by differences in administrative, clerical, and other support staff time. Case management at the two SHMOs sponsored by HMOs (Medicare Plus II and Seniors Plus), for example, did not include activities associated with utilization review and discharge planning, which were performed by HMO personnel for SHMO members. In contrast, Elderplan and SHP included discharge planning and utilization review in their case management activities.

The SHMOs had wide variation in the percentage of their members who received case management services (see Table 7.1). The number who were eligible (all those who were severely impaired shown on Table 7.1) can be compared to the number who actually received services at each site. For example, Medicare Plus II was able to keep the number receiving services well below the number eligible for each year. Elderplan also showed a similar pattern except for 1989.

Not all members eligible for chronic care services actually received services, for reasons that were not clear. Each site established its own procedures for service authorization to control costs and thus had ways of controlling costs below the generally authorized amounts. Members could receive services above the authorized amount if they were willing to pay for the nonauthorized services. The extent to which this occurred will be the subject of a later report by the evaluators.

In other situations, case managers worked closely with individual members and caregivers to plan benefit utilization in order to spread the available benefits throughout the 5-year period. In still other situations, the SHMOs reported that members and/or caregivers were reluctant to accept the benefits offered. For example, some were reluctant to accept an authorized home-maker into the home or in other cases, there was a mismatch between the type of homemaker available and the preference of the members and/or caregiver. Generally, the SHMOs reported good relationships with the members and caregivers with whom they were working and reported general high levels of satisfaction with the chronic care and case management services. Overall, the reasons for and effects of low long-term care service use at some of the sites could not be fully understood using aggregate site data, and will be addressed in later analyses.

Case management costs represented a small portion of overall SHMO expenditures ranging from 2% to 3% of the SHMO budgets in 1989 (about $7-11 pmpm). Seniors Plus had the highest proportion of its members using chronic care and case management services (see Table 7.1) and yet were able to keep their case management costs at a low level, by having a high patient to case manager ratio. Elderplan also had low case management costs, but had fewer members using case management services than any other site.

Chronic Care Services.   There were substantial variations across sites in chronic care utilization rates and patterns. These variations were attributable, in part, to differences in SHMO site benefits, eligibility criteria for services, case management procedures, and the proportion of members receiving services as discussed earlier (see Table 7.1). The same pattern as the Medicare nursing home service utilization was revealed in a comparison of non-Medicare-covered chronic care nursing service utilization across the four sites. Table 7.4 shows that in 1989, Seniors Plus had the lowest chronic nursing home service use rates and somewhat higher home and homemaker utilization. SHP had the reverse pattern with high nursing home use and lower home health and homemaker use. SHP's and Seniors Plus chronic care nursing home utilization were expected to be higher, because both plans had higher proportions of eligible members. In spite of higher proportions eligible for services, Seniors Plus was generally able to control its chronic care utilization. Elderplan had the highest chronic care utilization in both nursing home and homemaker services, but the lowest number certified as needing care and receiving services. Medicare Plus II also had a consistently high use of chronic care nursing home and homemaker services in comparison to other sites. The total chronic care expenditures per member per month also varied across the sites ($19-$44 pmpm in 1989).

Expanded Care Services.   Benefits and utilization of expanded care services such as pharmacy, dental, transportation, and other services varied across sites. Prescription use rates ranged from 18-19 scripts per member per year at Medicare Plus II and SHP in 1989. It is not known how these prescription use rates compare with those of other Medicare HMOs that offer drug benefits, but anecdotal reports by HMOs suggest that other HMOs also have high rates. The SHMOs all reported a number of efforts to control prescription costs over the 5-year period. Two sites (Elderplan and SHP)

TABLE 7.4
Utilization of Expanded Care Services Across S/HMO Sites per 1,000 Members per Year

	1985	1986	1987	1988	1989
Elderplan					
Dental Office Visits	443	257	391	235	361
Outpatient Prescriptions	15,060	18,172	15,594	6,674	NA
Optometry and Audiology Visits	1,191	645	613	167	348
Eyeglasses & Hearing Aids, and					
Durable Medical Equipment (Pieces)	585	297	285	282	96
Emergency Response System (Months)	41	24	9	7	7
Medical Transportation (Round Trips)[a]	2,235	2,162	1,223	523	996
Medicare Plus II					
Dental Office Visits	NA	NA	NA	NA	NA
Outpatient Prescriptions	13,912	15,660	18,141	22,506	18,756
Optometry and Audiology Visits	NA	NA	NA	NA	NA
Eyeglasses, Hearing Aids, and	609	408	346	308	329
Durable Medical Equipment (Pieces)					
Emergency Response System (Months)	0	15	28	64	76
Medical Transportation (Round Trips)[a]	39	75	98	176	156
SCAN Health Plan					
Dental Office Visits	–	–	–	–	NA
Outpatient Prescriptions[b]	19,305	20,693	21,673	20,288	17,556
Optometry and Audiology Visits	–	–	77	–	335
Eyeglasses, Hearing Aids, and	804	686	1,549	322	221
Durable Medical Equipment (Pieces)					
Emergency Response System (Months)	20	33	108	110	65
Medical Transportation (Round Trips)[a]	109	571	518	246	223
Seniors Plus					
Dental Office Visits	1,778	1,140	–	29	121
Outpatient Prescriptions	–	–	–	–	–
Optometry and Audiology Visits	2,017	1,713	–	1,580	1,397
Eyeglasses & Hearing Aids and	–	–	219	303	295
Durable Medical Equipment (Pieces)					
Emergency Response System (Months)	71	74	86	103	130
Medical Transportation (Round Trips)[a]	839	803	715	962	1,063

SOURCE: S/HMO Demonstration projects; quarterly reports. *Note:* These are unaudited data. Elderplan and Medicare Plus II data based on authorizations. All other sites based on actual utilization.

[a]Includes ambulance, ambulette (i.e., invalid coach), and private care service (with or without assistance).

[b]Decrease in utilization was due to reduction in the benefit levels so that the utilization reported is only what SCAN covered.

offered dental benefits and Seniors Plus offered preventive dental benefits until 1989. Utilization rates for eyeglasses, hearing aids, and durable medical equipment were 96–329 units per 1,000 members per year. The expenditure rates for expanded care ranged from $24–$52 pmpm in 1989, and a large proportion of these expenses were for the prescription drug benefits.

Consumer Satisfaction and Disenrollment

Another component of the evaluation examined the consumer satisfaction of SHMO members with a randomly selected Medicare fee-for-services comparison group in each SHMO geographical area and of those SHMO members who disenrolled. Preliminary data from this analysis shows that SHMO members and their comparison groups were well satisfied with their health and medical services (Newcomer, Weinstock, & Harrington, 1989). The primary area where differences occurred was that SHMO members were more satisfied with the wait in the physicians office and with the financial benefits of the SHMOs, and less satisfied with being able to obtain appointments quickly, how thorough the doctors were, continuity in seeing the same doctors, or having their questions answered. For those individuals who had used nursing home or home care services, the SHMO members appeared generally more satisfied than comparison group members (Newcomer, Weinstock, & Harrington, 1989).

Another indicator of satisfaction is the disenrollment rates from the SHMOs. Generally the SHMO disenrollment rates were slightly lower than those for HMOs. The rates varied across projects, and were lower for the SHMOs sponsored by established HMOs, and higher for the SHMOs sponsored by long-term care organizations. When individuals were asked the major reasons for disenrollment, the primary reason was that disenrollees considered the premiums to be too high, or they cited other financial reasons (47% of disenrollees). Others were dissatisfied with their physician and medical services (45%). There was also some evidence of higher disenrollment rates among the impaired at the two SHMOs sponsored by the long-term care organizations (Harrington, Weinstock, & Newcomer, 1989). The findings suggested that the SHMOs should focus greater efforts on preventing disenrollment among the impaired elderly.

Overall Financial Experience

Revenues were from primarily Medicare payments (77%–86%), but also included subscriber premiums, Medicaid, copayments, and other sources. The average revenues varied across site and were based in part on the age, gender, disability status, and location of the members. Total average expenditures, including financial reserves, ranged from $267–684 pmpm in 1985, to $331–$404 pmpm in 1989. During the period of 1985–1988, the average expenditures declined (except at Medicare Plus II), in part, because the projects lowered their marketing and administrative costs. Even though Medicare Plus II was the most successful of the SHMO projects in reaching its membership goals, in having low marketing and administrative costs and maintaining low service utilization, Medicare Plus II was the only project that showed losses over the 5-year period, (including $2 million in losses in 1989) (see Harrington & Newcomer, 1991).

The projects were more expensive to start-up than expected, and the financial losses were greater than expected. SHP lost $4 million in the first 3 years and then achieved a $1.2 million financial gain in the fourth and fifth years of the demonstration. Seniors Plus had overall losses of $1.9 million over the 5 years (even though it had a small net gain in year four). Elderplan had about $11 million in losses in the first 4 years and broke even in the fifth year. Medicare Plus II had $4 million in losses for the 5-year period. The two sites that were not sponsored by HMOs (SHP and Elderplan) had the largest start-up costs and incurred large debts but were able to make payments on their debts during the fourth year of operation.

Because of lower-than-expected Medicare and Medicaid enrollments during the first 3 years of operation, the SHMOs (except Kaiser) overestimated their total revenues. Low revenues and high administrative costs related to SHMO start-up were especially problematic for the new HMOs (Elderplan and SHP). The SHMOs underestimated the marketing effort needed and these costs became high for the three SHMOs with low enrollments as they attempted to reach their enrollment goals.

In general, the financial losses experienced by the SHMOs were not related to the delivery of long-term care services, but rather were primarily related to acute care utilization and costs. Overall, all the SHMOs were able to control their chronic care utilization and expenditures by a combination of methods. These methods included: (a) limiting benefits in terms of total dollar amounts with sizable copayments, (b) using case managers to limit eligibility to those who were impaired, (c) using case managers to limit chronic care service use, and (d) developing contractual arrangements with providers for chronic care services. In this sense, the SHMOs were successful in staying within their budgets. Whether these types of limited chronic care benefits and strict utilization controls are attractive to enough healthy individuals so that adequate numbers can be enrolled without adverse selection is still an open question, at least at sites where there is heavy Medicare HMO competition.

The revenues and losses of each SHMO had important impacts on its sponsor/partner. Although the SHMOs brought in new revenues, which were important to each of the sponsors/partners, the losses and opportunity costs were greater than expected at a time when all of the sponsors/partners were experiencing some financial difficulties of their own. In retrospect, the sponsors/parent organizations, except for KP Northwest, reported that they did not understand the potential financial problems involved in sponsoring the SHMO demonstration projects. All four of the organizations that undertook the demonstrations experienced some unexpected form of financial problems unrelated to the demonstration during the initial period of the demonstration. These financial problems contributed to the pressures for the SHMOs to achieve greater efficiency and tighten utilization controls during the period of full financial risk.

CONCLUSIONS

Congress approved language in the 1991 budget reconciliation act that gave the current SHMO demonstrations a waiver for continued operation and authorized the establishment of four new demonstration projects. Thus, Congress and the President expressed their support for the concept of the SHMOs and for continued study of this type of plan. Even though efforts are being made to continue these demonstrations, there are a number of inherent problems that have yet to be resolved in the program design and operation.

There are several problems that limit potential membership in SHMOs. Individuals joining a SHMO demonstration must be willing to change to an SHMO physician. Moreover, joining a SHMO may reduce their insurance options. Individuals who give up their supplemental health insurance when they join a SHMO (because they do not want to pay premiums both for the SHMO and a supplemental policy) and later develop a chronic illness may not be able to purchase another supplemental insurance policy should they wish to leave the SHMO. Private insurance companies are allowed to screen potential members for preexisting medical conditions and to deny coverage if such conditions exist. If medical conditions occur, SHMO members have limited options of remaining in a SHMO or joining another HMO (because HMOs are not allowed to screen members for health conditions). Moreover, many older people do not have high enough incomes to be able to afford the extra premiums required by the SHMOs.

The relatively small long-term care benefit package ($6,250–$12,000) offered by the SHMOs limits the value of the model for insurance purposes of protecting individuals from catastrophic long-term care costs. On the other hand, if the SHMO premiums were raised in order to increase the size of the long-term care benefit package, the number of individuals willing to enroll would no doubt be reduced.

From the consumer and caregiver perspective, individuals must weigh a number of factors in decisions to join a SHMO or to remain enrolled in a SHMO. These decisions take into account the premium costs, their perceived risk for needing long-term care services, the acute and long-term care benefits offered, their satisfaction with the providers and case managers, their experience in obtaining services needed, and many other considerations. As the SHMOs encounter greater pressures to control costs, they become less distinguished from their HMO competitors and may have greater difficulty selling their product, especially to healthy elderly. The ability of the SHMOs to offer a desirable long-term care service package at a reasonable price will strongly influence their future success.

Looking to the future, the ultimate test remains whether the four established SHMOs can become viable financial organizations or product lines within larger HMO organizations and survive after the SHMOs demonstration period is over. Presumably the SHMOs will be able to make use of their initial experience to bring greater efficiencies to the management of the program along with greater accuracy in financial planning. SHMOs also need to have a larger membership if they are to obtain economies of scale or greater efficiency. Their ability to enroll larger numbers has not proven to be an easy task. Large, expensive marketing efforts were not as successful as expected. Moreover, the two HMO sponsored plans have appeared reluctant to develop a large membership until they had more experience with the demonstration and a clearer understanding about the status of the enrollees after the demonstration period is over.

The real future of SHMOs to a great extent hinges on the future of the Medicare capitated HMO plans (paid on a monthly rate adjusted for age, gender, and geographical region). Since the late 1980s, many HMOs have suggested that the Medicare capitated reimbursement rates were too low and have been reluctant to expand their Medicare enrollment. Thus, the overall number of Medicare enrollees in HMOs has not grown as rapidly as when the program first began in 1985. The demonstration project has reinforced the awareness of the difficulties in controlling hospital and physician costs which are key components of the overall costs for both HMOs and SHMOs. Currently, HMOs can develop high-option SHMO plans with long-term care services either under their Medicare capitation contract or as a new SHMO demonstration project. Even though many HMOs may find this approach attractive as a service to their Medicare members, most will continue to be reluctant as long as the financial risk of such projects appears to exist. Under these conditions, the SHMO concept must be viewed as an exciting approach with a financial risk attached both for providers and for potential members. Thus, the development of this model will need considerable more time before it will be accepted on any widespread basis.

ACKNOWLEDGMENT

The research for this study was supported by the Health Care Financing Administration (Contract No. HCFA 85–034/CP).

REFERENCES

Fox, P. D., Heinen, L., & Steele, R. J. (1986). *Determinants of HMO success.* Contract No. BHMORD-240-83-0095. Washington, DC: Office of Health Maintenance Organizations.

Hamm, L. V., Kickham, T. M., & Cutler, D. A. (1982). Research, demonstrations, and evaluations. In R. J. Vogel, & H. C. Palmer (Eds.), *Long-term care: perspectives from research and demonstrations.* Health Care Financing Administration, Washington, DC: U.S. Government Printing Office.

Harrington, C., Estes, C. L., Newcomer, R. J. (1985). *Long-term care of the elderly: public policy issues.* Beverly Hills, CA: Sage Publications.

Harrington, C., & Newcomer, R. J. (1985). Social health maintenance organizations: An innovative model for the aged, blind, and disabled. *Journal of Public Health Policy, 6*(2), 204–222.

Harrington, C., & Newcomer, R. J. (1991). Social health maintenance organizations' service use and costs, 1985–1989. *Health Care Financing Review, 12,*(3), 37–52.

Harrington, C., Newcomer, R. J., & Friedlob, A. (1989a, September). Medicare Beneficiary Enrollment in S/HMO. In R. J. Newcomer, C. Harrington, & A. Friedlob (Eds.), *Social/health maintenance organization demonstration evaluation: Report on the first thirty months.* (Contract No. HCFA 85-034/CP). Washington, DC: U.S. Government Printing Office.

Harrington, C., Weinstock, P., & Newcomer, R. J. (1989, September). *Consumer satisfaction, disability and service use of S/HMO disenrollees.* Paper presented at the annual meeting of the Gerontological Society of America, Minneapolis, MN.

Kane, R. A., & Kane, R. L. (1987). *Long-term care: Principles, programs, and policies.* New York: Springer.

Kemper, P., Applebaum, R., & Harrigan, M. (1987, Summer). Community care demonstrations: What have we learned? *Health Care Financing Review, 8,* 87–100.

Leutz, W. N., Greenberg, J. N., Abrahams, R., Protlas, J., Diamond, L. M., & Gruenberg, L. (1985). *Changing health care for an aging society: Planning for the social health maintenance organization.* Lexington, MA: Lexington/Heath.

Luft, H. S. (1987). *Health maintenance organizations: Dimensions of performance.* New Brunswick, NJ: Transition Books.

Manton, K., Tolley, D., Vertress, J., Newcomer, R., & Harrington, C. (1990). *Assessment of selection bias in four social health maintenance organizations.* Durham, NC: Duke University Press.

Newcomer, R. J., Harrington, C., & Friedlob, A. (1989). *Social/health maintenance organization demonstration evaluation: Report on the first thirty months.* (Contract No. HCFA 85-034/CP). Washington, DC: Government Printing Office.

Newcomer, R. J., Harrington, C., & Friedlob, A. (1990a). Social health maintenance organizations: Assessing their initial experience. *Health Services Research, 25*(3), 425–454.

Newcomer, R. J., Harrington, C., & Friedlob, A. (1990b). Awareness and enrollment in the Social/HMO. *The Gerontologist, 30*(1), 86–93.

Newcomer, R. J., Weinstock, P., & Harrington, C. (1989). *Comparison of the consumer satisfaction of medicare beneficiaries in S/HMO and fee-for-service.* Paper Presented at the annual meeting of the Gerontological Society of America, Minneapolis, MN.

Pearlin, L. I., Mullan, J. T., Semple, S. J., & Skaff, M. M. (1990). Caregiving and the stress process: An overview of concepts and their measures. *The Gerontologist, 30*(5), 583–594.

U. S. General Accounting Office (GAO) (1988, November). *Long-term care for the elderly: Issues of need, access, and cost* (Report No. HRD-89-4 to the Subcommittee on Health, Committee on Ways and Means, House of Representatives). Washington, DC: U.S. General Accounting Office.

U. S. Senate. (1989, January 28). *Developments in aging: 1988, Vols. 1-3.* (Report No. 100-291 of the Special Committee on Aging, United States Senate). Washington, DC: U.S. Government Printing Office.

Weissert, W. G. (1985). Seven reasons why it is so difficult to make community-based long-term care cost-effective. *Health Services Research, 20*(4), 423–433.

Weissert, W. G. (1988). The national channeling demonstration: What we knew, know now, and still need to know. *Health Services Research, 23*(1), 175–187.

Yordi, C. (1988). Case management in the social health maintenance organization demonstrations. *Health Care Financing Review, Annual Supplement,* 83–88.

Yordi, C. (1990). *Case management practice in the S/HMO demonstrations.* Oakland, CA: Berkeley Planning Associates.

Zawadski, R. T. (1983). The Long-term care demonstration projects: What they are and why they came into being. *Home Health Care Services Quarterly, 4*(3/4), 3–19.

Are SHMOs Remedies
to Bureaucracy?

Diane Brannon
The Pennsylvania State University

Providing care for dependent elders consumes large and increasing amounts of resources from this society. We pay for it, and in more striking ways than we can even imagine, our children will pay for it with their time, their energy, and their direct and indirect monetary contributions. All of these contributions represent lost opportunities for those in our society who have struggled hard to achieve such opportunities. Women and the nonwealthy, of course, bear the brunt of caregiving costs. This fact alone makes elder care a problem of social structure even while it is one of family structure.

Charlene Harrington reported on an experiment in the organization and financing of acute and long-term care services to the elderly. As a publicly supported experiment, the Social Health Maintenance Organizations (SHMOs) are an attempt to rationalize the formal care system by increasing access to a range of services under payment mechanisms that encourage cost containment. Key to the expectation that more appropriate service utilization will result is the meshing of acute and long-term care services under a single organization and the use of client case management.

This section is an attempt to put the policy developments Harrington has described in the context of a sociological framework, focusing on the uneasy interface between families and the formal health care system. The goal is to examine this uneasy interface in search of a more refined answer to the question of to what problem is the SHMO a potential solution. In so doing, I introduce another aspect of social structure, bureaucracy, as it affects elder care. I begin by recognizing my reliance upon the thinking of sociologist Eugene Litwak, whose book *Helping the Elderly: The Complementary Roles of Informal Networks and Formal Systems* (1985) outlines the awkwardness with which nursing homes as bureaucratic organizations substitute for families as primary groups.

In thinking about how I would approach this topic, it occurred to me that I am prepared neither to idealize family and other informal caregiving nor to defend the care provided by formal systems. I am reminded of a statement made last year at the Retirement Research Foundation's meeting on autonomy in long-term care. Geriatrician Joanne Lynn shared her physician father's position that the concerns of families of the elderly should be taken seriously by health care providers because, the statement went, "families visit grave sites, physicians do not." Implied here is the power of familial attachment. Someone else in attendance pointed out, however, that not all families visit gravesites. Implied here are the myriad of involuntary and voluntary ways in which that attachment is incomplete in modern family life.

FAMILIES AS CAREGIVING SYSTEMS

Families as caregiving systems are neither simple nor stable social forms (Pearlin, Mullan, Semple, & Skaff, 1990). The Pearlin et al. (1990) conceptual model of Alzheimer's caregiver stress clearly depicts the multidimensional nature of family caregiving. Each individual familial system brings complexity to the occasion of elder care, complexity derived from many sources in its own social history and current context. Some of these sources of complexity are: (a) the family's dual histories (families of origin), (b) its relationship patterns, (c) its network of loosely and tightly held beliefs, (d) its size and gender distribution, and (e) its internal allocations of wealth and status.

Likewise, family caregivers change. They move away, get married, get divorced, get sick, hurt, stressed, strained, or they, themselves, get old and frail. In some situations, they cross the line and become abusive. The thorough treatment of family caregiving among gerontologists (Zarit, 1989) has made clear that although family care of frail elders is valued and pervasive in our society, it is far from a perfect solution to the problem of caring for dependent elders.

BUREAUCRACIES AS CAREGIVING SYSTEMS

Formal long-term care of the elderly, it has been noted by many, does not represent the failure of family care. Rather we have come to recognize, or perhaps it would be more accurate to say envision, a continuum of informal and formal, chronic and acute care services for the elderly. It is not a really a continuum at all, however, in the sense of a linear system of components characterized by relatively smooth transitions in both directions. Instead, individuals and families face a significant step or discontinuity where care enters the realm of formal organizations. It is, in short, a very different ball game.

Litwak (1985) made the point that institutions are more efficient providers of personal care than are families. This efficiency, he noted, is derived not only from economies of scale, but also from routinizing care and eliminating nonessential services. Indeed, the nursing home research group of which I am a part has observed that the core routines carried out in resident care are decidedly, sometimes shockingly, assembly-line oriented (Smyer, Cohn, & Brannon, 1988). There is a reason they are called "care routines." Bureaucracies are excellent purveyors of the routine. That elderly nursing home residents are among the most complex patients to enter the health care system does not perturb the bureaucratic routine in the nursing home setting.

Despite their lack of sensitivity to individual differences, bureaucratic systems enjoy a kind of eminent domain in all aspects of social life outside the family. Their stability provides the infrastructure for American society that keeps working despite the most severe political traumas. They can be counted on, and that is not an insignificant virtue, as noted in Weber's original description of bureaucratic principles (Gerth & Mills, 1946).

CONTRASTING CAREGIVING STYLES

Understanding the structural differences between the experience of family care and that of formal care provided by bureaucratic systems seems fundamental to understanding the approach–avoidance phenomenon that characterizes social policy and service utilization in this country. Why clients or caregivers avoid seeking help from available formal support systems, thereby increasing the likelihood of a higher level of need, may be explained, in part, by looking at some of the major contrasts between bureaucracies and informal social structures such as families.

What is unique about familial care is that family members value other family members in a particularistic rather than universalistic fashion. No objectivity is claimed or expected and favoritism is normative. Hence, concerns about what is best for this particular elder in the context of this particular family take precedence over social policy concerns for equity and cost containment. The concept of family members as gatekeepers, for example, is a very awkward one. Standards and rules for family care are minimal and quality is a flexible concept negotiated, explicitly or tacitly, among family members. The individual's care plan, if you will, is individualized, but it is a function of not only his or her needs, but also the interplay of forces contributing to family complexity and instability mentioned previously. Caregiving roles develop in the family, approximating a division of labor, and they are reinforced by affective ties—love, guilt, and responsibility. Gender-role expectations substitute for qualifications in establishing and maintaining an orderly flow of caregiving work. Remuneration for services can only comfortably occur indirectly, through gift-giving or projected inheritance. Care is an expression of love in this context, or filial piety as Lucy Yu (this volume) suggested. The rights of individuals, either elders or their caregivers, are not well protected in the family context, but we assume that affective ties minimize the need for such protection.

When the elder or her caregiving family crosses the threshold of the health care system, he or she must adapt to norms and assumptions that are not just a little different, but very different from those that guide family caregiving. Depending on the point of entry, whether it is a harried hospital emergency room or a market-conscious home health agency, for contrast, the differences may be strikingly apparent or subtly disguised. The entire context has changed, however, and it is clearly felt.

What has changed? There are four aspects of bureaucracy pertinent: (a) formalization, (b) objectivity, (c) standardization, and (d) the hierarchical division of labor. These major functions (and dysfunctions) of bureaucracy are examined as they generally apply to providing care for the dependent elderly.

The first discontinuity one experiences when moving from a primary group to a bureaucracy is formalization. Let me give a few examples. First, you must meet certain criteria to be allowed to enter the system. There is no system for all seasons or all reasons. Eligibility determination is a shocking concept in the face of clear and present needs, especially when they are your own needs. Next, if you are admitted to a hospital, lets say, by virtue of your medical and insurance status, you are expected to confer titles and deference on people only a fraction your age and about whom you know nothing except that they have completed requirements for the practice of medicine or another health profession. In a bureaucracy, authority legitimately rests not in individual human beings but in positions that are defined by credentials and stated responsibilities. Affective, interpersonal responses are irrelevant.

The second feature of bureaucracy to consider is its objectivity. Bureaucratic organization in the form of administrative agencies became pervasive in American government during the Progressive Era when the goals and rhetoric of economic democracy enjoyed their hey-day. Rules limiting the power of the financial barons and administrative structures to enforce those rules and to promulgate new ones when loopholes were exploited became the framework of industrial democracy by the beginning of the 20th century. Herbert Kaufman's (1977) eloquent book *Red Tape: Its Origins, Uses, and Abuses* outlines this history and makes a convincing argument concerning bureaucracy's role in the protection of individual rights.

In the current context, we experience the equalizing effects of bureaucracy whenever our lives intersect with social or health policy. Although political and economic choices affect who has access to services, bureaucracy assures more or less equal treatment of those who do enter. With this equality comes routine treatment, however, which often seems like the lowest common denominator in terms of service adequacy. When resources are inadequate, equal treatment may not feel satisfactory. This objective, universalistic standard that results in undifferentiated and routine caregiving from a nursing home or home health agency may keep family members awake at night feeling guilty, but it is what makes formal care derived from public programs possible. The bureaucratic fact of the matter is that because everyone cannot be treated as special, it is only fair that no one be so favored.

Next let's consider the related issue of standardization of care as a consequence of bureaucratized care. Clearly, public policy cannot be flexible enough to provide optimal choices to all in need. Attempts by service recipients or providers to subvert program requirements in favor of individualized treatment eventually lead to fewer and fewer options. Standard operating procedures enter the picture both to increase efficiency and to establish control. The most pervasive effort at standardization in recent times is Medicare's shift from cost-based reimbursement to prospectively determined reimbursement standards. The need to control public expenditures in an equitable fashion resulted in the prospective payment system of transferring financial risk for medically unnecessary hospital use to the hospitals themselves. They, in turn, have increased their efforts to influence physicians' practice patterns.

It is impossible to decouple the issue of reimbursement from that of defining a range of options in the provision of care. With the exception of a carefully controlled allocation for charity care, formal caregiving systems, unlike family caregivers, will provide only what they are paid to provide. The maintenance of this economic rationality depends on adherence to the bureaucratic principle of control through standardization of decision making. Historically, this kind of control has been a precious commodity in health service organizations dominated by autonomous professionals.

The business side of health care administration, however, became more clearly articulated in 1980s. In today's environment, the social worker breaking the news that to a family that their dependent elder cannot stay in the hospital while awaiting a nursing home placement is on a firm bureaucratic footing when he or she defends this decision as part of standard operating procedures. He or she is wearing the bureaucratic coat of arms in referencing a set of rules identified as necessary for the economic survival of the hospital. Again, these bureaucratic principles keep the system afloat and accessible at the cost of individual hardship.

Hierarchy and its complexity is the final characteristic I mention. The division of labor and authority in hierarchical form is what enables complex organizations to function automatically. It is an incredible source of stability, control, and inflexibility. If a physician's written order is required for a service to be provided (i.e., reimbursed), then that service will not be rendered until that order is signed. Nurses know very well the consequences of violating such hierarchical divisions of labor.

I was privy to a discussion in a nursing home recently of whose responsibility it was—nursing or dietary—to put bibs on residents before serving them. Because this task had been added to the care routine at some point without explicit inclusion in anyone's job description, conflict was brewing and family visitors were finding their elders with laps full of cold oatmeal. The bureaucratic dysfunction, here, of course, is that the staff were hired to perform certain caregiving tasks under the supervision of a single person, not to care for people holistically or to work as part of a team. Consequently, when the nursing supervisor asked the dietary workers to put the bibs on residents as they served trays, she was ignored because she was not their direct superior. In brief, hierarchical division of labor guarantees that some level of care will be provided in formal care settings more or less automatically. It also guarantees that holistic, elder-centered care will not be the norm.

CAN SHMOS HELP?

How might SHMOs and other forms of integrated, case-managed systems serve to ease the discontinuity between family care and formal care? Are such programs potential remedies to the dysfunctional consequences of bureaucratic caregiving systems?

I think the concept of SHMOs has several things to offer in this regard. First, the single point of entry has the potential to ease the transition between the particularistic family support system and the objective, depersonalized health care system that aims to treat everyone the same. Counseling and education to help elders and their families adjust their expectations and understand their rights and options within the system may assist the transition. The incentive for comprehensive SHMO-type systems to provide such services is much clearer than for any single service provider.

The comprehensiveness—to overstate the case a bit—of the SHMO is appealing, from the individual's viewpoint, in the sense that membership has its privileges, and the assessment process to determine eligibility need not be repeated in full when needs change. Perhaps there are fewer humiliating hoops to jump through in search of reasonably appropriate and timely service options.

Finally, the case management component of the SHMO can serve as a remedy to bureaucratic complexity and impersonality. As advocate or service broker, the case manager can provide the crucial component of "someone to call when you need help." Knowing even the name of a single bureaucrat goes a long way toward helping us manage our aversion to bureaucracies.

What is perplexing about case management, however, especially in light of Dr. Harrington's findings regarding reduced service utilization, is whose remedy is it? Does the case manager serve the client and his or her family as service broker and/or advocate? Or does he or she serve the payor source to control utilization? In the case of prepaid capitation programs like SHMOs, or in the case of the Medicaid case management, cost containment goals compete directly with service brokerage and client satisfaction goals.

THE CRITICAL ROLE OF THE CASE MANAGER

If SHMOs and other forms of case managed care systems are to serve as remedies to bureaucratization, the effectiveness of the case managers who provide interface between elders, their families and the system are all-important. It is tempting, in the context of this discussion, to view the case manager as a transitional role, a kind of buffer between family care and the formal health system.

How well the case manager in a SHMO-type system will serve to buffer the transition to a formal health is likely multiply determined. Several probable factors can be identified even before the SHMO evaluations are completed. These include: (a) the size of the case manager's caseload, (b) the positioning of the case manager in the system, and (c) the professional status of the case manager personnel.

The SHMO client satisfaction analysis may provide a basis on which standards for case management can be developed. It will be important to know, for example, at what size caseload does the case manager himself or herself become, a narrowly functioning bureaucrat. Where should case managers be placed organizationally to maximize their effectiveness? Decentralization of the case management function might make it more accessible to consumers, but perhaps at the cost of the manager's being less well informed of system-wide resources and constraints on service availability. At this point in time, it is unclear what professional orientation and skill-set is called for in case management of the elderly. Physicians, nurses, and social workers serve case management functions in managed care systems. Which group, if any, creates the better buffer between informal and formal care systems?

The case manager's multiple roles, however, include not only that of buffer, but also those of broker and gatekeeper. These broker and gatekeeper functions are likely to often be in conflict and produce significant role-ambiguity and stress. These two roles require a thorough knowledge of the resources and constraints available in the service system. The broker seeks the most desireable arrangement from the point of view of the client, whereas the gatekeeper is a steward of the service system's resources. The case manager can serve neither as the single-minded family advocate nor as the system-serving bureaucrat. Although the social work profession has a long history of operating under such circumstances, the cost containment strategies of the 1980s have introduced other health care professionals to the art of juggling system and individual needs as well.

Managed care is becoming pervasive as a structural choice of public and private payers for health care. It would not take a totally cynical perspective to view it as the ultimate bureaucratic instrument for co-opting individuals in service of institutional needs. As the evaluations of these programs accumulate, we need to keep a watchful eye on how the dependent elderly feel about being not only cared for but managed by bureaucratic systems.

ACKNOWLEDGMENT

Presented at the Penn State Gerontology Center Conference on the Social Structure and Caregiving: Family and Cross-National Perspectives, October 22–23, 1990, University Park, PA.

REFERENCES

Gerth, H. H., & Mills, C. W. (1946). *From Max Weber: Essays in sociology.* New York: Oxford University Press.

Kaufman, H. (1977). *Red tape: Its Origins, uses, and abuses.* Washington, DC: Brookings.

Litwak, E. (1985). *Helping the elderly: The complementary roles of informal networks and formal systems.* New York: Guilford.

Pearlin, L., Mullan, J., Semple, S., & Skaff, M. (1990). Caregiving and the stress process: An overview of concepts and their measures. *The Gerontologist, 30,* 583–594.

Smyer, M., Cohn, M., & Brannon, D. (1988). *Mental health consultation in nursing homes.* New York: NYU Press.

Zarit, S. (1989). Do we need another "stress and caregiving" study? *The Gerontologist, 29,* 147–148.

Public Policy Issues Related to the SHMO Demonstrations and Alzheimer's Disease

George Niederehe
National Institute of Mental Health

As a psychologist whose work is centered predominantly in clinical research, I come to the task of discussing public policy relative to health care financing demonstrations as a virtual outsider to this area of research. Given my limited background in this domain, my thoughts regarding Dr. Harrington's chapter on Social Health Maintenance Organizations (SHMOs) are general rather than specific, and they stem from some loosely formulated ideas about the role of public policy around social and health care interventions for the aged. I must acknowledge that these ideas are rather impressionistic and represent personal musings about service programs in our society, rather than having a basis in any formal theory or conceptual framework of governance. This chapter considers the SHMO demonstrations first against the backdrop of these notions and then within the broader context of public policy issues affecting the seriously disabled elderly who are most in need of improved long-term care, using as a case example those suffering from Alzheimer's disease or related dementias (ADRD).

GENERAL PUBLIC POLICY QUESTIONS

Although this chapter does not go into such depth, a discussion about public policy relative to interventions for the aged would ideally draw upon the extensive scholarly literature pertaining to this topic, and take into account a number of relevant theoretical distinctions. Public policies, for example, may be categorized according to their domains of applicability; conventional groupings include health, mental health, long-term care, aging, and social welfare (Kane, 1986). SHMOs were intentionally designed to cut across or bridge such domains, and to attempt an integrated treatment of the social and health needs of the aged — a concept with great intrinsic appeal. Clearly, such an integrative approach is more widely needed within care systems for the aged. Our ideal discussion might note various other conceptual distinctions as well, such as that between policy adoption and policy implementation (Binstock, Levin, & Weatherly, 1985), and between the different levels of government that might be appropriate for various types of intervention (federal, state, municipal). We should also carefully consider the rationale, and indicators of specific need, for public policy actions vis-a-vis the aged (Davis, 1985).

This chapter, however, has a narrower scope, addressing a series of questions that may be less elegant theoretically, but perhaps more practice oriented (adopting an approach analogous in some ways to the "who-what-where-when-how" approach to news reporting). From this perspective, relative to any condition or set of conditions in which we are trying to intervene with a treatment program or system of services, public policy would seemingly need to consider a basic set of issues:

1. **Prevention of Need.** For example, what is the feasibility of preventive measures? How much resources should go into efforts to avoid occurrence of the condition versus caring for those already affected by it?
2. **Eligibility/Access.** Who should be entitled to receive the potential benefit of the public program? What steps should be taken to assure open and equitable access to it for all eligible persons?
3. **Delivery/Utilization.** What steps should be taken to assure that the targeted persons actually receive the intervention intended for them, or at least have full opportunity to avail themselves of it?
4. **Quality Control.** What monitoring or research must be done to assure that the program is conducted correctly *(treatment fidelity)*, and that it actually achieves its stated goals or produces the intended effects *(treatment efficacy)* without undue risk of adverse side effects (safety)?
5. **Cost.** Among many questions here, salient issues include: What are the costs of delivering the service? What is the cost-effectiveness ratio? What level of cost is justifiable for efforts to address the specific condition? What methods of financing should be used? Who should be responsible for paying those costs? How should the relative importance of this problem area be weighed against other public priorities?

Dr. Harrington's chapter — even its title — makes it clear that the SHMO demonstrations have been focused mainly on financing and service delivery issues, which correspond to the fifth and third categories, respectively, in the above list: cost, and delivery/utilization of services. Another way of stating this is that, basically, the projects have been oriented strongly toward cost-containment and feasibility questions.

In addition, we should consider the importance of various perspectives or primary points of view from which public policy can be written. Many policy-related dilemmas stem from the difficulties of weighing and balancing the interests of the following broad constituencies:

1. Patients.
2. Family.
3. Health care/social service providers.
4. Society (including government as its representative).

QUESTIONS REGARDING
THE SHMO DEMONSTRATIONS

Let us briefly consider the methodological and outcome aspects of the SHMO demonstrations relative to a set of questions based on the aforementioned background principles. This chapter does not attempt to discuss the SHMO data that were presented any more systematically than this. Although these are the sort of questions more typically asked about clinical-level treatment studies, perhaps by analogy they may have some relevance also to larger demonstrations.

First, who is included in the programs studied? This question pertains primarily to the projects' inclusion/exclusion criteria, as they relate to an underlying issue of external validity (or generalizability) of the findings. A particular concern here is whether these demonstrations will yield useful findings relative to the segments of the population most in need of long-term care services—those with significant degrees of impairment. Given that the demonstration SHMOs were allowed to place strong limitations on the number of impaired individuals that they had to include, how capable will the projects be of assessing the breadth of applicability of the SHMO approach relative to the total need in the elderly population? If the samples studied are not broadly representative of the population at risk, what do we stand to learn about where this type of service model fits within a broader continuum of necessary services?

Some of the concerns addressed by the demonstrations appear to get in the way of looking at other issues that the researchers seemingly also want to investigate within these samples. Obviously, as Dr. Harrington's chapter points out, one of the foremost issues addressed has been that of enrollment— whether the SHMOs could attract and retain enough enrollees with the appropriate characteristics to make this model workable and financially feasible. The good news is that they have been able to recruit adequate plan members to make the approach work. From a research perspective, however, the bad news is that, by definition, the projects have what in other contexts would be called a subject self-selection factor that must be dealt with in making any comparisons between the SHMO participants and others. For example, Dr. Harrington reported that enrollment has been driven largely by financial considerations and whether prospective enrollees are concerned about getting the long-term care benefits provided by the SHMOs. Do we therefore have to worry about a bias toward participants being a relatively less impaired and financially better-off segment within the general population? In addition, the data suggest that attrition/dropout has been higher in more impaired patients, and appears linked to both patients' finances and their satisfaction with the physical/medical services they received from the SHMOs. Such issues of possible sampling bias call into question the internal validity of comparing participants and others in terms of outcomes, and suggest that additional research is probably required in the future in order to handle such comparisons adequately.

A second question is: What services were needed by, and actually provided to, the participants? Information addressing this question is well described in Dr. Harrington's report. An adequate answer, however, depends importantly on tracking participants' use of outside services as well as SHMO-provided services. Furthermore, it is noteworthy (perhaps curious) that — although the novelty of the SHMO approach resides in its emphasizing coverage of chronic care needs — to date the critical variance seems to have occurred in the acute care, rather than chronic care, aspects of these programs.

The third and fourth questions ask: What is the quality of the care provided by the SHMOs, and what are the effects or outcomes of receiving these services? For instance, is institutionalization delayed, or are other treatment goals met? On these issues, by and large Dr. Harrington's chapter is tantalizing but frustrating — because the study has not yet reached the point at which the critical analyses can be done. The data at present from these demonstrations indicate only that the projects have been able to control costs. Whereas this aspect is highly important from a societal perspective, without being able to factor in other data on the quality and efficacy of the care rendered, it is a mystery how one can appraise the model from the viewpoint of the patient and family. One can, however, readily and strongly second Dr. Harrington's point that the measurement of outcomes in these kinds of studies needs further conceptual development; in HCFA-funded and other demonstrations on elderly populations undergoing deteriorative processes, patient mortality rates or declines in health status are not necessarily appropriate outcome measures. Delays in, or changes in the rates of, decline may be the best kinds of outcomes that can be achieved.

This consideration leads to a final question, namely: In the SHMO model, who ultimately is benefitting from structuring services in this way? Clearly, there are advantages for society and third-party payers in terms of costs, but in order to have a fully effective model, SHMOs have to demonstrate success in delivering a high quality of care and achieving outcomes that are clinically meaningful and acceptable to patients and families, as well as yielding cost savings for society and families.

SEEING THE DEMONSTRATIONS IN A BROADER CONTEXT

The foregoing points have been intended primarily to indicate certain limitations on what one can expect to come out of these demonstrations in terms of findings, rather than to criticize Dr. Harrington or her colleagues regarding their evaluation of the projects—the design for which was not a matter that they controlled. She and her colleagues have an imposing and unenviable challenge in their task of extracting scientifically rigorous findings from these large projects.

Furthermore, though SHMOs certainly can be evaluated from other perspectives, the comments above have emphasized questions of SHMOs' relevance to that segment of the elderly population that is significantly impaired and most in need of long-term care. Continuing in that vein, let's now turn to some considerations of public policy regarding the seriously disabled elderly, specifically, persons with Alzheimer's disease or other dementias who represent a large portion of the impaired elderly. Several federal advisory bodies have formulated policy recommendations regarding this subpopulation, its needs, and other questions surrounding dementing diseases. Although the range of public policy issues considered by these advisory groups is much broader than simply those on which SHMOs have focused and includes topics not specifically related to Dr. Harrington's chapter or to health care financing demonstrations, the deliberations and conclusions of these groups may provide the very context within which the SHMO demonstrations can usefully be seen from some alternate vantage points.

RESEARCH RESOURCES FOR ALZHEIMER'S DISEASE

One large set of questions concerns the extent of public resources that should be put into research on service systems for the elderly impaired due to dementing illnesses, and where these resources should come from. At the national level, such resource questions are ultimately determined by our elected representatives in the legislative branch of government. However, in making decisions about appropriations, our lawmakers rely heavily on information from the executive branch about which social problems are foremost and what research avenues can feasibly be pursued at a given time.

Within the U. S. Department of Health and Human Services (DHHS), these questions are addressed through the Council on Alzheimer's Disease, an outgrowth of efforts that began in 1983 when Secretary of HHS Margaret Heckler established a Task Force on Alzheimer's Disease, composed of the heads of a number of agencies (Cutler, 1986). The principal report of the Task Force (U. S. DHHS, 1984) described current research on Alzheimer's disease and related dementias, and recommended future directions important for advancing the research agenda. The continuing work of the Task Force led to 1986 legislation (Title IX of Public Law 99–660, the Alzheimer's Disease and Related Dementias Services Research Act of 1986), creating the DHHS Council on Alzheimer's Disease along similar lines and essentially continuing the activities begun by the Task Force. The membership of the Council includes the officials and agencies shown in Table 1.

The Council functions to allow various federal agencies involved in ADRD research or services to share information about their activities and initiatives, coordinate efforts, and collaboratively determine priorities. The Council advises Congress annually in a report of the progress that has been made in ADRD research and of the areas of greatest promise, as well as of the plans that various agencies are following for research on services for ADRD patients and their families. Recent reports of the Council have made it clear that, with federal support, an exciting number and volume of efforts are being made to explore possible causes of Alzheimer's disease, to develop better diagnostic and treatment methods, and to improve the existing system of caring for ADRD patients and their families.

TABLE 1
Membership of the DHHS Council on Alzheimer's Disease

Assistant Secretary for Health
Surgeon General
Assistant Secretary for Planning and Evaluation
Director, National Institute of Allergy and Infectious Diseases
Director, National Institute of Mental Health
Director, National Institute of Neurological Disorders and Stroke
Director, National Institute on Aging
Commissioner on Aging, Administration on Aging
Administrator, Agency for Health Care Policy and Research
Administrator (or designee), Health Care Financing Administration
Administrator (or designee), Health Resources and Services Administration
Director (or designee), National Center for Health Statistics
Director, National Center for Nursing Research
Medical Director (or designee), Office of Geriatrics and Extended Care,
    Department of Veterans Affairs

Figure 1 shows the overall level of federal funding for ADRD research over recent years, which totaled $130 million in Fiscal Year 1989, and rose to approximately $231 million for Fiscal Year 1991. Appropriations to be expended during Fiscal Year 1992 have been estimated at approximately $280 million. These are impressive increases from a mere $4 million in 1976, and $20 million only 10 years ago. Although these figures do not provide a breakdown of the relative amounts of resources devoted to basic biomedical forms of research versus those going into social and health services research related to dementing disorders, it is clear that the lion's share of funds have been provided in the biomedical category.

To put these figures in another perspective, however, the amount being appropriated and expended on ADRD research is relatively small compared with some of the other "big ticket" medical disorders, as indicated in Fig. 2. Whereas those researching Alzheimer's disease generally disavow making competitive comparisons with these other research areas, juxtaposing these kinds of figures does provide a useful frame of reference for what might be possible or appropriate regarding ADRD research support. There clearly is room for arguing that, in terms of their relative social importance and the resources currently being allocated for their investigation, Alzheimer's disease and related dementias are underemphasized within the federal funding scheme and deserve greater attention. A subsidiary implication, given the relatively small proportion of the available funding that is directed toward

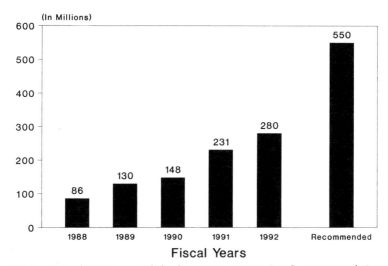

Federal ADRD Research Funding
1988 - 1992 vs. Panel's Recommendations

FIG. 1. Federal ADRD research funding: 1988–1992 vs. Panel's recommendations.

Comparative Research Support
on Major Disorders, FY 1991

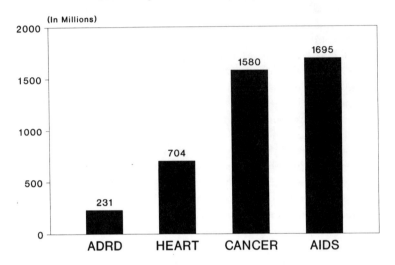

FIG. 2. Comparative research support on major disorders, FY 1991.

service system questions, is that the absolute amount of support provided for research on services for ADRD victims has been very limited, perhaps shortchanged.

Often certain public policy issues, such as funding priorities and levels and programmatic directions within service systems, can be addressed more directly and forcefully by those outside the executive branch of government than by the agencies within it. Accordingly, the same legislation that established the Council also established a second, but nonfederal, group called the Advisory Panel on Alzheimer's Disease. This nongovernmental group consists of 15 experts, with three members appointed to represent each of five areas; biomedical research, health services research, clinical services provision, health care financing, and public voluntary organizations interested in Alzheimer's disease. Thus constituted to provide a balance among various areas of concern and with representation across a wide geographic distribution, the Advisory Panel has been mandated to advise both DHHS and Congress from 1988 to 1992 regarding both research priorities and public policy actions pertinent to Alzheimer's disease, including recommendations about systems of care for ADRD patients. The group has thus far issued three reports.

In each report, relative to the above issues of research resources, the Advisory Panel recommended both that overall funding for ADRD research be increased, and that greater priority be placed on supporting services-related and financing research relevant to ADRD. If implemented (as represented in Fig. 2), the Panel's most recent recommendations would increase federal funding for ADRD biomedical research to an annual level of $500 million, provide some support for construction of additional research facilities, and raise ADRD services research funding by $25 million immediately, and by $50 million within 3 to 5 years. Included in the latter increase would be $10 million for establishing up to ten health services research centers devoted to ADRD studies.

Various of the Panel's recommendations made an obvious impact on the 101st Congress' considerations of these issues, and were incorporated into relevant legislative proposals, such as the Comprehensive Alzheimer's Assistance, Research and Education (CARE) Act introduced by Representative Edward Roybal and Senator Larry Pressler, and the Alzheimer's Disease Research and Training Act sponsored by Senators Howard Metzenbaum and Charles Grassley and Representative Olympia Snowe. During its second session, this Congress pooled selected elements from these pieces of legislation together with elements from several related bills and passed them as the Home Health Care and Alzheimer's Disease Amendments of 1990. Many of the Panel's recommendations, however, remain to be acted on in the future. As noted earlier, ADRD research appropriations were increased substantially in Fiscal Year 1991, but not to the levels recommended by the Panel (see Fig. 2).

Such funding proposals raise "big picture" concerns among some observers that increased allocations for ADRD research may compete against other research priorities within gerontology (Blazer, 1990). In a rejoinder, members of the Panel have suggested that a disease-specific approach be seen as one of the few ways available to increase total federal appropriations for age-related disorders (Larson, Katzman, Brody, & Drachman, 1990).

APPROPRIATE SERVICES FOR VICTIMS OF ALZHEIMER'S DISEASE

Numerous public policy questions concern the scope of services and organizational features that the overall care system should embody in order to meet the needs of ADRD patients and their families. The first report of the Advisory Panel on Alzheimer's Disease (1989) gave a broad national overview of both research and services for ADRD patients, and provided various recommendations that have subsequently been incorporated into legislative proposals under consideration in Congress. Its second or 1990 report (Advisory Panel on Alzheimer's Disease, 1991) expanded on many of the prior recommendations and, in addition, addressed personnel recruitment and staff training as critical problems to be faced in providing an acceptable quality of long-term care to ADRD patients. In describing various design features of the long-term care system that the group considered desirable, the Panel's reports have touched on nearly all the public policy realms mentioned earlier, including issues of eligibility/access, delivery/utilization, quality control, and cost.

In its most sweeping recommendation about services, the Panel endorsed the concept of a public (or national) insurance plan, providing universal coverage for at least basic health care needs. In regard to eligibility, the Panel proposed a system that includes and is sensitive to those suffering from Alzheimer's disease but is not constructed exclusively for these individuals. The Panel's position has been that the system should embody eligibility criteria tied to dysfunction and dependency rather than to the patient's age or diagnosis. It proposed modifying existing criteria, which screen potential beneficiaries for degrees of incapacity in activities of daily living (ADLs), to make them more sensitive to the unique deficits of ADRD patients, who typically suffer not from physical inability to perform these activities but require supervision or cueing to assure appropriate ADL performance and personal safety.

The Panel noted the need for a comprehensive care system that embodies a continuum of care options. In addition, in the Panel's opinion, the patient's family must be acknowledged and treated as central in the process of care. To overcome access and service delivery barriers to adequate care, the system also needs care providers sensitive to cultural and linguistic differences, particularly in multiethnic, multiracial localities.

If we return to the previously mentioned issue of where SHMOs might fit within the broader system of care for ADRD patients, presumably their potential value would be in achieving a more cost-effective delivery of services. Cost, financing, and cost-containment considerations have been prominently featured in the Panel's reports. The group recognizes that any workable long-term plan will have to incorporate multiple cost-containment strategies, such as income-related cost sharing (copayment requirements), gradating of entitlements for services according to levels of disability (or targeted benefits), capitation (centrally featured in the SHMOs), and pread-mission screening or case review mechanisms. Relative to such cost controls, however, the Panel emphasized the importance of assuring quality of care and access to care regardless of socioeconomic status. Assuming that coverage will involve public/private sharing in some form, the Panel also recommended that insurance coverage of Alzheimer's disease not be excluded from private insurance plans, as all too often is the case today. Furthermore, the Panel recognized that current financing mechanisms are too heavily slanted toward institutional care and may favor unnecessary or premature institutionaliza-tion; desiring to have greater balance in emphasis, the Panel encouraged expansion of home care options.

The Panel's first two reports pointedly discussed another concept of keen public policy interest: case management. As regards one issue that has concerned policymakers, the Panel has maintained that case management as a formal service tends to support informal caregiving by family and friends rather than to supplant it. A related issue that engendered considerable controversy and debate among Panel members has been whether case managers should be assigned the dual responsibilities of acting both as gatekeepers (i.e., containing the costs of services) and also as patient advocates. The majority of members have held that patient advocacy must be primary for case managers, and that it is not feasible to expect them to also concern themselves about cost control. Other members, however, have staunchly maintained that there is no insurmountable problem, and in fact considerable efficiency, in having the same individuals performing these dual functions, and that it is unrealistic to expect systems to be designed in any other way.

The Panel members have debated without resolution whether to suggest an incremental plan for implementing over time various aspects of the kind of system of care that they view as necessary, versus simply recommending the general systemic features to strive for while letting Congress work out the implementation details — as part of what many foresee will eventually be more sweeping long-term care reform legislation.

In terms of promoting services-oriented research, the Advisory Panel has suggested greater attention to the needs for better methods of evaluating outcomes in impaired populations, and has recommended that studies be conducted of the seeming underutilization of services by caregivers of ADRD patients. Among other systemic and clinical-level issues on which the Panel recommended services research were: (a) alternative techniques for clinical management of mental, emotional, and behavioral problems in ADRD; (b) clarification of which services most effectively meet the needs and expectations of ADRD patients and their families, including family-focused interventions such as respite care and caregiver support groups; (c) critical features to be included in the design of special care units for ADRD patients in institutions; and (d) effective ways of combining professional and informal support services.

OTHER POLICY CONCERNS

In terms of the public policy areas mentioned at the outset of this chapter, the focus of the Advisory Panel has moved progressively toward questions related to quality of care and access to services. As already mentioned, the 1990 report emphasized personnel recruitment and staff training issues in recognition of how critical these topics are to providing a better quality of long-term care to ADRD patients. Likewise, the Panel's 1991 report (Advisory Panel on

Alzheimer's Disease, 1992) deals primarily with values and goals in ADRD
care. Among the quality of care, treatment efficacy and cost themes
considered, major attention is given to the difficult and values-laden dilemmas that frequently must be faced in treating ADRD patients. For
instance, should greater priority be given to assuring ADRD patients' safety
or to attempting to promote their continued autonomy of function? This
dilemma is exemplified concretely in decisions about when psychopharmaco-
logical treatments or use of physical restraints are justified in care of nursing
home residents who present difficult-to-manage behavioral problems as
symptoms of their dementia. Another question to be considered is whether the
clinical approach to severely impaired ADRD patients should be a custodial
one that attempts primarily to ease the deteriorative and dying process, or a
more active form of intervention that emphasizes maximizing the patient's
level of functioning. Whereas these sorts of questions are of obvious salience
to the clinician, recognition of the underlying values that are being served by
various responses to these care situations is of equal importance to public
policy formulations that affect the process of care. A question framed more
directly in policy terms concerns resource allocation along the course of
Alzheimer's disease. In what relative proportions should treatment resources
be allocated to early-stage versus late-stage, more highly impaired patients?

The Panel is preparing a 1992 report that addresses ethnic, cultural, and
minority group issues both in services-oriented and clinical and biomedical
studies of dementia. Among the issues discussed, the inclusion of minority
patients in service systems—especially access to care and delivery of services
to these groups—clearly is a central theme.

NEEDS OF FAMILIES

SHMOs are oriented toward producing one particular kind of benefit for
caregivers and families of impaired elderly, namely, better control over the
costs of care and, perhaps, a reduction in the burden that stems from financial
pressures. As the Advisory Panel (1991) has pointed out, very little empirical
research has been done to establish the typical effects of ADRD care on
families' finances.

We should also ask, from a broader perspective than a strictly financial one:
What do these family members need? What other stresses do they typically
experience and what steps have been proven effective in helping them?

Research related to such caregiving issues in Alzheimer's disease has been
supported by a number of federal agencies, including the National Institute
on Aging, Administration on Aging, National Center for Nursing Research,
Health Care Financing Administration, Department of Veterans Affairs, and

others. The Mental Disorders of the Aging Research Branch of the National Institute of Mental Health (NIMH), in particular, has supported a great deal of clinically oriented research in Alzheimer's disease and related dementias, including many studies on family caregiving and stress in these disorders. In terms of the directions that seem to be emerging in this particular field, several are particularly relevant to the theme of the present volume. Caregiving research seems to be moving particularly toward studies of comprehensive models of the factors involved in producing stress within the caregiving process (e.g., Pearlin, Mullan, Semple, & Skaff, 1990), and toward intervention studies (Zarit, 1989; Zarit & Anthony, 1986).

As a major subtheme within the first of these research areas, there is now a growing body of research addressing what the NIMH Aging Branch staff has termed the *mental health/physical health interface*. Researchers are applying new research techniques from the burgeoning neuroscientific fields to the study of long-term effects of caregiving stress on family members of ADRD patients. One leading research group has found deteriorative immune system changes and other long-term physical health effects in caregivers, as well as the depressive and other psychiatric symptoms that have been more widely recognized (Kiecolt-Glaser, Dura, Speicher, Trask, & Glaser, 1991). These and other caregiving issues need to be studied more fully, especially in ethnic minority and lower socioeconomic groups.

Likewise, particularly in the intervention research area, there needs to be increasing attention to interventions with, and other studies of, the *families* of patients, above and beyond the typical focus on caregivers as individuals. Family dynamics need to be investigated as the systems and contexts within which dementing illnesses and many of the associated problems of caregiving unfold (Fruge & Niederehe, 1985; Lebowitz & Niederehe, 1992; Niederehe & Fruge, 1984; Zarit, Orr, & Zarit, 1985).

Several volumes are available as resource materials that can inform attempts to move in these research directions. These include a volume edited by the NIMH Aging Branch staff in which leading researchers discuss the current state of research on caregiving stress and suggest needed directions for future studies (Light & Lebowitz, 1989). More recently, an NIMH workshop held in March, 1990, on the mental health implications of caregiving in Alzheimer's disease has provided an update and expansion on emerging research findings in this area of investigation. The papers from this meeting are currently being edited and should soon be available as another useful resource volume for researchers (Light, Niederehe, & Lebowitz, in press). In addition, it should be noted that, under the leadership of Katie Maslow, a number of policy questions related to Alzheimer's disease, including the organization of services for ADRD patients and their families, have been organized and discussed very usefully in several volumes published by the Congressional Office of Technology Assessment (1987; 1990).

CONCLUSION

Historically, many other proposals in addition to those discussed here have been put forward as ways to improve or reorganize the service system for ADRD patients and other elderly with long-term care needs — few of which have been concretely implemented on any largescale basis. Undoubtedly, many more ideas will enter the general debate, and many more demonstrations will be done, before major changes are enacted.

If, however, we refer to the Advisory Panel reports for criteria against which to evaluate how well various service programs may serve the seriously impaired long-term care population, we note that the SHMO projects incorporate several features that the Advisory Panel has cited as important for adequate care of dementia patients. These features include provision of a continuum of care, an emphasis on case management, eligibility criteria tied to dysfunction and dependency rather than to the patient's age or diagnosis, and cost containment. It is not yet clear, however, whether the SHMO projects have successfully combined their efforts at cost control with certain other features that the Panel emphasized must be considered conjointly, particularly means of assuring quality of care and access to care regardless of socioeconomic status.

Of course, the very fact that the SHMO demonstrations are taking place and being evaluated is consistent with the Panel's recommendations that greater priority be placed on supporting services-related and financing research that is at least potentially relevant to ADRD. In addition, several points raised in Dr. Harrington's chapter resonate strongly with suggestions put forward in the Panel's reports. In particular, researchers need to develop better methods of evaluating outcomes in impaired populations and to study more carefully the seeming underutilization of services by caregivers of ADRD patients.

As a system of financing care, SHMOs depend a great deal on what subordinate sets of services are available and how well these serve the SHMO members. Data from the current demonstrations have indicated that the likelihood of disenrollment depends on members' satisfaction with the services provided as well as on financial concerns. Thus, the success of SHMOs is intimately linked with the development and refinement through research of effective services.

In turn, at the national level, it is undeniable that enactment of an effective public long-term care system of the sort advocated by the Advisory Panel ultimately will revolve around the Nation's cost concerns about that care, and whether effective ways of containing those costs have been found. One can only hope that some potential solutions, such as providing services through SHMOs, may prove capable in the long run of addressing these cost concerns, so critical to improving long-term care arrangements for the very impaired elderly.

REFERENCES

Advisory Panel on Alzheimer's Disease. (1989). *Report of the Advisory Panel on Alzheimer's Disease, 1988-1989.* (DHHS Publication No. ADM 89-1644). Washington, DC: U. S. Government Printing Office.

Advisory Panel on Alzheimer's Disease. (1991). *Second report of the Advisory Panel on Alzheimer's Disease, 1990.* (DHHS Publication No. ADM 91-1791). Washington, DC: U. S. Government Printing Office.

Advisory Panel on Alzheimer's Disease. (1992). *Third report of the Advisory Panel on Alzheimer's Disease, 1991.* (DHHS Publication No. ADM 92-1917). Washington, DC: U. S. Government Printing Office.

Binstock, R. H., Levin, M. A., & Weatherly, R. (1985). Political dilemmas of social intervention. In R. H. Binstock & E. Shanas (Eds.), *Handbook of aging and the social sciences* (2nd ed., pp. 569-618). New York: Van Nostrand Reinhold.

Blazer, D. (1990). What should the federal government do about Alzheimer's disease? Report of the Advisory Panel on Alzheimer's Disease. *Journal of Gerontology: Medical Sciences, 45*(1), M1-2.

Cutler, N. E. (1986). Public response: The national politics of Alzheimer's disease. In M. L. M. Gilhooly, S. H. Zarit, & J. E. Birren (Eds.), *The dementias: Policy and management* (pp. 161-189). Englewood Cliffs, NJ: Prentice-Hall.

Davis, K. (1985). Health care policies and the aged: Observation from the United States. In R. H. Binstock & E. Shanas (Eds.), *Handbook of aging and the social sciences* (2nd ed., pp. 727-744). New York: Van Nostrand Reinhold.

Fruge, E., & Niederehe, G. (1985). Family dimensions of health care for the aged. In S. Henao & N. P. Grose (Eds.), *Principles of family systems in family medicine* (pp. 165-191). New York: Brunner/Mazel.

Kane, R. A. (1986). Senile dementia and public policy. In M. L. M. Gilhooly, S. H. Zarit & J. E. Birren (Eds.), *The dementias: Policy and management* (pp. 190-214) Englewood Cliffs, NJ: Prentice-Hall.

Kiecolt-Glaser, J. R., Dura, J. R., Speicher, C. E., Trask, O. J., & Glaser, R. (1991). Spousal caregivers of dementia victims: Longitudinal changes in immunity and health. *Psychosomatic Medicine, 53,* 345-362.

Larson, E. B., Katzman, R., Brody, E. M., & Drachman, D. A. (1990). Letter to the editor. *Journal of Gerontology: Medical Sciences, 45*(3), M120.

Lebowitz, B. D., & Niederehe, G. (1992). Concepts and issues in mental health and aging. In J. E. Birren, R. B. Sloane, & G. D. Cohen (Eds.), *Handbook of mental health and aging* (2nd ed., pp. 3-26). New York: Academic Press.

Light, E., & Lebowitz, B. D. (Eds.) (1989). *Alzheimer's disease treatment and family stress: Directions for research.* (DHHS Publication No. ADM 89-1569). Washington, DC: U. S. Government Printing Office.

Light, E., Niederehe, G., & Lebowitz, B. D. (Eds.). (in press). *Alzheimer's disease caregivers: Future directions for research and treatment.* New York: Springer.

Niederehe, G., & Fruge, E. (1984). Dementia and family dynamics: Clinical research issues. *Journal of Geriatric Psychiatry, 17,* 21-56.

Office of Technology Assessment, U. S. Congress. (1987). *Losing a million minds: Confronting the tragedy of Alzheimer's disease and other dementias.* (OTA Report No. BA-323). Washington, DC: U. S. Government Printing Office.

Office of Technology Assessment, U. S. Congress. (1990). *Confused minds, burdened families: Finding help for people with Alzheimer's and other dementias.* (OTA Report No. BA-403). Washington, DC: U.S. Government Printing Office.

Pearlin, L. I., Mullan, J. T., Semple, S. J., & Skaff, M. M. (1990). Caregiving and the stress process: An overview of concepts and their measures. *The Gerontologist, 30,* 583-594.

U. S. Department of Health and Human Services. (1984). *Alzheimer's disease: Report of the Secretary's*

Task Force on Alzheimer's Disease. (DHHS Publication No. ADM 84-1323). Washington, DC: U. S. Government Printing Office.

Zarit, S. H. (1989). Issues and directions in family intervention research. In E. Light & B. D. Lebowitz (Eds.), *Alzheimer's disease treatment and family stress: Directions for research* (pp. 458-486). (DHHS Publication No. ADM 89-1569). Washington, DC: U. S. Government Printing Office.

Zarit, S. H., & Anthony, C. R. (1986). Interventions with dementia patients and their families. In M. L. M. Gilhooly, S. H. Zarit, & J. E. Birren (Eds.), *The dementias: Policy and management* (pp. 66-92). Englewood Cliffs, NJ: Prentice-Hall.

Zarit, S. H., Orr, N. K., & Zarit, J. M. (1985). *The hidden victims of Alzheimer's disease: Families under stress.* New York: New York University Press.

8

Québec Home-Care Services: A Program at the Local Community Level

Louise Lévesque
University of Montreal

In the early 1970s, the Canadian Province of Québec underwent a major reform of its health and social services system. Many characteristics of that reform had a profound impact on the delivery of home-care services that served a mainly elderly population. Among these characteristics were the establishment of a network of Local Community Services Centers (CLSCs) and, later, the implementation of a model program of home-care services throughout that network. That model program has thus been influenced by the CLSCs' line of action. The first part of this chapter is devoted to a review of the contextual development and the implementation of that model program and the services it offers. In the second part, I pinpoint some of its orientations, mainly the fact that the coordination is done at the local community level and that cooperation with community groups and informal networks is strongly encouraged. I also examine some vulnerable aspects of that program, particularly the growing threat in terms of a shift of resources away from prevention and toward providing home-care services in place of acute hospitalization and the limited availability of services. That situation is due to the slow growth in budgets compared to increase of the aged population and the persistent mentality of being hospital and medically oriented. In the third part, I review some research carried out on family caregivers that reveal that home-care services are not used by many of them, suggesting — at least in part — the limited visibility and availability of these services. This presentation is based mainly on official reports, on work done by two authors (Bozzini, 1988; Lesemann & Nahmiash, 1990a, 1990b) in the field of social and health policies; it is also based on my clinical experience with the caregivers of the demented elderly.

PROGRAM DEVELOPMENT, IMPLEMENTATION, AND SERVICES

The Contextual Development

Although home-care services in Québec were established in 1964, their intensive development is relatively recent, dating only to the late 1970s. The demographic situation, the legislation, and the orientation adopted by the Canadian government in the health field are all factors associated with that late development (Lesemann & Nahmiash, 1990b). In terms of demographic trends, it has only been since 1978 that Québec's population is considered an "aging nation," according to the United Nations' criterion of 8% or more of the population being 65 or over. The demographic pressure exerted by the increase of that age group started later than in some European countries. For example, in 1981, Québec's population aged 65 or over was 8.7%, whereas in France, Britain, and Sweden, the percentages were, 13.9, 15.4, and 16.4 respectively, (Statistique Canada, 1984). However, in 2001, the percentage of those aged 65 years or over will reach 12%; in that age group, persons 80 and older will represent 21.5% (Kergoat & Lebel, 1987). The rate of institutionalization in Québec is 7%, (Gouvernement du Québec, 1990) which puts the province ahead of France (5%), the United States (5.3%), Great Britain (5%), and Australia (5.9%).

Alternatively, in terms of legislation and orientation, the whole Canadian health system was initially geared toward hospital and medical services. Lesemann and Nahmiash (1990b) described the development and turning points in that system. In 1957, the hospital insurance system was established, followed by the creation of a public universal health insurance in 1966. Home-care services were not covered by this public insurance. In Canada, the federal government's health legislation and orientation exert a strong influence on the provincial health programs. Although the provinces have exclusive jurisdiction in the health and social services field (this explains why each provincial health system varies to a certain extent), the federal government shares the cost, but ties its grants to preferred national orientations and requires that the provincial programs meet the criteria of universality, accessibility, free services, public management, and interprovincial transferability.

Given the demographic trends and the high cost of hospital services, it was only at the end of the 1970s that incentives to develop home-care services were created. The federal government introduced a bill in 1977 whereby it offered grants to the provinces so that they could develop services that would be less costly than those provided in the hospital (Lesemann & Nahmiash, 1990b). That federal legislation led to the first Québec home-care policy established as a complement to other social policies (e.g., income security). It emphasizes, among others things, the prevention of institutionalization (Lesemann & Nahmiash, 1990b).

At about the same time, Québec's major reforms in health and social services as recommended by the Castonguay health commission (Castonguay, 1967–1972) were implemented. Those reforms make the Québec system different from the other provincial systems in several respects. The public sector is much more present than in the other provinces and the establishment of a network of Local Community Services Centers (CLSCs) has no equivalent in other Canadian provinces and "represents a somewhat unique experience in the Western world" (Bozzini, 1988, p. 346). It is important to point out that the Québec policy on home-care services, which was developed in the late 1970s, was implemented throughout the network of CLSCs; that network now extends to all areas of the Province.

The Implementation of the Home-Care Programs Within the CLSCs

The CLSCs make up the main body that has been given a mandate to provide home-care services. There are a few exceptions such as day centers or day hospitals that also receive funding from the provincial home-care budget. The implementation of the home-care program in the CLSC network has fashioned and colored its orientation. In other words, the home-care program is closely related to the CLSCs' development and characteristics. A few remarks about their development and a description of some of the characteristics that have influenced the home-care program seem appropriate, especially for those people not familiar with the Québec system.

CLSCs Development

The development of CLSCs was slow and painful. They were born in the context of the new health emphasis of the 1960s (holistic approach, demedicalization of health, community participation in health matters, individual and consumer rights, preventive versus curative orientation) as well as a "general left-oriented sociological discourse" (Bozzini, 1988, p. 352). Many CLSC practitioners held these beliefs and were strongly committed to prevention, community participation, and local autonomy. This emphasis was seen as a socialist threat by many doctors and conservative groups (Bozzini, 1988). In addition, there was resistance of people in the well established health-related institutions (hospitals, social services centers, etc.) who felt threatened with a loss of some of their resources and power over the health system. Such debates convinced the different governments to slow down the development of the CLSC network and to approve only modest budgets for it, especially in the difficult economic period of the early 1980s. In 1985-1986, the budget per capita (in real dollars) of the CLSCs created since 1981 was about half the budget of those opened between 1972-1977 (Gouvernement du Québec, 1987). To date, important disparities are still observed between the new CLSCs and the oldest ones (Fédération des CLSC du Québec, 1990a). However, the existence of the CLSCs is not questioned any more and the differences in ideology have smoothed out (Bozzini, 1988).

The CLSC network completed in 1988, is made up of 158 centers supplemented by 194 service points where the main services are provided and 124 fall points where some CLSC professionals provide services for a few hours a week. In total, there are 476 different points where services are offered. In 1989, the CLSCs were open for an average of 60 hours a week (Fédération des CLSC du Québec, 1990a). According to 1984 data (Table 8.1), the centers are largely known to the public (84%) and nearly 22% of the population use their services (Fédération des CLSC du Québec, 1985). However, this percentage increased to 38% in 1988-1989 (Fédération des CLSC du Québec, 1990a). As one can see, there is an increased penetration of the services even in a context where private polyclinics mostly owned by doctors are numerous and where the medical care is free. Table 8.1 also shows that people with different levels of formal education are aware of or use the services. Bozzini (1988) comments that "the CLSCs do not correspond to the

TABLE 8.1
Degree of Penetration of CLSCs in 1984

Awareness	
Awareness of the existence of CLSCs	84%
According to educational level	
0-7 years	76%
8-12 years	76%
13-15 years	87%
16 and more	89%
Users	
In % of the total population	22.6%
	38%[a]
In % of the population aware of CLSCs	27%
According to educational level	
0-7 years	28%
8-12 years	32%
13-15 years	19%
16 and more	27%

[a]figure for 1988-1989

Note: From *La clientèle réelle et potentielle des CLSC* (p. 9) by the Fédération des CLSC du Québec, 1985, Montréal, Spring, and from *Le réseau des CLSC, en 1990* (p. 1) by the Fédération des CLSC du Quebec, 1990a, Montréal, November. Adapted by permission.

North-American image of community health centres as ghetto clinics; they cater to all social categories" (p. 356).

CLSCs Characteristics in Relation to Home Care

Integration and Comprehensiveness. The CLSCs form a network established to deliver integrated and comprehensive front line health, social, and community services (Fédération des CLSC du Québec, 1990b). Indeed, all these services are available in the same CLSC. Primary health or social services take the form of consultation, prevention, referral, and so on; walk-in clinics exist in many centers. Many other forms of services are provided: home-care services, school health and social services (screening, health education, individual social intervention, contraception, etc.), occupational health, mother and child services, and mental health services, and so on. Specific activities are conducted with some target groups like abused women, adolescents, and handicapped persons, and so on. (Fédération des CLSC du Québec, 1990a). Community organization is an important component and most CLSCs have community organizers. In the CLSCs, a strong preoccupation is to ensure the quality of the local social milieu and to support networks of community groups. The emphasis is on developing, mobilizing, or supporting self-help groups, education groups, and advocacy groups. In doing so, the CLSCs serve as catalysts in the organization of community resources and groups; they contribute to their creation, development, and coordination in sharing of information, identifying community needs and gaps in services. When a group becomes autonomous, the CLSC leaves the group on its own. The CLSCs orientation is to make the local population responsible for the quality of life in the neighborhood.

Multidisciplinarity, Prevention, and Globality. The working team is multidisciplinary (nurses, social workers, physicians, occupational therapists, etc.) and promotes prevention (group education and information on important health and social issues such as hypertension, abuse, etc). Moreover, based on one of the key concepts from the Castonguay health commission's report (Castonguay, 1967–1972), the CLSCs have adopted a global approach which means, essentially, that health problems are assessed from a bio-psycho-social and environmental perspective. The professionals do not limit the assessment of a potential user of services to his medical condition or to his level of functional autonomy. Some people tend to request services in medical terms, whereas their demands are often correlates of social and environmental problems. The CLSC's are organized to intervene in those areas or to inform appropriate official bodies at the municipal or provincial level.

Autonomy and Local Orientation. The CLSCs are autonomous bodies within the Health and Social Service System, with their own board of directors; they are not "filials of hospitals." Autonomy also exists at the local level. Indeed, there is some diversity among the local programs offered, depending on the characteristics and the needs of the local community served by the CLSC. However, there are mandatory provincial programs decided at the Ministry level; one of these is the home-care program.

Local Participation. The participation of local citizens is encouraged at the management level as well as in the program activities. Four local citizens are elected to the board of directors of each CLSC, in order to represent the CLSC users. In addition, there are representatives of the CLSC personnel as well as representatives of local health and social institutions and community groups. In all, the citizens form the majority on the board.

Bozzini (1988) summarized what a CLSC is in these terms: "A CLSC is an institution providing basic primary health and social services with a community orientation as the basic framework" (p. 348). The CLSC Federation (Fédération des CLSC du Québec, 1990b) wishes the centers to be at the core of local community dynamics, which means that their activity is at the community level and is geared to the local population's needs. It is in such a context of integrated and comprehensive front line services, offered by a multidisciplinary team that has a strong community orientation and favors local participation, that a model program of home-care services was implemented. An overview of the home-care services provided in that context follows.

Home-Care Services Provided in the CLSC

In CLSCs, home-care services are the most important ones in terms of allocated protected budget. The objective of these services is to maintain people in their home environment as long as they desire. They also play an important role in relieving acute hospital beds occupied by the chronically ill elderly and overcrowded emergency rooms in large city hospitals where many elderly people go. There are two broad categories of home-care services: regular ones and special ones.

The Regular Services

There are four main types of regular services: (a) health services (personal hygiene services are part of these services), (b) social services, (c) community services, and (d) housekeeping services. These regular services are offered mostly to the elderly; other groups included are the physically or mentally handicapped and those who need post-hospitalization care. An average of 1 hour and 10 minutes of services per week for regular home care was delivered in 1989 (Fédération des CLSC du Québec, 1990a). The professional team consists of nurses, physicians, social workers, homemakers, community workers, occupational therapists, and so on. Volunteers and community groups take an active part in those services. Some examples of community services are: community organization for security issues, friendship visits to the isolated elderly (one person or couples), meals at home, shopping for homebound elderly people, and nonprofit cooperatives for housekeeping services organized with the help of the CLSC.

Special Services

With a view to preventing the inappropriate use of hospital emergency departments or to diminishing the ongoing bed crisis in acute hospitals, three special services were created starting in 1986–1987 in some designated CLSCs, at the request of the Ministry. First, the home intensive care service named SIMAD offers between 12–18 hours of services per person, per week. Second, the service called 24/7 (24 hours a day, 7 days a week) offers care for the terminally ill, for those with substantial functional losses, or for people in need of emergency services outside the regular CLSC hours. It is a service accessible to everybody by phone when the CLSC is closed; however, most users of the home intensive care service (SIMAD) are on the list of the 24/7 service. A nurse assesses each phone request and decides if the person needs a nurse's visit at any time of the evening or night, an ambulance to go to the hospital or only information and counseling by phone. Third, the home-psychogeriatric service is designed to prevent inappropriate institutionaliza-tion of the aged who have cognitive deficits or adaptation problems. A specialized multidisciplinary team covers one region and offers counseling and information to the CLSC professionals or to the caregivers of cognitively handicapped people. The specialized team helps the latter to know the community services more fully and to be aware of the specialized mental health hospital resources for the mentally impaired. The team also helps the caregivers give more effective care to the cognitively impaired.

In 1989–1990, Québec devoted 123 million Canadian dollars to home-care services; of that amount, 98 million were given to the regular services and 25 million to the intensive care service (Gouvernement du Québec, 1990). It must be noted that nearly a fifth of the budget for home-care services is thus reserved for a service that provides an alternative to hospitalization.

PROGRAM ORIENTATION AND VULNERABILITY

The Orientation

In looking at the list of services offered, one can see that the home-care program is integrated, comprehensive, and given by a multidisciplinary team whose characteristics are in line with the CLSCs' orientation. Moreover, the program's strength comes from the fact that the CLSCs are autonomous bodies based at the heart of the local community where home-care services are implemented. Those responsible for the delivery of home-care services are thus in a good position to know the service requirements, to set up services that are innovative and responsive to the local community characteristics and needs, and to establish a close interaction between the home-care staff and the community.

Local Coordination

The home-care program is coordinated at the community level with other resources (those given by private agencies or those available in health establishments such as day centers) for each user. The program is thus quite decentralized and, according to Lesemann and Nahmiash (1990b), the "aspect of local coordination is one of the strongest points in favor of the Quebec home-care system" (p. 8).

Because each region has its CLSC, the home-care program is found throughout the province. The CLSC promotes a system of auto-reference, that is, citizens may refer themselves rather than depending on a referral from a professional such a physician. Such a system increases the likelihood that home-care services will correspond to the needs of the elderly and of their caregivers because it is not a question of medical needs only, but also of social and nursing ones. An assessment for services is done at home, usually by a nurse. A treatment and a service plan are recommended to the multidisciplinary team who then makes the final decision; the plan is regularly reassessed. In case of emergency, immediate attention is given to the person before the recommended plan is submitted to the multidisciplinary team.

Cooperation with Community Groups and Informal Network

In addition, the home-care program services provided are based on the cooperation of organizations and volunteers, as illustrated by the types of services described earlier (e.g., nonprofit cooperatives for housekeeping). This is possible because of the CLSCs' community orientation to train and support volunteers and community groups. As for the actual caregiving and the support offered to caregivers, the home-care program approach consists of promoting an efficient articulation between the informal family network and the services themselves; it consists also of a partnership system based on intensive interaction. Moreover, in keeping with their community orientation, home-care services strive to support family members in their caregiving activities to help them strengthen their informal network and to make use of community resources.

Vulnerable Aspects

However impressive the foregoing description may be, the home-care program is in a relatively vulnerable position in terms of its orientation and the availability of services they can offer. This fragile position can be chiefly attributed to two problems that are closely related: (a) the presence of a persistently strong hospital-oriented system, and (b) a context of financial restrictions. Let us discuss these two problems in more detail.

Threat to the Preventive and Community Orientation

The special services, although potentially an innovative addition to home care, has been implemented in a way that poses a threat that the preventive and community-oriented approach of the home-care program. The special services have the specific purpose of reducing the number of acute hospital and emergency department beds often used by elderly persons. In other words, these services were hospitalization replacements. Although the CLSCs received budgets for these services, they received them at a time when many of them were experiencing difficulty providing even the regular home care services. Furthermore, the budgets allocated to the CLSCs have been modest, especially for newer programs or services, and growth has been slowed due to periods of economic slow down. According to a 1987 government report (Gouvernement du Québec, 1987), when the CLSCs received new mandates (home-care special services), they were asked to do more without being given adequate funding. In 1986, the CLSC Federation estimated that to offer adequate home services, the budget would have to be four times as great (Roy, 1986).

Such circumstances led to the risk of offering special home-care services at the expense of regular home-care services, particularly preventive and community-oriented ones. This means that the elderly and their caregivers who are not in a crisis situation or in one that would require hospital services if home care were not available, will receive fewer services than they need or will be put on a waiting list because they are not considered priority cases. If that threat materializes, we will have a home care system much less oriented to community and prevention and much more oriented to the substitution of institutional services and intensive care. I am not opposed to using home-care services in place of acute care beds, but my concern is that this step is being taken at the expense of other preventive home-care services.

Limited Availability of Services

Regular home-care services are experiencing difficulties, especially in terms of availability of services. In a free health system where the demand exceeds supply and where the aged population is increasing, priority criteria should be established for the use of the regular services. The four types of regular home services offered are affected in different ways by the context of limited resources with its inevitable consequence of having to set user criteria. Let us review the four regular home services within the framework of economic restraints and user criteria.

Health Services. Even though everyone has a right to health services, screening criteria that are often considered are the risk of institutionalization, a crisis situation, and if the aged person is without family. The latter situation has been noted in another Canadian study where the quantity of home-care services is negatively correlated to the presence of a spouse or to the number of family members (Chappell & Blanford, 1987). Indeed, it seems to be an international pattern. Even in Denmark where home-care services to the elderly are numerous, potential family assistance is taken into consideration in the allocation of home care (Jamieson, 1989). Moreover, in order to diminish the waiting list and to serve more people, the CLSCs have adopted a policy of crumbling the services, that is, they give services to more elderly people but for fewer hours. According to a 1990 CLSC Federation statement (Fédération des CLSC du Québec, 1990a), when the mean hours of services are calculated according to the needs of the population, the number is 5 hours per person, per week, not the 1 hour and 10 minutes that is currently available.

Social and Community Services. These services are in a variable position. The policy and the service orientation of each CLSC determines how much of the budget will be allocated to social and community services as part of the home-care program. If a CLSC is strongly oriented toward a preventive and a community home-care approach, more resources will be given to the social and community services. If, as mentioned by Lesemann and Nahmiash (1990b), "intensive home care and medically urgent clients are being given priority (beds replacement orientation), socially-oriented services and preventive services becomes less of a priority" (p. 6). In my own view, there is now considerable danger that social and community services will suffer as CLSCs narrow their focus to hospital beds replacement services.

Housekeeping Services. Within the regular services offered by the CLSCs, the housekeeping services are the ones most affected by the lack of financial resources; consequently, their availability is more limited than health services. Even though housekeeping services are essential to home care, there is a temptation to give them secondary importance, especially when the demand for intensive home-care service is high. At the moment, there is a clear tendency in favor of giving priority for housekeeping services to those people who have the lowest socioeconomic status. Most CLSCs do a financial assessment before offering housekeeping services and the person who can pay must at least pay what he is able to afford. In an effort to solve this problem, some CLSCs have helped to set up nonprofit cooperatives that deliver housekeeping services and have encouraged self-help groups or voluntary groups to participate in housekeeping services. Other CLSCs have a list of reliable private agencies where a caregiver or an elderly person may have those services at the best price–quality ratio. Moreover, the CLSCs will intervene in the area of housekeeping services in analyzing the support that is given to the elderly and their caregivers by the whole family system. Family meetings are held, if needed, in order to strengthen that support or to organize it in a more efficient way. However, what happens if a caregiver or an elderly person does not want to pay, because he is at the limit of his financial capacity, or if he refuses the support of the rest of the family? The chances are that his situation will deteriorate to the point where he will need intensive health services or intensive home care.

Thus, housekeeping services are in a grey area, in the sense that they are not part of the universal health and social services and are available only to the most needy (Dumont Lemasson, 1988; Lesemann & Nahmiash, 1990b). The status of housekeeping services is definitely an important issue and it should be considered carefully whenever home-care services are discussed.

Possible Changes

Until now, I have pointed out that even though the home-care program is implemented from a local community perspective, it has been increasingly oriented toward hospital replacement services (e.g., intensive care service-SIMAD) and the availability of services is limited as well. However, this situation may yet be partly corrected. In a white paper[1] (Gouvernement du Québec, 1990) published at the time of this writing, the Ministry of Health and Social Services recognizes the lack of resources for home-care services. A series of actions are proposed, notably, to inject 200 million Canadian dollars into the home-care services budget (40 million per year for 5 years). This measure means that the home-care budget will increase from 123 million (the 1989–1990 budget) to 323 million and that stability will be ensured. However, we do not yet know whether the Ministry or the CLSC will decide how the budget will be divided between home-care regular services and home-care special services. Moreover, the status of housekeeping services is not clarified in the white paper. This publication also calls for strengthening community groups by giving them more representation (e.g., more seats on different

---

[1]In Canada, a "white paper" designates the step that immediately precedes the making of a law (thus, it is much more important than a regular government report).

ministerial committees and at the community level), full autonomy in regard
to their orientation and approaches, and increasing their budget by $8 million
a year over 5 years. That would mean an increase from $50 million dollars to
$90 million. Moreover, their budget will be for a 3-year period rather than an
annual one.

Now that we have seen one side of the coin, the structure of home-care
program, let us move to the other side, the caregivers' use of these services as
found in research.

RESEARCH FINDINGS
IN REGARD TO CAREGIVERS

Formal Support to Caregivers

Results from two research studies are reported (other studies on home care to
caregivers are currently underway). The first one (Jutras, Veilleux, &
Renaud, 1989) was conducted with a random provincial sample of 249
caregivers of elderly people who had suffered severe functional losses.
Collected through a phone interview, the data show that the family is by far
the greatest source of support for the caregiver and the care receiver. Support
from the CLSC home-care services is minimal and from the community
groups, almost nonexistent. Services most frequently used by the caregivers
are medical consultations (very rarely at home) for the care recipient.

The second study (Cossette, 1989) was done with a convenience sample of
89 Montreal caregivers of persons suffering from an obstructive chronic
pulmonary disease at a moderate or severe stage. Only four caregivers benefit
from home-care services. Of course, there are limits to the inferences one can
draw from these research but they lead to similar conclusions: Caregivers are
not making extensive use of formal services (either public or private) and help
received by caregivers comes essentially from the informal network, not from
the formal support network. According to a recent white paper (Gouvernement du Québec, 1990). Between 70% and 80% of the care to the elderly
people is given by the family. That observation warrants particular mention
because some professionals in the health and social field feel that the family
should serve as a resource in the organization of home services and should do
more in terms of caregiving.

In these two research studies, the reasons for low utilization of home-care
services were not examined. However, possible explanations can be put
forward: the limited availability of such services, the families' perception of
home-care services as a rare commodity, and the lack of knowledge that these
services existed. In regard to the last possible explanation, a recent provincial

survey (Fédération des CLSC du Québec, 1991) conducted with a random sample of 1,664 respondents sheds some light on this point. Nearly 57% of the respondents were not aware of the existence of the home-care program and among those who knew of its existence, 43% were current or past users of the home-care services. However, the awareness increases among two groups potentially more interested in home-care services. Among the respondents aged 65 years or over, 61.2% were aware of the home-care program and among those aged between 45 and 64, where the possibility of being an adult-child caregiver can happen, the percentage of respondents was 49.5 (the sample percentages of these two groups of respondents are not given in the report). Overall, these figures show that the degree of awareness can still be increased.

Renaud, Jutras, and Bouchard (1987) found that only 4% of respondents surveyed (not exclusively elderly persons) had availed themselves of a community group during the preceding year, even though 60% knew of the existence of such a group in their neighborhood and its action is part of the CLSCs policy. It seems that this problem cuts across all age groups and is not limited to the elderly.

The Assessment of the Need for Services

In a free health system, where the demand exceeds the supply, the difficult task of evaluating the need for services amounts to accepting the demand, refusing it, limiting the service, or using a waiting list. One study (Lesemann & Chaume, 1989) done with a convenience sample of 196 Montreal caregivers might provide a little insight in respect to that issue. The sample consisted of caregivers of very dependent elderly people who were already receiving an average of 6 hours of home-care services a week. The study reveals an important difference between the assessment done by the professionals of the services and the one done by members of the research team, even if both parties used a very similar assessment tool. The assessment tool concerned mainly the functional status of the care receiver. One hundred percent of the elders were judged by the service agencies to be very dependent. When interviewed by a researcher, 50% of the caregivers described their elders as slightly dependent.

According to the authors, in the context of a free health-care system where the emergency of the situation and the number of needs are criteria for judging the priority of requests for services, caregivers might feel justified in insisting on the deficits of the sick person and on the more negative side of the situation. This can happen with the more or less implicit collaboration of the professional. In the context of a research interview, caregivers might be less inclined to describe their situation as dramatic and might even want to point out their ability to deal with the situation. The role and the status of the interviewer may bring the respondent to emphasize different aspects of his situation. However, this interpretation must be viewed with caution. Other factors could contribute to the difference in respondents' answers: the difference in interviewing techniques, the reliability of the instrument, and the fact that the two assessment tools were not exactly the same.

Overall, from research reported earlier, the support given by the families far exceeds support given by the home-care services and there is a low utilization of these. However, it seems that no research has been done to identify the reasons of this low utilization. There is also a lack of evaluation of home-care programs. Until now, the quality and the efficacy of that program has not been rigorously evaluated by the CLSCs. They have instead put their efforts into the development and expansion of their services and protection of their fragile position within the health system, leaving little time for evaluative research. The principal criterion for judging the home-care program is the evidence that interested persons remain at home as long as they wish.

SUMMARY AND CONCLUSION

In summary, what can we say about home-care programs in Québec? The network of CLSCs spread throughout the province provides the structure for its implementation and, therefore, the program is community-oriented and locally based. The program is committed to work in close collaboration with community groups, volunteers and the family network. Home-care services do exist in every CLSC but their availability is limited because restricted funding does not permit them to meet all the demands. Moreover, the program must be on its guard against the danger of becoming more oriented toward hospital replacement services and consequently allocating less resources for preventive community-based services. These vulnerable aspects of the program might be lessened present if the recent white paper's (Gouvernement du Québec, 1990) recommendation to increase their budget is adopted. However, housekeeping services will still be in a grey area and the least available. The fact that the community groups will have their budget increased may help to improve these services. If the trend to use nonprofit cooperatives to provide housekeeping services increases, it will help to make those services more affordable than in the private sector.

In addition to the problem of limited resources, the mentality of being hospital and medically oriented constitutes a threat to the community focus of the home-care program. Rather than providing prevention and support, there is a persistent risk of becoming more and more a hospital replacement service. The primary goal of community home-care services is not to delay or prevent institutionalization, although this might indeed be a consequence of these services. Their primary goal is, rather, to offer conditions that will not only enable the person to stay in his or her home, but that will ensure an acceptable quality of life. It cannot be too strongly stated that a home-care program should not be organized so as to serve the needs of the hospital system. In Québec, we need a shift toward strengthening the preventive and community-based characteristics of the home-care program. A greater extent of home-care services for acute care beds replacement should not be offered at the expense of other preventive home-care services.

At the research level, longitudinal studies are most needed in order to portray the pattern of utilization of home-care services and to identify the factors associated with possible patterns of use. At present, we can only speculate that patterns might vary over time, from the beginning of the caregiving situation to the admission to a nursing home, or to death at home. We know, for example, that there is a steady decline in demented persons' cognitive capacity and that their dysfunctional behaviors also change as time goes on. Other changes that must therefore be anticipated are related to the caregivers' difficulties in managing the dysfunctional behaviors, to the caregivers' coping skills and to the resources received from the informal network. One or all of these changes may influence the type, the number and the timing of the need of home-care services. We do not know if the effects of offering preventive home-care services are different from those obtained when services are given in a crisis situation. On the one hand, the caregiving function of the family in the home is considered critical; on the other hand, the quality of this function has been the subject of very few studies. Moreover, it would be of interest to conduct a study in both a free health system and in a private one, in order to compare patterns of utilization of services and barriers to that utilization. Such a study would help to identify, among other things, the influence of a free health system on user expectations and patterns of utilization.

REFERENCES

Bozzini, L. (1988). Local community services centers (CLSCs) in Quebec: Description, evaluation, perspectives. *Journal of Public Health Policy, 9,* 346–375.

Castonguay, C. (1967–1972). *Rapport de la commission d'enquête sur la santé et le bien-être social* [Report on the inquiry commission on health and welfare]. Québec: Editeur officiel du Québec.

Chappell, N. L., & Blanford, A. A. (1987). Health service utilization by the elderly persons. *Canadian Journal of Sociology, 12,* 195–215.

Cossette, S. (1989). *Prédiction en sciences infirmières de la santé des femmes soignant leur conjoint atteint d'une maladie pulmonaire obstructive chronique* [Prediction in nursing sciences on the health of wives giving care to a spouse affected by a chronic obstructive pulmonary disease]. Unpublished master's thesis, Université de Montréal, Montréal, Québec.

Dumont Lemasson, M. (1988). Politique du maintien à domicile [Home-care policies]. In Association pour la santé publique du Québec (Ed.), *Proceedings of the symposium on Le maintien à domicile: à la recherche d'un nouvel équilibre* [*Proceedings of the symposium on Home-care: Finding a new balance*]. (pp. 76–79). Montréal: Association pour la santé publique du Québec.

Fédération des CLSC du Québec (1985). *La clientèle réelle et potentielle des CLSC* [*CLSCs actual and potential clientèle*]. Montréal, Spring.

Fédération des CLSC du Québec (1990a). *Le réseau des CLSC, en 1990* [CLSCs network in 1990] (Press release). Montréal, November.

Fédération des CLSC du Québec (1990b). *Le défi local!* (Mémoire sur l'avant projet de loi sur les services de santé et les services sociaux) [*The local challenge!* (Report on the preliminary project for legislation on health and social services)]. Montréal, January.

Fédération des CLSC du Québec (1991). *Les perceptions des Québécois et des Québécoises à l'égard des services de maintien à domicile offerts par les CLSC* [*Perception of Quebecers regarding home-care services provided by local community services centers (CLSCs)*]. Montréal, January.

Gouvernement du Québec (1987). *Rapport du comité de réflexion et d'analyse des services dispensés par les CLSC* (Brunet Report) [*Report of the committee of reflection and analysis of services provided by CLSCs*]. Québec: Ministère de la Santé et des Services Sociaux, March.

Gouvernement du Québec (1990). *Une réforme axée sur le citoyen* (livre blanc) [*Reform centered on the citizen* (White Paper)]. Québec: Ministère de la Santé et des Services Sociaux, December.

Jamieson, A. (1989). A new age for older people? Policy shifts in health and social care. *Social Science and Medicine, 29,* 445–454.

Jutras, S., Veilleux, F., & Renaud, M. (1989). *Des "partenaires" méconnus: les aidants des personnes âgées en perte d'autonomie* [*Unrecognized partners: People helping elderlies losing their autonomy*] (Research Report). Université de Montréal, Groupe de recherche sur les aspects sociaux de la prévention, Montréal, Québec.

Kergoat, M.-J., & Lebel, P. (1987). Aspects démographiques et épidémiologiques [Demographic and epidemiological aspects]. In M. Arcand & R. Hébert (Eds), *Précis pratique de gériatrie* [*Handbook of geriatrics*] (pp. 17–27). Saint-Hyacinthe, Québec: Edisem.

Lesemann, F., & Chaume, C. (1989). *Familles-Providence: la part de l'Etat* [*Providential families: The government's share*]. Montréal: Les Editions Saint-Martin.

Lesemann, F., & Nahmiash, D. (1990a, May). *Home care in Canada: Home-based or institution-based?.* Paper presented at the International Seminar Shifts in the Welfare Mix, University of Montreal, Montreal, Quebec.

Lesemann, F., & Nahmiash, D. (1990b, May). *Case study: The organization of home care services for the elderly in Montreal: Case study of a local community service center: CLSC Metro.* Paper presented at the International Seminar Shifts in the Welfare Mix, University of Montreal, Montreal, Quebec.

Renaud, M., Jutras, S., & Bouchard, P. (1987). *Les solutions qu'apportent les Québécois à leurs problèmes sociaux et sanitaires* [*Quebecers' solutions for their social and health problems*] (Recherche 6, Commission d'enquête sur les services de santé et les services sociaux). Québec: Les Publications du Québec.

Roy, J. (1986). *Bilan du maintien à domicile dans les CLSC I: problématique des services* [*Report on home-care in CLSCs I: Problematic of the services*]. Montréal: Fédération des CLSC du Québec.

Statistique Canada. (1984). *Les personnes âgées au Canada* [*Elderlies in Canada*]. Ottawa: Statistique Canada.

The Direction of Home-Based Community Care in Québec: The Effects on Caregiving Families

Carol J. Whitlatch
The Pennsylvania State University

It is no small task to develop and implement a comprehensive system of care that provides basic primary health and social services to a large, diverse, and rapidly aging population. In addition to this already formidable task, imagine designing the system so that it is responsive to unique community needs and stresses prevention and high quality of care. These objectives reflect the intent of the Canadian Province of Québec in establishing a network of Local Community Service Centers (CLSCs) and model program of home-care services.

In her chapter describing Québec's comprehensive health system, Louise Lévesque examines the hazards of creating and maintaining this system in the face of initial opposition, overwhelming demand, and increasing costs. In addition, budget constraints, along with provincial mandates to expand services, have led to a shift away from preventative and community-oriented services. Lévesque observes that Québec's system is shifting away from home and preventative care and becoming more focused on intensive care and the substitution of institutional services. She further posits that this shift would likely have a negative impact on caregivers and other potential consumers in need of home-based rather than immediate or hospital care.

This section expands on the topic of home-based community service provision by reflecting on the main characteristics of Québec's system. Although home-based services can benefit a variety of consumers, this chapter emphasizes the manner in which services affect caregivers. First, the CLSCs' role as community organizer will be described: Does this role consistently and effectively promote and facilitate a responsibility by the local population to provide a high quality of life? Next, the interrelationship between service provision and utilization is discussed to emphasize the importance of ongoing needs assessments to insure appropriate service provision. Finally, the financial dilemma common to many health-care agencies is considered; that is, the problem of securing adequate program funding and containing costs during a time of rising health-care costs. This section concludes with a discussion of the direction of home-care services in assisting caregivers who support older community-dwelling family members.

Community Organization

Community organization is an integral part of Québec's CLSC system. In discussing community organization, three main points will be addressed: (a) the development and promotion of autonomous community organizations, (b) the provision of a "high quality of life" to community residents, and (c) local participation in the program development and implementation.

Promoting Local Organizations. An important component of Québec's CLSCs is to promote the local organization of self-help, education, advocacy, and other groups. These groups serve multiple, diverse, and needy populations. This type of consumer advocacy at the grass roots level can be very effective in developing caregiver programs. In the United States, for example, the Alzheimer's Disease Association and California's system of Caregiver Resource Centers were initially formed in response to the needs of caregivers. The success of these caregiver programs is due, in large part, to the solid foundation that was built through strong local organization. On the other hand, and considering the stresses of caregiving (Deimling & Bass, 1986; George & Gwyther, 1986; Zarit, Reever, & Bach-Peterson, 1980), it may well be that caregivers who are overwhelmed may have neither time nor energy to unite for their cause. Considering the time it takes to achieve change in governmental programs, caregivers and other consumers who wish to benefit from their efforts should focus on developing and promoting local community organization.

Providing a "High Quality of Life." A second component of the CLSC's role as community organizer is in the evaluation of providing a *high quality of life* for community residents. In order to evaluate high quality of life, the CLSCs must clearly define this subjective term. Is high quality of life the provision of preventative health-care services and assisting individuals to remain in their homes? Is it a reflection of consumer satisfaction, or service utilization? Or is it a specific standard by which all individuals should live; that is, adequate food, shelter, health care, and so on. In any case, the CLSCs as well as other home-care programs should have a clear understanding of their purpose and obligations to the community they serve.

   Local Participation.   A final component of community organization is the participation of local citizens on the CLSC's Board of Directors. To insure quality of services at the local level, the CLSCs might consider electing citizens specifically affected by CLSC service provision; that is, caregivers, recipients of other services, and so on. Again, however, it could be that many recipients of CLSC services may be too stressed to take an active role on the CLSC's Board.

   Although it remains unclear whether developing local programs is a feasible goal for the CLSCs, it is important to recognize the significance of community input for CLSC program development and implementation. Local input allows each autonomous CLSC to develop innovative programs that are responsive to needs of the local community. As a result, differences in rural and urban service delivery can be managed at the local level. The CLSCs must also follow the guidelines and mandates established by the province. Thus, CLSCs must accommodate both the needs of the local community and provincial service requirements.

   The effectiveness of local community input to program development and implementation has been demonstrated by California's system of Caregiver Resource Centers (CRCs). Funded by California's Department of Mental Health and overseen by Family Survival Project based in San Francisco, this system of 11 CRCs provides multiple services to a broad range of caregivers. Considering California's diverse population needs and geography, each CRC has been developed to meet the needs of its local community (Friss, 1990). In addition, and similar to Québec's CLSCs, the CRCs must also follow state mandates for service provision. In both the CLSCs and CRCs, local flexibility in program development and implementation has enabled more effective service provision for caregivers.

Service Provision and Utilization

The home-care services provided by the CLSCs have multiple functions. As mentioned, one important function is to help maintain persons in their home as long as they desire. According to Kane and Kane (1976), home-care services provided to the elderly are critical in enabling these elderly to remain out of institutions. Although it is not widely tested whether home care is more cost effective in comparison to institutional care, there is some evidence that supports this assumption (National Fund for Research into Crippling Disease, 1974 cited by Kane & Kane, 1976).

   A second function of CLSC home-care services is to relieve acute hospital beds and overcrowded emergency rooms, as Lévesque points out in her chapter. As a result, Québec's CLSCs are providing intensive care services at the expense of other community and preventative care services. In addition, caregivers who are not in a crisis situation are likely to be underserved. Unfortunately, as noted by Lévesque, the loss of preventative services is an enduring problem for this population. Indeed, the present medical system is designed to respond to an individual's acute care needs. Simultaneously, this system fails to address adequately the elderly's long-term care needs that result from chronic disease processes (Blieszner & Alley, 1990). Considering the universality and permanence of scarce fiscal resources, it is unlikely that there will be support for arguments in favor of preventative and noncrisis service provision.

A strength of the CLSC's service delivery model is that social and health services are offered within one agency. It has been noted that coordination between independent social and health service agencies can be problematic (Kane & Kane, 1976). The result of poor coordination is that patient care can become fragmented and inadequate. Because the CLSCs furnish both social and health services, effective coordination is more likely.

Underutilization of Services.   Although numerous home-care services are available to caregivers, these services are underutilized. Past research has shown that caregivers underutilize respite and other services even when they are available (George, Gwyther, Fillenbaum, & Palmore, 1986). One possible explanation is that the available services may be unreliable or inappropriate (Zarit, 1990). Caregivers of dementia patients have reported difficulties with services including unreliable or untrained workers, rigid and complicated procedures for receiving services, and a lack of control over how and when services were delivered (MaloneBeach, Zarit, & Spore, in press). In addition, many potential consumers may be unaware of services, as was the case in Québec. Thus, the manner in which services are organized, promoted, and delivered may determine rates of caregiver service utilization (Zarit, 1990).

It is not uncommon for caregivers to receive a great proportion of assistance from informal rather than formal sources (Friss, 1990; Friss & Whitlatch, 1991). Among elderly individuals, family members are the most constant source of support (Kane & Kane, 1976). Considering that CLSC services are underutilized by caregivers, it would be important to strengthen the informal network in supporting the impaired individual in their home. Lévesque appropriately suggests conducting an assessment of the informal network in order to improve its functioning. Periodic assessments of the network would allow a more effective coordination between the informal and formal sources of support.

Needs Assessments.   To assist in the organization and delivery of appropriate formal home-care services, agencies should consider performing periodic needs assessments within their specific communities. It is likely that a community's needs will shift, especially considering changing demographics. In addition, as has occurred in Québec, mandates for service requirements change as do budget amounts and allocations. Effective and ongoing needs assessments will enable service providers to allocate their scarce resources to the services the community most requires.

There are important issues to consider when performing a needs assessment on a caregiving population. First, it is important to survey a broad and random group rather than only those who have received services. Granted caregivers who have received services are easier to contact and more likely to respond. However, they represent a subgroup of the total population of caregivers; that is, a population that includes caregivers who do not receive services. To insure a comprehensive picture of the needs of the caregiving population, service providers must seek out and survey those caregivers who have not received services.

Once a community's needs have been assessed and programs have been developed and implemented to meet these needs, periodic program evaluations are in order to insure that the program's goals are being met. In the case of the CLSCs, little has been done in terms of evaluating the quality and efficacy of the home-care services. Instead, CLSC programs have been expanded with minimal emphasis on evaluative research to guide this expansion.

Considering that funding for supportive and preventative services will continue to be limited, it may be in the best interest of service agencies to implement periodic program evaluations. Information gained from these evaluations would provide guidance for improving programs and for funding allocations. It would be important, however, that the program goals were clearly defined. A principal criterion for judging home-care programs is "the evidence that interested persons remain at home as long as they wish." It could prove challenging to determine whether a client has remained at home "as long as they wish."

In general, it is imperative that home-care agencies are able to justify the methods by which they provide services. This can be accomplished through regular assessment of community needs, service utilization patterns, and program goals. If these assessments are designed effectively, home-care services available to caregivers will be more supportive, useful, and consistently available.

The Financial Dilemma Facing CLSCs

Since the late 1980s, Québec's CLSCs have experienced multiple financial difficulties. Since their inception, and as a result of their early socialist orientation, the CLSCs have had modest and restricted budgets. Periods of economic slowing have only aggravated these inconsistent patterns of funding. In addition, the CLSCs received new mandates to serve additional target groups without the provision of adequate funding. In fact, before these mandates were handed down, the CLSC Federation estimated that to offer adequate home services, the CLSC budget would need to be four times greater (Roy, 1986).

As is true in the United States, the increasing cost of health care is a major budgetary dilemma facing supportive and preventative programs. Also in common with the United States and other countries, Québec's elderly population is rapidly increasing. The fact that there will be more persons over the age of 75, who require a majority of the services, is even more serious in terms of costs (Kane & Kane, 1976).

Lévesque proposes one solution to contain costs by training volunteers to provide supportive services (e.g., friendly visiting, counseling, minor housework, etc.). This strategy would allow the early detection and resolving of problems that might be more costly later had they gone undetected. Unfortunately, a volunteer work force is not always as dependable as one that is paid. A home-care agency relying too heavily on volunteers would likely experience frequent turnover and, as a result, inconsistent and ineffective service provision.

A second solution to aid cost containment is a family partnership where caregivers and agencies share responsibility for the care of the older adult. As part of this partnership, service agencies would conduct periodic family meetings to coordinate care responsibilities between family members and agency staff. The family's informal support network would also be assessed and, if necessary, strengthened to guarantee that it is supportive rather than destructive to the caregiver. As noted by Lévesque, close coordination between the caregiver, service agencies, and informal network is crucial to insuring that caregivers receive the services they require.

Coordination between family and service agency is an important component of the Caregiver Resource Centers (CRCs) in California. Every 6 months, caregivers who receive CRC services are interviewed to determine if the mix of services they receive is still appropriate. If necessary, the caregiver's care plan is modified to meet the caregiver's changing needs. In some cases staff may suggest a family meeting be held to strengthen the caregiver's informal network. Overall, close coordination between service agencies and family caregivers can be very useful in insuring both effective service provision and supportive informal networks.

The Direction of Home-Care Services

Québec's system of CLSCs has been designed to provide nearly every service needed to maintain an older adult in their own home. In addition to these home-care services, CLSCs are mandated to provide health and social service assistance to a diverse population with multiple, complex, and costly needs. Have the CLSCs been successful in meeting these goals? Considering that they have had to struggle with inconsistent budget allocations, increasing health costs, serving an older and ailing population, and pressure to provide hospital replacement services, Québec's CLSCs have accomplished a great deal.

On paper, the CLSC system is committed to improving the lives of caregivers. In reality, due to recent shifts in program mandates, a system is now in place that is driven by issues of cost containment. The focus of CLSC service provision has shifted away from prevention and caregiving in order to provide hospital replacement and intensive care services.

The shift in service delivery that has occurred in Québec has policy implications for home-based community services everywhere. The economic and demographic trends seen in Canada are occurring throughout the world. Similarly, health-care costs will undoubtedly continue to rise. Sadly, any shift away from preventative care will negatively affect caregivers and other consumers in need of home-based rather than immediate or hospital care.

Unfortunately, there is no answer to this dilemma. Older adults will continue to prefer living at home and family members will continue to provide their care. It would be to everyone's advantage if service agencies and families would coordinate their efforts in maintaining older adults in the community. If this coordination is impossible, caregivers will have fewer preventative services available to them. In the end, older adults may be forced to use the hospital replacement and intensive care services that supplanted their preventative services.

ACKNOWLEDGMENT

This research was partially supported by National Institute on Aging Grant T32 AG00048 to The Pennsylvania State University.

REFERENCES

Blieszner, R., & Alley, J. M. (1990). Family caregiving for the elderly: An overview of resources. *Family Relations, 39*, 97–102.
Deimling, G. T., & Bass, D. M. (1986). Symptoms of mental impairment among elderly adults and their effects on family caregivers. *Journal of Gerontology, 41*, 778–784.
Friss, L. (1990). A model state-level approach to family survival for caregivers of brain-impaired adults. *The Gerontologist, 30*, 121–125.
Friss, L., & Whitlatch, C. J. (1991). Who's taking care: A statewide study of family caregivers. *American Journal of Alzheimer's Care and Related Disorders and Research, Sept./Oct.,* 16–26.

George, L. K., & Gwyther, L. P. (1986). Caregiver well-being: A multidimensional examination of family caregivers of demented adults. *The Gerontologist, 26,* 253–259.

George, L., Gwyther, L., Fillenbaum, G. G., & Palmore, E. (1986, November). *Respite care: A strategy for easing caregiver burden?* Paper presented at the annual meeting of the Gerontological Society of America, Chicago, IL.

Kane, R. L., & Kane, R. A. (1976). *Long-term care in six countries: Implications for the United States.* U.S. Department of Health, Education, and Welfare; National Institutes of Health, Washington, DC.

MaloneBeach, E. E., Zarit, S. H., & Spore, D. S. (in press). Case management as an approach to dementia: An exploratory study. *Journal of Applied Gerontology.*

National Fund for Research into Crippling Disease. (1974). *Care with dignity — An analysis of the costs of care for the disabled.* London. (cited in Kane & Kane, 1976)

Roy, J. (1986). *Bilan du maintien à domicile dans les CLSC I: Problématique des services* [Report on home-care in CLSCs I: Service problems]. Montréal: Fédération des CLSC du Québec.

Zarit, S. H. (1990, March). *Methodological considerations in caregiver interventions and outcome research.* Paper presented at the NIMH Workshop on the Mental Health of Family Caregivers in Alzheimer's Disease and Related Dementia, Chevy Chase, MD.

Zarit, S. H., Reever, K. E., & Bach-Peterson, J. (1980). Relatives of the impaired elderly: Correlates of feelings of burden. *The Gerontologist, 20,* 649–655.

9

Barriers to the Use of Formal Services Among Alzheimer's Caregivers

Joseph T. Mullan
University of California, San Francisco

Researchers have documented that caring for a family member with a progressive dementing illness increases caregiver distress (George & Gwyther, 1986; Pruchno & Resch, 1989; Zarit, Todd, & Zarit, 1986); and they agree that use of formal services may alleviate such distress. They remain puzzled, however, about why caregivers do not use more of the services available to them and why some caregivers take advantage of formal services but others do not (Brody, 1988; Montgomery, Kosloski, & Borgatta, 1990). Generally, caregivers underutilize formal services, even those provided at low cost (Caserta, Lund, Wright, & Redburn, 1987; Conrad, Hanrahan, & Hughes, 1990; Lawton, Brody, & Saperstein, 1989; Montgomery & Borgatta, 1989; Oktay & Volland, 1990). Perhaps clinicians and practitioners are correct: Barriers to the use of services are social and psychological as well as economic (Brody, 1988). Thus, especially as community budgets shrink and access to services becomes increasingly difficult, we must understand the social and psychological barriers to service use in order to devise effective intervention programs (Zarit, 1989).

The most common model of service use has been borrowed from studies of medical utilization (Andersen & Newman, 1973). At the individual level, it specifies three classes of predictors. First is the presence of medical needs that are seen as requiring attention. But even when medical needs exist, utilization of services occurs only when certain predisposing characteristics, such as positive attitudes toward the helpfulness of medical care, are also present. Finally, even those with medical needs and a predisposition to use services must have some enabling characteristics, such as adequate income or insurance coverage, which will allow them access to the services they need. At the system level, needed services must be available in the community.

241

Although this model alerts us to sets of characteristics plausibly related to utilization, it does not clearly specify the conditions under which some characteristics are more important than others, nor does it clarify the relationships among these sets of variables so that one can test alternative causal models (Mutran & Ferraro, 1988).

In fact, the model leaves much unexplained even when it is applied to the use of medical services, particularly among the elderly (Wolinsky & Arnold, 1988). And its problems are amplified when researchers apply it to the use of non-medical services arranged, not by care recipients, but by family caregivers. Recently, researchers have addressed some of the limitations of the model, by taking into account the characteristics of both care recipient and caregiver and by beginning to look at the relationship between informal social resources and use of formal services (Bass & Noelker, 1987; George, 1987; Noelker & Bass, 1989). One problem with the model is clear: Although the model assumes a need for services, what constitutes a need for nonmedical services is far from obvious (Chappell, 1987). Caregivers will vary in their definitions of optimal functioning for themselves and those for whom they care (Cohler, Groves, Borden, & Lazarus, 1989). Their use of services will depend on their ways of viewing the problems they face.

This chapter builds on previous modifications of the medical utilization model by placing the decision to use services within a stress framework (Pearlin, Mullan, Semple, & Skaff, 1990). First, it briefly traces the processes involved as caregivers decide that formal services can assist them in managing their relatives' care. Then it analyzes data from a large ongoing study of Alzheimer's caregivers in order to examine a broad range of psychosocial factors that may be related to service use. Finally, it extends the analysis by considering some well-defined conditional effects inherent in the use of the Andersen and stress models.

THE STRESS FRAMEWORK

The condition of the patient affected by dementia has a dual function in this framework. On the one hand, the cognitive deficits and functional impairments represent the patient's needs. But, equally important, these patient needs represent *primary stressors* for the caregivers and their families, that is, they place demands on the family to provide care (Pearlin, Mullan, Semple, & Skaff, 1990). Caregivers must evaluate the patient needs, assess their own capacities to provide appropriate care, and then set up a strategy for dealing with these primary stressors.[1]

---

[1]The stress framework places the decision to use formal services within the broader context of caregivers' lives. In this respect, it shares many features with other attempts to provide a

Moreover, as the disease progresses, the situation becomes more complex, because the primary stressors may create *secondary strains* or exacerbate already existing strains in caregivers' lives.[2] The secondary strains might include economic hardships, family conflict, difficulty maintaining social connections, and a variety of intrapsychic strains, such as role overload, anger, and depression (Pearlin et al., 1990). As these strains develop, a new cycle of planning and self-assessment may occur. That is, caregivers may re-evaluate their resources and devise continuing strategies for care: They may care for the patient entirely alone, decide to institutionalize, share caregiving with other family members, arrange other informal help, and/or form a variety of linkages to formal services (Noelker & Bass, 1989). In addition, as caregivers adjust to the patients' growing needs, the secondary strains—the caregivers' own problems and needs—may begin to require attention. Absorbed as they are in meeting the needs of the patient, they may fail to realize the pressing nature of their own problems (MaloneBeach, Zarit, & Spore, 1992). At this point, a difference may emerge between their sense of their situation and the view professionals take of it. As Brody has argued, and as much of the caregiver literature attests, professionals can often recognize that caregivers, whom they have treated as their partners in caring for the patient, are becoming their clients as well (Brody, 1988).

When caregivers are dealing with primary stressors or secondary strains, they may turn to formal services for help. In order to understand the barriers to use of formal services, the extended stress model I employ takes into account seven types of characteristics of the caregiving situation. First are *background characteristics,* such as gender or education that may affect use directly, or indirectly influence other factors that affect use. Second, *economic resources* such as income or economic strain may facilitate or impede service use. Third is the *caregiving context,* for example, the relationship of caregiver to patient or the length of time the patient has needed care. This context forms the basis for strategies of informal help and service use. Fourth, there are informal *social resources* that can influence the necessity or likelihood that formal services will be used (Noelker & Bass, 1989). These include friends and family who may provide instrumental assistance, emotional support, and information about services; or who may create conflictive situations. Fifth, the *physical health* of the patient and caregiver may require medical care, which in turn may link caregivers with other formal services. Sixth are the *primary stressors,* the configuration of patient characteristics that indicate need for

---

conceptual framework for the study of family members who provide care to frail elderly (e.g., Cohler et al., 1989; Romeis, 1989; Schulz, 1990).

[2]It should be emphasized that in calling experiences such as overload "secondary," I am not suggesting that they are less important in their consequences, only that they follow in part from the primary stressors, in this case, the cognitive and functional impairments of the demented family member.

help: cognitive decline, functional impairments, or problematic behavior. Finally, *intrapsychic strains* such as overload, anger, or depression may be secondary strains, that is, problems and needs of caregivers that may at times lead them to seek help from formal services, and may at other times incapacitate them and make service use less likely.[3]

It is important to note that the applications of the Andersen model have focused on behavioral and demographic variables that are surrogates for a set of important predisposing factors, such as beliefs and attitudes, that are not directly measured in this as in most studies. These factors include knowledge of available services and how to access them, beliefs and attitudes about formal care, norms around caregiving responsibilities and the acceptability of using formal care, and concerns and beliefs about the safety and quality of nonfamily care. These factors are influenced by background characteristics and presumably explain in part why the typical background variables affect service use (Ward, Sherman, & LaGory, 1984).

SAMPLE

The data are drawn from the first wave of a multi-wave study of 555 caregivers in the San Francisco and Los Angeles areas. For the most part, the caregivers were recruited from people who had telephoned or joined their local Alzheimer's Associations (formerly ADRDA). We attempted to contact all those who described themselves as the primary family member providing home care for a spouse, parent, or parent-in-law with Alzheimer's or another progressive dementia. During a screening call, we verified that these criteria were met. When the contact persons did not consider themselves the primary caregivers, we asked for the name and phone number of the family members who had primary responsibility for providing care. When caregiving was shared, we chose the spouse whenever possible. Most interviews were conducted in caregivers' homes and lasted between $1\frac{1}{2}$ and 2 hours.

Table 9.1 presents the baseline characteristics of the sample, separately for spouses and adult children. In many ways it is similar to samples from other caregiver studies: Mainly Caucasian and tending toward the better educated and wealthier segment of the presumed caregiver population. Nevertheless, there is enough variability in the key characteristics to allow for an analysis of

---

[3]I have included overload as a secondary strain in this chapter, although it was considered a subjective indicator of a primary stressor in the Pearlin et al. (1990) overview of caregiver stress. I do this in order to differentiate clearly the condition of the demented family member from the consequences to the caregiver of those stressors. This emphasis is useful in extending Andersen's utilization model because that framework has tended to focus on the characteristics of the identified patient and has ignored caregivers or other informal supports. (See Noelker & Bass, 1989, for a critique of the Andersen model.)

TABLE 9.1
Sample Characteristics (N = 555)

Variable		Spousal Caregivers (n = 326) N	Percent		Children Caregivers (n = 229) N	Percent
City	S.F.	182	56		118	52
	L.A.	144	44		111	48
Caregiver Relationship	Wife	190	58	Daughter	173	76
	Husband	136	42	Son	37	16
				Dtr-in-law	18	8
				Son-in-law	1	–
Marital Status	Married	326	100		132	58
	Div./Sep.	–	–		44	19
	Widowed	–	–		18	8
	Never Marr.	–	–		35	15
Living with AD Patient	Yes	323	99		139	61
	No	3	1		90	39
Race	White	284	87		183	80
	Black	24	7		35	15
	Asian	6	2		6	3
	Hispanic	12	4		5	2
Resp. Education	Less than HS	60	18		14	6
	High School	95	29		58	25
	Some College	71	22		73	32
	College Grad	45	14		40	18
	College +	54	17		44	19
Variable		N	Mean		N	Mean
Resp. Age		325	70		228	51
Patient Age		326	72		229	80
Duration of Years Caregiving		323	2.8		229	3.2
Household Income (in thousands)		312	39		223	31

service use. The advantage of a sample drawn from those who contact Alzheimer's Associations in large metropolitan areas rich in services is that we can examine a broad segment of caregivers who have some familiarity with the disease and the possibility of making linkages with outside agencies to obtain information or help. The disadvantage, of course, is that we cannot say anything about those who are very isolated, alienated from sources of formal help, or otherwise disinclined to seek information from such organizations.

The following analyses are based on interview data from 520 spousal and adult child caregivers. It excludes 18 daughters-in-law and 1 son-in-law, as well as 16 other cases with incomplete data on the variables of interest.

MEASURES

Service Use

Caregivers were asked which of 16 services they had used in the past year, and how often they had used each one. Because this chapter focuses on barriers to service use, rather than volume of use, the primary dependent variable is whether caregivers had used any of the services in the prior year. Table 9.2 presents the distributions of service use in the prior year and, for comparison, in the prior month. Along with overall use, the table indicates caregivers' use of nine of the most frequently used services.

This group of caregivers is generally not averse to using services. Only 15% had not used a service in the past year; more than three quarters had used one in the past month. In general, a relatively large proportion of these caregivers uses respite services. The most commonly used service is a support group, with 40% having attended one in the past year and about a quarter in the past month. The second most commonly used service in the past year is an attendant or companion (31%); it is the most commonly used service in the past month (29%). Almost a quarter have used adult day care; 19% a senior center, and 15% have been to counseling.

Caregivers were also asked why they hadn't used services if they thought that some services might have been helpful. Half replied that they did not need them, whereas 20% cited cost, 17% replied that their AD relative acted up or opposed the help, 9% said that they didn't know about the service, 7% responded that they didn't know how to obtain the services, and 5% worried about the poor quality of services. (The reasons for nonuse were not tied explicitly to any specific service.) These responses constitute a sensible, if incomplete, set of reasons for not using services and correspond to reasons commonly reported in other research (Krout, 1983; MaloneBeach et al., 1992).

TABLE 9.2
Service Use ($N = 520$)

Service	Past Year	Past Month
Any Service	84%	77%
Support Group	41%	26%
Attendant/Companion	31%	29%
Housekeeper	24%	21%
Adult Day Care	23%	20%
Senior Center	19%	14%
Visiting Nurse	17%	9%
Counseling	15%	8%
Transportation	14%	11%
Home Delivered Meals	8%	7%

Predictors of Service Use

Background Characteristics.   Table 9.3 presents the means and standard deviations of the explanatory variables for the 520 cases included in the analysis. The background characteristics consist of demographic and status questions such as caregiver race, gender, education, and age. (Patient age was omitted because it was so highly correlated with caregiver age.)

Economic Resources.   These consist of two measures. First is the total amount of money available to caregivers. This includes not only their household income, but also any financial help they report receiving from other family members. For adult children, it also counts the patient's income. As noted earlier, this is a fairly well-off group of respondents, having almost $40,000 a year available from all sources. At the same time, it is important to note that there is considerable variability among respondents (SD = $26,000), with one quarter having $17,000 or less available from all sources. Income Adequacy is a report of whether caregivers have any money left at the end of a month, ranging from *not enough to make ends meet* = 1 to *some left over* = 3. On

TABLE 9.3
Explanatory Variables: Means and Standard Deviations (N = 520)

	Mean	(SD)		Mean	(SD)
Background			Social Resources		
Location (SF = 1)	0.55	(0.50)	Help with Care (=1)	0.37	(0.48)
Race (White = 1)	0.84	(0.37)	Help with Chores (=1)	0.27	(0.44)
Gender (Male = 1)	0.32	(0.47)	Family in Household	0.70	(1.11)
Caregiver Age (Yrs)	62.20	(13.05)	Phone Contacts/Month	11.44	(7.36)
Education (Yrs)	13.90	(2.81)	Emotional Support	3.28	(0.51)
			Fam Conflict: CG or PT	1.46	(0.70)
Economic Resources			Fam Conflict: Illness	1.49	(0.71)
Income (Thousands)	39.46	(26.70)	Physical Health		
Income Adequacy	2.44	(0.67)	CG Health	2.98	(0.79)
			Relative's Health	2.96	(0.95)
Caregiving Context			CG Chronic Conditions	1.43	(1.35)
Type of Caregiver					
Spouse (=0)	0.61	(0.49)	Primary Stressors		
Child (Apart = 1)	0.15	(0.36)	Cognitive Difficulties	2.20	(0.88)
Child (Home = 1)	0.24	(0.43)	Functional Impairment	2.76	(0.78)
			Problem Behaviors	1.98	(0.58)
Years Helping	2.97	(2.30)			
Work Status			Intrapsychic Strains		
Not Working (=0)	0.66	(0.47)	Overload	2.58	(0.93)
Full-time (=1)	0.23	(0.42)	CG Anger	2.43	(0.75)
Part-time (=1)	0.11	(0.32)	CG Competence	3.38	(0.55)
			Depression	1.83	(0.73)

average, they report having slightly more than "just enough" money left at month's end; about 45% report having some difficulty: they have "just enough" or do not have enough "to make ends meet."

Caregiving Context. Type of Caregiver consists of two dummy coded variables that indicate whether the caregiver is an adult child living apart from or residing in the same home as the parent with Alzheimer's. Spouses are the referent category. Most of the caregivers in the sample are spouses (60%). Of the adult child caregivers, most live with their parent. On average, caregivers have been providing help for almost 3 years. Most do not work outside the home: only 10% of spouses work full-time and 6% part-time, whereas 40% of adult child caregivers work full-time and 18% work part-time.

Social Resources. Help with Care is a dummy coded variable that indicates whether the caregiver reports having "a friend or relative who helps look after" the AD patient "on a *regular* basis," for example who stays with (him or her) or who helps (him or her) do things like bathing or dressing. Almost 40% report having such regular help. Help with Chores is a similar question inquiring whether the caregiver has a regular source of help with household tasks. One quarter of respondents reported that they do have help.

Family in Household is simply the number of family members, excluding the AD patient, living in the same household as the caregiver. It may be a surrogate measure of the number of people, usually children, who are available to help with tasks or caregiving at any particular time, even if they do not regularly help out. Phone Contacts is the number of the caregiver's telephone calls, in a typical month, with family and friends, some of whom may not be close by. It may be an indirect measure of the extensiveness of their network and thus of their ability to obtain information about formal services.

Emotional Support measures the availability of persons whom the caregiver perceives as trustworthy, caring, uplifting, or generally supportive ($\alpha = .84$). Caregivers feel supported by others, with only 10% not generally endorsing the items. Caregiver family conflict, a secondary role strain, is measured by two scales. The first measures the amount of conflict with family members concerning their treatment of the caregiver or the patient (Family Conflict: CG or PT), for example, not showing enough respect for the patient, or not providing enough help to the caregiver ($\alpha = .86$). The second (Family Conflict: Illness) involves conflict over the severity of the patient's illness, for example, the seriousness of memory problems or need for care ($\alpha = .80$).

Physical Health. This includes standard questions concerning physical health, from *poor* = 1 to *excellent* = 4. Caregivers reported that both they and the patients are in generally good health. In addition, caregivers indicated the number of chronic health conditions for which they had been treated in the previous 5 years (range: 0-7). They averaged a little more than one such condition.

Primary Stressors. Cognitive Difficulties measures the problem (from *No difficulty* = 0 to *Can't do at all* = 4) patients have with seven different skills such as remembering recent events and knowing what day of the week it is (α = .86). They are reported by the caregivers and are taken from standard clinical instruments such as the Mini-Mental State Exam (Folstein, Folstein, & McHugh, 1975). Caregivers reported a significant degree of impairment: on average, it is fairly difficult for patients to perform these skills.

Functional Impairment measures how much patients depend on caregivers for help (from *not at all* = 1 to *completely* = 4) with IADL tasks such as cooking, taking medications, doing housework (Lawton & Brody, 1969), or with ADLs such as eating, bathing, and grooming (Katz, Ford, Moskowitz, Jackson, & Jaffe, 1963). The average level of functional impairment is considerable, with patients depending on others "quite a bit" for help with these everyday activities (α = .89).

Problematic Behaviors is a 14-item scale that represents the frequency in the prior week that the caregiver dealt with a variety of troublesome behaviors such as incontinence, agitation, and inappropriate sexual behavior (α = .79). Caregivers reported having to deal with such behaviors once or twice a week.

Intrapsychic Strains. Overload is a three-item scale that measures the sense of being worn out or fatigued by necessary tasks (α = .80). Anger is a five-item scale which indicates feelings of tension, frustration, and anger about caregiving (α = .82); note that these feelings may or may not have been directed at the patient. Caregiving Competence is a four-item scale which assesses the respondents' perceptions of the adequacy of their performance in the caregiver role (α = .74). Depression is a summary measure of the depressive symptoms experienced in the previous week (α = .86). It is taken from standard items found in such scales as the HCL (Derogatis, Lipman, Covi, & Rickles, 1971).

ANALYSIS

This chapter focuses on the factors that either prevent the use of potentially helpful services, or make their use less likely. Because the focus is on a skewed dichotomous variable — service use versus nonuse — and not on volume of use, we employ logistic regression analysis to predict the odds of service use. Although the distribution of the outcome variable is skewed, there is still a sizable minority of caregivers who did not use any services in the prior year.

The predictors of service use are those variables identified by extensions of the Andersen model outlined earlier: background characteristics, economic resources, the caregiving context, the social resources available, medical problems of the patient and caregiver, primary stressors which place demands on caregivers' and their families' capacities, and the intrapsychic strains that may result from the demands of the caregiving situation.

The odds of service use in the previous year is the dependent variable. First, we begin with a main effects model, asking whether certain factors make people unable or unwilling to use services generally. Then, we test whether certain conditional effects occur; here we add multiplicative terms to the equation much as one would in a multiple regression model.

The major complication in the following analysis is that the data are cross-sectional, so that some of the predictor variables may stand in a reciprocal relationship with service use, being both its causes and its consequences. We expect, for example, that one factor that motivates the use of services is feeling overloaded. At the same time, to the extent that services are successful, feelings of overload should eventually decrease. We deal with this problem by estimating the logistic regressions in two ways. First, we omit the experiential variables most likely to be affected by service use, for example, overload, anger, competence, family conflict, emotional support, and depression. Then, we reestimate the equations adding these variables so that we can determine what effect their inclusion has on the other variables in the model. Fortunately, as we shall see, their inclusion has little effect on the substantive statements we would wish to make about the other variables. However, one should be somewhat cautious about how confidently one interprets the effects of these experiential variables since they could be consequences of service use as well as causes. Until subsequent waves of data are examined, we have no way of disentangling these reciprocal effects. What we can begin to do now is to test whether the data are at least consistent with the model, which assumes that these experiences may be causally related to the use of formal services.

PREDICTORS OF SERVICE USE:
MAIN EFFECTS

Table 9.4 presents the results from the main effects logistic regression analyses, estimated with and without the experiential variables in the equations. It includes only the significant predictors of service use in the past year. The first two columns present the main effects model without the experiential variables; the second two columns present the significant predictors, including the experiential variables (e.g., emotional support, overload, caregiver competence, caregiver anger, depression, family conflict over illness

TABLE 9.4
Predictors of Service Use: Main Effects Models (N = 520)

	Without Experiential Variables		With Experiential Variables	
	Coefficient	Odds Ratio	Coefficient	Odds Ratio
San Francisco	0.7294**	2.07	0.7434**	2.10
Education	0.1801***	1.20	0.1740***	1.19
Income	0.0200**	1.02	0.0198*	1.02
Number in Household	−0.4674****	0.63	−0.4561****	0.63
CG Chronic Conditions	0.2663*	1.31	0.1710	1.19
Functional Impairment	0.6561*	1.93	0.6246*	1.87
Family Conflict: PT or CG	−	−	0.8865**	2.43
Emotional Support	−	−	0.6517*	1.92

These are effects net of the other variables in the equations: Background characteristics, economic resources, caregiving context, social resources, physical health, primary stressors, and intrapsychic strains.
*$p < .05$; **$p < .01$; ***$p < .005$; ****$p < .001$

issues, and family conflict over the treatment of the caregiver or patient). In each model, the first column is the metric coefficient and associated significance level. For ease of interpretation, the second column contains the odds ratio (the exponentiated coefficient); its interpretation is analogous to that of a multiple regression coefficient except that the outcome is the odds of service use. For example, location is a predictor of service use: the odds of caregivers from San Francisco using a service are twice the odds of those from Los Angeles.

It is important to remember that these odds ratios are adjusted for the other independent variables, such as patient impairment, socioeconomic status, social resources, and so on. Thus, this location difference may be due to the availability or accessibility of services in the areas, or to the caregivers' attitudes, knowledge, or concerns about the quality of services.

As expected, those with lower incomes are less likely to use services. This positive relationship makes sense, because most services require significant out-of-pocket expenditures and are not typically covered by insurance or entitlement programs. In our sample, 70% of those using services reported that they must pay at least some of the costs themselves, and of those, almost one third reported that it is at least fairly difficult to pay for the services.

Education is also positively related to increased service use, independent of the amount of income caregivers have. Education, of course, is an omnibus variable that may be a surrogate for a set of interconnected characteristics, such as knowledge, attitudes, beliefs, and norms about using formal services.

The more chronic medical conditions caregivers report, the more likely they are to use services. This may reflect a greater willingness to acknowledge a need for help among those with a chronic condition, because they have learned to accept help from formal services, or it may mean that those with chronic conditions experience greater needs themselves.

A greater number of people in the household decreases the probability of service use, suggesting that the presence of an available group of possible helpers may reduce the need for formal services. It is worth noting again that this availability effect is independent of having a regular source of help with care or chores.

Also as expected, patient functional status is clearly related to use. Overall, greater functional impairment leads to increased likelihood of using formal services.

The second two columns present the significant predictors of service use when the seven experiential variables are added to the first equation. Two issues need to be noted. First, the general results of the initial analysis remain even when these variables are added to the equation: with one exception, the same predictors are significant and at the same magnitude. The exception is caregiver's chronic medical conditions, which is no longer a significant predictor. This suggests that the added variables intervene between chronic conditions and service use and explain why chronic conditions lead to increased use of formal services; that is, chronic conditions lead to use because caregivers facing these illnesses are more distressed. Conversely, the fact that the other predictors remain significant suggests that they do not have their effects through these added variables; for example, the number of family members in the caregiver's household decreases service use independent of the caregiver's sense of emotional support or report of family conflict.

The second issue of note is that only two of the added variables have direct effects on service use. Feeling emotionally supported increases the likelihood of using services. But having family conflict around the treatment of the patient or caregiver also increases service use, which suggests that caregivers may turn to formal help when the psychological cost of obtaining family help increases. Conflict around the severity of the illness does not affect service use. None of the intrapsychic strains (e.g., caregivers' overload, competence, anger, or depression) appears to directly affect overall service use.

To summarize the main effects model: those from San Francisco are more likely to use formal services. As expected, patient functional impairment is a predictor of service use, with those providing care for more impaired family members more likely to use services. When we turn to those socioeconomic characteristics that may interfere with the use of formal services, a relative lack of money and education is clearly related to nonuse.

The caregiver's informal social resources affect service use in complicated ways. Conflict with family members over how they or the patient are treated leads caregivers to turn outside the family for help. At the same time, however, there is evidence that having more family members in the household decreases the likelihood of turning to formal services for help. Feeling emotionally supported increases service use: People who feel relatively disconnected from a supportive and trustworthy set of relationships may find it difficult to make contact with agencies and to allow strangers to help care for their relative with Alzheimer's. What is missing from this picture is the possibility that other psychological strains may be barriers to service use: for example, we have not found that strains such as role overload or depression affect the likelihood of using services.

PREDICTORS OF SERVICE USE: CONDITIONAL EFFECTS

Perhaps one of the reasons that researchers have found only need variables significant in utilization studies is that we have not specified our models properly (Rundall, 1981). The Andersen model (Andersen & Newman, 1973) has typically been tested as a main effects model, when in fact it is inherently a conditional one. The need variables drive the entire process of seeking help. When there is no need, or low need, caregivers have little reason to use formal services. It is only when significant needs arise that a factor such as income can become an enabling variable. Similarly, as we attempt to integrate the extensions of the Andersen model within a stress framework, we face an inherently interactive model. For example, strains should be related to service use only when there is already some need for such services. The direction of effects is less predictable, however. On the one hand, feeling depressed or worn out can delay or inhibit service use. Caregivers who feel depressed or overloaded may not even attempt to reassess patients' declining abilities and mobilize themselves to search for appropriate services. On the other hand, increases in depressive symptoms or feelings of burnout may motivate caregivers to search for some help or respite for themselves.

To test these conditional effects, two sets of multiplicative terms were added to the logistic equations predicting service use. The first set tests conditional effects implied by the Andersen model: that the effects of income and education would vary by the needs of the patient. We test this by adding two multiplicative terms to the equation (functional impairment by income and functional impairment by education). Only the interaction with education was significant, and so the model was reestimated with the income interaction omitted. The first two columns of Table 9.5 contain the logistic coefficients and odds ratios of the conditional model in which functional impairments condition the impact of education.

The second set of conditional effects is implied by the stress framework: Strains will affect use under conditions of high demand on caregivers, when, for example, caregivers must provide care to someone who is severely

TABLE 9.5
Predictors of Service Use: Conditional Models ($N = 520$)

	Without Depression Interaction		With Depression Interaction	
	Coefficient	Odds Ratio	Coefficient	Odds Ratio
San Francisco	0.8446**	2.33	0.8177**	2.27
Education	−0.3166	−	−0.273	−
Income	0.0212**	1.02	0.0241**	1.02
Number in Household	−0.4328***	0.65	−0.4564***	0.63
CG Chronic Conditions	0.1784	−	0.1661	−
Functional Impairment	−1.736	−	−0.2648	−
Family Conflict: PT or CG	0.9039**	2.47	0.9376**	2.55
Emotional Support	0.6467*	1.91	0.7742**	2.17
Depression	0.1636	−	2.0973**	−
Impairment−Education	0.1879**	−	0.1666*	−
Impairment−Depression	−	−	−0.7091*	−

These are effects net of the other variables in the equations: Background characteristics, economic resources, caregiving context, social resources, physical health, primary stressors, and intrapsychic strains.

*$p < .05$; **$p < .01$; ***$p < .005$

functionally impaired. To test this, we added two multiplicative terms to the previous equation (impairment by depression and impairment by overload). Only the depression interaction was significant and the final model is presented in the second two columns of Table 9.5.

Before discussing the meaning of the conditional effects, it is important to point out that they do not change the direction or size of the other main effects, those not involved in the interactions. For example, location, income, number of family in household, family conflict, and emotional support remain predictors of service use in the presence of the interactions.

The results of the interactions are as expected: The effects of both education and depression depend on the level of impairment. Education increases the likelihood of using services among those whose relatives are more impaired. Depressive symptoms decrease use when more impairment exists. Figure 9.1 presents the results of this conditional model in a somewhat different form. It presents the odds ratios for education and depression under low, medium, and high levels of functional impairment (the lower quartile, median, and upper quartile). The odds ratios for education and depression contrast the lower versus upper quartile scores in the sample. For education, this difference is 4 years; for depression, it is one scale point.

There is a clear pattern to the conditional effects. Education has a more powerful positive influence as functional impairments increase. For example, at low impairment, the odds of a college graduate using services are almost 1.5 times those of a high school graduate. At high impairment, the odds of a

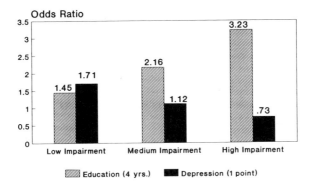

FIG. 9.1 Odds ratios by level of patient impairment.

college graduate are more than three times those of a high school graduate. Depression has a more powerful negative effect as impairment increases. At low impairment, an increase in depression (from the lower quartile to the higher) increases the odds of service use by almost 1.75. At medium impairment, the odds are about even, and at high impairment, an increase in depression decreases the odds of service use, to almost three quarters of what it is among those lower in depression. Education, whatever it represents, enables caregivers to respond to impairment by enlisting the aid of formal services. Being depressed appears to block this possibility.[4]

THE PROBLEM OF RECIPROCAL EFFECTS

This is a convenient point to underscore again the necessarily tentative nature of the effects associated with the experiential variables, those characteristics that could be consequences of service use.[5] Analysis of subsequent waves of these data may help us disentangle this issue, but we should not be too sanguine about obtaining a definitive answer from data of this kind. Even under the controlled conditions of psychotherapy research, it is sometimes difficult to demonstrate effects of this magnitude on depression; it has been

---

[4]I also tested, in a more exploratory way, a number of other possible conditional effects, none of which was significant. For example, there is no evidence in these data that the predictors of service use differ by location (S.F. vs. L.A.) or relationship to the demented family member (spouse vs. adult child), nor do I find the same kinds of conditional effects if I substitute problem behaviors or cognitive status for functional impairment.

[5]Over time, other characteristics may be affected by service use as well, for example, whether a caregiver continues working, or even continues in the caregiver role at all. Thus, some characteristics that we normally treat as stable may change in response to the caregiver's ability to access services. Only longitudinal data with larger samples can clarify these transitions in and out of the caregiver role, and other changes in the configuration of informal and formal helpers.

even more difficult in service intervention studies (Zarit, 1989). It would be surprising if, in this study, the use of any service in the past year leads to systematic decreases in depression of a magnitude to measurably affect this analysis. As in most such cross-sectional examinations, the zero-order correlation between depression and service use is positive ($r = .09$), even stronger between depression and counseling ($r = .19$). Finally, this same line of causal reasoning would suggest that family conflicts are also a consequence of service use. It is true that some families may have more conflict if the primary caregiver decides to use formal services, but then this effect should show up in the other family conflict scale that asks about conflicts concerning the seriousness of the illness; and it doesn't. We expect then, that some service use leads to some decreases in strains, but it seems unlikely that the depression effects we observe are consequences simply of having used any of 16 services in the prior year.

MOVING BEYOND THE ANDERSEN MODEL

This chapter presents an attempt to integrate models of service use and the stress process. Past extensions of the model of service use (Bass & Noelker, 1987) have suggested that the characteristics of the caregiver as well as care recipient should be included, and that information about the amount and kind of social resources should be considered. These issues are particularly central to any study of Alzheimer's caregivers, for they emphasize two obvious but important points. First, the family is the link between the Alzheimer's patient and the world of formal services—to study these family caregivers is to study the conditions under which informal care provides linkages to formal care or substitutes for it (George, 1987). Second, our study of service use needs to be grounded in our understanding of caregivers' lives. The stress framework places the decision to use care in the larger context of the caregiver's set of strategies for responding to the changing nature of the disease (the primary stressors), as well the emergence over time of secondary strains, some of which may be in other sectors of the caregivers' lives. Besides alerting us to the changing nature of both the patient and caregiver, the stress model also focuses attention on the underlying causal models of formal service use (Mutran & Ferraro, 1988), suggesting that we begin to attend to a number of concerns: the conditional nature of some of these relationships, the indirect effects of the background and predisposing characteristics, and the many gaps in our understanding of the help-seeking process. In this regard, I note briefly how little we understand the so-called predisposing variables, the knowledge, attitudes, beliefs, and norms that provide the basis for caregivers' decision making (Harel, Noelker, & Blake, 1985; Krout, 1983).

We also have little but anecdotal knowledge and our own experience of how difficult it may be to try to use formal services. It can take a major effort to investigate the services available in an area, to determine how they may meet needs, to assess their quality, and to learn how to gain access to them. Caregivers may confront a mosaic of services offered by a staggering variety of public and private agencies. Navigating through this complexity may itself constitute an ongoing strain for caregivers, and a strain probably worth measuring in our future studies.

These data suggest that there are barriers to service use at both the individual and system levels. Disparities exist in service use by socioeconomic status, even within this fairly wealthy sample. It is likely that we are underestimating these effects, because caregivers at the low end of the income and educational distributions are underrepresented in our sample. Similarly, it is striking that lack of social support surfaces as a barrier among these caregivers, almost none of whom is truly isolated. For example, the lower quartile of emotional support in this sample still contains caregivers who generally feel supported. The conditional effects we found underscore the truism that it is better to have than not to have. As patient impairment increases, the less well educated become progressively less likely to respond by using formal services. The effect of depression in blocking service use with increased patient impairment is troubling, for it suggests what clinicians have long suspected, that some caregivers who may most need help, cannot bring themselves to seek or accept it.

Exploring the linkages between informal care and formal service use appears central to our understanding of caregivers, but we are just beginning to unravel the complicated ways that these forms of care interact (George, 1987; Noelker & Bass, 1989). In this sample, having available helpers in the house decreases the need to turn to formal services, but as the emotional cost of dealing with family members increases, so does the likelihood of turning to formal help. Finally, it appears that not feeling emotionally supported decreases the likelihood of using formal services.

As we move closer to caregivers' experiences and away from the use of surrogate variables, we must begin to study the reasons people give for not using services. Our studies must eventually develop measures of some of these beliefs, attitudes, values, and concerns that family members express about their own responsibilities as caregivers, as well as their beliefs about strangers' ability and motivation to care properly for their family member.

It is also important to remind ourselves from time to time that reluctance to use formal care is expectable. Given the tireless, and sometimes heroic, efforts that family members expend in providing in-home care, we should not be surprised when they are reluctant to turn over some of the care to strangers, people who cannot know what their demented relative is like, and who are unlikely to bring the same commitment to caring for their relative as family members can.

ACKNOWLEDGMENTS

Support for this work was provided by the National Institute of Mental Health grant #MH42122. This chapter has benefitted from the collaboration of Dr. Leonard I. Pearlin, Dr. Shirley Semple, Dr. Marilyn Skaff, and Jane Karp (University of California, San Francisco); Drs. David Lindeman and William Jagust (Northern California Alzheimer's Disease Center, University of California, Davis); Dr. Carol Aneshensel (School of Public Health, University of California, Los Angeles). We are grateful for the generous help provided by William Fisher, Executive Director of the Bay Area Alzheimer's Association, and by Peter Braun, Executive Director of the Los Angeles Alzheimer's Association.

REFERENCES

Andersen, R., & Newman, J. F. (1973). Societal and individual determinants of medical care utilization in the United States. *Milbank Memorial Fund Quarterly, 51*(1), 95-124.

Bass, D. M., & Noelker, L. S. (1987). The influence of family caregivers on elder's use of in-home services: An expanded conceptual framework. *Journal of Health and Social Behavior, 28,* 184-196.

Brody, E. M. (1988). The long haul: A family odyssey. In L. F. Jarvik & C. H. Winograd (Eds.), *Treatments for the Alzheimer patient: The long haul* (pp. 107-122). New York: Springer.

Caserta, M. S., Lund, D. A., Wright, S. D., & Redburn, D. E. (1987). Caregivers to dementia patients: The utilization of community services. *The Gerontologist, 27,* 209-214.

Chappell, N. L. (1987). The interface among three systems of care: Self, informal, and formal. In R. A. Ward & S. S. Tobin (Eds.), *Health in aging: Sociological issues and policy implications* (pp. 159-179). New York: Springer.

Cohler, B. J., Groves, L., Borden, W., & Lazarus, L. (1989). Caring for family members with Alzheimer's disease. In E. Light & B. D. Lebowitz (Eds.), *Alzheimer's disease treatment and family stress: Directions for research* (pp. 50-105). Rockville, MD: U.S. Department of Health and Human Services.

Conrad, K. J., Hanrahan, P., & Hughes, S. L. (1990). Survey of adult day care in the United States. *Research on Aging, 12*(1), 36-56.

Derogatis, L. R., Lipman, R. S., Covi, L., & Rickles, K. (1971). Neurotic symptom dimensions. *Archives of General Psychiatry, 24,* 454-464.

Folstein, M. F., Folstein, S. E., & McHugh, P. R. (1975). Mini-mental state: A practical method for grading the cognitive state of patients for the clinician. *Journal of Psychiatric Research, 12,* 189-198.

George, L. K. (1987). Easing caregiver burden: The role of informal and formal supports. In R. A. Ward & S. S. Tobin (Eds.), *Health in aging: Sociological issues and policy implications* (pp. 133-158). New York: Springer.

George, L., & Gwyther, L. (1986). Caregiver well-being: A multidimensional examination of caregivers of demented adults. *The Gerontologist, 26,* 253-259.

Harel, Z., Noelker, L., & Blake, B. F. (1985). Comprehensive services for the aged: Theoretical and empirical perspectives. *The Gerontologist, 25,* 644-649.

Katz, S., Ford, A. B., Moskowitz, R. W., Jackson, B. A., & Jaffe, M. W. (1963). Studies of illness in the aged: The index of ADL, a standardized measure of biological and psychosocial function. *Journal of the American Medical Association, 185,* 914-919.

Krout, J. A. (1983). Knowledge and use of services by the elderly: A critical review of the literature. *International Journal of Aging and Human Development, 17,* 153–167.

Lawton, M. P., & Brody, E. M. (1969). Assessment of Older People: Self-Maintaining and Instrumental Activities of Daily Living. *The Gerontologist, 9,* 179–186.

Lawton, M. P., Brody, E. M., & Saperstein, A. R. (1989). A controlled study of respite service for caregivers of Alzheimer's patients. *The Gerontologist, 29*(1), 8–16.

MaloneBeach, E. E., Zarit, S. H., & Spore, D. L. (1992). Perceptions of caregivers to cognitively impaired elders: Use of and satisfaction with case-managed services. *Journal of Applied Gerontology, 11,* 146–159.

Montgomery, R. J. V., & Borgatta, E. (1989). The effects of alternative support strategies on family caregiving. *The Gerontologist, 29*(4), 457–464.

Montgomery, R. J. V., Kosloski, K., & Borgatta, E. (1990). Service use and the caregiving experience. In D. E. Biegel & A. Blum (Eds.), *Aging and caregiving* (pp. 139–159). Newbury Park, CA: SAGE Publications, Inc.

Mutran, E., & Ferraro, K. F. (1988). Medical need and use of services among older men and women. *Journal of Gerontology, 43*(5), S162–171.

Noelker, L. S., & Bass, D. M. (1989). Home care for elderly persons: Linkages between formal and informal caregivers. *Journal of Gerontology, 44*(2), S63–70.

Oktay, J. S., & Volland, P. J. (1990). Post-hospital support program for the frail elderly and their caregivers: A quasi-experimental evaluation. *American Journal of Public Health, 80*(1), 39–46.

Pearlin, L. I., Mullan, J. T., Semple, S. J., & Skaff, M. M. (1990). Caregiving and the stress process: An overview of concepts and their measures. *The Gerontologist, 30,* 583–594.

Pruchno, R. A., & Resch, N. L. (1989). Aberrant behaviors and Alzheimer's disease: Mental health effects of spouse caregivers. *Journal of Gerontology, 44,* S177–S182.

Romeis, J. C. (1989). Caregiving Strain: Toward an enlarged perspective. *Journal of Aging and Health, 1,* 188–208.

Rundall, T. (1981). A suggestion for improving the behavioral model of physician utilization. *Journal of Health and Social Behavior, 22,* 103–104.

Schulz, R. (1990). Theoretical perspectives on caregiving. In D. E. Biegel & A. Blum (Eds.), *Aging and caregiving* (pp. 27–52). Newbury Park, CA: SAGE Publications, Inc.

Ward, R. A., Sherman, S. R., & LaGory, M. (1984). Informal networks and knowledge of services for older persons. *Journal of Gerontology, 39*(2), 216–223.

Wolinsky, F. D., & Arnold, C. L. (1988). A different perspective on health and health services utilization. In G. Maddox & M. P. Lawton (Eds.), *Annual Review of Gerontology and Geriatrics, 8,* 71–101.

Zarit, S. H. (1989). Intervention with frail elders and their families: Are they effective and why? In M. A. P. Stephens, J. H. Crowther, S. E. Hobfoll, & D. L. Tennenbaum (Eds.), *Stress and Coping in Later-Life Families* (pp. 241–266). New York: Hemisphere.

Zarit, S. H., Todd, P., & Zarit, J. (1986). Subjective burden of husbands and wives as caregivers. *The Gerontologist, 26,* 260–266.

Understanding Barriers
to Caregivers' Use of Formal Services:
The Caregiver's Perspective

Mary Ann Parris Stephens
Kent State University

Based on research that has been conducted since the early 1980s, practitioners and researchers in gerontology are now acutely aware of the role that the family plays in the long-term care of older adults, and the toll that intensive caregiving efforts often place on the family, especially the primary caregiver. In response to the needs of these family members, a variety of programs and services have been designed to help alleviate the stresses associated with giving care to a disabled or chronically ill older adult. The purposes of this section are two-fold. First, the contribution highlights current knowledge about caregivers' use of services aimed at reducing their stress and burden. Second, it suggests some potential ways that research in this area could be refined to more adequately address important practical questions concerning service delivery, as well as to address a variety of intriguing social psychological phenomena.

Throughout this discussion, research on the use of formal services by older adults is used as a point of comparison. In recent years, a great deal of research attention has been given to this issue, especially in the United States and other developed countries with extensive government-sponsored human service programs. Research interest in this issue has been stimulated by both practical and theoretical concerns. On the practical side, research has attempted to determine the degree of client coverage that a given service program enjoys, that is, whether the intended clients of a program are actually being served, as well as to evaluate the effectiveness of these programs in achieving their stated goals. On the theoretical side, service utilization has been conceptualized as a type of help-seeking behavior that has a number of inherently interesting properties for social scientists. Current research on the use of formal services by caregivers seems to be guided by practical and theoretical concerns similar to those that catalyzed research into service use by older adults, and thus research on caregivers may be examined profitably against the rich backdrop of research and theory on elders' service use.

USE OF FORMAL CAREGIVER SERVICES

The formal services that have been designed for caregivers can be categorized into two basic types, psycho-educational and respite (Zarit, 1990). Psycho-educational programs refer to those that are designed to enhance caregivers' abilities to cope with caregiving responsibilities, such as counseling, psycho-therapy, and support groups. In contrast, respite programs include those that provide new resources that relieve caregivers of some portion of routine care activities, including in-home services, adult day care, and institutional respite. Placing these services in a theoretical context, the psycho-educational programs can be thought of as the formal provision of emotional support, and respite programs can be thought of as the formal provision of instrumental support.

The most consistent finding concerning caregivers' use of formal services is that not many caregivers use these services, and those that do, do not use them very much. Studies have begun to indicate that large portions of caregivers to older adults with dementia, as well as caregivers to those with a variety of other illness conditions, do not use formal services at all (George, 1987; Noelker & Bass, 1989; Office of Technology Assessment, 1990; Swan & Estes, 1990).

The data reported in the Mullan chapter (this volume) are somewhat inconsistent with other findings reported in the gerontological literature. Specifically, approximately 85% of caregivers in his sample used formal services of some kind. It is likely, however, that this high rate of service use is a function of either the sampling procedures used to recruit respondents (i.e., through caregivers' contact with the Alzheimer's Association), or the fact that the study was conducted in two large, metropolitan areas that have a rich array of services, including some of the first caregiver programs. Thus these data are not necessarily a reflection of more general trends among caregivers.

In the larger literature on caregivers' use of formal services, it appears that the lack of service use is not evenly distributed across various categories of caregivers. In fact, it seems to be the most socially isolated caregivers and those who are giving the most intensive levels of care who are not partici-pating in the formal service system (George, 1987; Office of Technology Assessment, 1990).

An experimental evaluation of the effects of respite care on the well-being of dementia caregivers revealed a pattern of low usage of these services

(Lawton, Brody, & Saperstein, 1989). Specifically, participants in the experimental group had several forms of respite care made available to them over the course of a year. Only about half took advantage of these service opportunities at all. Of those who used in-home services, the median amount of use was less than one hour per week, and among those who used either adult day care, or nursing home respite, the median use was less than one day per month (Lawton et al., 1989). Despite these low rates of use, many of these caregivers indicated that respite services are among the services most needed (Lawton et al., 1989). However, evaluations of the effectiveness of formal services more generally in alleviating caregivers' feelings of stress and burden have yielded largely disappointing results (George, 1987; Lawton et al., 1989; Zarit, 1990).

Clearly, if services are provided and few caregivers are taking advantage of them, it is important to understand why. The case of dementia caregivers provides an interesting illustration of this problem. Despite the generally high levels of distress among these individuals, their rate of formal service use is lower than that for caregivers to older adults with other illness conditions (Office of Technology Assessment, 1990). Consequently, much of the research on service utilization has concentrated on dementia caregivers, and the present chapter focuses solely on this group.

In 1990, the Office of Technology Assessment issued a report on linkages between the formal service system and people with dementia and their families. As a part of this reporting effort, a survey was conducted in Cuyahoga County, Ohio, to identify caregivers' reasons for not using formal services. Lack of knowledge of services was the reason most frequently named. Other reasons that centered on the service system included not knowing how to make arrangements for formal services, the cost of services, and the fear of future illness-related costs that made caregivers reluctant to spend money for formal services in the present. Some caregivers stated that they felt no need for service assistance, either because they did not feel burdened, or because they did not regard their relative with dementia as having a disease. Other caregivers expressed concerns about criticisms from others if they were to seek outside help, and still others expressed discomfort or embarrassment over their relative's behavior, which they wanted to hide even from service providers. Fear that their relative would be upset if an outsider were to help with care and feelings of discomfort at making decisions for their relative were reasons offered by other caregivers for their reluctance to use formal services. Many of the same reasons offered by these caregivers for not using formal services were also mentioned by caregivers in the sample reported by Mullan (this volume), and in studies reported by other researchers (Swan & Estes, 1990).

Although these reports have offered some valuable insights into the reasons why dementia caregivers say they do not seek assistance from formal agencies, the atheoretical nature of the research limits a more comprehensive understanding of the phenomenon of help-seeking behavior, or in this case, the failure to seek help (Harel, Noelker, & Blake, 1985). The lack of theory makes it difficult to know the broader context to which these reasons apply, or how to proceed on the basis of this information. Because the literature on elders' use of formal services has a longer history, it might prove useful to trace this history in order to advance research on caregivers' use of services.

APPROACHES TO UNDERSTANDING MEDICAL SERVICE USE

Structural Approaches

Research on elders' use of services has been a rich and relatively profitable arena for studying service utilization, especially those services involving health care. Perhaps one key to its success has been that many researchers have shared a common theoretical framework for conducting their investigations. The Andersen model of service utilization (Andersen & Newman, 1973) has guided much of this work. This model assumes that differential use of health services is a function of three classes of structural variables: (a) personal characteristics such as gender, age, and ethnicity that may predispose individuals to seek care; (b) enabling factors such as low socioeconomic status, lack of health insurance coverage, and other barriers to health care; and (c) need-for-care factors such as subjectively determined and objectively assessed health status.

One strength of this model is that it permits study of both the personal and social resources of older adults as predictors of service use, rather than focusing on one or the other of these domains. Another strength of this model lies in its relative flexibility in incorporating new predictor constructs. Most recently, it has been modified to include the personal and social resources of the caregiver as additional factors influencing the kinds and amounts of formal health-care services that are used in support of the older person (Bass & Noelker, 1987; Noelker & Bass, 1989; Soldo, Agree, & Wolf, 1989).

Across a wide range of studies, a high degree of consistency in findings has emerged. Need for services appears to be the strongest predictor of service use, although in certain studies, some predisposing and enabling factors have been shown to affect service use (Branch et al., 1981; Chappell & Guse, 1990; Coulton & Frost, 1982; Holtzman, Braunger, & James, 1987; Rivnyak, Wan, Stegall, Jacobs, & Li, 1989; Wolinsky, Coe, & Mosely, 1987; Wolinsky et al., 1983). However, this consistent pattern generally accounts for only small portions of variance in service use. This pattern of results has been found both when the older adults' needs are considered alone (for example, the older person's level of functional impairment), and when their needs are considered in the context of their caregiver's needs (e.g., caregiver's level of stress) (Bass & Noelker, 1987; Brown, Potter, & Foster, 1990; McAuley & Arling, 1984; Stoller, 1989). Although this model of service use has yielded some valuable information about what kinds of people use formal services, its perspective is largely structural, and, as such, it offers little insight into the process by which older adults decide to seek services, or decide not to do so (Wan, 1989).

Reflecting on this matter, McCaslin (1988, 1989) has argued that rather than trying to find better ways to classify older people, we need to focus on the processes used by these individuals in making decisions about service use. Through such a decision-making approach to the problem, the limitations and objectionable features of the existing service system that inhibit use by people for whom the services were intended may be better understood.

Cognitive Approaches

Cognitive models of decision making in health-related contexts could offer some guidance into the development of a problem-solving approach to the study of service use. Social scientists interested in health have made the distinction between illness (health problems that limit normal activities) and illness behavior (actions taken when a person defines him or herself as ill, which includes seeking help from a health-care professional) (Kasl & Cobb, 1966; Mechanic, 1968). This distinction takes into account the possibility that individuals may experience similar states of ill health, and yet engage in very different behaviors in an attempt to manage these conditions. Health decision-making theories have conceptualized illness behaviors as products of complex judgment processes. A key assumption in these theories is that the way a person cognitively represents (or labels) his or her health status, influences the health-related actions that this person takes (Leventhal, Nerenz, & Steele, 1984; Rakowski, 1984). These approaches assume that individuals actively process information that is available to them and that, through this process, they construct a view or representation of behavior and experience. Information processing systems integrate current stimulus information with information that is coded in memory. Thus, our experience of the world and ourselves, our emotional reactions to these experiences, and our coping responses are created by this cognitive system.

In the context of illness, these theories assert that individuals make a series of decisions, each of which is determined by the way information is organized and represented. A key decision is whether the individual judges himself or herself to have an illness, which is largely determined by his or her cognitive representation of current and past information. Cognitive representations of illness necessarily rely heavily on current stimulus information in the form of somatic symptoms, for example, nausea, dizziness, and skin discoloration. However, they also make use of past information such as one's memory of previous illness episodes.

The outcome of this decision process, in the form of a cognitive representation of one's own health status, has a direct bearing on subsequent decisions that the individual makes about illness behaviors, or the extent to which he or she has needs for health care. Put simply, if a person labels their symptoms as an illness, he or she is more likely to seek health-care services than another person who does not label the same symptoms as an illness. Even in the presence of objective and defined symptoms, there is marked variability in individuals' cognitive representations of their own states of health and illness, and in their subsequent health-related actions. Variability in the labeling process and in seeking health care is further increased when signs and symptoms are vague and ambiguous (Leventhal et al., 1984).

This cognitive approach to understanding illness behavior extends the more traditional structural approach in several ways. First, it emphasizes the role of the potential user of medical services as an active agent in the health-care process, rather than as a passive reactor. Second, it recognizes the complexity of the decisions that the individual must make both about his or her state of health and about ways to cope with health problems. Third, it allows for the possibility that even in the presence of objectively similar situations, individuals will represent their health conditions in markedly different ways and will engage in a wide variety of behaviors in an attempt to cope. Such an approach to understanding service use among dementia caregivers might provide valuable insight into this perplexing problem.

A COGNITIVE APPROACH TO UNDERSTANDING CAREGIVERS' USE OF FORMAL SERVICES

It has been noted that predicting caregivers' formal service use is already proving to be a more difficult undertaking than predicting health service utilization by the elderly (George, 1987). Thus, an important question to consider is: How can our understanding of utilization behavior among dementia caregivers profit from theory and research on illness behavior and medical service use? More precisely, how can the study of caregivers' service use profit from past research in order to achieve a fuller understanding of why caregivers do or do not use the services they frequently say they need?

One approach to answering this question is analogous to that suggested by McCaslin (1989) concerning elders' use of medical services, namely, to examine the ways caregivers make judgments about their own needs for formal services. To accomplish this, a cognitive model of mental health decision making similar to that used to describe decisions concerning somatic health, might be employed. Such an approach would be concerned with how an individual represents or labels their own mental health status as a key to understanding their use of formal services. That is, knowing whether an individual labels himself or herself as having a psychological problem will help determine whether this person seeks services that are designed to alleviate this problem.

It is likely that the judgments leading to caregivers' perceptions of needs for help involve an even more complex process than judgments about the need for medical care. The increased complexity of this decision process, over that used by older adults in seeking health care, is due in large part to the fact that caregivers are making decisions about different kinds of needs. Whereas the literature on elders' health-care utilization focuses on decisions individuals make on the basis of somatic signs and symptoms, the literature on caregivers' service use is concerned primarily with decisions made on the basis of psychological signs and symptoms. Such psychological symptoms have been the most consistently documented negative effects of caregiving stress (Schulz, Visintainer, & Williamson, 1990), and their alleviation is the target of most services and programs designed for caregivers (Zarit, 1990).

Because psychological symptoms are more often vague and ambiguous than are somatic symptoms, the process of appropriately labeling emotional states can be a more difficult task. For example, emotional states typically have no readily available or well-defined criteria for evaluation by the average individual who is experiencing them. As such, bodily dysfunction and even physical pain are more easily identified than is psychological pain. To complicate this situation further, because many emotional states have concomitant physical manifestations, their distinction from somatic dysfunction is sometimes hard to detect. In addition to these ambiguities that are a natural part of affect, societal values, norms, and expectations about these emotions enter into the labeling process. For example, although much progress has been made in recent years to destigmatize mental illness, many segments of society still regard psychological problems as signs of weakness. As such, individuals may be reluctant to label themselves as experiencing psychological distress out of fear for what others might think about them.

In the case of caregivers whose experiences of psychological distress are most often moderate and transient (Schulz et al., 1990; this volume), psychological symptoms are even more ambiguous and thus, the problem of appropriate labeling becomes increasingly difficult. This is not to suggest that caregivers are necessarily inaccurate in their responses to self-report inventories measuring psychological distress. In fact, they might be quite accurate in reporting symptoms, which enables researchers and practitioners to assess and label their psychological states. Despite their ability to report symptoms, caregivers may have difficulty in placing appropriate labels on their own mental health status, especially in the absence of any objective information. That is, they may not perceive that they have a psychological problem even though the more objective research or clinical indicators suggest that they do. Conversely, they might label themselves as psychologically troubled when the more objective indicators suggest only mild or moderate levels of distress. This is a key difference between the structural approach where an outsider (researcher or clinician) makes the judgment about the caregiver's psychological status and needs for service support, and the decision approach where the caregiver makes those judgments about him or herself.

Figure 1 depicts some of the basic elements that would likely be involved in caregivers' decisions to seek formal services for themselves. It is important to emphasize that psychological well-being has many determinants, only one of which is caregiving (Pearlin, Mullan, Semple, & Skaff, 1990). This point is illustrated in the figure by indicating that experiences in the caregiver role, as well as those occurring in caregivers' other roles are all important antecedent conditions in the decision-making process.

Despite the ambiguous information involved in decisions about emotional states, individuals do make evaluations concerning their own psychological status. Ultimately, they judge whether they are experiencing psychological distress or not. This decision may be made either explicitly or implicitly, and may involve various degrees of conscious awareness. Even if a caregiver determines that he or she is distressed, the labels that are applied to these psychological states may not be the same ones that a mental health professional would use to diagnose the same symptoms. Nonetheless these labels have significance for the individual. For example, a caregiver might describe his or her depressive symptoms as "being down in the dumps," or as "being

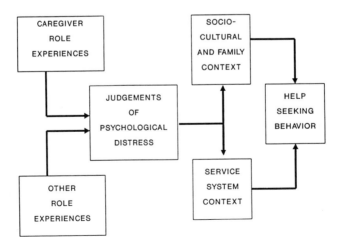

FIG. 1. Caregivers' decision-making about utilizing formal services.

worn out." Although vague and imprecise, these labels carry valuable meaning that can bear on subsequent decisions about formal service use.

Clearly, the judgment that one is experiencing psychological distress is not the only factor in caregivers' decisions to seek help from formal services. A host of situational or contextual factors could come into play to either facilitate or impede such help-seeking. In Fig. 1, these contextual factors are classified into those that reflect the sociocultural and family milieu of the caregiver, and those that reflect characteristics of the formal service system.

Many of the reasons offered by caregivers in the studies conducted by the Office of Technology Assessment (1990), by Mullan (this volume), and Swan and Estes (1990) for not using formal services can be conceptualized as contextual factors in the decision to use services. For example, concerns about criticisms from others regarding relinquishing some caregiving responsibilities to an outsider, or concerns about upsetting the relative with dementia if such help were sought, could be classified as sociocultural and family factors. Other factors in this category include the availability of intimate relationships for sharing feelings and for discussing ways to cope with these feelings. Additionally, this category could include values, norms, and expectations of the caregivers' demographic and reference groups about how to deal with emotional problems. In contrast, the context of the service system includes the availability, quality, and cost of services that are in the caregiver's local community, as well as the effectiveness of the marketing strategies used by service organizations to make their services known.

The outcome of this complex process is a decision by the caregiver about whether or not to seek some form of assistance from the formal service system. Given that a caregiver judges that he or she is experiencing distress, the best possible outcome of this process is the case where the various contextual factors facilitate formal service utilization. However, it is all too possible that an individual could judge that he or she is experiencing distress, but that the barriers created by society, family or the service system itself, are too formidable to permit the use of needed services.

In considering this approach to service utilization by caregivers, one caveat should be stated. It is conceivable that a person might judge that he or she was experiencing good psychological adjustment, and seek formal services for other reasons, such as the need for patient care while the caregiver works, or the desire to gain information that might prevent caregiver burn-out in the future. However, the most common motivation for seeking formal services is probably the desire to reduce psychological symptoms, either by learning new coping behaviors for managing the stress of caregiving, or by having sufficient time away from caregiving responsibilities to permit one's personal resources to be replenished.

One of the most intriguing findings in the study reported by Mullan (this volume) is the relationship between caregivers' levels of depression and their service use. Caregivers experiencing relatively greater depression, especially those with the more impaired care recipients, tended to use fewer formal services. Although those caregivers who did not use formal services were given the opportunity to explain their reasons, using the perspective developed in the present chapter, specific investigation might be undertaken to understand how caregivers make decisions about their own mental health status, and how these decisions affect subsequent decisions about formal service use.

From a decision-making perspective, it would be important to determine whether caregivers scoring relatively higher on the more objective indicator of depression also labeled themselves as experiencing significant distress and as needing help in dealing with this distress. These self-labeled states may be better predictors of service use than the labels that researchers derive from standardized measures, even though these measures rely on self-reported symptoms.

It would also be useful to know how the beliefs and values of various families, and racial and ethnic groups concerning such issues as mental health and filial obligations, influence the decision to seek and use formal services. Additionally, caregivers' perceptions about and attitudes toward available services would need to be considered as part of the decision-making process. Such factors may be useful in differentiating among those caregivers who label themselves as experiencing similar levels of psychological distress, and who either do or do not use formal services. Through such an approach, a fuller understanding of how caregivers make decisions about seeking help from formal services may be achieved.

The intent of this section has not been to offer a theoretical model for the study of service utilization by caregivers, or even to offer a specific agenda for future research. Instead, its principal aim has been to suggest a framework for conceptualizing caregivers' service use that could capture the complexity of this deceptively simple problem. The cognitive decision-making approach offered here underscores the importance of examining this problem from the point of view of the caregiver. It views the act of seeking help from a formal service organization as a culmination of a highly idiosyncratic process of gathering, organizing, and evaluating information about the self, significant others, and the formal service environment. The complexity of this phenomenon cannot be adequately reflected by the traditional social variables that are most often used in structural analyses of service utilization. Perhaps by examining this process from the caregiver's decision-making perspective, research could identify the critical conditions that either promote or impede formal help-seeking.

The decision-making orientation could be useful in addressing some very important practical and theoretical issues. On the practical side, if we could better understand the psychosocial barriers to formal service use from the perspective of the caregiver (the potential client), we could refine our efforts at public education, information and referral, outreach, and case management accordingly. Efforts could be directed at overcoming these barriers through modifications of programs and services, as well as through changes in marketing strategies. In so doing, services might be more optimally used by those caregivers who need them. However, given the wide variability in caregivers' experiences of distress and burden, and in the family, social, and service contexts that caregiving takes place, it should not be expected that all dementia caregivers (even those with the most severely impaired patients) will choose to seek help from formal services.

On the theoretical side, there are a number of intriguing problems for social scientists. Understanding how people represent psychological symptoms and act on these representations would be an extremely interesting endeavor and would make a major contribution to our knowledge about mental health and mental health services. Furthermore, by conceptualizing service use as help-seeking behavior, the literature on social support could be extended to include formal support systems.

REFERENCES

Andersen, R., & Newman, J. F. (1973). Societal and individual determinants of medical care utilization in the United States. *Millbank Memorial Fund Quarterly, 51,* 95–124.

Bass, D. M., & Noelker, L. S. (1987). The influence of family caregivers on elder's use of in-home services: An expanded conceptual framework. *Journal of Health and Social Behavior, 28,* 184–196.

Branch, L., Jette, A., Evashwick, C., Polansky, M., Rowe, G., & Diehr, P. (1981). Toward understanding elders' health service utilization. *Journal of Community Health, 7,* 80–91.

Brown, L. J., Potter, J. F., & Foster, B. G. (1990). Caregiver burden should be evaluated during geriatric assessment. *Journal of the American Geriatric Society, 38,* 455–460.

Chappell, N. L., & Guse, L. W. (1990). Linkages between informal and formal support. In K. S. Markides & C. L. Cooper (Eds.), *Aging, stress, and health* (pp. 5–23). New York: Wiley and Sons.

Coulton, C., & Frost, A. K. (1982). Use of social and health services by the elderly. *Journal of Health and Social Behavior, 23,* 330–339.

George, L. (1987). Easing caregiver burden: The role of informal and formal supports. In R. A. Ward & S. S. Tobin (Eds.), *Health in aging: Sociological issues and policy directions* (pp. 121–139). New York: Springer.

Harel, Z., Noelker, L., & Blake, B. F. (1985). Comprehensive services for the aged: Theoretical and empirical perspectives. *The Gerontologist, 25,* 644–649.

Holtzman, J. M., Braunger, A., & James, C. (1987). Health-care needs of older women and minorities: Implications for education and training programs. In G. Lesnoff-Caravaglia (Ed.), *Handbook of Applied Gerontology.* New York: Human Sciences Press.

Kasl, S. V., & Cobb, S. J. (1966). Health behavior and sick-role behavior. *Archives of Environmental Health, 12,* 246–266.

Lawton, M. P., Brody, E. M., & Saperstein, A. R. (1989). A controlled study of respite service for caregivers of Alzheimer's patients. *The Gerontologist, 29,* 8–16.

Leventhal, H., Nerenz, D. R., & Steele, D. J. (1984). Illness representations and coping with health threats. In A. Baum, S. E. Taylor, & J. E. Singer (Eds.), *Handbook of psychology and health: Vol. IV. Social psychological perspectives* (pp. 219–252). New Jersey: Lawrence Erlbaum Associates.

McAuley, W. J., & Arling, G. (1984). Use of in-home care by very old people. *Journal of Health and Social Behavior, 25,* 54–64.

McCaslin, R. (1988). Reframing research on service use among the elderly: An analysis of recent findings. *The Gerontologist, 28,* 592–599.

McCaslin, R. (1989). Service utilization by the elderly: The importance of orientation to the formal system. *Journal of Gerontological Social Work, 14,* 153–174.

Mechanic, K. (1968). *Medical sociology: A selective view.* New York: Free Press.

Noelker, L. S., & Bass, D. M. (1989). Home care for elderly persons: Linkages between formal and informal caregivers. *Journals of Gerontology: Social Sciences, 44,* S63–70.

Office of Technology Assessment. (1990). *Confused minds, burdened families: Finding help for people with Alzheimer's and other dementias* (OTA-BA-403). Washington, DC: U.S. Government Printing Office.

Pearlin, L. I., Mullan, J. T., Semple, S. J., & Skaff, M. M. (1990). Caregiving and the stress process: An overview of concepts and their measures. *The Gerontologist, 30,* 583–591.

Rakowski, W. (1984). Health psychology and late life: The differentiation of health and illness for the study of health-related behaviors. *Research on Aging, 6,* 593–620.

Rivnyak, M. H., Wan, T. T. H., Stegall, M. H., Jacobs, M., & Li, S. (1989). Ambulatory care use among the noninstitutionalized elderly. *Research on Aging, 11,* 292–311.

Schulz, R., Visintainer, P., & Williamson, G. M. (1990). Psychiatric and physical morbidity effects of caregiving. *Journal of Gerontology: Psychological Sciences, 45,* P181–191.

Soldo, B. J., Agree, E. M., & Wolf, D. A. (1989). The balance between formal and informal care. In M. G. Ory & K. Bond (Eds.), *Aging and health care: Social science perspectives* (pp. 77–92). London: Routledge.

Stoller, E. P. (1989). Formal services and informal helping: The myth of service substitution. *The Journal of Applied Gerontology, 8,* 37–52.

Swan, J. H., & Estes, C. L. (1990). Changes in aged populations served by home health agencies. *Journal of Aging and Health, 2,* 373–394.

Wan, T. (1989). The behavioral model of health-care utilization by older people. In M. Ory & K. Bond (Eds.), *Aging and health care: Social science and policy perspectives* (pp. 54–76). London: Routledge.

Wolinsky, F. D., Coe, R. M., Miller, D. K., Prendergast, J. M., Creel, M. J., & Chavez, M. N. (1983). Health services utilization among the noninstitutionalized elderly. *Journal of Health and Social Behavior, 24,* 325–337.

Wolinsky, F. D., Coe, R. M., & Mosely, R. R. (1987). The use of health services by elderly Americans: Implications from a regression-based cohort analysis. In R. A. Ward & S. S. Tobin (Eds.), *Health in aging: Sociological issues and policy directions.* New York: Springer.

Zarit, S. H. (1990). Interventions with frail elders and their families: Are they effective and why? In M. A. P. Stephens, J. H. Crowther, S. E. Hobfoll, & D. L. Tennenbaum (Eds.), *Stress and coping in later-life families* (pp. 241–265). New York: Hemisphere.

10

Family Caregiving Policies: Insights from an Intensive Longitudinal Study

Rosalie A. Kane
Joan Dobrof Penrod
University of Minnesota

It is platitudinous to state, but true and important to contemplate, that family members provide the bulk of community-based long-term care to the elderly and disabled. Moreover, research has established that this so-called informal care is often given at considerable physical, psychic, and social cost to the caregiving family member (Brody, 1981; Cantor, 1983; Pearlin, Mullan, Semple, & Skaff, 1990; Zarit, Reever & Bach-Peterson, 1980). Large-scale national surveys have confirmed the incidence and prevalence of family caregiving, which is widely believed to enable two comparably disabled people to live in the community for each person who lives in a nursing home (Kane & Kane, 1987).

Numerous smaller studies, some cross-sectional and some longitudinal, have investigated family caregivers and found associations among characteristics of caregivers (such as gender, age, marital status, living situation, relationship to the care receiver, labor force participation, other demands on caregivers' time) with characteristics of care receivers (such as gender, age, martial status, living situation, functional abilities, and cognitive abilities) and finally, with characteristics of the care situation such as the amount and type of care given by family members, nature of caregivers' backup support from other family members, amount and type of so-called formal care delivered by paid caregivers (Clipp & George, 1990; Krause, 1990; Soldo, Wolf, & Agree, 1990; Stone, Cafferata, & Sangl, 1987; Wan & Weissert, 1981; Young & Kahana, 1989). Family caregiving is widely agreed to be stressful (George & Gwyther, 1986; Horowitz, 1985; Pruchno, Kleban, Michaels, & Dempsey, 1989; Schulz, Visintainer, & Williamson, 1990; Zarit et al., 1980).

As a society, we rely on the labor of family caregivers. Without it, we can safely assume more people would be in nursing homes or the equivalent residential care at great public cost. Married older people or widowed people with adult children living nearby are less likely to enter a nursing home than those who never married, who never had children, or who have no nearby children (Doty, 1986; Soldo & Myllyluoma, 1983). The National Channeling Demonstration showed that providing publicly subsidized community-based long-term care services leads to no wholesale replacement of family care. Although some slight substitution effect was noted, most often family members realigned their tasks and continued to spend substantial time giving care (Christianson, 1988; Stephens & Christianson, 1986). A few studies also point out that family care frequently continues even after a relative enters a nursing home and, to some extent, nursing home staff relies on that assistance (Stoller & Earl, 1983).

In connection with a large-scale, longitudinal study of Medicare beneficiaries after they leave the hospital, researchers at the University of Minnesota sought to add both breadth and depth to the study of family care, including family care associated with the aftermath of acute health-care episodes in older people, and ongoing family care. These studies are shaped by a desire to inform the public policy debate about policies toward family caregivers. This chapter discusses the design of these studies and presents preliminary findings.

POLICY CONTEXT

Actual and proposed public policy regarding family caregiving is ambiguous and ambivalent. Contradictory pronouncements are common. On the one hand, it is often stated that families need relief from their freely assumed burden of informal care. On the other hand, it is also frequently stated that incentives (both carrots and sticks) are needed to make sure that family members fulfill obligations they otherwise will attempt to escape. A midway position between believing family members do much too much and believing they do much too little is to support provisions that would ease the lot of those who voluntarily decide to give care to elderly and disabled relatives. The purpose of such support to family members is both pragmatic and humanitarian. Family support efforts are a means to the end of keeping family caregivers longer at their jobs, and are also designed to relieve burdens and mitigate stress, desirable ends in themselves.

Concrete suggestions for family policies fall into several categories.

• **Direct services to family caregivers.** These include Information and Referral (I&R) programs, educational programs for family caregivers, support groups for family caregivers, and mental health services for family caregivers (who have been shown to have high prevalence of depression, particularly if they care for persons with Alzheimer's disease).

• **Respite services.** Also conceptualized as direct services for family caregivers, respite services are formal services provided to the care receivers to offer them relief. The services may be provided in the care receiver's home, at day care centers, or in residential settings such as nursing homes. They may be as brief as a few hours or as extended as a few weeks. They may be planned and regular, or organized to respond to emergencies of the caregiver. Advocates of respite services have varying views of the extent to which the programs should be subsidized, what fees may be appropriate for the service, and, indeed, the actual goals of the respite (Montgomery, 1990).

• **Financial incentives.** Positive financial incentives range from direct payment of the family caregivers to tax incentives for those who give care to elderly relatives (Linsk, Kehiger, & Englund, 1990). A variant of paying family caregivers is providing money or vouchers to the disabled older person, who may then elect to hire a family member. Credit banks that promise future care for oneself in exchange for present care for a relative have also been explored. Direct payment of family members may be general or limited to those who would otherwise be in the work force. Spouses are sometimes perceived as categorically inappropriate for payment, whereas other programs will pay a spouse if he or she leaves the labor force to give care.

• **Legal requirements.** Although their constitutionality is in question, various states have toyed with requiring family members such as adult children and even grandchildren to be financially responsible for some of the nursing home bill, an obligation that presently is limited to spouses. Presumably such strategies could also be explored for home care.

• **Eligibility policies for in-home formal care.** Policies about eligibility for and characteristics of formal care inevitably effect informal care, either because family members are left by default to cover the uncovered, or because information about family is taken specifically into account when an individual's eligibility for a particular program is established. Families could be eliminated at the source through policies that provide direct care to elderly people in their homes and the community. If free or affordable (that is, subsidized) care is available and acceptable, family members are exempted from duty. If nursing homes were perceived as better places to live and less financially disadvantageous, perhaps family members would struggle less to keep their relatives at home. Implicit or explicit assumptions about what care family members are expected to provide govern the decisions made by hospital discharge planners and by case managers in community care (Doty, 1990).

In community long-term care programs (usually funded by Medicaid waivers and/or other state money), home-care plans tend to be made by locally designated case managers based on a comprehensive, multidimensional assessment of the client's needs and resources. An emerging policy issue is simply this: What information about family members should be collected as part of the assessment, and how should it be used to determine what service the older person gets? A corollary question is: What expectations for family-provided care, if any, should be built into care planning? Can decision rules be formulated, or is it completely an individualized matter? Present policies require that family care not be replaced, but as yet no decision algorithms are available to titrate formal and family care. Indeed it is not always clear how the availability and assistance of family affects eligibility for community programs: Family help could be a prerequisite for some programs and for others those with family help go to the bottom of the list.

Coherent policies about family caregiving are difficult to develop as long as their goals remain imprecise or contradictory. The following goals may be identified: (a) to engage persons in giving family care who are not doing so; (b) to maximize the amount and duration of care given by family members, including those already serving as caregivers; (c) to enable family members to give more skilled and effective care, which should benefit the care receiver; (d) to make the job of family caregivers easier, less stressful, or less burdensome; and (e) to assure that the exercise of family care is appropriate and equitable, which in turn means relieving some families of their responsibilities in part or completely. The problem is complicated by the multitudinous patterns of family care involving different degrees of consanguinity in the family caregiver's relationship to the person needing care, differing life stages and competing obligations for family caregivers, and different demands of the job itself. It is highly possible that public policies to relieve, on the one hand, and provide incentives to continue on the other, need to coexist and be targeted to different groups.

Although family caregiving is a favorite research topic for gerontologists and much has been learned about the phenomenon, the body of research informs the public policy debate in only the most general way. Policy-makers know that the expansion of community-based long-term care benefits must be conceived as a partnership with family members, who will continue to volunteer their care. It would be naive to predicate a public policy on paying persons to do everything family members now do free. Even in Great Britain, Canada, and Scandinavian countries where community-care benefits are well established, such programs are perceived as augmentation to rather than replacement of family care. Lacking, however, is a strategy for family caregiving based on social goals for the well-being of people of all ages, intergenerational equity, principles of cost-effectiveness, and an understanding of the likely effectiveness of various strategies that are possible. Such a strategy should also be based on an understanding of why families behave as they do, and the kinds of incentives that are meaningful to them.

UNIVERSITY OF MINNESOTA STUDIES

We use two sources of data, singly and in combination, to examine family caregiving. The first is the National Post-Acute Care (PAC) Study, a longitudinal study of 2,610 elderly hospital dischargees, that permits an examination of family care for a large number of people in the context of rich information about clinical condition and health-care utilization. The second is the Heinz Study of Patterns of Family Care; a study of a subset of 307 family caregivers of sample members in the PAC study. This intensive study permits a much more detailed examination of family caregiving in the sample both through analysis of carefully post-coded responses to open-ended questions and through learning the story behind a particular family's experience with care. The two study designs are briefly summarized below.

National Post-Acute Care Study

The University of Minnesota National Post-Acute Care Study, performed under a grant from the Office of Assistant Secretary for Planning and Evaluation (ASPE) of the Department of Health and Human Services and the Health Care Financing Administration (HCFA), includes a 1-year longitudinal study in three metropolitan areas of Medicare patients with diagnosis-related groups (DRGs) that are associated with heavy use of post-acute care paid for by Medicare. Stimulated by the goal of understanding how Medicare's prospective hospital payment by DRG affects the patients, the post-acute care study set out to answer two general questions: (a) What accounts for the type and frequency of post-acute care (including rehabilitation, nursing home, Medicare-funded home care, and other home care) received by Medicare beneficiaries; and (b) How does the post-acute care affect patient outcomes (including place of residence) 6 weeks, 6 months, and 1 year after the initial hospitalization.

The sample was drawn from Medicare beneficiaries hospitalized in three Metropolitan areas (Pittsburgh, Twin Cities, and Houston) and discharged with DRGs representing five kinds of conditions: (a) stroke; (b) congestive heart failure; (c) hip, femur, and pelvis fractures with procedures; (d) chronic obstructive pulmonary disease, and (e) hip replacements and major joint procedures of the lower extremities. These conditions were chosen to include medical and surgical conditions that account for much Medicare funded post-acute care and are characterized by diverse post-acute care arrangements. Analysis of the five major DRGs done by The Rand Corporation using a file of 20% of all Medicare Part A discharges in 1984–1985 revealed that more than 50% of all Medicare post-acute care was accounted for by those five DRGs. In addition, there was a lot of variability in the type of post-acute care delivered to patients in these five DRGs (and most notably within the stroke and hip fracture DRGs), including no Medicare covered post-acute care, care classified as rehabilitation, and skilled nursing home care. Thus, these DRGs were ideal for answering the core questions of the Post-Acute Care study.

The three metropolitan areas selected differ markedly in health-care practice patterns. Pittsburgh is characterized by voluntary hospitals and relatively little prepaid care; the Twin Cities have high penetration rates of Medicare HMOs; and Houston has considerable representation of proprietary hospitals. All hospitals discharging persons in the five DRGs were invited to participate; 19 out of 19 possibilities participated in Pittsburgh, 18 out of 20 possibilities participated in the Twin Cities, and in Houston only 15 of an eligible 31 hospitals agreed to participate. Thus, the sample reflects the variability in health practice patterns Medicare beneficiaries face across the country.

Sample members were enrolled at the time of discharge from the hospital and interviewed and observed in person by the study staff within 72 hours before their discharge from the hospital. Data sources for the study include the patient discharge interview, in person patient interviews 6 weeks, 6 months, and 1 year post discharge, telephone interviews with the family caregiver designated by the patient as primary immediately following each of the patient follow-up interviews, and a full record review of the hospital chart using a modified Medisgroups approach. Information about major health care utilization come directly from Medicare fiscal intermediaries and Medicaid management information systems.

The resultant patient information includes patient perspective on the hospital discharge planning process, family care prior to hospitalization, demonstrated functional capacity at discharge and at each interview thereafter, self-reported functional status at several time periods (before hospitalization, at discharge, 2 weeks after discharge, and in the 2 weeks before the 6-week, 6-month, and 1-year interviews), use of formal services, cognitive status, affective status, and social functioning. The interviews with the family caregiver yielded the total number of hours of care given by the primary provider during the same 2-week post-hospital time intervals for which the patients' functional status is available, breakdown of the kind of tasks provided by family, demographic information about the primary caregiver, family burden on several dimensions, and some relatively detailed questions about economic impact of family care and effect on labor force participation, added at the particular request of HCFA.

Study of family care was not, of course, the purpose of the PAC study, but the information about the extent of family care and its perceived burdens was needed as possible predictors of client outcomes. Family burden was also of interest as a dependent variable that might be associated with various patterns of post-acute care. As a source of information about family care, the PAC data set has the following strengths:

1. A relatively large and longitudinal sample of elderly Medicare beneficiaries following an acute care hospitalization.
2. A sample of caregivers and care receivers drawn from persons discharged from hospitals, rather than preselected from persons known to give family care.
3. An opportunity to study family care of older persons in relationship to acute illness episodes, that may or may not be superimposed on a longstanding pattern of family care. We will be able to divide our sample into persons with a history of family caregiving before the focal hospitalization and those whose career of family care for the particular patient began after the hospitalization.
4. The availability of much fuller objective information about the older person's medical condition and health-care utilization than is usually available for studies of family care.

Heinz Study of Patterns of Family Caregiving

With funding from the Vira I. Heinz Endowment, the University of Minnesota has conducted an in-depth study of family caregiving for a subset of subjects in the PAC Study. The sample was limited to the DRG clusters for hip fracture and stroke because of our assumption that many patients leaving hospitals with those conditions would need at least some post-acute care in response to temporarily or permanently changed functional status.

The Heinz subsample was enrolled consecutively in each metropolitan area until at least 50 hip-fracture patients and 50 stroke patients were selected for a total of 150 persons discharged from hospitals with strokes and 150 discharged from hospitals with hip fractures. An additional criterion for inclusion in the Heinz sample was that the elderly person had not been admitted to the hospital from a nursing home. Clients were followed regardless of their destination on leaving the hospital. The family member designated as primary caregiver was interviewed 6 weeks after the patient's discharge from the hospital, 6 months later, and 1 year later.

The intensive interviews with family caregivers were designed to explore the decision-making process when the patient left the hospital as well as after any subsequent hospitalizations, nursing home or rehabilitation center stays; the history of family caregiving; how the respondent became selected or self-selected as primary caregiver; detailed description of the tasks performed; the extent of backup available to the primary caregiver in terms of financial help or help with caregiving tasks; aspects of family care the respondent perceived as difficult or stressful; interactions with formal caregivers; effects of giving care on the relationship with the care receiver, relationships with other family caregivers, family financial status, and employment of the family caregiver; positive aspects of giving care; legal planning and advance directives; and attitudes towards proposed public policies. Whereas the Post-Acute Care study measures caregiver burden through closed-ended standardized measures, the Heinz study used open-ended questions to explore the caregiving experience that were then meticulously post-coded.

Like the PAC study to which it is appended, the Heinz study affords a view of a sample of family caregivers of elderly recently experiencing an acute hospital stay, and it contains information about formal care as well as informal care. In conjunction with the detailed information that the PAC study provides on the patient's functional status at each time period, the family caregivers objective level of help at each time period, and the information from the chart audit during the focal hospitalization, the Heinz data set has the following advantages:

1. It provides sufficient depth in its qualitative data to explore the motivations and incentives that affect family caregivers.
2. It may produce methodological insights because it permits comparisons of responses to forced choice questions in the PAC study to the open-ended post-coded questions in the Heinz data set. For example, PAC asked respondents if they had any difficulty locating or affording various kinds of services, whereas the Heinz study post-coded the responses to a relatively unstructured discussion of the respondent's experience with formal care. Similarly, level of caregiver burden was assessed in the PAC study with the Montgomery Burden Scale. The level of burden thus measured can be compared to the qualitative measure of burden based on the open-ended Heinz interviews.

PRELIMINARY FINDINGS

Post Hospital Movement

Without having detailed multivariate analyses, the larger PAC study suggests several messages about persons leaving the hospitals with common discharge diagnoses, and these messages are relevant for considering informal care.

First, patients discharged from hospitals experience substantial change in the first several months as they move across post-acute care modalities such as rehabilitation facilities, nursing homes, and home care (sometimes truncated by rehospitalizations) and as they move from a relative's home back to their own or vice versa. When the 2,610 patients enrolled in PAC study were considered, investigators found 37% of the stroke patients and 32% of the hip patients had made at least one move in addition to the hospital discharge. At the 6-month interview, movement was still occurring, including returns to nursing homes.

Those patients who did not enter rehabilitation programs or nursing homes use home-care services to a limited extent at hospital discharge. Formal care use tapers off over time. Home nursing, personal care, and homemaking services are most frequent. The therapies, day care, and meal services are infrequently used.

Not all of the Medicare patients discharged from the hospital are in need of long-term care and those that are have varying levels of need. The PAC study identified patients who need long-term care from the sample when need is defined with varying thresholds of cognitive and physical impairments. A conservative threshold of three ADL deficiencies or four errors on the MSQ yields 38% of the people in the PAC sample needing care at a level that would qualify them for nursing home admission in most states.

Family care for the 2,610 PAC patients varied in intensity but was a definite presence. Immediately following patient discharge, 31% of caregivers provided over 5 hours of care per day and 20% provided more than 8 hours a day.

Characteristics of the Patients and the Caregivers in the Heinz Study

From preliminary analyses of the Heinz caregiver sample we can generate a more detailed picture of the 307 caregivers and the 307 care receivers at the 6-week interview in the more detailed Heinz caregiver study. Table 10.1 indicates that the family caregivers tended to be older people themselves (median age = 59 yrs), married, and female. About one half of the caregivers were adult children of the care receiver and about one third are spouses. Approximately 56% of the caregivers were not employed. Interviews indicate that about 10% stopped working or decreased employment hours as a result of caregiving responsibilities. At the 6-week interview, about 13% of caregivers and patients shared a household compared to 10% prior to the hospitalization.

Most of the caregivers in this sample (54%) provided care for more than a year prior to this hospitalization. On the other hand, consistent with the relatively independent functional status of patients prior to this hospitalization, about 35% of the caregivers performed no caregiving tasks prior to this acute episode. Clearly, the hospital brings together patients with family caregivers who are new to the job and a larger group whose families will be offering a continuation of care.

TABLE 10.1
**Heinz Caregiver Study: Characteristics of Family Caregivers at
6-Week Interview**

Characteristic	Percent (n = 307)
Gender	
Male	28%
Female	72%
Age[1]	
21 years or younger	1%
22 years to 35 years	4%
36 years to 50 years	22%
50 years to 65 years	25%
66 years to 70 years	17%
over 70 years	7%
refusals	24%
Relationship to patient[1]	
Spouse	28%
Adult children	51%
Grandchildren	3%
Other relatives/non-relatives	18%
Living with patient	13%
Marital status[1]	
Married	61%
Widowed	4%
Divorced	7%
Never married	5%
missing	25%
Employment status	
Not employed/retired	56%
Employed full time	30%
Employed part time	14%
Duration of family caregiving	
Began with this hospitalization	39%
Less than a year before hospitalization	7%
More than a year	54%
No family care before hospitalization	35%

[1]Percentages may not sum to 100 due to rounding errors and refusals.

Table 10.2 describes the demographic characteristics of patients in the Heinz study. They were predominately female and over the age of 75. Based on the caregivers' reports, about 10% of the patients were on Medicaid at the 6-week interview.

Table 10.3 presents patient functional status over the study year. As is clear from Table 10.3, most patients were functioning better at one year post hospitalization than at discharge. At discharge, 23% of the patients had between one and three impairments in activities of daily living (ADLs) and 74% had more than three impairments. Cognitive status was measured by the Short Portable Mental Status Questionnaire (MSQ), which asks patients to answer ten questions. At the 6-week interview about one third were sufficiently impaired to get four or more wrong on the test. By the 12-month interview, however, the percentage with four or greater incorrect had dropped to 21% on the mental status measure.

TABLE 10.2
Heinz Caregiver Study: Characteristics of Patients
at 6-Week Interview

Characteristic	Percent (n = 307)
Gender	
Male	32%
Female	68%
Age[1]	
65 years to 69 years	15%
70 years to 75 years	23%
76 years to 80 years	18%
81 years to 85 years	23%
86 years to 90 years	14%
Over 90 years	6%
Living situation before hospitalization[1]	
Own home	83%
Family home	11%
Board & care home	5%
Marital status[1]	
Married	51%
Widowed	38%
Divorced	3%
Never married	7%
missing	1%
Patients on Medicaid	11%

[1]Percentages may not sum to 100 due to rounding errors and refusals.

TABLE 10.3
Heinz Caregiver Study: Patient Functional Status Over Time

	Before Hospital (n = 307)	At Discharge (n = 307)	6 Weeks (n = 305)	6 Months (n = 260)	12 Months (n = 208)
ADL Impairments[1]					
none	66%	3%	30%	40%	49%
1 impairment	19%	7%	26%	24%	20%
2 impairments	8%	6%	9%	10%	8%
3 impairments	2%	10%	8%	6%	4%
4 impairments	3%	43%	14%	12%	8%
5 impairments	2%	31%	14%	9%	11%
Cognitive Impairments					
0 to 1 errors on MSQ	not measured	42%	46%	51%	63%
2 to 3 errors on MSQ	not measured	24%	29%	26%	16%
4 to 10 errors on MSQ	not measured	34%	25%	23%	21%

[1]Percentages may not sum to 100% due to rounding errors. Prior hospitalization ADL's were measured by self-report. At all other time periods ADL's and cognitive impairments were measured by patient demonstration.

The Family Caregiving Situation

Most family caregivers in the sample identified at least one person who helped them with caregiving tasks over the year. At discharge, about half had two helpers. Some of the respondents had larger networks of helpers (see Table 10.4). Over time the number and perhaps the need, for additional helpers for a primary family caregiver decreases. Consistent with this pattern, primary caregivers with no helpers increased over time. It is likely those caregivers cared for patients who gradually improved. However, they may reflect a subgroup of caregivers who, for whatever reason, become increasingly isolated over time. Future analyses will investigate this issue.

TABLE 10.4
Heinz Caregiver Study: Family Caregiving Network Over Time

Number of helpers available to primary caregiver	Percent Reporting		
	6 Weeks (n = 307)	6 Months (n = 300)	12 Months (n = 281)
None	8%	19%	26%
One helper	29%	27%	23%
Two helpers	24%	27%	22%
Three helpers	20%	15%	17%
Four helpers	13%	8%	7%
Five helpers	4%	3%	2%
Six or more helpers	4%	2%	3%

Caregivers indicated that having helpers was not the same as having another person available to assume the primary caregiver's responsibilities. Despite the large number of family caregivers who had help with tasks, 34% believed that no one was available to replace them if they were no longer able to be the primary caregiver. In interviews, most caregivers who perceived they had no replacement cited no one available due to distances or competing demands of potential caregivers. They said that there was literally no other adult in the family to assume the tasks.

Primary caregivers were asked how they came to be selected for the role. Selection or self-selection as primary caregiver was usually the result of several factors. However, unless ill, spouses considered their role as primary caregiver to be automatic and self-evident. Combinations of proximity and lack of other family accounted for most selections. Affection was rarely mentioned as a reason for becoming the primary caregiver. However, it may be the case that spouses and those family living with or close to the patient did not perceive the need to identify affection — perhaps it goes with out saying for many caregivers.

Informal Caregiving Over Time

Family members provided a wide variety of types of help during each time period. Table 10.5 presents the number of family caregivers reporting that they helped with a specific task over time and further broken down depending on whether the patient lived in the community (including own home, other home, and board and care homes) or in an institution (nursing home, hospital, or rehabilitation facility). As Table 10.5 indicates, help given to care receivers was greatest 2 weeks post discharge and decreases over time. The most frequent type of assistance given by families was supervision of safety, shopping and errands, business assistance, transportation, meal preparation, cleaning, and laundry. Assistance with activities of daily living was less frequently given by families. Many patients received family help with medications, physical therapy, and exercises, especially in the first 6 weeks. Feeding help was rarely given by the family. Notably, feeding help is more frequent when the patient is in an institution. This reflects a combination of greater need for this type of assistance for less functionally able care receivers. In addition, feeding, errands, and laundry are tangible assistance families can give to institutionalized relatives. Feeding can easily be done if visits are at meal time. As the table shows, the relative frequencies for these categories are highest and stay that way for the institutionalized subgroup.

Table 10.6 indicates the hours of family care over time for patients living in the community at the time of the interview. Given that 40 hours in a 2-week period is equal to one half time job, and 80 hours in a 2-week period is a full

TABLE 10.5
**Heinz Caregiver Study: Family Caregiver Tasks Over Time by Patient Location
(Community or Institution[1])**

	Percent of Patients Receiving Help							
	2 weeks post hospital		6 weeks		6 months		12 months	
Tasks	n = 242 Comm.	n = 65 Inst.	n = 242 Comm.	n = 65 Inst.	n = 254 Comm.	n = 37 Inst.	n = 226 Comm.	n = 40 Inst.
Bathing/ showering	47%	11%	30%	17%	32%	3%	20%	5%
Dressing	44%	20%	30%	22%	28%	8%	21%	8%
Grooming	40%	30%	32%	31%	29%	30%	4%	25%
Feeding	10%	26%	4%	15%	7%	16%	24%	23%
Toileting	35%	25%	16%	23%	21%	11%	13%	8%
Transferring	37%	31%	17%	26%	19%	3%	12%	3%
Walking	49%	22%	27%	20%	32%	22%	26%	8%
Supervising safety	60%	39%	54%	40%	52%	35%	47%	18%
Giving medicines	38%	8%	34%	15%	32%	5%	28%	5%
Medical procedures	11%	2%	11%	5%	9%	3%	8%	5%
P.T./exercises	28%	22%	19%	20%	13%	14%	9%	0
Meal preparation	45%	12%	35%	22%	37%	8%	24%	8%
Cleaning	48%	25%	36%	31%	37%	8%	28%	8%
Laundry	51%	51%	36%	43%	40%	27%	32%	38%
Shopping/ errands	79%	74%	74%	77%	70%	78%	67%	75%
Transportation	62%	26%	72%	40%	65%	35%	63%	38%
Reading to pt.	12%	15%	12%	20%	13%	22%	12%	25%
Business/ finances	53%	70%	46%	65%	50%	65%	46%	68%
Heavy chores	32%	25%	31%	23%	32%	14%	28%	15%

[1]Community includes care receivers living at home, family home, and board and care homes. Institution includes those in nursing homes, hospitals and rehabilitation facilities.

time job, these data show that about half of the caregivers are working at caregiving as a half time job or more at the 6-week interview. The hours of caregiving gradually fall off over the course of the year as expected. At 12 months, only 27% are reporting over 40 hours per 2-week period compared to 37% at the 6-week interview.

Formal Care

Table 10.7 highlights formal care for the care receivers before the hospitalization and over the course of the year. The most frequently used types of

TABLE 10.6
**Heinz Caregiver Study: Hours of Family Caregiving over Time for Patients
Living in the Community**

Number of Hours[a] over 2 weeks	6 Weeks (n = 180)[b]	6 Months (n = 166)[c]	12 Months (n = 173)[d]
0	12%	14%	19%
less than 10	19%	16%	23%
10 to 20	18%	18%	17%
21 to 40	14%	19%	15%
41 to 60	11%	14%	9%
61 to 80	5%	4%	3%
greater than 80	21%	16%	15%

[a]Percentages may not sum to 100 due to rounding errors.
[b]Missing cases = 62
[c]Missing cases = 47
[d]Missing cases = 53

formal care in the post hospital period are visiting nurse services, homemakers, and physical therapy. The use of formal care decreases over time in all categories except day care. When given the opportunity to comment on services, few family caregivers reported difficulty in finding or affording formal care services. Few reported dissatisfaction with services received. Nursing homes and paraprofessional services engendered the most discontent.

Family caregivers were asked about how giving care affected them in several key areas: relationships with the care receiver, other family members, work and finances. These were explored with open-ended questions followed by probes to elicit detailed discussion. The responses were then post-coded in categories of effects.

Tables 10.8 shows the effects of caregiving on the relationships with the patient by duration of caregiving. A larger proportion of inexperienced caregivers (those giving care only since the focal hospitalization) compared to experienced (those giving care before the acute episode) perceive the relationship as unchanged over the year. Additionally, experience seems to make a difference in how difficult caregiving is for the caregiver. Experienced caregivers were somewhat more likely to report discomforts related to caregiving than inexperienced caregivers. However, multivariate analyses are necessary to identify the source of the difference. It may be that experienced caregivers are also caring for the most functionally disabled care receivers.

The location of the care receiver in an institution or in the community has some effect on the relationship between the caregiver and the care receiver. Overall, as Table 10.9 indicates, almost half of the caregivers interviewed at 6 weeks and more than half of the caregivers interviewed at 6 months perceived the relationship as unchanged, regardless of patient location. At 12 months after hospital discharge, some change in the relationship is reported

TABLE 10.7

Heinz Caregiver Study: Formal Care Use over Time by Patients Living in the Community

Type of Formal Care	Before Hospital (n = 307)	6 Weeks (n = 242)	6 Months (n = 254)	12 Months (n = 226)
Homemaker	26%	15%	27%	23%
Home health aid	8%	17%	15%	10%
Visiting nurse	9%	32%	11%	5%
Meals delivered	9%	7%	7%	6%
Transportation	13%	5%	7%	4%
Day care	4%	0%	1%	1%
Outpatient rehab	2%	3%	2%	1%
Physical therapy	4%	27%	6%	2%
Occupational therapy	1%	7%	2%	1%
Speech therapy	2%	5%	2%	1%

TABLE 10.8

Heinz Caregiver Study: Effects of Caregiving on Relationship Between Caregiver and Care Receiver by Duration of Caregiving

	Percent Reporting					
	6 weeks		6 months		12 months	
Effect[a]	Inexp. (n = 185)	Exper. (n = 119)	Inexp. (n = 183)	Exper. (n = 114)	Inexp. (n = 172)	Exper. (n = 107)
No effect	37%	69%	60%	61%	38%	56%
Emotionally closer	22%	22%	17%	17%	31%	22%
Emotionally more distant	8%	4%	11%	4%	14%	13%
Pity	3%	1%	2%	0	8%	28%
Worry	5%	7%	6%	6%	5%	3%
Anger or resentment	13%	8%	9%	4%	9%	5%
More time together	5%	3%	3%	1%	2%	3%
Role reversal	11%	6%	7%	6%	10%	5%
Patient is helpful	4%	2%	3%	1%	2%	1%
Patient more dependent	9%	4%	5%	6%	10%	0
Relationship worse (no specifics)	5%	1%	4%	2%	4%	8%
Relationship improved (no specifics)	2%	2%	4%	3%	4%	0

[a]Respondents were asked to discuss how family caregiving affected their relationship with the patient and answers were later coded. Columns do not sum to 100% because respondents could give more than one response.

TABLE 10.9
Effects of Caregiving on Relationship Between Primary Caregiver and Patient by Location of Patient in Community or Institution[a]

Effect[a]	6 weeks		6 months		12 months	
	Comm. (n = 242)	Inst. (n = 65)	Comm. (n = 254)	Inst. (n = 37)	Comm. (n = 226)	Inst. (n = 40)
No effect	45%	46%	54%	57%	48%	35%
Emotionally closer	24%	14%	17%	11%	26%	28%
Emotionally more distant	6%	8%	7%	19%	11%	23%
Pity	1%	5%	1%	3%	1%	8%
Worry	5%	8%	5%	11%	3%	8%
Anger or resentment	10%	15%	8%	3%	8%	5%
More time together	4%	3%	2%	0	3%	0
Role reversal	9%	9%	7%	5%	8%	10%
Patient is helpful	3%	3%	2%	3%	2%	0
Patient more dependent	6%	12%	6%	5%	6%	13%
Relationship worse (no specifics)	2%	8%	4%	3%	3%	0
Relationship improved (no specifics)	2%	2%	3%	5%	2%	0

[a]Institution includes nursing home, hospitals and rehabilitation facilities. Community includes patient home, family/caregiver home and board and care homes.
[b]Respondents were asked to discuss how family caregiving affected their relationship with the patient and answers were later coded. Respondents could give more than one response.

by more caregivers of patients in institutions than those who live in the community. However, this difference is likely to be a result of several factors such as patient functional status and caregiver experience.

The PAC study collected information from spousal and nonspousal caregivers about the direct financial effects of caregiving. Spouses make up the greatest proportion of caregivers providing financial assistance, followed by daughters. Between 15% and 23% of caregivers provided financial assistance. Caregivers were asked at the 12-month interview to assess the degree of financial sacrifice incurred in helping the patient financially. Of the 417 caregivers who reported providing financial assistance, the majority said no financial sacrifice was entailed, whereas 12% reported considerable or major sacrifice. These data suggest that there is a subgroup of caregivers who provide direct financial assistance and most do not view it as a burden.

Overall, the message from caregivers about the effects of caregiving seems to be variation. The effects can be simultaneously positive and negative for caregivers. In addition, there are subgroups, such as those we have discussed, and others: caregivers in the labor force, caregivers responsible for more than one care receiver, experienced and inexperienced caregivers, and those who are alone. Attention to the variation in patterns and perceptions and subgroups created by the variations is a necessary part of framing policy for family caregiving.

DISCUSSION

The preliminary findings we present in this chapter describe some of the basic characteristics and features of the caregiving experience over time. These data and other longitudinal approaches to studying the caregiver experience are available to look at one of the central questions for researchers and policymakers: What happens to care givers and care receivers over time under varying circumstances?

From our vantage point at the intersection of acute and long-term care, we note that the experience of caregiving immediately after a hospitalization may be different from other points of time in a caregiving trajectory. In addition, family caregivers with previous experience may face quite different challenges than those who are new to the tasks. These differences may in turn suggest specific interventions that would be useful in the post acute period and not at other times, and for inexperienced caregivers and not experienced ones. Our data also show alot of patient transitions in the first 6 weeks after hospital discharge, moves to and from nursing homes, rehabilitation facilities, and family home to own home. Interventions can be focused on these transition points as well at hospital discharge. It appears that family members are physically present during a hospitalization and that professionals may fail to capitalize on this availability to prepare family members for the likely changes that will occur during the next 6 weeks and to discuss their possible roles.

In further analyses of these data, we plan to identify subgroups for further study — for example, caregivers with other care recipients, caregivers who themselves need care, patients who have not discussed the post-hospital plan with anybody (either professionals or family members), caregivers with long histories of family caregiving, caregivers with no backup, caregivers who believe that there is nobody to take their place, caregivers in the labor force, and caregivers who get no pleasure from the role. We also plan methodological studies that compare family caregivers' responses about stresses and burdens on open-ended Heinz interviews with their responses to forced choice questions in the PAC study.

Above all, we argue the merit of including medical data and linking acute episodes to long-term care needs and plans. Samples of caregivers of patients after an acute hospital stay provide variation that can complement past studies with samples of caregivers selected because they are known to give care.

ACKNOWLEDGMENTS

This chapter is based on the design and preliminary analyses from a study on Patterns of Family Caregiving Over Time, which is funded by the Vira I.

Heinz Endowment of Pittsburgh, Pennsylvania. The study builds on a longitudinal data set created for the National Post-Acute Care Study funded by the Office of the Assistant Secretary for Planning and Evaluation (ASPE) and the Health Care Financing Administration (HCFA). Colleagues collaborating on the study include Michael Finch, Robert Kane, and Jon Christianson. The larger Post-Acute Care Study is directed by Robert Kane and managed Michael Finch.

REFERENCES

Brody, E. M. (1981). Women in the middle and family help to older people. *The Gerontologist, 21,* 471–480.
Cantor, M. H. (1983). Strain among caregivers: A study of experience in the United States. *The Gerontologist, 23,* 597–604.
Christianson, J. B. (1988). The evaluation of the National Long-Term Care Demonstration: The effects of Channeling on informal caregiving. *Health Services Research, 23,* 99–118.
Clipp, E. C., & George, L. K. (1990). Caregiver needs and patterns of social support. *Journal of Gerontology: Social Sciences, 45,* S102–111.
Doty, P. (1986). Family care of the elderly: The role of public policy. *The Milbank Memorial Fund Quarterly, 64*(1), 34–75.
Doty, P. (1990, December). *Family caregiving and access to publicly funded home care: Implicit and explicit influences on decision making.* Paper presented at Family Caregiving in Long-Term Care: Next Steps for Public Policy, Morgantown, WV.
George, L. K., & Gwyther, L. P. (1986). Caregiver well-being: A multidimensional examination of demented adults. *The Gerontologist, 26,* 253–259.
Horowitz, A. (1985). Family caregiving to the frail elderly. In M. P. Lawton & G. Maddox (Eds.), *Annual review of gerontology and Geriatrics* (Vol. 5., pp. 194–246). New York: Springer.
Kane, R. A., & Kane, R. L. (1987). *Long-term care: Principles, programs and policies.* New York: Springer.
Krause, N. K. (1990). Perceived health problems, formal/informal support, and life satisfaction among older adults. *Journal of Gerontology: Social Sciences, 45,* S193–205.
Linsk, N. L., Kehiger, S. M., & Englund, S. (1990, December). *Compensation of family care for the elderly.* Paper presented at Family Caregiving in Long-Term Care: Next Steps for Public Policy, Morgantown, WV.
Montgomery, R. J. V. (1990, December). *Examining respite care: Promises and limitations.* Paper presented at Family Caregiving in Long-Term Care: Next Steps for Public Policy, Morgantown, WV.
Pearlin, L. I., Mullan, J. T., Semple, S. J., & Skaff, M. M. (1990). Caregiving and the stress process: An overview of concepts and their measures. *The Gerontologist, 30,* 583–594.
Pruchno, R. A., Kleban, M. H., Michaels, J. E., & Dempsey, N. P. (1989). Mental and physical health of caregiving spouses: Development of a causal model. *Journal of Gerontology: Psychological Sciences, 45,* P192–199.
Schulz, R., Visintainer, P., & Williamson, G. M. (1990). Psychiatric and physical morbidity effects of caregiving. *Journal of Gerontology: Psychological Sciences, 45,* P181–191.
Soldo, B. J., & Myllyluoma, J. (1983). Caregivers who live with dependent elderly. *The Gerontologist, 23,* 605–611.
Soldo, B. J., Wolf, D. A., & Agree, E. M. (1990). Family, households, and care arrangements of frail older women: A structural analysis. *Journal of Gerontologist: Social Sciences, 45,* S238–249.

Stephens, S. A., & Christianson, J. B. (1986). *Informal care of the elderly.* Lexington: D.C. Health.

Stoller, E. P., & Earl, L. L. (1983). Help with activities of everyday life: Sources of support for the noninstitutionalized elderly. *The Gerontologist, 23,* 64–70.

Stone, R., Cafferata, G. L., & Sangl, J. (1987). Caregivers of the frail elderly: A national profile. *The Gerontologist, 27,* 616–626.

Wan, T., & Weissert, W. G. (1981). Social support networks, patient status, and institutionalization. *Research on Aging, 3,* 240–256.

Young, R. F., & Kahana, E. (1989). Specifying caregiver outcomes: Gender and relationship aspects of caregiving strain. *The Gerontologist, 29,* 660–666.

Zarit, S. H., Reever, K. E., & Bach-Peterson, J. (1980). Relatives of the impaired elderly: Correlates of feelings of burden. *The Gerontologist, 20,* 649–655.

Methodological Issues Confronting Research on Service Use Among Caregiving Families

Aloen L. Townsend
Kent State University

This section presents a critique of literature on later-life caregiving and service utilization in order to highlight some of the methodological challenges and dilemmas confronting research on longitudinal patterns of service use among caregiving families. It also proposes some directions for future work. The contribution is organized around three major questions: (a) How is longitudinal defined, (b) What is meant by patterns of service use, and (c) What do we mean by caregiving families?

How is Longitudinal Defined?

Obviously, the appropriate study design depends on the researcher's purposes. One major limitation of present work on service use, however, is the predominant reliance on cross-sectional studies. Longitudinal studies, such as those presented at this conference, are an important advance.

Two closely related decisions that must be made in designing any longitudinal study are how long the study should last and how often to make assessments (Campbell, 1988). Existing studies, both panel and cross-sectional ones with retrospective data, vary widely in the timespan used to assess service utilization.

In deciding on the appropriate time frame, there are advantages and disadvantages to both longer and shorter periods and to greater and fewer data collection points. One of the disadvantages of shorter studies (particularly when combined with more data collection waves) is less likelihood of services being used either at all or extensively or of any change in status occurring.

Another disadvantage of short periods is that all possible variations in service use (e.g., home care versus nursing-home care) are less likely to occur at any given point. Consequently, the researcher is less likely to have sufficient cases for analytical purposes in any one condition and is less able to determine longer range patterns.

On the other hand, one of the advantages of shorter periods is less likelihood of missing short-term, acute, or transitory phenomena. There is also greater likelihood that constructs being measured in a given data collection wave are contemporaneous or closely proximate in time, and there is less opportunity for selective biases in self-report and recall to affect the study. If one is only interested in stable care arrangements, the limited likelihood of change in status occurring becomes an advantage rather than a disadvantage of shorter periods.

Longer periods of time entail greater expenditures in cost, effort, and time; have greater likelihood of sample attrition; and run more risk of missing short-term intervening states. They also have advantages, however. The likelihood increases of seeing a larger magnitude of service use or of change in use. More individuals are likely to experience service use or change in use. Longer designs also provide more opportunity to prospectively identify predictors of subsequent outcomes, with less reliance on retrospection.

Longitudinal designs (particularly panel designs) provide an opportunity to study variability in patterns of service use and its correlates over time and to examine the reliability of our measures. They also enable us to estimate prevalence rates more accurately, draw stronger causal inferences about the longitudinal nature of relationships (and their mathematical form), and identify potential biases related to selective sample attrition (such as the unique characteristics of older people who receive care in their own homes for extended periods of time). Panel designs can model individual-level as well as aggregate-level change, and they more realistically represent families' caregiving careers.

The decisions about what time frames and measurement points to include are not simple ones to make. One of the most vexing issues is deciding on the basis for these decisions. For some purposes, the care recipient's characteristics or status may be most critical, but for other purposes the primary caregiver, the informal care network, or formal services may be the entity one chooses to assess. The most useful time span may differ, for example, depending on whether one wants to predict subsequent service use from changes in the care recipient's health, the family caregivers' stress, the composition of the informal care network, or prior service use.

What Constitutes Patterns of Service Use?

Defining patterns of service use, like decisions about longitudinal designs, is really more complicated than first appearance reveals. The meaning of services must be clarified, then the meaning of use, and finally the meaning of patterns.

What is Meant by Services?   One of the most common problems with research on service use is the confounding of services with the sites at which they are delivered or with their providers (Evashwick, Rowe, Diehr, & Branch, 1984; Kane & Kane, 1989). For example, "home care" and "visiting nurse" are two common illustrations of vague, compound services.

Another common issue is whether informal as well as formal care providers are included in defining services (George, 1987). Quasiformal arrangements, including regular paid helpers such as a housekeeper hired privately rather than through an agency, or assistance from groups such as churches, pose special problems as to whether they should be included and whether they should be classified as informal or formal services (Soldo, Agree, & Wolf, 1989).

Most current research includes a very restricted range of services. Within the formal arena, there has been a predominance of attention to medical services, with relative neglect of other types such as social services, mental health services, or personal care assistance.

Existing studies also tend to treat services as either unidimensional or as independent of each other. This latter practice is becoming even more questionable with the increase in case management systems and health maintenance organizations (HMOs, and their social service oriented cousins, SHMOs), where services are more likely to be interdependent (Kane & Kane, 1989; Mechanic, 1989). When services are treated as unitary, current research typically categorizes and combines them on the basis of convenience or untested assumptions of similarity rather than on empirical or theoretical grounds.

Another challenge is the difficulty of defining the target of service or, in other words, specifying who is the client (George, 1987). If services are restricted to those directed to the care recipient, research may underrepresent services for the caregiver; if services are defined as targeted solely to individuals, we may neglect services for families or other groups. Decisions about how clients are defined affect not only how services are operationalized, but also the sorts of outcomes and predictors that are included in our research. When data are collected from service providers or funders, researchers are especially vulnerable to recording and categorizing decisions made according to the provider's or funder's rules about what constitutes a service.

Little effort has been directed toward assessing similarities and differences across service settings, especially those that are represented by general categories, such as HMOs, senior centers, or nursing homes. Studies that focus globally on such multiservice sites obscure potentially important distinctions within these sites in the services provided and used and in the characteristics of the setting (Krout, 1983; Mechanic, 1989). Within the category of home care, many potentially important distinctions across living arrangements are also presently overlooked.

An allied difficulty with existing research has been the lack of a common metric across services to describe and compare their nature and characteristics (Soldo et al., 1989). The missing common language is especially noticeable between informal and formal care. Informal helpers may be assisting with the same tasks as formal helpers, but often this informal help is not even considered a service. For example, how does one compare the assistance with meals given by formal providers such as Meals on Wheels or nutrition sites with that provided by a family member?

Formal services vary widely in their availability and accessibility. Availability and accessibility ought to be broadly defined, including physical, political, economic, organizational, psychological, social, and geographic dimensions. Conclusions about the nature, volume, and intensity of service use would be more illuminating if both the local and broader service contexts were better specified (Gilford, 1988; Kane & Kane, 1989; Soldo et al., 1989). A creative combination of large-scale, nationally representative data and local or regional studies is needed for this task.

What is Meant by Use?   The second dilemma one must grapple with in defining patterns of service use is how to operationalize use. In many studies, it is defined dichotomously as any contact or as receiving at least one service within a given period.

Alternative conceptions of service use, in terms of frequency (how often), intensity (how much), or duration (how long services are used), are less common (Krout, 1983; Soldo et al., 1989). Regularity (i.e., consistency) of service use is especially neglected in current research. In addition, measures of volume of use (for example, number of physician visits) often confound intensity and duration (Day, 1984).

Little attention has been paid to the purpose (e.g., prevention, treatment, information) for which services are used (Branch et al., 1981; Wolinsky, Coe, & Mosely, 1987). Purpose indirectly affects definitions of use, as illustrated by studies that omit people who inquire about but don't use a service.

All too often, initial use is not distinguished from reuse of services (e.g., first admission vs. readmission, new vs. reopened cases, initial vs. followup visits; Kane & Kane, 1989). Current research also usually lacks information about who initiated the use. Even more common is lack of information about the termination of service use (Krout, 1983), including when a service was terminated, by whom, for what reason, and whether service is continuing but being transferred to another site or provider. Both reuse and cessation raise the tricky question of what constitutes a unit of service or how to delineate when a service episode begins and ends.

Finally, the question of what defines use is intimately related to the source of the data. Corroborating evidence from a second source is not commonly part of a study design. In addition, different service settings and payment mechanisms define and record use in very different ways (McKinlay, 1972). Researchers too often fail to acknowledge that alternative methods of collecting data might lead to quite different results and conclusions.

What Constitutes a Pattern? A number of general methodological issues arise from this question. For example, are we interested in linear or nonlinear relationships between our predictors and service use? Do we want to treat the variables quantitatively or qualitatively (as in typologies of service users)? Are we interested in the aggregate level or in individual-level processes and, if group-level processes are the focus, what is the basis for aggregating?

Do we wish to look for commonalities or for heterogeneity? Are we going to examine interactive or exponential relationships as well as the more common additive ones? Will we include reciprocal (i.e., nonrecursive) relationships in our models or only the typical unidirectional ones?

Only occasionally have researchers explicitly confronted the fact that measures of service use are often distributed nonnormally (Wolinsky et al., 1987). It is not uncommon for there to be a large number of nonusers or low users, for example, whereas at the high end a few cases may use a disproportionate amount of services.

Especially needed are prospective, multivariate, and causal models of service use, where there are appropriate statistical controls and where a causal sequence is postulated (Branch & Stuart, 1985; Kane & Kane, 1989; McAuley & Arling, 1984; Soldo et al., 1989; Wan, 1987). Service use research is just beginning to grapple with the question of whether such models should be specific to a given service, setting, provider, time, population, or geographic locale or whether the models are intended to be more general (Evashwick et al., 1984; Gilford, 1988; Kane & Kane, 1989). General models have been an implicit assumption behind many of the current studies, such as those that aggregate measures of use across a variety of services. Given the heavy reliance on empirically derived models of service use, more theoretically based models are sorely needed.

Beyond these general methodological decisions about the types of patterns to be considered, patterns can also be described in terms of their focus on within-services versus across-services issues. For any given service, for example, one can look at patterns distinguishing users from nonusers. Indeed, use versus nonuse of a service has been the primary theme in prior research. In many studies, however, nonusers are a mixture of people who have never used the service, haven't used it in the specified time period, or are using it but below some criterion level.

Other within-service patterns on which research is needed include short-term versus long-term use, selective use (that is, the use of some services rather than or more than others), and stable versus unstable use. This latter topic would encompass people who drop out of services; refuse services; lose eligibility (including financial eligibility); transfer to a different service, provider, or setting; no longer need services; or are dropped by the provider for reasons other than the above. Thus, stability of service use can be defined either in terms of the regularity of use among users (for example, uninterrupted versus erratic use) or as continued use versus exit from use.

A whole different array of patterns come into focus when the perspective shifts from within a service to across services. Now, patterns such as sequential versus simultaneous use of services, providers, or service settings can be examined. Similarly, segregated versus integrated use can be studied, as in patterns representing whether care providers are performing the same tasks or different tasks. Such patterns are at the heart of the current debate about formal service substitution for informal care.

Another pattern across services is that of interdependence versus autonomy. Many studies treat each service, provider, and setting as if it were independent of any others. In reality, factors such as third-party payment mechanisms, DRGs, and managed care systems alter the likelihood of using certain services, providers, or settings. A closely related but distinct pattern is that of coordination versus fragmentation across services.

The organization of service delivery systems and of funding mechanisms constrain the options and shape all of these patterns, both within and across services (Gilford, 1988; Kane & Kane, 1989; Mechanic, 1989; Soldo et al., 1989). Unfortunately, such macrolevel factors are generally incorporated as introductory or concluding comments rather than as predictor variables in research on service use.

Regardless of whether one looks within or across service systems, there are several areas of research that are conspicuously neglected. First, current studies focus much more on service events than on processes (Kane & Kane, 1989; Krout, 1983; McKinlay, 1972; Mechanic, 1989). Thus, little attention is paid to the decision-making processes underlying service use, including decisions about whether to initiate, continue, alter, or terminate services, as well as decisions about the nature of the services needed.

Second, analyses of the quality or value of services is a neglected area. For example, research is needed on the pros and cons, costs and benefits, or strengths and weaknesses of; the ethical dilemmas associated with; and the values attached by various parties to particular patterns of service use (Kane & Kane, 1989; Soldo et al., 1989). Current research on service use also has devoted significantly more energy to measuring the quantity than the quality of services (McKinlay, 1972; Mechanic, 1989).

What Do We Mean by Caregiving Families?

The last major question provoked by existing research is what we mean by caregiving families. Caregiving has been operationalized in numerous ways

(Barer & Johnson, 1990). Most often, however, it is defined as assistance with activities of daily living (ADL). Some studies also include assistance with instrumental activities, some don't define caregiving at all, and some define the term imprecisely (for example, specifying help with ADL tasks, but not which ones). Other facets of caregiving, such as supervision, companionship, or emotional support are rarely covered.

Caregiving is often operationalized as the total number of ADL tasks with which help is provided, rather than in terms of the intensity and frequency of help required or the duration of care provided. An issue that is receiving increasing attention is the specificity versus generality of caregiving experiences depending on the nature of the care recipient's impairment (Montgomery, Kosloski, & Borgatta, 1990). Little is known about how the services needed or used differ depending on whether the care recipient suffers from Alzheimer's disease or another health condition, for example.

In defining caregiving, the researcher also faces the question of the point at which to enter the caregiving process. Unfortunately, the onset of informal care arrangements is even more likely to be missed than the onset of formal services. The researcher must also struggle with the difficult decision about what constitutes an appropriate control or comparison group.

Family, like caregiving, is a term that can be defined in various ways. Too often, current research reduces family caregiving to a design with only one informant, typically the primary caregiver. Even when studies do look beyond the efforts of a single family caregiver, the availability and involvement of other family members is often inferred from measures of family structure (such as number of adult daughters) rather than measured directly.

Studies that assess the quantity or extensiveness of family support still generally neglect the quality of informal caregiving relationships. Thus, much still needs to be learned about the affective quality and the reliability of family care (Walker & Thompson, 1983).

Despite substantial evidence that family caregiving is not usually the undertaking of a solitary family member (Tennstedt, McKinlay, & Sullivan, 1989; Townsend & Poulshock, 1986), measures of informal care arrangements remain rudimentary. Most often they consist of the number of informal caregivers or the kin relationship of the primary caregiver. Individual characteristics of care recipients and caregivers are far more likely to be used as predictors of service use than interpersonal or systemic variables are.

Lastly, by focusing so many of our studies on primarily White, middle class, urban or suburban families, research on service use has been less sensitive to potential heterogeneity among caregiving families than it should be. Among the understudied groups are the poor, the oldest-old, racial and ethnic minorities, people living in rural areas, and the mentally ill or mentally retarded elderly (Gilford, 1988; Krout, 1983; Townsend & Harel, 1990; Wolinsky et al., 1987). Cross-national studies provide an important counterbalance to the common tendency to overgeneralize from distinctively American results to universal experiences.

Conclusion

Obviously, no one study can address all the issues raised in this discussion. Nevertheless, research provides several promising models for ways to expand and refine our understanding of families' caregiving experiences and their patterns of both informal and formal service use over time. Although the difficulties of such longitudinal research can seem formidable, the rewards to the field will be tremendous.

REFERENCES

Barer, B., & Johnson, C. (1990). A critique of the caregiving literature. *The Gerontologist, 30,* 26–29.

Branch, L., Jette, A., Evashwick, C., Polansky, M., Rowe, G., & Diehr, P. (1981). Toward understanding elders' health service utilization. *Journal of Community Health, 7,* 80–91.

Branch, L., & Stuart, N. (1985). Towards a dynamic understanding of the care needs of the noninstitutionalized elderly. *Home Health Care Services Quarterly, 6*(1), 25–37.

Campbell, R. (1988). Integrating conceptualization, design, and analysis in panel studies of the life course. In K. W. Schaie, R. Campbell, W. Meredith, & S. Rawlings (Eds.), *Methodological issues in aging research* (pp. 43–69). New York: Springer.

Day, S. (1984). Measuring utilization and impact of home care services: A systems model approach for cost-effectiveness. *Home Health Care Services Quarterly, 5*(2), 5–24.

Evashwick, C., Rowe, G., Diehr, P., & Branch, L. (1984). Factors explaining the use of health care services by the elderly. *Health Services Research, 19,* 357–382.

George, L. (1987). Easing caregiver burden: The role of informal and formal supports. In R. Ward & S. Tobin (Eds.), *Health in aging: Sociological issues and policy directions* (pp. 133–158). New York: Springer.

Gilford, D. (1988). *The aging population in the twenty-first century: Statistics for health policy.* Washington, DC: National Academy Press.

Kane, R. L., & Kane, R. A. (1989). Transitions in long-term care. In M. Ory & K. Bond (Eds.), *Aging and health care: Social science and policy perspectives* (pp. 217–243). New York: Routledge.

Krout, J. (1983). Knowledge and use of services by the elderly: A critical review of the literature. *International Journal of Aging and Human Development, 17,* 153–167.

McAuley, W., & Arling, G. (1984). Use of in-home care by very old people. *Journal of Health and Social Behavior, 25,* 54–64.

McKinlay, J. (1972). Some approaches and problems in the study of the use of services — An overview. *Journal of Health and Social Behavior, 13,* 115–152.

Mechanic, D. (1989). Epilogue: Future challenges in health care for an aging population. In M. Ory & K. Bond (Eds.), *Aging and health care: Social science and policy perspectives* (pp. 244–255). New York: Routledge.

Montgomery, R., Kosloski, K., & Borgatta, E. (1990). Service use and the caregiving experience: Does Alzheimer's disease make a difference?. In D. Biegel & A. Blum (Eds.), *Aging and caregiving: Theory, research, and policy* (pp. 139–159). Newbury Park, CA: Sage.

Soldo, B., Agree, E., & Wolf, D. (1989). The balance between formal and informal care. In M. Ory & K. Bond (Eds.), *Aging and health care: Social science and policy perspectives* (pp. 193–216). New York: Routledge.

Tennstedt, S., McKinlay, J., & Sullivan, L. (1989). Informal care for frail elders: The role of secondary caregivers. *The Gerontologist, 29,* 677–683.

Townsend, A., & Harel, Z. (1990). Health vulnerability and service need among the aged. In Z. Harel, P. Ehrlich, & R. Hubbard (Eds.), *The vulnerable aged: People, services, and policies* (pp. 32–52). New York: Springer.

Townsend, A., & Poulshock, S. W. (1986). Intergenerational perspectives on impaired elders' support networks. *Journal of Gerontology, 41,* 101–109.

Walker, A., & Thompson, L. (1983). Intimacy and intergenerational aid and contact among mothers and daughters. *Journal of Marriage and the Family, 45,* 841–849.

Wan, T. (1987). Functionally disabled elderly: Health status, social support, and use of health services. *Research on Aging, 9,* 61–78.

Wolinsky, F., Coe, R., & Mosely, R. (1987). The use of health services by elderly Americans: Implications from a regression-based cohort analysis. In R. Ward & S. Tobin (Eds.), *Health in aging: Sociological issues and policy directions* (pp. 106–132). New York: Springer.

Family Caregiving: Integrating Informal and Formal Systems for Care

Steven H. Zarit
The Pennsylvania State University
Leonard I. Pearlin
University of California

Family caregiving has become, in many ways, the pivotal issue in later life. Following a decade of intensive research, a broad consensus has been established on the stressfulness of caregiving and the disruptions it causes in people's lives. This research has made a compelling case for improving the availability and quality of services to families. Much less agreement can be found on what type of programs and policies are needed, and about the effectiveness of current programs. We examine the fundamental question of integration of informal and formal services, that is, how families and service providers work together, or fail to do so, and the implications of current policies for coordination of their efforts. We then consider several issues in determining the effectiveness of programs and services for caregivers.

THE INTERFACE OF FORMAL AND INFORMAL CARE

Caregiving takes place at the critical juncture of age-associated disabilities, family relationships, health care, and social policies. A caregiving family defines the boundaries of its relationships, obligations, and responsibilities, while searching for scarce resources to manage often overwhelming demands. At the points that families interface with health providers and social agencies, procedures and policies have the potential to support the families' efforts significantly, or to add another layer of complexity and stress.

Informal and formal systems of care do not exist side-by-side as separate or independent processes, but are brought together usually through the efforts of informal caregivers. In this integration, informal caregivers play an important executive function in arranging and monitoring care. Even in instances when a case manager takes on some portion of these functions, the informal caregiver reserves ultimate decision-making and oversight responsibilities.

This linking activity becomes part of the complement of tasks carried out by informal caregivers and imposes varying amounts of demand on time and energy. The caregivers' efforts will determine to what extent the systems interface adequately. Once the systems are integrated, they can have synergistic or entropic effects. In a synergistic system, an informal caregiver who is skillful at initiating the links will get relief from well-conceived formal services, which will in turn facilitate better functioning of the informal system, including the linking activity. The interface will be characterized by entropy, when the time and effort expended in linking and monitoring services further depletes the informal caregiver. The key is to find a proper balance of assistance that interfaces in supportive and mutually compatible ways.

At the heart of the question of interface are issues of what the responsibilities of family and government ought to be and how formal service programs can best be integrated with informal or family caregiving. Some societies have achieved considerable consensus on elder care and the relation of informal and formal services. In Sweden, for example, it is widely accepted that the government should provide care to any elder who needs it, and that no family should have to take on more responsibilities than they want (Hokenstad & Johansson, 1990). Although growth of the older population and a slowdown in the Swedish economy has put pressure on many features of the welfare system, most of the public debate centers around more efficient use of resources, rather than change of basic principles. It is also worth noting that these policies have not led families to abandon their elders, or to rely exclusively on public services. Instead, families still provide alot of care for disabled elders in Sweden, but an extensive, integrated service network is available to supplement the family and to take over when informal caregivers are unavailable or unable to assist.

At the other extreme are countries in which almost all responsibility remains with the family. Public policy in South Korea, for example, remains strongly influenced by Confucian ideals of family responsibility for elders. Development of programs or services to assist families has been minimal. In fact, a basic social security program has only recently been implemented. As a result, families assume responsibility for all of an elder's needs: housing, financial support, and providing care when it is needed.

Because it is unlikely that policies would be adopted in the United States that reflect these extremes of either relieving families of all responsibility or placing the entire load upon them, the challenge is to work out a satisfactory integration of formal and informal helping. Policy discussions, however, have often avoided examination of basic principles of what kind of interface there should be. In the decade of the 1980s, the dominant ideology was to reduce the role of government and to privatize many activities previously carried out by government. In that climate, few people have been willing to argue that government has a positive role, or to offer comprehensive or systematic approaches to the issue of family care (or the larger question of long-term care of the elderly). Instead, much of the debate has centered on specific programs or policies, often raised by pressure groups, that address one type of program or group of caregivers, but do not examine the larger issue of what type of relationship families and government should have and how they can work together.

Drawing upon the work of Litwak (1985), Noelker and Bass (1989) developed a useful typology for the interface of formal and informal assistance, based on whether tasks are shared or segregated between agency and family. The types of relationship they propose are: (a) kin independence — the family provides all the assistance without any formal services; (b) formal service specialization — agencies perform one or more care tasks, although families may provide by themselves or jointly with agencies some other tasks; (c) dual specialization — families and formal service providers assist with different tasks, and do not overlap in their responsibilities; (d) supplementation — formal services assist with tasks that the family also performs; (e) substitution — formal agencies assist with all needed tasks. This framework is helpful for considering how families and formal services interact and for the larger issue of what goals formal services and policies should have.

As Kane discusses in her chapter in this volume, current policies take often contradictory approaches to the interface of family and formal services. Goals of policies may alternatively be to encourage families to become involved as caregivers, to relieve them of some or all of their responsibilities, or to sustain them in the caregiving role. The competing views that these different goals represent may result in unexpected or paradoxical outcomes. As an example, it has often been proposed that programs should be targeted at families at the point when they are considering institutionalization. By providing some relief at that point, nursing home placement would be delayed or prevented. Paradoxically, however, offering formal services at that point in their caregiving career may actually make institutional care more acceptable (see e.g., Scharlach & Frenzel, 1986). Rather than giving families relief, these programs may provide sufficient emotional distance so that caregivers are more likely to take the next step.

The problems of contradictory goals and policies are evident in the descriptions of innovative programs by Harrington and Lévesque in this volume. The Social Health Maintenance Organizations, or SHMOs, have at their core the dual goals of controlling costs through a capitation system and providing necessary long-term care services. The tension between those objectives is apparent. It is further complicated by the fact that costs of medical care, particularly hospital utilization and prescription medication, were quite large, and that nursing home costs at two sites also exceeded projections. Medical care remains at the forefront of the model, with the social component as an add-on to business as usual. Thus, potential savings that might accrue from a more integrated system of long-term care were not realized.

The system in Québec described by Lévesque experienced similar tensions between high costs of medical and institutional care and the ideal of developing a true preventive community care system. A key feature of the Québec system is the principle of universal and free access to health and long-term care. As with the SHMOs, however, rising costs of medical care has led to cost containment pressures that restrict or limit community and preventive approaches.

The trend in the United States toward capitation models, as in the SHMOs, in more usual HMOs, and of course in Medicare's DRG approach to reimbursing hospitals, represents a major shift in the relationship among providers, consumers, and government. Implicitly, capitation approaches are stating that we cannot trust physicians, hospitals, laboratories and other providers (including social services) to do only what is necessary. Rather than having the responsibility for determining what services will be given to be solely in the provider–consumer relationship, these services must now fit under a larger fiscal umbrella. When the provider (whether physician, social worker, or other professional) must both assess need and limit costs, that will necessarily change and complicate his or her relationship with consumers. It is a system that raises to the forefront the question of whose interests the provider is serving.

Several implications of this change in health care can be identified for families. One of the most complex questions is access to services. Despite the attention to this problem by the aging service network, which has promoted information and referral programs and case management, significant barriers to accessing services can be found in many communities. The usual situation is multiple agencies have overlapping responsibilities and varying eligibility and payment procedures. Single gatekeepers may be found for certain groups of users, usually lower income, but that remains the exception.

Although it is generally believed that a patchwork system of programs and eligibilities can be very confusing and inefficient, there can also be limitations of systems with single gatekeepers, such as overbureaucratization of services. Who the gatekeeper is will determine which services are given priorities. Thus, when physicians are actual or de facto gatekeepers (as when cost of medical services crowd out other programs or if physicians do not encourage access to social services in a timely way), one set of interventions are given precedence over others. There may frequently be nonmedical alternatives in chronic care that are overlooked, but may be equally appropriate and effective (e.g., Cummings, 1987). In contrast, some gatekeepers have too little status or prestige to be effective. They also may have little clinical training for making complex assessments and determination of need, as is the case in some case management programs.

We usually consider access to services and the interface of formal and informal helpers solely from an organizational or management perspective, but there are also important psychological dimensions of this process. Three important issues are assertiveness, control, and trust. In care systems that actively seek to control costs, families may be faced with the task of becoming advocates for their relative or for themselves in order to obtain necessary services. The need to take on this assertive stance adds one more layer to the complexity of caregivers' lives. Knowing when to push a provider to do more or to go over that provider's head is a critical problem for anyone in a bureaucratic system. Whenever obstacles are put in place to restrict access, however, it results in some caregivers who become excessively combative, working the system to get what they need, and others who are too passive to obtain needed assistance. At least some individuals decide it is easier to do everything themselves than to deal with bureaucratic procedures (MaloneBeach, Zarit, & Spore, in press).

A related issue is the extent to which families feel in control of decisions about services. The complex rules that currently govern eligibilities and cost-sharing for services often leave families feeling confused and out of control (MaloneBeach et al., in press). They do not know what help they can get, or even what the rules of the game are. Additionally, services are sometimes provided in a way that further undermines control. As an example, families receiving in-home services are often given little say over who will come out to their home or when that person will come (MaloneBeach et al., in press). A different person may be sent for each home visit, even when the person receiving help has dementia and will generally adjust more poorly to a lot of change. The events of caring for an elder often leave families feeling that they have little control, which has consequences for their psychological well-being (Pagel, Becker, & Coppel, 1985). A service system that further undermines feelings of control or self-efficacy will not be able to achieve its larger goals of utilizing services efficiently or relieving stress on caregivers.

A third psychological dimension is trust. For families to accept services, they must have a sense that the person making the recommendations understands their circumstances and is looking out for their or their relative's best interest. The process of matching people to services as it is typically conceived in case management is brief—a need is identified through a rational assessment process and then appropriate services are recommended.

People do not take good advice, however, unless they have implicit trust in the advice-giver. For some elders and their families, development of a helping relationship with providers may be necessary before they can make adequate use of services. As an example, families who were most satisfied with case managed services noted one person in the care system who they had developed a special relationship with (MaloneBeach et al., in press). This person often was not the case manager, but may have been an aide or even a driver. Nonetheless, families were able to use these relationships to explore personal concerns and also for arranging what kinds of help they needed.

In summary, families play a critical role in initiating and sustaining the link between informal and formal care systems. In planning policies and services, we need to consider how these systems are linked from both an organizational and psychosocial perspective. In an era of scarce resources and ever-growing demand, a premium will be placed on cost effective and efficient programs. Yet a mean-spirited or grudging approach to the needs of families can actually place new burdens on them, and, in the end, increase service use and other costs. Perhaps the most basic question is how we conceptualize the relationship—how much help should be available, how should costs be shared, what role will families have in determining their own need for services, and to what extent will families feel empowered in the process of obtaining help.

EVALUATING THE EFFECTIVENESS OF SERVICES

At the heart of an effective interface of informal and formal care systems is a set of programs and services that are successful in achieving their objectives, including providing relief for families. Although most research on caregiving has addressed issues pertaining to stress, only limited attention has been given to evaluating the effects of programs and other interventions. Ongoing studies of that sort are needed to develop an empirically based care system, where the assumptions we make about what will be helpful are tested. There are certainly risks involved in this approach. As Anne Martin Mathews suggested in this volume, premature conclusions from limited or flawed research may foreclose certain options or proscribe the debate over programs.

An example of this problem is the response to the respite study conducted by Lawton, Brody, and Saperstein (1989). In that study, respite services were associated with high consumer satisfaction and a small delay in use of institutional care, but no differences in well-being or subjective burden between experimental and control subjects. When this investigation was published in *The Gerontologist,* it was accompanied by an editorial by Callahan (1989), which challenged the conclusions about the effectiveness of respite care. This editorial has been influential in shaping a climate of opinion that is skeptical about the benefits of respite.

A careful examination of the study reveals that several facets of the research design may have accounted for the relatively circumscribed findings. In the study, participants were recruited for a general investigation of caregiving, and then randomly assigned into a group that had a case manager to assist them in obtaining respite and a control group given lists of community services. The case manager had a small subsidy to pay for respite services, although it was based on ability to pay, and some higher income participants apparently did not qualify. The results indicate that respite use was relatively low in the experimental group. Users of day care received a median of 10 days of service over a 1-year period, whereas subjects using in-home care had a median of 63 hours of service in 1 year. Complicating this finding of low service use, many subjects in the control group used respite services that they arranged on their own.

Given these findings, a set of different conclusions emerges than reached either by Lawton et al. (1989) or Callahan (1989). First and foremost, the study was not an effective test of respite. The experimental group had a low rate of use, which may not have differed much from controls. Rather than evaluating respite, the study tests the benefit of a case management approach to link people to respite services. As in other case management studies (e.g., Applebaum, Christianson, Harrigan, & Schore, 1988), clear advantages of that approach were not found.

Low rate of service use has been identified as a major concern in caregiving interventions (e.g., Gwyther, 1989). Reluctance of some family members to use this type of assistance may have similarly contributed to the outcome in the Lawton et al. study. Another factor, however, is that subjects were recruited initially not because of their interest in or need for respite, but because they were caregivers. This sampling strategy was used to allow for random assignment, but introduced other problems. In effect, a low rate of service use may have reflected subjects' current needs. In any event, it would seem that the experiment did not adequately test the benefits of respite care.

Subject selection procedures is related to another outcome of the study, the lack of effects on caregivers' well-being. By recruiting a diverse sample of caregivers, the researchers included subjects with adequate well-being and low subjective burden at baseline. As a result, the probability of demonstrating treatment effects was reduced, because these individuals could not show much additional improvement. Similar floor and ceiling effects have been noted in other caregiver intervention studies (e.g., Haley, Brown, & Levine, 1987; Zarit, Anthony, & Boutselis, 1987).

The strengths of the Lawton et al., (1989) study should not be overlooked. Although not accomplishing its major goal of demonstrating unequivocably the benefits of respite, it stands as the largest scale and best study to date. It was a well-conceived project that used innovative design and measurement approaches. The fact that some aspects of the research did not function as

intended is instructive for the next steps that should be taken in field studies
of major interventions such as respite.

From this study and other intervention research conducted in the past few
years, several possible directions for new studies emerge. New studies can
address both the needs of caregivers and, by basing their approach on theory,
examine propositions about the relation of stress to various mediating factors.

The Need for Powerful Interventions

A principle consideration is that interventions need to be powerful. Caregiving is sufficiently complex and demanding to warrant sophisticated and
skilled intervention.

As an example, the support group literature has found that short-term
treatments that provide some general information to caregivers and encourage them to use new approaches for managing stress are perceived as
helpful but do not have much impact on the burdens of care or well-being
(e.g., Haley et al., 1987; Toseland, Rossiter, & Labreque, 1989; Toseland,
Rossiter, Peak, & Smith, 1990; Whitlatch, Zarit, & von Eye, 1991; Zarit et
al., 1987). Given the relatively low intensity of these interventions (presenting
new information, encouraging mutual support), the findings are not surprising, and should not be interpreted as discouraging. Rather, they represent an
expected outcome, in light of the magnitude of treatment provided.

For respite or other community services, there has been a tendency to
design treatments to demonstrate both potential benefits to families, and
cost-saving features of the treatment, when compared, for example, to
institutional care (e.g., Carcagno & Kemper, 1988). Unfortunately, this
approach often results in provision of relatively low levels of treatment in
order to keep costs low. There needs, instead, to be consideration of how
much treatment is needed to make a significant difference, and to assure that
the resources are available in the demonstration program for implementing
that level of effective intervention. An effective research design is to vary
systematically the amount of intervention available, so as to determine
sufficient levels.

A corollary is that there must also be consideration of whether or not the
treatment is implemented. Do participants in a support group, for example,
actually receive new information or support from other group members? Or
do participants in a program of community-based services actually use those
services in expected amounts? This type of information can serve both as a
reliability check on the intervention and as the basis for a process analysis to
identify features of treatment that are most likely associated with improvement.

Conceptualization of Benefits of Treatments

Another important direction in caregiving research is to develop better conceptualizations of the benefits of interventions. It is clear both from treatment studies and from theoretical papers on caregiving (e.g., Pearlin, Mullan, Semple, & Skaff, 1990) that a multivariate framework is needed for considering the effects on caregivers' lives. Given the multiple ways in which caregiving may affect someone's life, a single intervention will influence only some of those changes. Interventions, then, need to identify or target more specifically what effects are likely to occur. Global measures of well-being or burden will be too general to identify the main effects of most treatments.

As an example of this approach, the effects of a very potent intervention, institutional placement, on caregivers of dementia patients was examined (Zarit & Whitlatch, in press), using data from the ongoing longitudinal study of Pearlin and his associates (1990). A major advantage of this study is its differentiation of processes and consequences of caregiving. Building on this perspective, institutionalization was conceptualized as having primary and secondary effects. Primary effects were those immediate changes likely to occur because the caregiver is no longer spending the time or effort in daily activities, such as feeling overwhelmed or experiencing time pressure. Secondary effects included changes in appraisal of their role performance and well-being. The results were that caregivers who placed their relative in a nursing home had significantly decreased scores on measures of primary effects compared to caregivers who were still providing care in the community, but there were no differences on the indicators of secondary effects.

A major limitation in the current literature is the emphasis on measures of caregivers' mood or well-being. Although there are advantages of measures of well-being for understanding caregivers' experience (see, e.g., George & Gwyther, 1986), there are also drawbacks, particularly when used as indicators of treatment outcome. As noted earlier, a major problem in using mood or well-being measures is that an unselected sample of caregivers will have quite varied scores at baseline, leading to floor or ceiling effects.

Schulz, in his chapter in this volume, calls attention to two other important features of depressed mood in caregivers: its episodic pattern and possible self-regulating processes used by caregivers. Given the episodic pattern observed by Schulz, it might be more appropriate to consider future recurrences as an outcome measure, rather than the usual measure of changes in scores from baseline to post treatment. By pointing out possible self-regulating mechanisms, Schulz suggests that many caregivers may respond actively to increased feelings of distress by making alterations in their situations. Seeking help before they become highly distressed would be one such step. Thus, to the extent that caregivers take actions to head off a worsening of their own circumstances, measures of mood will be relatively insensitive to the potential benefits of these actions.

Smyer, in his chapter in this volume, raises another important distinction, that individual differences characterize the structure of change in mood. Evidence for this type of variability is found in a study by MaloneBeach, Zarit, and Farbman (1990). Patterns of change in mood over a 14-day period were analyzed for a sample of caregivers of dementia patients. Four distinct patterns emerged. Some respondents had stable, low scores of negative mood over the entire period. A second group had generally stable mood, but with one or two episodes of high distress. A third group was highly variable, with scores of negative affect at times exceeding positive affect. Finally a small group had continually high negative affect scores, indicating considerable distress. Given these findings, it is clear that how people might be changing in response to an intervention is more complex than indicated by a comparison of means at pre- and post-treatment.

Finally, whereas most of the intervention research has used measures of well-being or mood, the treatments have seldom been focused on these dimensions. Providing information or respite may not have direct or consistent effects on depression or other emotions, yet may have other valuable consequences.

Several possible directions for treatment research are apparent. Interventions that focus on mood need to differentiate between individuals who currently do and do not have problems in that area. If the goal of a treatment is to reduce caregivers' feelings of depression, then subjects should be selected who are depressed (i.e., who can show benefits from the treatment). The treatment, in turn, should include potent interventions for depression. An alternative approach would be to conceptualize treatment as preventing future occurrences of depressed feelings. In that case, caregivers who are currently not depressed would be appropriate subjects. Because not all subjects would be expected to become depressed during the followup period if no treatment were provided, estimates of the benefits of treatment would have to be adjusted accordingly. If, for example, we estimated that 30% of a group of caregivers were at risk of becoming depressed during a 1-year period, then the treatment effect could be demonstrated only for this portion of the sample. Then, if 30% of control and 15% of experimental subjects were depressed after one year, that would not be a large effect in terms of the overall sample, but would represent a 50% reduction of depression among those at risk. A power analysis and estimate of the sample size needed under these conditions must take into account the fact that only a portion of the sample is at risk in the first place.

Intervention research also needs to identify other appropriate measures of outcome besides mood and well-being. Some alternatives are feelings of efficacy or mastery over certain aspects of the caregiving situation, and role strain or conflict. As examples, successful outcomes of day care for some caregivers would be that they are able to continue working, or that they no longer feel as trapped in the caregiver role. Another alternative to measures of psychological distress is to consider the threats to well-being that caregivers perceive in their current situation. This approach takes into account the observation that many caregivers seek help so that the situation does not get out of hand, rather than because they are immediately distressed.

Satisfaction of caregivers with services is another appropriate dimension for evaluating outcome. Despite Callahan's (1989) criticism of this approach, caregivers' satisfaction can provide useful information about how well an intervention has been implemented and which features of an intervention may be helpful or not helpful. Satisfaction measures can also clarify the problem of why caregivers underutilize services.

As these suggestions indicate, consideration of outcome measures must include evaluation of the goals that caregivers have for themselves. Toseland and his associates (Toseland et al., 1989; 1990) have used a goal attainment approach with some success in research on support groups. An individualized approach to goals is particularly appropriate in evaluating new treatments, or as a step toward developing more general measures. Although there are also limitations, for example, the difficulties in generalizing across individuals and samples and the possibility for nonspecific effects of treatment to influence these ratings, more of this kind of work is needed to determine what kinds of help caregivers want.

An overriding theme in these observations is that caregiving cannot be viewed from a pathology perspective, in which it is expected that caregivers share some common problems. Rather, the process of caregiving represents the diversity of human experiences. Although the risks to individuals are considerable, the particular costs or vulnerabilities will differ, and many people will head off the more extreme or unacceptable consequences by learning new coping responses, institutionalizing their relative or otherwise taking steps to rearrange care responsibilities.

Finally, an important consideration that is largely neglected in the caregiving literature is the goals and status of the care recipient. It is conceivable that certain interventions that are helpful to caregivers could have adverse effects on care recipients. Little is known about what older people want for themselves, or how they would choose between various care alternatives. We also know little about the effects of interventions such as day care or overnight respite on care recipients. Inclusion of the care recipient's perspective seems an important next step even though it complicates the research process.

New Directions for Interventions

There are currently many good suggestions about possible approaches to assist caregivers and some excellent demonstration programs throughout the country. Two approaches that have received relatively less attention, but may potentially have considerable benefits, warrant our attention.

First, as Mullan in this volume and others have noted, perhaps the most stressful event for caregivers is dealing with disruptive behavior. Often overlooked, however, is the amount of disruptive behavior that is at least in part the result of the interaction between caregiver and recipient. Observations of caregivers suggest that confrontive and authoritarian approaches may increase the amount of behavioral problems, whereas calmer, non-confrontive approaches that provide stimulation, distraction, or emotional support can have a calming effect under some circumstances (see Niederehe & Funk, 1987; Zarit, Orr, & Zarit, 1985).

Preliminary studies suggest caregivers are able to learn behavioral approaches that reduce targeted problems considerably (Pinkston & Linsk, 1984). Further work of this type is warranted. Because of new regulations in nursing homes limiting the use of restraints and medications, systematic application of behavioral approaches in those settings is also timely.

Second, the literature has not discussed to any extent one critical group in long-term care—physicians. Physicians' costs take a significant portion of expenses in social health maintenance approaches. We need to consider how physicians fit, and fail to fit, in long-term care approaches. A particular focus is decisions about management of chronic disabilities. There may be times when medical approaches, such as tests and medications, have a lower payoff for the care recipient and family than nonmedical services and interventions (Cummings, 1987). Although likely to be controversial, examination of physicians' role and decisions in long-term care is long overdue.

CONCLUSIONS

The complexity of caregiving, particularly, the diversity of family structure and process and the various ways that formal and informal helpers may interact, present a major challenge to researchers. Approaches that assess individual differences in goals and responses, or that carefully target groups of caregivers selected on key characteristics relevant to treatment appear promising. Attention must also be given to the magnitude of the intervention, and how well it is implemented. Finally, the expectation that effective community-based long-term care services will be inexpensive or divert costs from other areas such as nursing homes is probably unrealistic. The need for long-term care services for family caregivers and the importance of how they interface with the formal system must be articulated as part of the national debate over allocation of limited resources.

REFERENCES

Applebaum, R. A., Christianson, J. B., Harrigan, M., & Schore, J. (1988). The evaluation of the national long-term care demonstration: The effect of channeling on mortality, functioning, and well-being. *Health Services Research, 23*(1), 143–160.

Callahan, J. J., Jr. (1989). Play it again Sam—There is no impact. *The Gerontologist, 29,* 5–6.

Carcagno, G. J., & Kemper, P. (1988). The evaluation of the national long-term care demonstration: An overview of the channeling demonstration and its evaluation. *Health Services Research, 23*(1), 1–22.

Cummings, N. A. (1987). The future of psychotherapy: One psychologist's perspective. *American Journal of Psychotherapy, 41*(3), 349–356.

George, L. K., & Gwyther, L. P. (1986). Caregiver well-being: A multidimensional examination of family caregivers of demented adults. *The Gerontologist, 26,* 253–259.

Gwyther, L. P. (1989, August). Overcoming barriers: Home care for dementia patients. *Caring, VIII*(8), 12–16.

Haley, W. E., Brown, S. L., & Levine, E. G. (1987). Experimental evaluation of the effectiveness of group intervention for dementia caregivers. *The Gerontologist, 27,* 376–382.

Hokenstad, M. C., & Johansson, L. (1990). Caregivers for the elderly in Sweden: Program challenges and policy initiatives. In D. E. Biegel & A. Blum (Eds.), *Aging and caregiving: Theory, research, and policy* (pp. 254–269). Newberry Park, CA: Sage.

Lawton, M. P., Brody, E. M., & Saperstein, A. R. (1989). A controlled study of respite services for caregivers of Alzheimer's patients. *The Gerontologist, 29,* 8–16.

Litwak, E. (1985). *Helping the elderly: The complementary role of informal networks and formal systems.* New York: Guilford.

MaloneBeach, E. E., Zarit, S. H., & Farbman, D. (1990, November). *Daily variability in stressors and mood of family caregivers.* Paper presented at the meetings of the Gerontological Society of America, Boston, MA.

MaloneBeach, E. E., Zarit, S. H., & Spore, D. (in press). Caregivers' perceptions of case management and community-based services: Barriers to service utilization. *Journal of Applied Gerontology.*

Niederehe, G., & Funk, J. (1987, August). *Family interaction with dementia patients: Caregiver styles and their correlates.* Paper presented at the 95th annual convention of the American Psychological Association, New York City.

Noelker, L. S., & Bass, D. M. (1989). Home care for elderly persons: Linkages between formal and informal caregivers. *Journals of Gerontology, 44,* 563–570.

Pagel, M. D., Becker, J., & Coppel, D. B. (1985). Loss of control, self-blame, and depression: An investigation of spouse caregivers of Alzheimer's disease patients. *Journal of Abnormal Psychology, 94*(2), 169–182.

Pearlin, L. I., Mullan, J. T., Semple, S. J., & Skaff, M. M. (1990). Caregiving and the stress process: An overview of concepts and their measures. *The Gerontologist, 30,* 583–594.

Pinkston, E. M., & Linsk, N. L. (1984). *Care of the elderly: A family approach.* New York: Pergamon.

Scharlach, A. E., & Frenzel, C. (1986). An evaluation of institution-based respite care. *The Gerontologist, 26,* 77–82.

Toseland, R. W., Rossiter, C. M., & Labrecque, M. (1989). The effectiveness of peer-led and professionally-led groups to support caregivers. *The Gerontologist, 29,* 465–471.

Toseland, R. W., Rossiter, C. M., Peak, T., & Smith, G. C. (1990). Comparative effectiveness of individual and group interventions to support family caregivers. *Social Work, 35,* 209–217.

Whitlatch, C., Zarit, S. H., & von Eye, A. (1991). Efficacy of interventions with caregivers. *The Gerontologist, 31,* 9–14.

Zarit, S. H., Anthony, C. R., & Boutselis, M. (1987). Interventions with caregivers of dementia patients: Comparison of two approaches. *Psychology and Aging, 2,* 225–232.

Zarit, S. H., Orr, N. K., & Zarit, J. M. (1985). *The hidden victims of Alzheimer's disease: Families under stress.* New York: New York University Press.

Zarit, S. H., & Whitlatch, C. J. (in press). Institutional placement: Phases of the transition. *The Gerontologist.*

Author Index

Note: Page numbers in *italics* denotes full bibliographical reference.

Subject Index

Activities of daily living (ADL) (*see* Functional impairments)
Acute medical services (Acute Care) (*See* Medical care)
African Americans, 4, 48, 50–51, 55–56, 62, 70–72, 158
Age (of caregivers), 12–13, 21–22, 41, 45, 82, 108, 123–124, 127, 129–130, 132, 134–136, 141, 144–146, 178–179, 218, 245, 247, 273, 281–283
Alzheimer's Association, 164, 244–245, 262
Alzheimer's Disease (*see also* Dementia), 3–4, 7–8, 70–71, 75–76, 107, 119–120, 122–125, 128, 138, 141, 151, 160, 164, 166, 194, 201, 205–214, 234, 242, 244, 246, 248, 253, 256, 275, 299
 Advisory Panel, 208–212, 214
 Council on, 206, 208
 Federal research funding, 206–207, 209
 Services Research, 206, 208–209
Analytic strategies, 86, 164, 249, 250–256, 280
Andersen Model, 241–242, 244, 253, 256, 264–265

Behavior problems (*see also* Memory & Behavior Problems Checklist), 7, 18–19, 20, 25–26, 77, 94–95, 99, 123–124,

126–132, 134–135, 137–138, 152, 211–212, 231, 244, 249, 254, 314
Burden (*see also* Stress and Strain), 3, 7, 12, 18, 22–25, 27, 31, 34, 52, 68, 70–72, 75, 77, 80, 85, 88, 91–96, 98–100, 108, 159, 162, 263, 271, 274, 276, 278, 280, 289, 308–311

California Caregiver Resource Centers (CRCs), 234–235, 238
Cancer, 4, 76, 78–79, 83–93, 95, 98, 110
Capitation, 174–175, 179, 190, 199, 210, 306
Caregivers, 3–4, 6–7, 9, 11, 13, 16–21, 23–27, 48, 50, 53–59, 61–62, 67–68, 70, 72, 75, 80–83, 87–89, 92–97, 99–100, 107–108, 111, 114–116, 119–134, 136, 138, 141–142, 144, 151–153, 156–157, 159–167, 173, 194–195, 211, 213–214, 224, 227–228, 233–236, 238, 239–244, 246–247, 253, 255–256, 261–263, 265–271, 274–276, 280–282, 284–285, 290, 295, 304, 307, 309, 311–313
 Age (*see* Age)
 Education (*see* Education)
 Employment (*see* Employment)
 Gender (*see* Gender)
 Income (*see* Income)
 Marital status (*see* Marital status)
 Non-kin, 15, 25, 71, 109